Abraham Lincoln

Abraham Lincoln

MATTHEW PINSKER

Dickinson College

CQ PRESS

A Division of Congressional Quarterly Inc.
Washington, D.C.

CQ Press
1255 22nd Street, N.W., Suite 400
Washington, D.C. 20037

202-729-1900; toll-free, 1-866-4CQ-PRESS (1-866-427-7737)

www.cqpress.com

♾ The paper used in this publication meets the minimum requirements of the American National Standard for Information Sciences—Permanence of Paper for Printed Library Materials, ANSI Z39.48-1992.

Cover illustration by Talia Greenberg
Design by Karen Doody
Composition by Jessica Forman
Editorial development by the Moschovitis Group, Inc.,
    New York, N.Y.

Printed and bound in the United States of America

06 05 04 03 02   5 4 3 2 1

Library of Congress Cataloging-in-Publication Data

Pinsker, Matthew.
    Abraham Lincoln / Matthew Pinsker.
        p. cm.— (American presidents reference series)
Includes bibliographical references and index.
    ISBN 1-56802-701-X (alk. paper)
    1. Lincoln, Abraham, 1809-1865. 2. Presidents—United States—Biography. 3. United States—Politics and government—1861-1865. I. Title. II. Series.
    E457 .P575 2002
    973.7'092—dc21

                                    2002011582

For Rachel
Love is eternal.

Contents

Preface

One of the problems in writing about Abraham Lincoln is that it is nearly impossible to outdo his prose. The Gettysburg Address is only ten sentences—a mere 272 words. Yet even the best scholarly dissections are longer, less elegant, and usually far more confusing. Not every Lincoln utterance was that compact or poetic, but his written statements are models of persuasive clarity. The truth is that Lincoln authors always seem to suffer in comparison with Lincoln, the author.

This book attempts to overcome that pitfall by embracing it. Each chapter covers a critical aspect of Lincoln's life or presidency with original commentary and with primary source documents. Most of these documents come from the body of Lincoln's critical speeches and political letters. In this fashion, the eloquent subject is allowed to speak for himself. Readers will also find numerous selections from Lincoln's contemporaries—candid observations about him recorded in diaries, letters, and recollections.

The timing for this volume could not be better. The past several years have seen a veritable revolution in the way scholars can access materials about the great president. Fully searchable digital archives contain all of Lincoln's collected works and most of his incoming correspondence. Several publishers have undertaken the valuable task of reprinting and annotating important recollections about Lincoln originally published after his assassination. A determined retired couple from Virginia has even gone to the trouble of building a database of tens of thousands of Civil War court-martial cases to help document Lincoln's legendary use of the presidential pardon.

These advances underscore a surprising fact about Lincoln scholarship. Historians have been working with a complete set of documents from the Lincoln presidency for only about fifty years. Angered by the gossip mongering of Lincoln's earliest biographers, Lincoln's son, Robert, took actions in the years following the assassination that effectively closed off access to the president's papers until the late 1940s. Thus, despite the ongoing national dialogue about Abraham Lincoln, many facts about him have remained elusive. Furthermore, enduring myths of the rail-splitting icon have obscured the work of many modern scholars.

This volume attempts to set the record straight. The first chapter offers a sketch of Lincoln's life, emphasizing his self-made story and displaying his major attempts at autobiographical writing. Chapter 2 reviews Lincoln's electoral track record, pointing out that his extraordinary success as a political candidate and party leader often gets overlooked. Chapter 3 includes analyses of the major policies of the Lincoln administration in an attempt to synthesize some of the most important insights of recent scholarship. Chapter 4 offers a compact narrative of the Civil War with Lincoln at or near the center of the action. Chapter 5 has several shorter sections that build on important new work by other leading scholars, offering insight into Lincoln's relationships with major institutions. The final chapter explores the myths and realities of the assassination conspiracy that ended Lincoln's life; it also includes several evocative documents from the diary of John Wilkes Booth and the trial of his co-conspirators.

In the course of writing this book, I received superb research assistance from Ryanne Shuey, who has been one of my most promising students and has a bright future in whatever field she chooses. Valerie Tomaselli and Catherine Carter of the Moschovitis Group offered wonderful patience and professionalism in their roles as editors and coordinators for this project. Sabra Ledent performed the important task of copy editing, and several members of the CQ Press team helped improve the book: Christopher Anzalone, Molly Lohman, Sally Ryman, and others whose names have probably remained hidden from me in the scrum of postproduction. Above all others, however, I owe a special debt of gratitude to Professor Gabor Boritt, a legend in the Lincoln field and a wonderful mentor and friend.

On a personal level, I drew support, as always, from my parents and my sister Beth, all of them accomplished writers, critics, and members of our lifelong mutual admiration society. I began this project about the time of my engagement and completed it shortly after my marriage. In that sense, I will always remember the book fondly as my one safe harbor from wedding planning and as my first extended intellectual offering dedicated completely to Rachel, my muse now and forever.

Matthew Pinsker
Dickinson College

Lincoln in Washington, D.C., November 8, 1863.

Introduction

T ry to imagine any discussion of the U.S. presidency or the U.S. federal government that does not feature Abraham Lincoln prominently. He set practically every major standard for the office—from crisis leadership to public communication to party management. He rests at or near the top in all surveys of scholars rating the presidents.

DEMOCRATIC ICON

In fact, if there is still an American civil religion—a true faith in the democratic process—then Lincoln appears to be its greatest icon. He seems more human than George Washington or any of the other Founders, yet equally critical to the story of the nation's development. And in a modern culture that continually frets over the perceived absence of character in national leaders, Lincoln's story seems to embody the ultimate triumph of integrity.

How this exalted status came about is easy enough to explain. According to the traditional consensus, Lincoln deserves credit for several of the most important achievements in American political leadership. He kept the Union together and won the war. He freed the slaves. He preserved democracy. He wrote some of the most eloquent speeches in history.

Union and Victory

The day after Lincoln was inaugurated in March 1861, he received a memo detailing an impending supply crisis at Fort Sumter, a small federal military command in the bay outside of Charleston, South Carolina. States from the Deep South, such as South Carolina, had seceded from the Union after Lincoln's controversial election, and now he faced the daunting task of either persuading or compelling them to return to the national fold. He tried both methods and ended up spending most of the next four years struggling to keep certain important slave states within the Union coalition while employing the federal military to destroy the other rebels, or Confederates, who refused to return peacefully. The challenge proved far greater than expected. Balancing border state moderates with fiery Yankee abolitionists was nearly impossible. On the military front, the president was forced to work through several generals before finding an effective commander in the unlikely figure of Gen. Ulysses S. Grant, whose life up to that point had been thoroughly undistinguished. During the long months of uncertainty, Lincoln endured repeated criticism, even contempt, but ultimately his thoughtful, balanced approach to the crisis proved successful. Despite a tragic cost—more than 620,000 combatant deaths alone—the Union was maintained and victory was achieved.

Freedom

At bottom, the secession dispute revolved around the fate of slavery. Leading white Southerners feared that Lincoln and the Republican Party planned to dismantle the institution that they considered the cornerstone of their society and wealth. At first, President Lincoln attempted to dispel those fears, especially as he cultivated border slave states such as Maryland, Kentucky, and Missouri. But once the war proved bloodier than anyone had anticipated, and once slaves demonstrated their willingness to escape from their masters, Lincoln adjusted his strategy, using the Emancipation Proclamation to endorse the principle of immediate abolition in rebel territories. By the war's end, he also became committed to lobbying for the Thirteenth Amendment, which would guarantee an end to slavery across the nation and mark a new beginning for black freedom in America.

Democracy

Although the war was fundamentally about slavery, the trigger for the conflict was the Southern response to the election of 1860. Simply put, for the first (and only) time in American history a significant minority of the country refused to accept the results of a presidential contest. Although some leaders wanted compromise in the form of various constitutional amendments to protect the status of slavery and thus reassure nervous Southerners, Lincoln refused to bend on this issue. He had been elected on a Republican platform that solemnly pledged to limit the extension of slavery. He stuck to this position that slavery was inherently wrong and stubbornly insisted that elections mattered, a principle he upheld even more courageously in 1864 when he went ahead with a reelection campaign in the midst of the ongoing military stalemate. For him, secession was the essence of chaos. Although he exhibited fewer inhibitions about suppressing legal and civil liberties, Lincoln proved to be an absolutist on the subject of the democratic process.

Eloquence

With Lincoln, it is impossible to separate his actions from his words, because the speeches and public papers of his presidency define his decision making with a degree of brilliance rarely seen in politics. To some scholars, for example, the Gettysburg Address was nearly as important to the war's outcome as the Battle of Gettysburg itself. In an era when presidents were not public communicators, Lincoln excelled at the art of reaching beyond Capitol Hill and influencing the minds of the national electorate. Reprinted in newspapers across the North, his clear, evocative statements mobilized popular opinion. During a long contest in which public morale swung wildly with news from the battlefield, this ability to define the terms of the conflict proved critical to the maintenance of the Union coalition.

Add to this laundry list of greatness the fact that Lincoln grew up in humble surroundings on the edge of the American frontier and one has the true makings of national mythology.

Without a doubt, various critics have raised nagging questions over the years about the realities behind many of these claims. Some dismiss Lincoln's petty politicking. Others condemn his meddling with Union military strategy. A few label him a wartime dictator. There is even the occasional scholar who challenges his authorship of certain well-known public papers.

Mostly, there are lingering doubts about Lincoln's attitudes on race. It is no coincidence that the area of Lincoln's record that still fuels the most heated debate is his outlook on the abolition of slavery. Skeptics, both during his lifetime and today, have questioned his commitment to black freedom. Lincoln himself confused the issue by acting and speaking in apparently contradictory fashion. For Americans still obsessed by race, the desire for clarity on his true intent only seems to increase over time.

Nonetheless, Lincoln's public image has not yet succumbed to the fate of so many other once-revered heroes. Despite the countervailing trends in this postmodern age, he remains a large and elusive figure who somehow retains the ability to inspire.

THE "REAL" LINCOLN AND THE HISTORICAL RECORD

Most Americans are content to let the iconic Lincoln provide some much-needed civic inspiration, but anyone who studies him cannot help but aspire to understand and explain the "real" Lincoln. Of course, at some level any historical Lincoln is an incomplete model, constructed out of fragmentary evidence and often designed to satisfy present-day concerns more than ideals of universal truth.

A reference guide, such as this one, can only attempt to find a workable balance through the presentation of competing arguments and evidence. In other words, what follows is a starting point for analysis, not a final judgment—which may seem like a strange admission of failure since Lincoln has been dead for nearly a century and a half.

The historical record, however, has been very much alive, dramatically altering knowledge of the great man's biography and the behind-the-scenes workings of his presidency. More than 16,000 books have been written about Lincoln, but, if anything, the pace of scholarship has been accelerating. Over the past decade, two books on Lincoln, one by Mark E. Neely Jr. and one by Garry Wills, have won the Pulitzer Prize. According to most accounts, the best single-volume biography of Lincoln ever published, a careful study by the noted historian David Herbert Donald, appeared in 1995.

Thus the final word on the real Lincoln, if it is coming, is still years away. As the bicentennial anniversary of his birth approaches in 2009, students of the great president are still sorting out a host of new insights on his life and times. "We cannot escape history," Lincoln once warned, but, to a surprising degree, he has.

Lincoln reads to his son, Tad, February 9, 1864.

CHAPTER ONE

A Self-Made Story

I was born Feb. 12, 1809, in Hardin County, Kentucky," Abraham Lincoln wrote in what was his first serious attempt at an autobiographical sketch, penned at the age of fifty on the eve of his 1860 presidential bid. "My parents were both born in Virginia, of undistinguished families," he noted (Basler 1953, 3:511; see Document 1.1). The embodiment of the "self-made man," Lincoln never invested much energy in celebrating his background. He believed that his father's ancestors were lapsed Quakers who had migrated to Virginia from eastern Pennsylvania (see Documents 1.2 and 1.3). His father, Thomas, had told him a few stories about his grandfather, also named Abraham, who had moved his wife and five young children to Kentucky but was killed by Indians while clearing land for their farm. Lincoln was aware that the catastrophe had created "narrow circumstances" for his father's family, but he seemed unable to muster much sympathy for him, recalling on more than one occasion that Thomas Lincoln "grew up litterally without education" (Basler 1953, 4:60, 3:511; see Documents 1.1 and 1.2). He noted dismissively in print that his father became a "wandering laboring-boy" in rural Kentucky who "never did more in the way of writing than to bunglingly write his own name" (Basler 1953, 4:60).

About his mother, Lincoln was even more reticent. Nowhere in his letters or speeches is there anything more than a few matter-of-fact statements about Nancy Hanks Lincoln, who died from a disease called the "milk sickness" when he was only nine years old. After her son became president, friends and neighbors gossiped that she had been illegitimate, and possibly her son as well. Lincoln's law partner William H. Herndon and other historians have since speculated that he was ashamed of these stories and therefore closed off discussion about his mother, but not much proof exists for this theory. Instead, it seems more probable that he simply remembered little about her, having transferred his feelings of maternal love to his stepmother, Sarah Bush Johnston, a widow who married Thomas Lincoln in 1819 when Lincoln was ten. About his father's second wife, he wrote affectionately that she had been a "good and kind mother" to him, although he also later lampooned her "want of teeth" (Basler 1953, 4:62).

The truth is that Lincoln appeared to have little attachment to any of his relations. He was one of three children, but the only one who survived to raise a family of his own. A younger brother succumbed as an infant and an older sister died in childbirth while he was still a teenager. His stepmother brought some of her children from a prior marriage into the Lincoln household and he grew up with cousins from his natural mother's side of the family, but most of those ties faded after he reached adulthood. He hardly ever visited once he left the family farm and even declined to see his dying father or attend his father's funeral in 1851.

Historians have long suspected that Lincoln felt misunderstood and unappreciated by his backcountry relatives, particularly his father with whom he seemed to have an especially tense relationship. Yet the testimony collected after Lincoln's assassination offers conflicting viewpoints about his coming of age experiences and family dynamics. His stepmother, for example, said he was "the best boy I ever saw" and claimed that his father was proud of his intellect and "never made Abe quit reading to do anything if he could avoid it" (Wilson and Davis 1998, 106, 109; see Document 1.4). But his cousin recalled that young Abe could be "rude" and that sometimes Thomas Lincoln would "slash him for neglecting his work by reading" (Wilson and Davis 1998, 39, 41).

Lincoln's own recollections are equally ambiguous. "There was absolutely nothing to excite ambition for education," he reported of his childhood, adding tartly, "If a straggler supposed to understand latin, happened to so-journ in the neighborhood, he was looked upon as a wizzard" (Basler 1953, 3:511). He estimated that altogether he enjoyed no more than a year of formal schooling, a fact he openly regretted. On the other hand, he recalled cheerfully that he had been big as a child, and that from age seven to twenty-three he was "almost constantly handling" an axe (Basler 1953, 4:61).

Some memories left him unsettled. In one of his personal sketches, Lincoln made the revealing decision to include a story about how he once shot and killed a wild turkey as a young boy while his father was away from home. What made the story especially unusual was the lesson he drew from the episode. He noted that he had "never since pulled a trigger on any larger game," a detail that a typical nineteenth-century American male raised in a rugged, frontier culture was unlikely to emphasize (Basler 1953, 4:62; see Document 1.2).

Unfortunately, it is difficult to resolve the unanswered questions about Lincoln's childhood or his relationship with his father, because hardly any direct, contemporary evidence remains on those elusive subjects. One of the first and only documents still available in his own childhood hand comes from the pages of a copybook he kept while learning how to spell (Basler 1953, 1:1–2):

> Abraham Lincoln
> his hand and pen
> he will be good but
> god knows When

Although the commonplace verses were not original to the young teenager, they still suggest a smart, sensitive boy with an affinity for wry humor that would become one of his trademarks as an adult (see Documents 1.5 and 1.6).

What is known for certain about Lincoln's childhood is that his family, like many others in early American history, moved several times as Thomas Lincoln struggled to secure good land and more freedom of opportunity (see Document 1.7). When Abraham was two years old, the family relocated to a new farm in Kentucky about ten miles from his birthplace. After he turned seven, the family made an even bigger move, across the Ohio River into the territory of Indiana, where slavery was prohibited. "This removal was partly on account of slavery," Lincoln recalled, "but chiefly on account of the difficulty of land titles in Kentucky" (Basler 1953, 4:61–62). Like many poor southern whites, his father, who owned no slaves and eventually joined an antislavery church, resented the economic and political power of slaveholders. At the time, southern Indiana was still largely unsettled by whites and appeared, according to Lincoln's recollection, as "a wild region with many bears" (Basler 1953, 3:511). His family remained there for just over thirteen years, through his mother's death, his father's remarriage, his teenage years, and his older sister's fatal pregnancy. In 1830 the Lincolns once again pursued what they hoped were better economic opportunities when the extended household journeyed over two hundred miles in ox-drawn wagons to a new settlement in central Illinois.

COMING OF AGE

Lincoln was twenty-one years old at the time of his family's arrival in Macon County in the spring of 1830. Up until this point in his life, with the exception of a single, eventful trip to New Orleans, he had stayed close to the family farms in western Kentucky and southern Indiana. During that trip along the Mississippi River, Lincoln had worked as a hand on a flatboat carrying supplies to the South's busiest port. It was a dramatic excursion. He saw his first major city and was nearly killed by a group of runaway slaves who attempted to rob his party as they traveled down the river.

Despite the obvious dangers, the world beyond his family's prairie homestead did not frighten him. Once his family had arrived safely in Illinois, Lincoln determined to strike out on his own. While his father and stepmother continued to seek a permanent farm in the central region of the state, he hired himself out again on another boat trip to New Orleans. Upon his return in the summer of 1831, he agreed to begin a new assignment for his flatboat employer, who had befriended him during the trip. This time he worked as a clerk in a store at New Salem, a small trading village near the Sangamon River and, not coincidentally, some distance from his parents. Within several months he had made a strong network of new friends, even though the store did poorly, and boldly announced himself as a candidate for the state legislature. Adding to his growing sense of ambition, Lincoln found himself selected captain of the local militia, which had been called out during a frontier Indian scare. The appointment, made possible by his new neighbors, gave him "more pleasure than any I have had since," he reported proudly in 1859 (Basler 1953, 3:512).

For Lincoln, however, the actual experience of Indian fighting proved far less dramatic than his selection as a company officer. He would later joke that his combat in the so-called Black Hawk War consisted largely of "charges upon the wild onions" and "a good many bloody struggles with the musquetoes" (Basler 1953, 1:510; see Document 1.8). Still, he valued the camaraderie, or the pay, well enough to reenlist twice—something many of his contemporaries, bored with service, avoided.

By the time Lincoln returned to New Salem in July 1832, the election for state legislature was practically upon him (in those days certain Illinois political contests were held in early August). The young candidate campaigned briefly, but found that he was too unknown across most of his district to earn a place in the legislature. After losing the race and his job—his employer's failing store had gone out of business—the young clerk and ex-militia captain suddenly found himself "without means" but anxious to stay in New Salem, because, in his own words, he had "nothing elsewhere to go to" (Basler 1953, 4:66; see Document 1.2).

Over the next few years, Lincoln struggled to make a living. Relying heavily on credit, he and a partner attempted to open their own grocery store in the small town, but the operation soon "winked out," according to Lincoln's sardonic recollection, leaving him with a crushing debt that took years to repay (Basler 1953, 4:64; see Document 1.2). At one point, the local sheriff even seized his horse and other personal items as part of the default proceedings on his unpaid business loans. During this period, Lincoln worked at several odd jobs, including stints as the local postmaster and deputy surveyor.

But haphazard personal finances were relatively common in early-nineteenth-century America, especially in the boom-or-bust culture of the western frontier, and Lincoln found that his early economic woes had no negative impact on his political career. He finally won election to the Illinois legislature in 1834 and continued to win reelection until he stepped aside after serving for eight years, or four terms (see Chapter 2). Actually, becoming a part-time lawmaker helped to spur Lincoln to consider making the law his full-time career. He began studying on his own to enter the legal profession, reading a handful of borrowed volumes on jurisprudence. He received his license to practice law in the autumn of 1836.

The next year was a critical one in young Lincoln's life. He moved from New Salem to Springfield, a town just designated by the state legislature—partly through Lincoln's own efforts—as the new capital of Illinois. At that time, Springfield was bigger than nearby New Salem, but no more than a small village by modern standards. As he had done once before when striking out on his own, Lincoln migrated toward a local grocery store, where he shared a room with another young man named Joshua Speed, who would become the closest friend of his life. The two bachelors lived together for about four years, cultivating a close-knit group of friends in the fast-growing community that Lincoln happily called a "busy wilderness" (Basler 1953, 1:79).

Like many young, single men of the era, they also attempted—quite awkwardly in some cases—to find wives. Gender differences loomed larger in those days, and the gender imbalance in Illinois at that time was striking. At first, Lincoln seemed painfully uneasy about all issues related to romance and sexuality. In 1837, for example, he was engaged, in some fashion at least, to a woman from Kentucky named Mary Owens. They had been introduced by her sister, a resident of New Salem, some years before and had conducted a long-distance relationship mainly through a series of dry letters. As the months passed, however, they appeared to reach a mutual understanding about marriage, a fact that Lincoln only seemed to fully comprehend in the spring of 1837 when Mary Owens suggested that it was time for her to move to Springfield. Frantically, he wrote and tore up a handful of messages before somewhat pathetically offering to "abide" by her decision if she actually preferred to leave him. Warning that there was a "great deal of flourishing about in carriages" around the new capital, Lincoln attempted to scare his would-be fiancée away by emphasizing his poverty (Basler 1953, 1:78). But his ploy did not work. Mary Owens visited Springfield in August to confront him in person. Apparently during their terse conversations, Lincoln could not bring himself either to propose marriage or to end the relationship. Then, on the day she left, he finally put in writing a half-hearted proposal, which she rejected. Lincoln later wrote that the entire affair left him "mortified" and that he feared he could "never be satisfied with any one who would be block-head enough to have me" (Basler 1953, 1:119; see Document 1.9).

Some historians believe that Lincoln's uneasiness stemmed in part from an earlier tragedy involving a lost love. After his assassination in 1865, several former New Salem residents told interviewers that he had once been infatuated with the daughter of a local tavern owner. Most described the young girl, Ann Rutledge, as beautiful and kind-hearted. She had actually been engaged to another man, but he had disappeared from New Salem under mysterious circumstances and, according to local gossip, Lincoln and Rutledge surreptitiously pursued a deeply romantic relationship while he was still a postmaster and novice legislator. The affair, however, was short-lived; Rutledge died in the summer of 1835 after a sudden illness. Lincoln himself never wrote anything about Ann Rutledge, and years later his widow would furiously deny the story, but the accumulation of recollected testimony suggests that the tale has at least some credibility.

The most important partnership that Lincoln forged in 1837 was with John Todd Stuart, a prominent attorney and local politician who had served with Lincoln during the Black Hawk War. Stuart accepted Lincoln as his junior law partner in April, the same month Lincoln arrived in Springfield. Stuart and Lincoln quickly emerged as one of the small town's premier law firms. Stuart had encouraged Lincoln to undertake his initial legal studies and proved to be an excellent first mentor for the novice attorney. He also helped to guide Lincoln's blossoming political career. Both men belonged to the Whig Party, a generally conservative, probusiness political movement that organized in opposition to the populist politics of the Jacksonian Democrats. By the end of the 1830s, Stuart had entered Congress and his junior partner had earned a role as Whig leader in the state house. Ultimately, the two allies dissolved their firm, but the episode once again proved that Lincoln's ability to cultivate quick friendships and capitalize on opportunities made him a figure capable of great professional and political success.

MARRIAGE AND CAREER

Lincoln's surefooted approach to his career contrasted sharply with his rather clumsy efforts at achieving personal happiness. It was not only his awkwardness around young women that proved frustrating. He also was a strangely sensitive young man, prone to brooding and depression, or what he termed the "hypo" (Basler 1953, 1:79). Some medical historians have since speculated that his emotional difficulties might have been exacerbated by brain damage suffered in a childhood accident when a horse fractured his skull and left him temporarily comatose—in his own words, "killed for a time" (Basler 1953, 4:62). Most traditional scholars embrace less dramatic explanations, looking toward culture more than biology. In New Salem, Lincoln spent long nights memorizing melancholy poetry and developed a fascination with Shakespearean drama, especially the dark tragedy *Macbeth*. And he was not alone. Despite the crude conditions in Illinois during this era, other young men shared interests in drama, poetry, and philosophical musings. Lincoln was, then, able to participate in both formal and informal debating societies and literary clubs throughout this period of his life, continuing his impressive course of self-education.

It should therefore come as no surprise that the woman Lincoln finally chose as his wife, Mary Todd, attracted him with her intellectual companionship as much as her physical beauty. She was better educated than he was and shared his passion for theater. More important, unlike most women of the age, she was a keen observer of the political scene. Mary Todd grew up in Lexington, Kentucky, a distant relative of his first law partner and the daughter of a prominent businessman who had been on good terms with Henry Clay, the nation's leading Whig politician. When one of her sisters married the son of Illinois's first territorial governor, Mary Todd began visiting Springfield and before long met her future husband. She understood politics well, and, according to her biographer, the couple first moved from friendship to romance while following the 1840 presidential contest, an exciting race that featured Whig candidate William Henry Harrison, the celebrated "Old Tippecanoe." Within a year, they began to make wedding plans.

In Springfield, Mary Todd lived with her sister and brother-in-law, Ninian and Elizabeth Edwards, a wealthy couple who occupied the center of the town's small social scene. For Lincoln, courting Mary Todd meant crossing an invisible class barrier, leaving behind his humble origins for a place among the social and political elite of his adopted hometown. During this period, he also joined forces with a new law partner, Stephen Logan, who was less political than Stuart but widely regarded as the most learned attorney then residing in Illinois. As he entered his early thirties, Lincoln had every reason to feel that he had finally arrived.

Yet it was not a seamless transition. For some reason, still unknown and much debated among scholars, Lincoln and Mary Todd broke off their engagement on New Year's Day 1841. Theories for the split range widely—from second thoughts to another woman to virginal anxieties—but the result was indisputable. The couple separated, and Lincoln fell into a severe depression. Nearly three weeks after the decisive confrontation, he noted to his former law partner Stuart that he did not have the "composure" to write long letters, and other Springfield residents commented in their correspondence on his distressing "Cat fits" (Basler 1953, 1:229n). Some recalled fearing that their friend would commit suicide.

Eventually, the two lovers reconciled and were married in a private ceremony in November 1842. Again, the circumstances surrounding their decision remain cloudy, but it appears that politics helped bring them together. Their renewed courtship coincided with a bizarre public feud that ensnared Lincoln and involved Mary Todd. Both had contributed to a Whig newspaper anonymous satiric letters that ridiculed a local Democrat named James Shields. When the hot-tempered public official challenged the author of the letters to reveal himself, Lincoln accepted responsibility and the two men nearly engaged in duel. Historian Douglas Wilson, an expert on Lincoln's early years, denies that the episode with Shields itself precipitated the reunion with Mary Todd, but he argues persuasively that many of Lincoln's actions during this period should be placed in the context of a young man striving to act honorably.

Whatever his exact motivation, Lincoln's marriage ushered in a new age of maturity and responsibility in his life (see Document 1.10). Nine months after the wedding, Mary Lincoln gave birth to their first son, Robert, and the couple, who had been living temporarily in a tavern, soon rented one home and then finally bought another, not too far from the courthouse and all-important state capitol building. Lincoln also made a surprising career move, leaving his comfortable partnership with Logan in 1844 and setting up a new firm, with himself as senior member and a young, recently licensed attorney, William Herndon, as his junior partner.

Herndon remained Lincoln's principal officemate for the next sixteen years. No one, other than his wife, had such familiarity with Lincoln's daily habits. According to Herndon, the mature Lincoln was easygoing, almost to the point of being careless. He kept no account books, simply dividing their fees evenly after receiving them. His silk "plug" hat was "an extraordinary receptacle" that he stuffed with papers, using it as an unofficial briefcase while he walked about town or rode out to nearby courthouses (Herndon and Weik 1983, 254). Occasionally, he was compelled to apologize to clients or fellow attorneys for misplacing documents, a problem that cropped up whenever he changed hats. Herndon recalled with exasperation that the future president would typically begin each workday by stretching out on a sofa, reading the daily newspapers out loud in order, he said, to better absorb their contents. On weekends, he allowed his children to run wild around the law office, a policy that drove his more nervous partner to distraction. Yet under Lincoln's leadership, the firm was still one of the busiest and most successful in antebellum Illinois.

Despite Lincoln's reputation as a good-natured storyteller, Herndon believed that the purpose of the endless stream of anecdotes was usually self-centered. He claimed that frequently Lincoln was "not even polite" about injecting his humorous tales into various conversations and did so precisely because he wanted to avoid responding to questions or unwanted requests from his listeners. Although Herndon admired Lincoln greatly, he had no illusions about what he considered to be his partner's numerous shortcomings. In his opinion, Lincoln did not research legal doctrines carefully enough and too often relied on his instinctive common sense and good judgment to argue their clients' cases. He also found the future president too slow in the courtroom and repeatedly urged him to speak before juries with "more vim" (Herndon and Weik 1983, 268–273; see Document 1.11). On political matters, he believed that Lincoln was too inherently conservative and took credit for pushing him toward a more radical view on issues like the need to abolish slavery.

From Herndon's perspective, and according to the recollections of many other Springfield residents, the Lincoln marriage was troubled. But this view can be overstated, because much of the testimony comes secondhand from figures, such as Herndon, the junior law partner, who clearly detested Mary Lincoln. Moreover, it can be countered by a significant body of evidence that testifies to the warmth of the connection between husband and wife. The Lincolns had four children, all sons, over the first ten years of their marriage; Robert (1843), Edward (1846), William "Willie" (1850), and Thomas "Tad" (1853). Childbearing in an age of relatively primitive health care took an enormous toll on nineteenth-century women, and Mary Lincoln appeared to suffer progressively after each pregnancy. She endured terrible headaches and other physical discomfort that may have left her short-tempered and prone to outbursts. She clearly became even more demanding and more difficult as she grew older. Her emotional stability was further challenged by the prolonged illness and death of her second son, Edward, in 1850 (from tuberculosis) and by the increasingly extended absences of her husband, who traveled frequently for his legal and political work in the late 1840s and 1850s.

The truth is that the Lincoln marriage was probably like marriages of any era—a fluid combination of passion and affection, hostility and boredom with the ultimate arrangement of feelings unknowable to anybody other than the two participants. The surviving personal letters that Lincoln wrote to his wife reveal a complicated, but still positive, portrait of their marriage. For example, he was elected to Congress in 1846 and initially brought his young family to Washington with him, a telling move. But annoyed over the distractions they created, he eventually arranged for his wife and two young boys to visit some of her relatives in Kentucky. Soon, however, he also regretted that decision. "I hate to stay in this old room by myself," he complained in a warm letter to his wife that also teased her gently about her weight and contained attentive questions about the children and her health (Basler 1953, 1:465–466; see Document 1.12).

During the twelve years between his service in Congress and his presidency, Lincoln continued to struggle to find a workable balance between family and career. Although he did not hold public office in this period, he was a prominent party leader, first for the Whigs and later, after 1854, for the new Republican movement. He was in near constant demand as a speaker, not just in central Illinois but, as the 1850s wore on, also across the North. Despite his easygoing demeanor inside the walls of the Lincoln and Herndon law office, Lincoln proved during this period to be a classic workaholic who always found time for political allies and clients, even at the cost of spending days and evenings at home. The impact on his family was noticeable. Willie and Tad, his youngest sons, were too young to express their feelings, but his eldest son, Robert, grew distant from his father and later claimed that he had hardly any serious contact with him. It is also easy to see in Mary Lincoln's behavior signs of a wife who felt abandoned and resentful and who initiated occasional scenes with her husband in order to gain much-needed attention.

LIFE IN WARTIME WASHINGTON

One might imagine that the family dynamic only worsened once Lincoln became president, but, in a surprising way, his wartime position created an interesting role reversal within the family. Unlike their days together in Illinois, he became the one essentially stuck at home, because it also was his office. Robert Lincoln spent most of the war away as a student at Harvard College. Mary Lincoln also began traveling frequently, on shopping expeditions and for extended vacations away from Washington's stifling summer heat. Meanwhile, although the president did what he could to leave the confines of the White House, he remained more emotionally and physically isolated than at any other time in his life.

Before 1861, Lincoln had always been quick to fill the gaps in his personal life with male camaraderie—swapping stories at the grocery store, in militia service, around the political cloakroom, or outside of the local courthouse. As president, he discovered that opportunities for such casual banter were rare and intimate friendships were hard to find. He had been elected with only 40 percent of the popular vote as the leader of the Republican Party, a new political movement that was itself split into various factions. As a consequence of his weak political position, Lincoln selected men for his cabinet who had been his principal rivals and filled his administration with representatives of his party's competing constituencies. It was a delicate balancing act. Surrounded by only a handful of younger loyal aides, he spent much of the war engaged in the thankless task of holding together support for his administration's most controversial policies. For someone who had been absent from the nation's capital and Washington politics for nearly twelve years, the challenge was enormous.

The loneliness of the presidency and the burdens of the office were not good for Lincoln's personal constitution. He entered national life as a vigorous-looking fifty-two-year-old, standing six feet four inches tall and weighing somewhere in the neighborhood of 185 pounds. He had campaigned for president as the "Rail-splitter," embodying the glorified image of a self-made frontiersman. But by the end of the conflict between North and South, his skin appeared sallow and unhealthy. He had aged considerably and numerous visitors to the White House commented on his haggard appearance. When questioned about his health, he replied sadly, "I must die sometime" (Pease and Randall 1925, 1:559–560).

Of course, the grave national tragedy that played out in the ten thousand military actions of the long war explained most of the worry etched on the president's sad face, but he also endured personal sorrow as well.

Willie Lincoln, his precocious twelve-year-old son, died of a respiratory illness believed to be typhoid fever in February 1862. That left only Tad, the youngest child, at home with his parents during the war. He was sweet natured, but also spoiled and rambunctious and, according to Jean Baker, Mary Lincoln's biographer, perhaps even slightly retarded. Although he was already eight years old when the fighting began, Tad did not read, write, or dress himself while the Lincolns lived in the White House. Moreover, a speech impediment, probably from a cleft palate, made him incomprehensible to practically everyone but his increasingly patient and doting father.

Mary Lincoln also watched over Tad closely, always bringing him along during her numerous trips, but she suffered greatly during the war and became more self-absorbed, depressed, and detached from reality. For the first time in her life, Mary Lincoln faced intense public criticism—for her shopping habits, her Kentucky-born Confederate relatives, her wartime socializing, even for her attempts to renovate the White House. In a sad coincidence that the First Lady perceived as an ominous sign, one of her most lavish state dinners took place in early 1862 just as Willie grew fatally ill. The sudden death of a second child unnerved Mary Lincoln. Her strain worsened with additional physical ailments brought on by a mysterious carriage accident in the summer of 1863—one that some suspected was the result of a botched assassination attempt on the president's life. According to Robert Lincoln, his mother's headaches intensified after recovering from her injuries and left her judgment diminished in the years that followed.

Despite everything, Lincoln somehow managed to find just enough inner peace to continue and lead the Union coalition to victory. After Willie's death and at Mary Lincoln's urging, the president initiated the practice of moving his household during the hotter season to a cottage at the nearby Soldiers' Home, a secluded retreat outside the city. Here he lived for a quarter of his presidency, partially escaping from the pressures of war and enjoying the banality of commuting to work, as he did each day, on horseback to and from the White House. Poet Walt Whitman, serving as a nurse at a local hospital, recorded in his wartime diary that he often exchanged pleasant nods with the "rusty and dusty" president (Whitman 1875–1876, 22–24; see Document 1.13).

Close friends, such as Sen. Orville Browning from Illinois, noted that Lincoln seemed to particularly relish his interaction with ordinary

Americans. Browning described scenes in his diary of the weary president taking therapeutic afternoon trips to nearby hospitals to visit with the wounded soldiers. Each week, Lincoln insisted that the White House be opened to any visitors who chose to come, seeking help with their problems, offering some new invention or assistance for the war effort, or even just hoping to gain an audience with their president. This basic humanity and lack of pretension became a permanent part of Lincoln's public persona and helped to explain his enduring popular appeal.

Although no one observed the president as closely as Herndon had done in Illinois, young White House aide John Hay kept a diary that reveals wonderful glimpses of Lincoln both in action and at ease. Hay slept at the White House, still known generally as the Executive Mansion, and noted, for example, that one evening the sleepless president sought company after midnight and wandered into the offices of his aides, who were still at work. Standing before them in his night-shirt, resembling "an enormous ostrich," Lincoln shared some comic verses from a poet he had been reading. Hay, only recently graduated from college, could not contain his awe and amusement. "What a man it is!" he exclaimed in his journal about a president who was both so noble and so human (Burlingame and Ettlinger 1997, 194; see Document 1.14).

LINCOLN'S ACCOMPLISHMENTS

Any sketch of Lincoln's life demands at least a summary of his presidency. As president, Abraham Lincoln accomplished three profound objectives. First, he provided the sophisticated, subtle leadership needed to maintain the Union and win the war. Second, after some hesitation, he also accepted responsibility for persuading the North that the war for the Union had also become, by necessity, a war for freedom (see Chapter 4). In doing so, he helped to ensure that slavery would be abolished in the United States. Third, Lincoln protected the functioning of democracy. By insisting that the results of the 1860 election be acknowledged and by forging ahead with the 1864 election despite the continued fighting (see Chapter 2), Lincoln demonstrated that in the American system popular government truly matters. In the meantime, while pursuing these goals Lincoln penned some of the most memorable speeches and public papers in modern history.

The fact that he accomplished so much explains why he was unable to achieve even more. Regardless of his various personal troubles or human failings, the president was the indispensable figure of the war. His enemies understood that, and one of them organized an assassination conspiracy to act on this realization. The plot succeeded just as the Confederate cause was finally collapsing. On April 15, 1865, at 7:22 in the morning, Abraham Lincoln died from gunshot wounds inflicted the previous night while he attended the theater with his wife. Almost immediately, he was elevated to iconic status within the American civil religion, guaranteeing that the Lincoln family name would be distinguished for decades to come.

SELECTED PRIMARY SOURCES

Burlingame, Michael and John R. Turner Ettlinger, eds. *Inside Lincoln's White House: The Complete Civil War Diary of John Hay.* Carbondale: Southern Illinois University Press, 1997.

Fehrenbacher, Don E., and Virginia Fehrenbacher, eds. *Recollected Words of Abraham Lincoln.* Stanford: Stanford University Press, 1996.

Miers, Earl S., ed. *Lincoln Day by Day: A Chronology 1809–1865.* Dayton, Ohio: Morningside, 1990.

Mitgang, Herbert, ed. *Abraham Lincoln: A Press Portrait.* 1956. Reprint, New York: Fordham University Press, 2000.

Pease, Theodore C., and James G. Randall, eds. *The Diary of Orville Hickman Browning.* 2 vols. Springfield: Illinois State Historical Society, 1925–1933.

Turner, Justin G., and Linda Levitt Turner, eds. *Mary Todd Lincoln: Her Life and Letters.* New York: Knopf, 1972.

Whitman, Walt. *Memoranda during the War.* Camden, N.J.: Walt Whitman, 1875–1876.

Wilson, Douglas L., and Rodney O. Davis, eds. *Herndon's Informants: Letters, Interviews, and Statements about Abraham Lincoln.* Urbana: University of Illinois Press, 1998.

SECONDARY SOURCES

Burlingame, Michael. *The Inner World of Abraham Lincoln.* Urbana: University of Illinois Press, 1994.

Donald, David Herbert. *Lincoln at Home: Two Glimpses of Abraham Lincoln's Domestic Life*. Washington, D.C.: White House Historical Association, 1999.

Guelzo, Allen C. *Abraham Lincoln: Redeemer President*. Grand Rapids, Mich.: Eerdmans, 1999.

Kempf, Edward J. *Abraham Lincoln's Philosophy of Common Sense: An Analytical Biography*. 3 vols. New York: New York Academy of Sciences, 1965.

Neely, Mark E., Jr. *The Last Best Hope of Earth: Abraham Lincoln and the Promise of America*. Cambridge: Harvard University Press, 1993.

Paludan, Phillip S. *The Presidency of Abraham Lincoln*. Lawrence: University Press of Kansas, 1994.

Randall, Ruth Painter. *Lincoln's Sons*. Boston: Little, Brown, 1955.

———. *Mary Lincoln: Biography of a Marriage*. Boston: Little, Brown, 1953.

RECOMMENDED READING

Baker, Jean H. *Mary Todd Lincoln: A Biography*. New York: Norton, 1987.

Not all historians accept Baker's generally positive interpretation of the Lincoln marriage, but her biography of Mary Lincoln stands as the most sensitive and sophisticated available.

Basler, Roy P., ed. *The Collected Works of Abraham Lincoln*. 9 vols. New Brunswick: Rutgers University Press, 1953.

This invaluable reference source is also available online with full text search capabilities through the efforts of the Abraham Lincoln Association (www.hti.umich.edu/l/lincoln/). Although sometimes cagey about his own past, Lincoln, in his own words, remains the best single starting point for any true student of his life.

Donald, David Herbert. *Lincoln*. New York: Simon and Schuster, 1995.

There are dozens of good biographies of Lincoln—and whole shelves of bad ones—but this contribution is widely regarded as the best researched and most reliable.

Herndon, William H., and Jesse W. Weik. *Herndon's Life of Lincoln*. 1889. Reprint, New York: Da Capo, 1983.

William Herndon was Lincoln's law partner and most tireless analyst. His judgments were not always sound, but his devotion to the pursuit of historical truth remains inspiring.

Nicolay, John G., and John Hay. *Abraham Lincoln: A History.* 10 vols. New York: Century, 1890.

No one reads ten-volume biographies anymore, but if they did, this would be one to tackle. Nicolay and Hay were Lincoln's top White House aides and had unparalleled access to his personal papers as they prepared this official history of his life and administration.

Wilson, Douglas L. *Honor's Voice: The Transformation of Abraham Lincoln.* New York: Knopf, 1998.

In a beautifully written study, Wilson meticulously examines competing testimony about Lincoln's early life, concluding that the search for honor ultimately guided his actions and transformed an immature, uncertain figure into a responsible young leader capable of greatness.

Winkle, Kenneth J. *The Young Eagle: The Rise of Abraham Lincoln.* Dallas: Taylor, 2001.

Winkle, a social historian, has produced a unique portrait of Lincoln that roots his family background and early experiences in the social and cultural trends of nineteenth-century America.

Document 1.1   Autobiographical Sketch (1859)

Lincoln prepared his first extended autobiographical sketch at the request of Jesse W. Fell, a newspaper editor from Bloomington, Illinois—and an ancestor of twentieth-century presidential candidate Adlai Stevenson. The sketch provided the basis for an article about Lincoln that appeared in the Chester County (Pa.) Times *on February 11, 1860, and was reprinted in Republican newspapers across the North. The purpose of the sketch and subsequent articles was to help familiarize Northern Republican audiences with Lincoln in preparation for his first presidential bid. It is interesting to note, then, how carefully Lincoln details his connections to different regions of the country and with various types of occupations.*

Dec. 20. 1859

J. W. Fell, Esq Springfield,

My dear Sir:

Herewith is a little sketch, as you requested. There is not much of it, for
the reason, I suppose, that there is not much of me.
If any thing be made out of it, I wish it to be modest, and not to go beyond
the materials. If it were thought necessary to incorporate any thing from
any of my speeches, I suppose there would be no objection. Of course it
must not appear to have been written by myself. Yours very truly

A. LINCOLN

I was born Feb. 12, 1809, in Hardin County, Kentucky. My parents were
both born in Virginia, of undistinguished families—second families, perhaps I should say. My mother, who died in my tenth year, was of a family
of the name of Hanks, some of whom now reside in Adams, and others in
Macon counties, Illinois. My paternal grandfather, Abraham Lincoln, emi-
grated from Rockingham County, Virginia, to Kentucky, about 1781 or 2,
where, a year or two later, he was killed by indians, not in battle, but by
stealth, when he was laboring to open a farm in the forest. His ancestors,
who were quakers, went to Virginia from Berks County, Pennsylvania. An
effort to identify them with the New-England family of the same name
ended in nothing more definite, than a similarity of Christian names in both
families, such as Enoch, Levi, Mordecai, Solomon, Abraham, and the like.
    My father, at the death of his father, was but six years of age; and he
grew up, litterally without education. He removed from Kentucky to what
is now Spencer county, Indiana, in my eighth year. We reached our new
home about the time the State came into the Union. It was a wild region,
with many bears and other wild animals still in the woods. There I grew
up. There were some schools, so called; but no qualification was ever
required of a teacher, beyond "*readin, writin, and cipherin,*" to the Rule
of Three. If a straggler supposed to understand latin, happened to so-journ
in the neighborhood, he was looked upon as a wizzard. There was
absolutely nothing to excite ambition for education. Of course when I
came of age I did not know much. Still somehow, I could read, write, and

cipher to the Rule of Three; but that was all. I have not been to school since. The little advance I now have upon this store of education, I have picked up from time to time under the pressure of necessity.

I was raised to farm work, which I continued till I was twenty two. At twenty one I came to Illinois, and passed the first year in Macon county. Then I got to New-Salem (at that time in Sangamon, now in Menard county[)], where I remained a year as a sort of Clerk in a store. Then came the Black-Hawk war; and I was elected a Captain of Volunteers—a success which gave me more pleasure than any I have had since. I went the campaign, was elated, ran for the Legislature the same year (1832) and was beaten—the only time I ever have been beaten by the people. The next, and three succeeding biennial elections, I was elected to the Legislature. I was not a candidate afterwards. During this Legislative period I had studied law, and removed to Springfield to practice it. In 1846 I was once elected to the lower House of Congress. Was not a candidate for re-election. From 1849 to 1854, both inclusive, practiced law more assiduously than ever before. Always a whig in politics, and generally on the whig electoral tickets, making active canvasses. I was losing interest in politics, when the repeal of the Missouri Compromise aroused me again. What I have done since then is pretty well known.

If any personal description of me is thought desirable, it may be said, I am, in height, six feet, four inches, nearly; lean in flesh, weighing, on an average, one hundred and eighty pounds; dark complexion, with coarse black hair, and grey eyes—no other marks or brands recollected.

Yours very truly
A. LINCOLN

Source: Abraham Lincoln to Jesse W. Fell, "Enclosing Autobiography," December 20, 1859, in *The Collected Works of Abraham Lincoln,* 9 vols., ed. Roy P. Basler (New Brunswick: Rutgers University Press, 1953), 3:511–512.

Document 1.2   Additional Autobiography
Written for John L. Scripps (1860)

During the nineteenth century, American political parties typically commissioned official campaign biographies of their presidential candidates. Journalist John Locke Scripps prepared one of Lincoln's campaign biographies in

1860, relying heavily on an autobiographical sketch written in the third person but prepared for him by Lincoln himself, probably in June 1860. For historians, the Scripps biography has special importance, because Lincoln read and corrected a draft before it went into print, noting several mistakes about the facts of his life and career.

Abraham Lincoln was born Feb. 12, 1809, then in Hardin, now in the more recently formed county of Larue, Kentucky. His father, Thomas, & grand-father, Abraham, were born in Rockingham county Virginia, whither their ancestors had come from Berks county Pennsylvania. His lineage has been traced no farther back than this. The family were originally quakers, though in later times they have fallen away from the peculiar habits of that people. The grand-father Abraham, had four brothers—Isaac, Jacob, John & Thomas. So far as known, the descendants of Jacob and John are still in Virginia. Isaac went to a place near where Virginia, North Carolina, and Tennessee, join; and his decendants are in that region. Thomas came to Kentucky, and after many years, died there, whence his decendants went to Missouri. Abraham, grandfather of the subject of this sketch, came to Kentucky, and was killed by indians about the year 1784. He left a widow, three sons and two daughters. The eldest son, Mordecai, remained in Kentucky till late in life, when he removed to Hancock county, Illinois, where soon after he died, and where several of his descendants still reside. The second son, Josiah, removed at an early day to a place on Blue River, now within Harrison [Hancock] county, Indiana; but no recent information of him, or his family, has been obtained. The eldest sister, Mary, married Ralph Crume and some of her descendants are now known to be in Breckenridge county Kentucky. The second sister, Nancy, married William Brumfield, and her family are not known to have left Kentucky, but there is no recent information from them. Thomas, the youngest son, and father of the present subject, by the early death of his father, and very narrow circumstances of his mother, even in childhood was a wandering laboring boy, and grew up litterally without education. He never did more in the way of writing than to bunglingly sign his own name. Before he was grown, he passed one year as a hired hand with his uncle Isaac on Wata[u]ga, a branch of the Holsteen [Holston] River. Getting back into Kentucky, and having reached his 28th. year, he married Nancy Hanks—mother of the present subject—in the year 1806. She also was born in Virginia; and relatives of hers of the name of Hanks, and of other names, now reside in Coles, in Macon, and in Adams counties, Illinois, and also in Iowa. The present subject has no brother or sister of the whole or half blood. He had a sister, older than himself, who was grown and married, but died many years ago, leaving no child. Also a brother, younger than himself, who died in infancy. Before leaving Kentucky he and his sister were sent for short periods, to A.B.C. schools, the first kept by Zachariah Riney, and the second by Caleb Hazel.

At this time his father resided on Knob-creek, on the road from Bardstown Ky. to Nashville Tenn. at a point three, or three and a half miles South or South-West of Atherton's ferry on the Rolling Fork. From this place he removed to what is now Spencer county Indiana, in the autumn of 1816, A. then being in his eigth year. This removal was partly on account of slavery; but chiefly on account of the difficulty in land titles in Ky. He settled in an unbroken forest; and the clearing away of surplus wood was the great task a head. A. though very young, was large of his age, and had an axe put into his hands at once; and from that till within his twenty third year, he was almost constantly handling that most useful instrument—less, of course, in plowing and harvesting seasons. At this place A. took an early start as a hunter, which was never much improved afterwards. (A few days before the completion of his eigth year, in the absence of his father, a flock of wild turkeys approached the new log-cabin, and A. with a rifle gun, standing inside, shot through a crack, and killed one of them. He has never since pulled a trigger on any larger game.) In the autumn of 1818 his mother died; and a year afterwards his father married Mrs. Sally Johnston, at Elizabeth-Town, Ky—a widow, with three children of her first marriage. She proved a good and kind mother to A. and is still living in Coles Co. Illinois. There were no children of this second marriage. His father's residence continued at the same place in Indiana, till 1830. While here A. went to A.B.C. schools by littles, kept successively by Andrew Crawford, —Sweeney, and Azel W. Dorsey. He does not remember any other. The family of Mr. Dorsey now reside in Schuyler Co. Illinois. A. now thinks that the agregate of all his schooling did not amount to one year. He was never in a college or Academy as a student; and never inside of a college or accademy building till since he had a law-license. What he has in the way of education, he has picked up. After he was twentythree, and had separated from his father, he studied English grammer, imperfectly of course, but so as to speak and write as well as he now does. He studied and nearly mastered the Six-books of Euclid, since he was a member of Congress. He regrets his want of education, and does what he can to supply the want. In his tenth year he was kicked by a horse, and apparently killed for a time. When he was nineteen, still residing in Indiana, he made his first trip upon a flat-boat to New-Orleans. He was a hired hand merely; and he and a son of the owner, without other assistance, made the trip. The nature of part of the cargo-load, as it was called—made it necessary for them to linger and trade along the Sugar coast—and one night they were attacked by seven negroes with intent to kill and rob them. They were hurt some in the melee, but succeeded in driving the negroes from the boat, and then "cut cable" "weighed anchor" and left.

March 1st. 1830—A. having just completed his 21st. year, his father and family, with the families of the two daughters and sons-in-law, of his step-mother, left the old homestead in Indiana, and came to Illinois. Their mode of conveyance was waggons drawn by ox-teams, or A. drove one of the teams. They reached the county of Macon, and stopped there some time within the same month of March. His father and family settled a new place on the North side of the Sangamon river, at the junction of the timber-land and prairie, about ten miles Westerly from Decatur. Here they built a log-cabin, into which they removed, and made sufficient of rails to fence ten acres of ground, fenced and broke the ground, and raised a crop of sow[n] corn upon it the same year. These are, or are supposed to be, the rails about which so much is being said just now, though they are far from being the first, or only rails ever made by A.

The sons-in-law, were temporarily settled at other places in the county. In the autumn all hands were greatly afflicted with augue and fever, to which they had not been used, and by which they were greatly discouraged—so much so that they determined on leaving the county. They remained however, through the succeeding winter, which was the winter of the very celebrated "deep snow" of Illinois. During that winter, A. together with his step-mother's son, John D. Johnston, and John Hanks, yet residing in Macon county, hired themselves to one Denton Offutt, to take a flat boat from Beardstown Illinois to New-Orleans; and for that purpose, were to join him—Offut—at Springfield, Ills so soon as the snow should go off. When it did go off which was about the 1st. of March 1831—the county was so flooded, as to make traveling by land impracticable; to obviate which difficulty the[y] purchased a large canoe and came down the Sangamon river in it. This is the time and the manner of A's first entrance into Sangamon County. They found Offutt at Springfield, but learned from him that he had failed in getting a boat at Beardstown. This lead to their hiring themselves to him at $12 per month, each; and getting the timber out of the trees and building a boat at old Sangamon Town on the Sangamon river, seven miles N.W. of Springfield, which boat they took to New-Orleans, substantially upon the old contract. It was in connection with this boat that occurred the ludicrous incident of sewing up the hogs eyes. Offutt bought thirty odd large fat live hogs, but found difficulty in driving them from where [he] purchased them to the boat, and thereupon conceived the whim that he could sew up their eyes and drive them where he pleased. No sooner thought of than decided, he put his hands, including A. at the job, which they completed—all but the driving. In their blind condition they could not be driven out of the lot or field they were in. This expedient failing, they were tied and hauled on carts to the boat. It was near the Sangamon River, within what is now Menard county.

During this boat enterprize acquaintance with Offutt, who was previously an entire stranger, he conceved a liking for A. and believing he could turn him to account, he contracted with him to act as clerk for him, on his return from New-Orleans, in charge of a store and Mill at New-Salem, then in Sangamon, now in Menard county. Hanks had not gone to New-Orleans, but having a family, and being likely to be detained from home longer than at first expected, had turned back from St. Louis. He is the same John Hanks who now engineers the "rail enterprize" at Decatur; and is a first cousin to A's mother. A's father, with his own family & others mentioned, had, in pursuance of their intention, removed from Macon to Coles county. John D. Johnston, the step-mother's son, went to them; and A. stopped indefinitely, and, for the first time, as it were, by himself at New-Salem, before mentioned. This was in July 1831. Here he rapidly made acquaintances and friends. In less than a year Offutt's business was failing—had almost failed,—when the Black-Hawk war of 1832—broke out. A joined a volunteer company, and to his own surprize, was elected captain of it. He says he has not since had any success in life which gave him so much satisfaction. He went the campaign, served near three months, met the ordinary hardships of such an expedition, but was in no battle. He now owns in Iowa, the land upon which his own warrants for this service, were located. Returning from the campaign, and encouraged by his great popularity among his immediate neighbors, he, the same year, ran for the Legislature and was beaten—his own precinct, however, casting it's votes 277 for and 7, against him. And this too while he was an avowed Clay man, and the precinct the autumn afterwards, giving a majority of 115 to Genl. Jackson over Mr. Clay. This was the only time A was ever beaten on a direct vote of the people. He was now without means and out of business, but was anxious to remain with his friends who had treated him with so much generosity, especially as he had nothing elsewhere to go to. He studied what he should do—thought of learning the black-smith trade—thought of trying to study law—rather thought he could not succeed at that without a better education. Before long, strangely enough, a man offered to sell and did sell, to A. and another as poor as himself, an old stock of goods, upon credit. They opened as merchants; and he says that was *the* store. Of course they did nothing but get deeper and deeper in debt. He was appointed Post-master at New-Salem—the office being too insignificant, to make his politics an objection. The store winked out. The Surveyor of Sangamon, offered to depute to A. that portion of his work which was within his part of the county. He accepted, procured a compass and chain, studied Flint, and Gibson a little, and went at it. This procured bread, and kept soul and body together. The election of 1834 came, and he was then elected to the Legislature by the highest vote cast for any candidate. Major John T. Stuart, then in full practice of the law, was also elected. During the canvass, in a private conversation he encouraged A. [to] study law. After the election he borrowed books of Stuart, took them home with him, and went at it in good earnest. He studied with nobody. He still mixed in the surveying to pay board and clothing bills. When the Legislature met, the law books were dropped, but were taken up again at the end of the session. He was re-elected in 1836, 1838, and 1840. In the autumn of 1836 he obtained a law licence, and on April 15, 1837 removed to Springfield, and commenced the practice, his old friend, Stuart taking him into partnership. March 3rd. 1837, by a protest entered upon the Ills. House Journal of that date, at pages 817, 818, A. with Dan Stone, another representative of Sangamon, briefly defined his position on the slavery question; and so far as it goes, it was then the same that it is now. The protest is as follows—(Here insert it) In 1838, & 1840 Mr. L's party in the Legislature voted for him as Speaker; but being in the minority, he was not elected. After 1840 he declined a re-election to the Legislature. He was on the Harrison electoral ticket in 1840, and on that of Clay in 1844, and spent much time and labor in both those canvasses. In Nov. 1842 he was married to Mary, daughter of Robert S. Todd, of Lexington, Kentucky. They have three living children, all sons—one born in 1843, one in 1850, and one in 1853. They lost one, who was born in 1846. In 1846, he was elected to the lower House of Congress, and served one term only, commencing in Dec. 1847 and ending with the inaugeration of Gen. Taylor, in March 1849. All the battles of the Mexican war had been fought before Mr. L. took his seat in congress, but the American army was still in Mexico, and the treaty of peace was not fully and formally ratified till the June afterwards. Much has been said of his course in Congress in regard to this war. A careful examination of the Journals and Congressional Globe shows, that he voted for all the supply measures which came up, and for all the measures in any way favorable to the officers, soldiers, and their families, who conducted the war through; with this exception that some of these measures passed without years and nays, leaving no record as to how particular men voted. The Journals and Globe also show him voting that the war was unnecessarily and unconstitutionally begun by the President of the United States. This is the language of Mr. Ashmun's amendment, for which Mr. L. and nearly or quite all, other whigs of the H.R. voted.

Mr. L's reasons for the opinion expressed by this vote were briefly that the President had sent Genl. Taylor into an inhabited part of the country belonging to Mexico, and not to the U.S. and thereby had provoked the first act of hostility—in fact the commencement of the war; that the place, being the country bordering on the East bank of the Rio Grande, was inhabited by native Mexicans, born there under the Mexican government; and had never submitted to, nor been conquered by Texas, or the U.S. nor transferred to either by treaty—that although Texas claimed the Rio Grande as her boundary, Mexico had never recognized it, the people on the ground had never recognized it, and neither Texas nor the U.S. had ever enforced it—that there was a broad desert between that, and the country over which Texas had actual control—that the country where hostilities commenced, having once belonged to Mexico, must remain so, until it was somehow legally transferred, which had never been done.

Mr. L. thought the act of sending an armed force among the Mexicans, was *unnecessary*, inasmuch as Mexico was in no way molesting, or menacing the U.S. or the people thereof; and that it was *unconstitutional*, because the power of levying war is vested in Congress, and not in the President. He thought the principal motive for the act, was to divert public attention from the surrender of "Fifty-four, forty, or fight" to Great Brittain, on the Oregon boundary question.

Mr. L. was not a candidate for re-election. This was determined upon, and declared before he went to Washington, in accordance with an understanding among whig friends, by which Col. Hardin, and Col. Baker had each previously served a single term in the same District.

In 1848, during his term in congress, he advocated Gen. Taylor's nomination for the Presidency, in opposition to all others, and also took an active part for his election, after his nomination—speaking a few times in Maryland, near Washington, several times in Massachusetts, and canvassing quite fully his own district in Illinois, which was followed by a majority in the district of over 1500 for Gen. Taylor.

Upon his return from Congress he went to the practice of the law with greater earnestness than ever before. In 1852 he was upon the Scott electoral ticket, and did something in the way of canvassing, but owning to the hopelessness of the cause in Illinois, he did less than in previous presidential canvasses.

In 1854, his profession had almost superseded the thought of politics in his mind, when the repeal of the Missouri compromise aroused him as he had never been before.

In the autumn of that year he took the stump with no broader practical aim or object that [than?] to secure, if possible, the re-election of Hon Richard Yates to congress. His speeches at once attracted a more marked attention than they had ever before done. As the canvass proceeded, he was drawn to different parts of the state, outside of Mr. Yates' district. He did not abandon the law, but gave his attention, by turns, to that and politics. The State agricultural fair was at Springfield that year, and Douglas was announced to speak there.

In the canvass of 1856, Mr. L. made over fifty speeches, no one of which, so far as he remembers, was put in print. One of them was made at Galena, but Mr. L. has no recollection of any part of it being printed; nor does he remember whether in that speech he said anything about a Supreme court decision. He may have spoken upon that subject; and some of the newspapers may have reported him as saying what is now ascribed to him; but he thinks he could not have expressed himself as represented.

Source: Abraham Lincoln, "Autobiography Written for John L. Scripps," c. June 1860, in *The Collected Works of Abraham Lincoln,* 9 vols., ed. Roy P. Basler (New Brunswick: Rutgers University Press, 1953), 4:60–68.

Document 1.3   Response to a Distant Relative (1848)

Throughout his career Lincoln occasionally received requests for information about his family, which he usually answered in terse or noncommittal fash-

ion. In this letter, responding to a New Englander who shared his surname (and was actually distantly related), then Congressman Lincoln offered a more expansive reflection on his family's background than he customarily provided.

Washington, March 6- 1848

Mr. Solomon Lincoln,

Dear Sir:

Your letter to Mr. Hale, in which you do me the honor of making some kind enquiries concerning me, has been handed me by Mr. Hale, with the request that I should give you the desired information. I was born Feb: 12th. 1809 in Hardin county, Kentucky. My father's name is *Thomas;* my grandfather's was *Abraham,*—the same of my own. My grandfather went from Rockingham county in Virginia, to Kentucky, about the year 1782; and, two years afterwards, was killed by the indians. We have a vague tradition, that my great-grand father went from Pennsylvania to Virginia; and that he was a quaker. Further back than this, I have never heard any thing. It may do no harm to say that "Abraham" and "Mordecai" are common names in our family; while the name "Levi" so common among the Lincolns of New England, I have not known in any instance among us.

Owing to my father being left an orphan at the age of six years, in poverty, and in a new country, he became a wholly uneducated man; which I suppose is the reason why I know so little of our family history. I believe I can say nothing more that would at all interest you. If you shall be able to trace any connection between yourself and me, or, in fact, whether you shall or not, I should be pleased to have a line from you at any time. Very respectfully

A. LINCOLN

Source: Abraham Lincoln to Solomon Lincoln, March 6, 1848, in *The Collected Works of Abraham Lincoln,* 9 vols., ed. Roy P. Basler (New Brunswick: Rutgers University Press, 1953), 1:455–456.

**Document 1.4   Lincoln's Stepmother
Recalls His Childhood (1865)**

Lincoln and his stepmother, Sarah Bush Johnston, grew attached to each other after her marriage to his widowed father in 1819. He always regarded her with affection. Sarah Lincoln remained in Illinois even after Thomas Lincoln died in 1851, living with her daughter. President-elect Lincoln visited her briefly in 1861 before leaving for Washington. After Lincoln's assassination in 1865, his former law partner, William H. Herndon, conceived of a plan to write Lincoln's biography and began conducting a series of interviews with various relatives and friends of the great man. He interviewed Sarah Lincoln on September 8, 1865, at her daughter's home. The following selection comes from his notes of that interview. Lincoln's stepmother died in 1869.

. . . Abe was about 9 ys. of age when I landed in Indiana—The country was wild—and desolate. Abe was a good boy: he didn't like physical labor—was diligent for Knowledge—wished to Know & if pains & Labor would get it he was sure to get it. He was the best boy I ever saw. He read all the books he could lay his hands on—I can't remember dates nor names—am about 75 ys. of age—Abe read the bible some, though not as much as said: he sought more congenial books—suitable for his age. I think newspapers were had in Indiana as Early as 1824 & up to 1830 when we moved to Ills—Abe was a Constant reader of them—I am sure of this for the years of 1827–28–29–30. The name of the Louisville Journal seems to sound like one. Abe read histories, papers—& other books—cant name any one—have forgotten. Abe had no particular religion—didn't think of that question at that time, if he ever did—He never talked about it. He read diligently—studied in the day time—didnt after night much—went to bed Early—got up Early & then read—Eat his breakfast—go to work in the field with the men. Abe read all the books he could lay his hands on—and when he came across a passage that Struck him he would write it down on boards if he had no paper & keep it there till he did get paper—then he would re-write it—look at it repeat it—He had a copy book—a kind of scrap book in which he put down all things and this preserved them. He ciphered on boards when he had no paper or no slate and when the board would get too black he would shave it off with a drawing knife and go on again: When he had paper he put his sums down on it. His copy book is here now or was lately (Here it is shown me by

Mr. Thos Johnson). Abe, when old folks were at our house, was a silent & attentive observer—never speaking or asking questions till they were gone and then he must understand Every thing—even to the smallest thing—Minutely & Exactly—: he would then repeat it over to himself again & again—sometimes in one form and then in another & when it was fixed in his mind to suit him he became Easy and he never lost that fact or his understanding of it. Sometimes he seemed pestered to give Expression to his ideas and got mad almost at one who couldn't Explain plainly what he wanted to convey. He would hear sermons preached— come home—take the children out—get on a stump or log and almost repeat it word for word—He made other Speeches—Such as interested him and the children. His father had to make him quit sometimes as he quit his own work to speak & made the other children as well as the men quit their work. As a usual thing Mr. Lincoln never made Abe quit reading to do anything if he could avoid it. He would do it himself first. Mr. Lincoln could read a little & could scarcely write his name: hence he wanted, as he himself felt the uses & necessities of Education his boy Abraham to learn & he Encouraged him to do it in all ways he could— Abe was a poor boy, & I can say what scarcely one woman—a mother— can say in a thousand and it is this—Abe never gave me a cross word or look and never refused in fact, or Even in appearance, to do any thing I requested him. I never gave him a cross word in all my life. He was kind to Every body and Every thing and always accommodate others if he could—would do so willingly if he could.

Source: Sarah Bush Lincoln, interview by William H. Herndon, September 8, 1865, in *Herndon's Informants: Letters, Interviews, and Statements about Abraham Lincoln,* ed. Douglas L. Wilson and Rodney O. Davis (Urbana: University of Illinois Press, 1998), 106–109.

Document 1.5   Lincoln's Reply to "Dictionary of Congress" Questionnaire (1858)

Responding to a form questionnaire that was sent to all present or former members of Congress, Lincoln offered the following terse summary of his career achievements on the eve of his famous campaign to unseat Illinois senator Stephen A. Douglas.

Brief Autobiography
June [15?] 1858

> Born, February 12, 1809, in Hardin County, Kentucky.
> Education defective.
> Profession, a lawyer.
> Have been a captain of volunteers in Black Hawk war.
> Postmaster at a very small office.
> Four times a member of the Illinois legislature, and was a member of the lower house of Congress. Yours, etc.,

A LINCOLN.

Source: Abraham Lincoln, "Brief Autobiography," c. June 15, 1858, in *The Collected Works of Abraham Lincoln,* 9 vols., ed. Roy P. Basler (New Brunswick: Rutgers University Press, 1953), 2:459.

Document 1.6   Earliest Known
Lincoln Documents (c. 1824–1826)
The earliest known writings by Abraham Lincoln appeared in a copybook he kept as a teenager while learning to spell. Editors of his collected works have tentatively dated the following selections 1824–1826, when Lincoln was between fifteen and seventeen.

Abraham Lincoln
his hand and pen
he will be good but
god knows When

Abraham Lincoln is my nam[e]
And with my pen I wrote the same
I wrote in both hast and speed
and left it here for fools to read

Source: Abraham Lincoln, "Copybook Verses," c. 1824–1826, in *The Collected Works of Abraham Lincoln,* 9 vols., ed. Roy P. Basler (New Brunswick: Rutgers University Press, 1953), 1:1–2.

Document 1.7   The Lincoln Family on the Move

Name (relationship)	Life span	Birthplace	Number of moves	Total distance
Mordecai (American-line founder)	1657–1727	Mass.	2	9 miles
Mordecai Jr. (great-great-grandfather)	1686–1736	Mass.	3	120 miles
John (great-grandfather)	1716–1788	N.J.	3	299 miles
Abraham (grandfather)	1744–1786	Pa.	2	576 miles
Thomas (father)	1778–1851	Va.	6	708 miles
Abraham	1809–1865	Ky.	6	1,098 miles

Source: Adapted from Kenneth J. Winkle, *The Young Eagle: The Rise of Abraham Lincoln* (Dallas: Taylor, 2001), 3.

Document 1.8   Lincoln Lampoons
His Military Experience (1848)

During the 1848 presidential campaign, Congressman Abraham Lincoln gave a speech from the floor of the House of Representatives that used humor to poke fun at the Democratic candidate, Sen. Lewis Cass from Michigan. Because Cass was running against an acknowledged war hero, Gen. Zachary Taylor, the Democrats tried vainly to tout Cass's military credentials. Lincoln would have none of it, and in responding to their claims, he offered a revealing tongue-in-cheek recollection of his own military past.

By the way, Mr. Speaker, did you know I am a military hero? Yes sir; in the days of the Black Hawk war, I fought, bled, and came away. Speaking of Gen: [Lewis] Cass' career, reminds me of my own. I was not at Stillman's defeat, but I was about as near it, as Cass was to Hulls surrender; and, like him, I saw the place very soon afterwards. It is quite certain I did not break my sword, for I had none to break; but I bent a musket pretty badly on one occasion. If Cass broke his sword, the idea is, he broke it in de[s]peration; I bent the musket by accident. If Gen: Cass went in advance of me in picking huckleberries [whortleberries], I guess I surpassed him in charges upon the wild onions. If he saw any live, fighting indians, it was more than I did; but I had a good many bloody struggles with the musquetoes; and, although I never fainted from loss of blood, I can truly say I was often very hungry. Mr. Speaker, if I should ever conclude to doff whatever our democratic friends may suppose there is of black cockade federalism about me, and thereupon, they shall take me up as their candidate for the Presidency, I protest they shall not make fun of me, as they have of Gen: Cass, by attempting to write me into a military hero.

Source: Abraham Lincoln, "Speech in the U.S. House of Representatives on the Presidential Question," July 27, 1848, in *The Collected Works of Abraham Lincoln*, 9 vols., ed. Roy P. Basler (New Brunswick: Rutgers University Press, 1953), 1:501–516.

Document 1.9   Early Romantic Troubles (1838)

In this letter to the wife of a fellow attorney and politician, Lincoln describes a botched romance he conducted with a woman named Mary Owens. The description of the affair, though intended to be humorous and self-deprecating, seems sophomoric and, in places, verges on cruel.

To Mrs. Orville H. Browning
Springfield, April 1. 1838.

Dear Madam:

Without appologising for being egotistical, I shall make the history of so much of my own life, as has elapsed since I saw you, the subject of this letter. And by the way I now discover, that, in order to give a full and inteligible account of the things I have done and suffered *since* I saw you, I shall necessarily have to relate some that happened *before*.

It was, then, in the autumn of 1836, that a married lady of my acquaintance, and who was a great friend of mine, being about to pay a visit to her father and other relatives residing in Kentucky, proposed to me, that on her return she would bring a sister of hers with her, upon condition that I would engage to become her brother-in-law with all convenient dispach. I, of course, accepted the proposal; for you know I could not have done otherwise, had I really been averse to it; but privately between you and me, I was most confoundedly well pleased with the project. I had seen the said sister some three years before, thought her inteligent and agreeable, and saw no good objection to plodding life through hand in hand with her. Time passed on, the lady took her journey and in due time returned, sister in company sure enough. This stomached me a little; for it appeared to me, that her coming so readily showed that she was a trifle too willing; but on reflection it occured to me, that she might have been prevailed on by her married sister to come, without any thing concerning me ever having been mentioned to her; and so I concluded that if no other objection presented itself, I would consent to wave this. All this occured upon my *hearing* of her arrival in the neighbourhood; for, be it remembered, I had not yet *seen* her, except about three years previous, as before mentioned.

In a few days we had an interview, and although I had seen her before, she did not look as my immagination had pictured her. I knew she was over-size, but she now appeared a fair match for Falstaff; I knew she was called an "old maid", and I felt no doubt of the truth of at least half of the appelation; but now, when I beheld her, I could not for my life avoid thinking of my mother; and this, not from withered features, for her skin was too full of fat, to permit its contracting in to wrinkles; but from her want of teeth, weather-beaten appearance in general, and from a kind of notion that ran in my head, that *nothing* could have commenced at the size of infancy, and reached her present bulk in less than thirtyfive or forty years; and, in short, I was not all pleased with her. But what could I do? I had told her sister that I would take her for better or for worse; and I made a point of honor and conscience in all things, to stick to my word, especially if others had been induced to act on it, which in this case, I doubted not they had, for I was now fairly convinced, that no other man on earth would have her, and hence the conclusion that they were bent on holding me to my bargain. Well, thought I, I have said it, and, be consequences what they may, it shall not be my fault if I fail to do it. At once I determined to consider her my wife; and this done, all my powers of discovery were put to the rack, in search of perfections in her, which might be fairly set-off against her defects. I tried to immagine she was handsome, which, but for her unfortunate corpulency, was actually true. Exclusive of this, no woman that I have seen, has a finer face. I also tried to convince myself, that the mind was much more to be valued than the person; and in this, she was not inferior, as I could discover, to any with whom I had been acquainted.

Shortly after this, without attempting to come to any positive under-standing with her, I set out for Vandalia, where and when you first saw me. During my stay there, I had letters from her, which did not change my opinion of either her intelect or intention; but on the contrary, confirmed it in both.

All this while, although I was fixed "firm as the surge repelling rock" in my resolution, I found I was continually repenting the rashness, which had led me to make it. Through life I have been in no bondage, either real or immaginary from the thraldom of which I so much desired to be free.

After my return home, I saw nothing to change my opinion of her in any particular. She was the same and so was I. I now spent my time between planing how I might get along through life after my contemplated change of circumstances should have taken place; and how I might pro-crastinate the evil day for a time, which I really dreaded as much—perhaps more, than an irishman does the halter.

After all my suffering upon this deeply interesting subject, here I am, wholly unexpectedly, completely out of the "scrape"; and I now want to know, if you can guess how I got out of it. Out clear in every sense of the term; no violation of word, honor or conscience. I dont believe you can guess, and so I may as well tell you at once. As the lawyers say, it was done in the manner following, towit. After I had delayed the matter as long as I thought I could in honor do, which by the way had brought me round into the last fall, I concluded I might as well bring it to a con-sumation without further delay; and so I mustered my resolution, and made the proposal to her direct; but, shocking to relate, she answered, No. At first I supposed she did it through an affectation of modesty, which I thought but ill-become her, under the peculiar circumstances of her case; but on my renewal of the charge, I found she repeled it with greater firm-ness than before. I tried it again and again, but with the same success, or rather with the same want of success. I finally was forced to give it up, at which I verry unexpectedly found myself mortified almost beyond endurance. I was mortified, it seemed to me, in a hundred different ways. My vanity was deeply wounded by the reflection, that I had so long been too stupid to discover her intentions, and at the same time never doubting that I understood them perfectly; and also, that she whom I had taught myself to believe no body else would have, had actually rejected me with all my fancied greatness; and to cap the whole, I then, for the first time, began to suspect that I was really a little in love with her. But let it all go. I'll try and out live it. Others have been made fools of by the girls; but this can never be with truth said of me. I most emphatically, in this instance, made a fool of myself. I have now come to the conclusion never again to think of marrying; and for this reason; I can never be satisfied with any one who would be block-head enough to have me.

When you receive this, write me a long yarn about something to amuse me. Give my respects to Mr. Browning.

Your sincere friend
A. LINCOLN

Source: Abraham Lincoln to Mrs. Orville H. Browning, April 1, 1838, in *The Collected Works of Abraham Lincoln*, 9 vols., ed. Roy P. Basler (New Brunswick: Rutgers University Press, 1953), 1:117–119.

Document 1.10   Lincoln's Transition to Adulthood

	Age	Location
Starting to work at home	7	Indiana
Hiring out for the first time	13–14	Indiana
Leaving home	22	Decatur, Ill.
Initiating a courtship	26–27	New Salem, Ill.
Choosing an occupation	27	New Salem
Marrying	33	Springfield, Ill.
Acquiring a new home	34	Springfield

Source: Kenneth J. Winkle, *The Young Eagle: The Rise of Abraham Lincoln* (Dallas: Taylor, 2001), 61.

Document 1.11   Herndon Recalls Lincoln as Lawyer (1888)

William H. Herndon served as Lincoln's law partner for over sixteen years before the latter left for Washington as president-elect in 1861. The two had formed an enormously successful partnership, one of the busiest and most respected in antebellum Illinois. Yet according to Herndon's recollection, published as part of his biography of Lincoln cowritten by Jesse W. Weik in 1888, Lincoln was almost careless in his professional demeanor and in the practice of the law. Herndon, who considered himself a serious intellectual, admired Lincoln, but did not always seem able to understand his partner's practical outlook or mischievous sense of humor.

. . . In the office, as in the court room, Lincoln, when discussing any point, was never arbitrary or insinuating. He was deferential, cool, patient, and respectful. When he reached the office, about nine o'clock in the morning, the first thing he did was to pick up a newspaper, spread himself out on an old sofa, one leg on a chair, and read aloud, much to my discomfort. Singularly enough Lincoln never read any other way but aloud. This habit used to annoy me almost beyond the point of endurance. I once asked him why he did so. This was his explanation: "When I read aloud two senses catch the idea: first, I see what I read; second, I hear it, and therefore I can remember it better." He never studied law books unless a case was on hand for consideration—never followed upon the decisions of the supreme courts as other lawyers did. It seemed as if he depended for his effectiveness in managing a law suit entirely on the stimulus and inspiration of the final hour. He paid little attention to the fees and money matters of the firm—usually leaving all such to me. He never entered an item in the account book. If any one paid money to him which belonged to the firm, on arriving at the office he divided it with me. If I was not there, he would wrap up my share in a piece of paper and place it in my drawer—marking it with a pencil, "Case of Roe vs. Doe.—Herndon's half."

On many topics he was not a good conversationalist, because he felt that he was not learned enough. Neither was he a good listener. Putting it a little strongly, he was often not even polite. If present with others, or participating in a conversation, he was rather abrupt, and in his anxiety to say something apt or to illustrate the subject under discussion, would burst in with a story. In our office I have known him to consume the whole forenoon relating stories. If a man came to see him for the purpose of finding out something, which he did not care to let him know and at the same time did not want to refuse him, he was very adroit. In such cases Lincoln would do most of the talking, swinging around what he suspected was the vital point, but never nearing it, interlarding his answers with a seemingly endless supply of stories and jokes. . . .

. . . I used to grow restless at Lincoln's slow movements and speeches in court. "Speak with more vim," I would frequently say, "and arouse the jury—talk faster and keep them awake." In answer to such a suggestion he one day made use of this illustration: "Give me your little pen-knife, lying on the table." Opening the blade of the pen-knife he said: "You see, this blade at the point travels rapidly, but only through a small portion of space till it stops; while the long blade of the jack-knife moves no faster but through a much greater space than the small one. Just so with the long, labored movements of my mind. I may not emit ideas as rapidly as others, because I am compelled by nature to speak slowly, but when I do throw off a thought it seems to me, though it comes with some effort, it has force enough to cut its own way and travel a greater distance." This was said to me when we were alone in our office simply for illustration. It was not said boastingly.

Source: William H. Herndon and Jesse W. Weik, *Herndon's Life of Lincoln* (1888; reprint, New York: Da Capo, 1983), 268–273.

Document 1.12   Letter to His Wife (1848)

When he first arrived in Congress in December 1847, Lincoln brought along his wife, Mary, and their two young sons, Robert and Edward. Before long, however, the new congressman felt overwhelmed and distracted and arranged for his family to visit with relatives in Kentucky. The following letter, addressed to Mary Lincoln, offers a fascinating glimpse inside their marriage, suggesting that there were affection and mutual interests but also occasional friction over differences in their personalities.

Washington, April 16- 1848-

Dear Mary:

In this troublesome world, we are never quite satisfied. When you were here, I thought you hindered me some in attending to business; but now, having nothing but business—no variety—it has grown exceedingly taste-less to me. I hate to sit down and direct documents, and I hate to stay in this old room by myself. You know I told you in last sunday's letter, I was going to make a little speech during the week; but the week has passed away without my getting a chance to do so; and now my interest in the subject has passed away too. Your second and third letters have been received since I wrote before. Dear Eddy thinks father is "*gone tapila* [.]" Has any further discovery been made as to the breaking into your grandmother's house? If I were she, I would not remain there alone. You mention that your uncle John Parker is likely to be at Lexington. Dont forget to present him my very kindest regards.

I went yesterday to hunt the little plaid stockings, as you wished; but found that McKnight has quit business, and Allen had not a single pair of the description you give, and only one plaid pair of any sort that I thought would fit "Eddy's dear little feet." I have a notion to make another trial to-morrow morning. If I could get them, I have an excellent chance of sending them. Mr. Warrick Tunstall, of St. Louis is here. He is to leave early this week, and to go by Lexington. He says he knows you, and will call to see you; and he voluntarily asked, if I had not some package to send to you.

I wish you to enjoy yourself in every possible way; but is there no danger of wounding the feelings of your good father, by being so openly intimate with the Wickliffe family?

Mrs. Broome has not removed yet; but she thinks of doing so tomorrow. All the house—or rather, all with whom you were on decided good terms—send their love to you. The others say nothing.

Very soon after you went away, I got what I think a very pretty set of shirt-bosom studs—modest little ones, jet, set in gold, only costing 50 cents a piece, or 1.50 for the whole.

Suppose you do not prefix the "Hon" to the address on your letters to me any more. I like the letters very much, but I would rather they should not have that upon them. It is not necessary, as I suppose you have thought, to have them to come free.

And you are entirely free from head-ache? That is good—good—considering it is the first spring you have been free from it since we were acquainted. I am afraid you will get so well, and fat, and young, as to be wanting to marry again. Tell Louisa I want her to watch you a little for me. Get weighed, and write me how much you weigh.

I did not get rid of the impression of that foolish dream about dear Bobby till I got your letter written the same day. What did he and Eddy think of the little letters father sent them? Dont let the blessed fellows forget father.

A day or two ago Mr. Strong, here in Congress, said to me that Matilda would visit here within two or three weeks. Suppose you write her a letter, and enclose it in one of mine; and if she comes I will deliver it to her, and if she does not, I will send it to her.

Most affectionately A. LINCOLN

Source: Abraham Lincoln to Mary Lincoln, April 16, 1848, in *The Collected Works of Abraham Lincoln,* 9 vols., ed. Roy P. Basler (New Brunswick: Rutgers University Press, 1953), 1:465–466.

Document 1.13   Walt Whitman Observes the President (1863)

During a period of the Civil War, poet Walt Whitman served as a nurse in one of the temporary hospitals set up around Washington. From his residence, he viewed President Lincoln passing in and out of the city to his summer cottage at the nearby Soldiers' Home. On August 12, 1863, Whitman recorded these vivid observations in his wartime journal.

I see the President almost every day, as I happen to live where he passes to or from his lodgings out of town. He never sleeps at the White House during the hot season, but has quarters at a healthy location, some three miles north of the city, the Soldiers' Home, a United States military establishment. I saw him this morning about 8 ½ coming in to business, riding on Vermont avenue, near L street. The sight is a significant one, (and different enough from how and where I first saw him.)

He always has a company of twenty-five or thirty cavalry, with sabres drawn, and held upright over their shoulders. The party makes no great show in uniforms or horses. Mr. Lincoln, on the saddle, generally rides a good-sized easy-going gray horse, is dress'd in plain black, somewhat rusty and dusty; wears a black stiff hat, and looks about as ordinary in attire, & c., as the commonest man. Lieutenant, with yellow straps, rides at his left, and following behind, two by two, come the cavalry men in their yellow-striped jackets. They are generally going at a slow trot, as that is the pace set them by the One they wait upon. The sabres and accoutrements clank, and the entirely unornamental *cortege* as it trots towards Lafayette square, arouses no sensation, only some curious stranger stops and gazes. I see very plainly ABRAHAM LINCOLN'S dark brown face, with the deep cut lines, the eyes, & c., always to me with a deep latent sadness in the expression. We have got so that we always exchange bows, and very cordial ones.

Sometimes the President goes and comes in an open barouche. The cavalry always accompany him, with drawn sabres. Often I notice as he goes out evenings—and sometimes in the morning, when he returns early—he turns off and halts at the large and handsome residence of the Secretary of War, on K street, and holds conference there. If in his barouche, I can see from my window he does not alight, but sits in the vehicle, and Mr. Stanton comes out to attend him. Sometimes one of his sons, a boy of ten or twelve, accompanies him, riding at his right on a pony.

Earlier in the summer I occasionally saw the President and his wife, toward the latter part of the afternoon, out in a barouche, on a pleasure ride through the city. Mrs. Lincoln was dress'd in complete black, with a long crape veil. The equipage is of the plainest kind, only two horses, and they nothing extra. They pass'd me once very close, and I saw the President in the face fully, as they were moving slow, and his look, though abstracted, happen'd to be directed steadily in my eye. He bow'd and smiled, but far beneath his smile I noticed well the expression I have alluded to. None of the artists or pictures have caught the deep, though subtle and indirect expression of this man's face. There is something else there. One of the great portrait painters of two or three centuries ago is needed.

Source: Walt Whitman, "August 12, 1863," *Memoranda during the War* (Camden, N.J.: Walt Whitman, 1875–1876).

Document 1.14   Hay Diary Recalls Lincoln Late at Night (1864)

White House aide John Hay, recently graduated from college, often slept at the White House in a small bedroom adjacent to his office. His diary entry for April 30, 1864, records a memorable scene late at night when the sleepless president sought some company with his secretaries.

April 30, 1864:

. . . A little after midnight as I was writing those last lines, the President came into the office laughing, with a volume of [Thomas] Hood's works in his hand to show [John] Nicolay & me the little Caricature "An unfortunate Bee-ing," seeming utterly unconscious that he with his short shirt hanging about his long legs & setting out behind like the tail feathers of an enormous ostrich was infinitely funnier than anything in the book he was laughing at. What a man it is! Occupied all day with matters of vast moment, deeply anxious about the fate of the greatest army of the world, with his own fame & future hanging on the events of the passing hour, he yet has such a wealth of simple bonhommie & good fellow ship that he gets out of bed & perambulates the house in his shirt to find us that we may share with him the fun of one of poor Hoods queer little conceits.

Source: John Hay, diary entry, April 30, 1864, in *Inside Lincoln's White House: The Complete Civil War Diary of John Hay*, ed. Michael Burlingame and John R. Turner Ettlinger (Carbondale: Southern Illinois University Press, 1997), 194.

Let the People Rejoice!

CAPITAL SHALL NOT OWN US!

LINCOLN ELECTED!

THE PEOPLE TRUE TO LIBERTY.

ILLINOIS REDEEMED!

SHE VOTES FOR LINCOLN.

She chooses Republican Legislature.

SHE REPUDIATES DOUGLAS.

GOD BLESS THE OLD KEYSTONE!!

GOD BLESS NEW YORK!

Lincoln carries all the Atlantic States but New Jersey.

AN AVALANCHE OF FREEMEN.

SHOUT BOYS SHOUT, VICTORY IS OURS, FREEDOM IS TRIUMPHANT.

A Republican newspaper celebrates Lincoln's presidential victory in 1860.

CHAPTER TWO

Campaigns and Elections

L incoln's track record in politics is often misunderstood. He lost a popular vote only once, in his first race for state representative, when he was just twenty-three years old, barely employed, and recently arrived in a new town. During a thirty-three-year career in electoral politics that spanned from 1832 until 1864, Lincoln appeared as a candidate on nine general election ballots. He ran for Illinois state representative six times (1832, 1834, 1836, 1838, 1840, 1854), for U.S. representative once (1846), and for president twice (1860, 1864). Although he fell short in two contests for U.S. Senate (1855, 1859), neither involved a direct popular election, because in those days state legislatures—not the general public—selected members of the upper body (see Documents 2.1, 2.2, and 2.3). Thus he could report honestly at the outset of his first presidential campaign that his rookie defeat in 1832 was "the only time I have been beaten by the people" (Basler 1953, 3:512).

Nonetheless, most Americans continue to regard Lincoln as someone more accustomed to failure than success in the years before his presidency. Such a view, however, vastly underestimates his well-tested electoral abilities. In many ways, he became the consummate political professional—developing a thick skin to endure negative attacks, cultivating a folksy charm to win over skeptical audiences, building a reputation as a powerful public debater, and even coming to terms with the importance of raising campaign funds. Above all, he tended to the chores of his trade with a diligence that bordered on obsession. Lincoln may have entered the White House with hardly any administrative experience, but he certainly knew as much as anyone about how to operate inside the nineteenth-century American political system.

Yet it would be equally misleading to define Lincoln as little more than a smooth political operator. He invested great faith in the moral potential of the democratic process. His first public statement, for example, loftily described his "peculiar ambition" as that of "being truly esteemed of my fellow men, by rendering myself worthy of their esteem" (Basler 1953, 1:9; see Document 2.4). Although winning esteem while remaining worthy of esteem proved more elusive than it appeared at age twenty-three, Lincoln never lost this conviction. For years he searched for an issue or cause that would realign the political forces, elevate his own politicking, and justify the abuse he endured from unkind rivals. Ultimately, the future president came to realize that slavery was the fundamental moral and political question of the age.

During the 1850s, Lincoln helped organize the new Republican Party in Illinois and focus public attention on the spreading evils of the peculiar institution. Through his tireless efforts, he emerged as a respected figure in regional politics. Still, the national press and public were largely surprised by his nomination for president in 1860 and by his emergence as an effective commander in chief. Many contemporaries remained bewildered when he became the first president since Andrew Jackson to win reelection, a feat made even more remarkable because it was accomplished in the midst of a lengthy Civil War. Yet by holding firm to the principle that popular government can achieve a moral purpose, Lincoln finally demonstrated that he was both esteemed and worthy.

LEARNING THE POLITICAL TRADE, 1832–1849

Explaining Lincoln's attraction to political life is not a simple matter. There was little about his background that encouraged ambition for public office. "I was raised to farm work," he once recalled (Basler 1953, 3:511). Yet he left the farm and his family almost as soon as he possibly could. The lanky twenty-two-year-old settled in the central Illinois trading outpost of New Salem where he worked for several months, according to his own description, "as a sort of Clerk in a store" (Basler 1953,

3:512). The job offered little in the way of salary but allowed the aspiring young man to meet practically everyone in the small community. He made friends quickly, both among the more rough-and-tumble crowd who were impressed by his surprising athleticism and with the handful of frontier businessmen and professionals who organized earnest debating societies and reading clubs, which the poorly educated Lincoln joined enthusiastically. In a transient society of self-made strivers, the young man fit in easily. However, it soon became apparent that getting along was not his only mission. Despite humble origins, Lincoln had dreams of forging a distinguished public career. In March 1832, less than eight months after his arrival, he announced his intentions to run for state representative.

What made that announcement especially audacious was the way it appeared to violate the custom of republican virtue, a tradition still widely celebrated in a nation then little more than fifty years old. Early-nineteenth-century Americans believed that candidates were supposed to "stand," not "run," for office. They expected gentlemen of distinction to emerge almost by consensus on polling days, without divisive or self-aggrandizing campaigns. Whatever canvassing took place was usually more social than political and typically involved alcohol as much as analysis. The overriding fear, nurtured since the colonial era, was that anyone who sought power too eagerly could not be trusted to exercise the restraint considered vital for the functioning of a representative system.

Lincoln entered the political arena just as these attitudes were evolving into a more practical approach that accepted the need for actual contests. For the first time in American history, organized mass political parties were taking shape and campaigns for office were beginning to include discussion of serious issues. The two most prominent party movements were the Democrats, who supported President Andrew Jackson, and the Whigs, who generally opposed his administration's policies. Over time, several other political and socioeconomic issues divided the two parties, but these differences varied widely by region. In many of the younger prairie states, such as Illinois, open partisan warfare did not erupt until the late 1830s, after Jackson had already returned to Tennessee. Consequently, Lincoln ran his first campaign without officially aligning himself with either side of the emerging national debate.

His neutrality may explain why he lost. Without an organization behind him and with his politicking limited to a few personal appearances and one public letter, the young candidate was forced to rely too heavily on support from his adopted hometown. And though the voters of New Salem certainly came through for their candidate, backing him by an overwhelming 98 percent, the rest of the district knew little about him and the future president finished eighth out of thirteen candidates. There was no shame in defeat, however, and like many first-time political losers, he gained valuable exposure from the attempt. Indeed, the pro-Jackson forces in Illinois soon approached the ambitious young man, offering him appointments as local postmaster and deputy surveyor. The positions represented a good deal for an aspiring politician: much-needed cash and some government experience, plus opportunities to travel the district and keep up with current events (at that time, newspapers were distributed by mail). Lincoln accepted the jobs but never joined the Democrats.

Instead, during the 1830s and 1840s he emerged as one of the leaders of the new Illinois Whig Party. He secured state legislative office on his second try in 1834 and continued to win reelection to the General Assembly of Illinois until he stepped aside after serving four terms. The biggest issues of the period revolved around regional economics, and Lincoln's support for commercial growth probably best explains his early affiliation with the Illinois Whigs, who were strongly identified with such policies. He backed an ambitious scheme to expand the state's transportation network (what were then called internal improvements), but when the national economy declined, the plan faltered and the state temporarily faced bankruptcy.

He also worked to switch the state capital from a village in southern Illinois to the town of Springfield, closer to the state's center (and within what was then part of his legislative district). Once the deal was approved, he moved himself to the new capital and, after a brief period of study, entered the legal profession. He quickly mastered the fine points of lawmaking and party organization, emerging as a floor leader of the Whigs in the state house.

Before long, however, he found that his new lifestyle had created a backlash among some former friends and neighbors in the surrounding farming communities. Only a few years removed from his days as a penniless store clerk, Lincoln was now criticized for being part of the "Springfield Junto," a disparaging reference to what was perceived as the arrogant local elite. His marriage in the autumn of 1842 to Mary Todd, the sister of one of Springfield's leading hostesses and the daughter of a wealthy Kentucky businessman, only fueled this growing jealousy.

It took Lincoln several years to find the right political balance between his frontier roots and the middle-class culture that he ultimately embraced. At first, he seemed inclined toward a rough, informal style. When he believed he had been smeared late in one of his legislative campaigns, Lincoln bitterly denounced his attacker as "a liar and a scoundrel" and threatened to "give his proboscis a good wringing" (Basler 1953, 8:429; see Document 2.5). While speaking to friendlier audiences, he developed the rustic orator's habit of telling earthy, sometimes crude, jokes in order to warm up the crowds. Unimpressed, a local Democratic newspaper accused him of having an "*assumed clownishness*" which it claimed did not "become him" (Mitgang 2000, 17–18; see Document 2.6). But, in fact, sarcasm was a particular weapon of the young politician. In an era in which personal honor was highly cherished, Lincoln was even challenged to a duel because of one of the satirical pieces he wrote occasionally for local newspapers poking fun at leading Democrats. Even though dueling was then illegal, Lincoln accepted the challenge and almost carried it out.

The aborted duel coincided with the thirty-three-year-old's much-delayed decision to marry and by most accounts marked the beginning of a newfound maturity in his approach to politics and life. Out of office for the first time in years, Lincoln nevertheless remained active in the political arena, managing state party affairs and maneuvering to win the Whig nomination for Congress. "Turn about is fair play" became his mantra as he urged local party members to adopt a policy of rotating their nominees—a decision that would have benefited him most because the incumbent was a fellow Whig unlikely to lose his seat (Basler 1953, 1:353; see Document 2.7). As part of his campaign for greater stature, Lincoln also established his own law firm, carefully choosing as his junior partner William H. Herndon, who was politically active and associated with those opposed to the ruling Springfield clique. Lincoln quickly expanded his law practice across central Illinois, participating in a frontier custom called "riding the circuit" in which attorneys and judges actually rode together from town to town, creating a kind of traveling courtroom for communities too small to sustain their own judicial system. In addition to providing business for the new firm of Lincoln and Herndon, riding the circuit also offered the ambitious would-be congressman a good opportunity to meet new friends in his prospective district.

Lincoln finally won his much-desired congressional seat in 1846, but his timing proved inauspicious. By the late 1840s, the Jacksonian era party system was losing steam. The divisive economic issues of the 1830s had been mostly resolved. Moreover, enthusiasm for the new-style popular campaigns was beginning to ebb. The political parties had developed a variety of innovative tactics to rally their supporters—everything from parades and bonfires to custom-made songs and snappy slogans such as "Tippecanoe and Tyler Too." Although turnout remained high in presidential contests, observers noticed declining interest in races for other offices. Lincoln's congressional contest, for example, hardly received any newspaper coverage.

The only serious controversy in the congressional campaign erupted when the Democratic nominee, a Methodist preacher named Peter Cartwright, apparently implied to some audiences that Lincoln was "an open scoffer at Christianity." This charge had been leveled against Lincoln before, but it assumed new life in view of his pious opponent. Crafting a measured response, Lincoln admitted in a public statement that he did not belong to any church and confessed that he had previously believed in a form of fatalism, but he vigorously denied the underlying accusation. "I do not think I could myself, be brought to support a man for office," he wrote, "whom I knew to be an open enemy of, and scoffer at, religion." The episode left such a bitter taste that he authorized local newspapers to reprint his statement even after he had successfully defeated Cartwright in the election (Basler 1953, 1:382; see Document 2.8).

The other negative factor affecting Lincoln was the changing political climate caused by the outbreak of the Mexican War. Most northern Whig politicians opposed the conflict, begun in the spring of 1846, disturbed by the controversial way in which it began and concerned about the consequences for the simmering national debate over slavery. They feared that any acquisition of Mexican territory would disrupt the delicate sectional balance that had been in place since the Missouri Compromise of 1820. The compromise had been so important because it maintained an even number of slave and free states while establishing geographic boundaries regulating any future extension of slavery. However, among voters, especially in states such as Illinois, such legalistic objections to the war proved unpopular in the face of growing patriotic fervor.

Although he avoided taking a stance on the issue while campaigning, Lincoln proved loyal to his national party leadership as a freshman member and stubbornly attacked the Democratic administration's conduct of the war. His position earned him savage criticism from his political enemies and a series of nervous rebukes from his law partner and other political allies back in Springfield. Frustrated by the second-guessing, overwhelmed by the workload in an age without congressional staff, and lonely for his wife and young boys, Lincoln eventually made the decision that "turn about" applied to him as well and left Congress voluntarily after a single term.

Leaving Capitol Hill, however, did not necessarily mean leaving politics. If anything, Lincoln's ambitions seemed to grow during this period. In the presidential campaign of 1848, he attended the Whig national convention in Philadelphia, where he worked behind the scenes to help select Gen. Zachary Taylor, a Mexican War hero whose background was considered an insurance policy against the party's unpopular antiwar record. The lame-duck congressman also undertook a major speaking tour in New England on behalf of the Whig nominee, a strange move for a prairie politician unless perhaps he was beginning to see a national horizon within his own future. After Taylor's election, Lincoln made a concerted effort to secure a lucrative and relatively powerful appointment in the new administration as commissioner of the general land office (see Document 2.9). Despite a frenetic campaign for the position that controlled government land sales, he was passed over. Declining a consolation offer to become governor of the Oregon Territory, Lincoln returned to his law practice in Springfield uncertain about his future in politics.

FACING THE POLITICAL CRISIS, 1850–1858

By this stage in his life, the forty-year-old former congressman might have easily walked away from the public arena, content to earn more money as an attorney and less abuse as a private citizen. Many historians believe that was his intention, because over the next five years he declined to run for any office and appeared almost indifferent to local Whig Party affairs. Lincoln himself later wrote that he was "losing interest in politics," but the repeal of the Missouri Compromise in 1854 finally "aroused" his interest once again (Basler 1953, 3:512).

This interpretation, however, surely understates his voracious political appetite. After years of studying the electoral trade, he had become a devoted practitioner who was hard-pressed to pass up any realistic opportunities for political advancement. A good example of his instinctive politicking comes from the correspondence of a Boston journalist who shared a stagecoach ride with Lincoln in 1847. The eastern reporter found his traveling companion so amusing that he worked a few scattered descriptions of the tall politician into his travelogue—of course, utterly unaware of his new friend's future greatness. The vivid images suggest how obsessive Lincoln must have appeared to many of his contemporaries. "Such a shaking of hands—such a how-d'ye-do—such a greeting of different kinds, as we saw, was never seen before," commented the reporter. "It seemed as if he knew every thing, and he had a kind word, a smile and a bow for every body on the road, even to the horses, and the cattle, and the swine" (Pratt 1937, 139–140). In this manner, during the five years of political "retirement" that followed his congressional service and as he rode the judicial circuit eagerly shaking hands and swapping stories, Lincoln—regardless of his exact intentions— was steadily improving his future electoral prospects by the sheer force of his relentless, folksy charm.

In addition, it was not politics that was losing its appeal so much as the Whig Party. New issues made the old partisan distinctions appear irrelevant and outdated. As predicted, the Mexican War unhinged the sectional consensus over slavery once the free territory of California applied for statehood. The subsequent controversy resulted in the Compromise of 1850, an elaborate legislative deal that most notably shifted the balance of power in the Senate in favor of the free states while offering tougher restrictions on fugitive slaves to the South. Both Whigs and Democrats endorsed the arrangement, further eroding the differences between the two national parties and alienating a growing body of activists on either side of the Mason-Dixon Line.

By the early 1850s, the weaker Whig Party had effectively collapsed in parts of the North, where abolitionists sought to forge a new anti-slavery coalition from the disgruntled elements of the old parties. Further complicating the political situation was the emergence of surprisingly powerful social movements, such as the nativists who opposed rising European immigration and the temperance advocates who decried the widespread abuse of alcohol. This impending sense of crisis exploded in 1854 when Sen. Stephen A. Douglas, a Democrat from Illinois, secured federal legislation that repealed the Missouri Compromise. Anxious to expand white settlements across the Great Plains, Douglas gambled that by removing old restrictions on slavery in the territories—essentially allowing residents to decide the issue for themselves via referendum—he would realign the sectional stalemate and enhance his own career.

What happened over the next few years sorely tested American public institutions and the mettle of political leaders from all factions. In many ways, Douglas, though diminutive in stature, was the towering figure of his age, a powerful and ambitious senator blessed with sharp intelligence and a feisty sense of political combativeness. The boldness of his "Nebraska bill" (the 1854 Kansas-Nebraska Act) catalyzed a host of changes, leading ultimately to a massive partisan realignment that swept over nativism and temperance, destroyed the Whigs, divided the Democrats, spawned the Republicans, and created a dangerous atmosphere in which sectional differences finally appeared irreconcilable. Navigating such treacherous political terrain required extraordinary ability and vision. Lincoln soon proved himself equal to the challenge. In the first place, he knew Douglas well, having practically grown up with him in the cloistered world of Springfield politics. For the next several years, Lincoln placed his career squarely in the shadow of the "Little Giant," as Douglas was called, elevating his own stature by repeatedly testing his better known rival. Second, he learned from his earlier disappointments as a Whig and approached the formation of the Republican Party in Illinois primarily as a challenge in coalition building. It was hard, time-consuming work, but he proved almost indefatigable in his efforts. Finally, he recognized that the future of slavery in America was too serious a subject to allow pettiness or sarcasm to create unnecessary distractions. He adopted a new, more sober approach to public speaking that impressed audiences with the power of his ideas and the moral force of his philosophy.

From 1854 until his death in 1865, Lincoln devoted more time and attention to politics and government service than any other facet of his life, including his lucrative legal career or his beloved family. His first move was to make a formal comeback in electoral politics as a candidate for state representative. Such a strategy might seem to be a strange step backward for a former congressman, but Lincoln understood that fragile coalitions require stable figureheads, and he was prominent enough as a local figure to unite the various elements of what were generally called the anti-Nebraska forces. There was no doubt, however, that he had bigger plans in mind than serving another term in the Illinois General Assembly. On several occasions during the fall campaign, when Senator Douglas spoke to audiences across Illinois, private citizen Lincoln conveniently showed up to rebut his claims. Their seemingly spontaneous debates were actually the result of months of preparation on Lincoln's part. Local newspapers reported that he had been observed poring over documents in the state library, and his law partner later recalled that he had never seen him take public speaking so seriously.

Lincoln had always received praise for his oratorical abilities, but the response to his standard stump speech in 1854 was overwhelming. Unlike many other public speakers of the day, Lincoln carefully refrained from hyperbole, pretentious allusions, or personal vindictive. Instead, in speeches that routinely lasted for hours, he patiently built arguments rooted in American history and based on the plainest, most homespun logic. "When the white man governs himself that is self-government," he declared, "but when he governs himself, and also governs another man, that is more than self-government—that is despotism" (Basler 1953, 2:266; see Document 2.10). He used simple, evocative language to persuade his listeners and not simply impress them. For example, he admitted that the proposal to allow the extension of slavery in the territories filled him with "hate," because it enabled "the enemies of free institutions, with plausibility, to taunt us as hypocrites." He tempered this outburst, however, by confessing that "Southern people" were "just what we would be in their situation" and that even if he had "all earthly power," he was unsure what to do with slavery in states where it already existed (Basler 1953, 2:255; see Document 2.10).

A careful dissection of Lincoln's principal 1854 speech yields great insight into his developing political strategy. Without a doubt, he considered slavery the overriding issue of the period. Despite the fact that he was a local candidate running for office in a free state, the future of slavery was all that he talked about on the stump. Clearly, however, he was still working his way through the implications of an American nation without race-based slavery. He simply could not yet imagine whites and blacks living together as equals. Some historians believe his reluctance on this topic was the product of his own racism. Others argue that his ambivalence reflected political realities, not personal prejudice. In either case, all sides agree that he was opposed to the extension of slavery, a position that became the central tenet of the new Republican movement.

Lincoln does not often receive credit for being a founder of the Republican Party, because he was slow to label himself a Republican. Yet he played a more active role in the organization's formation than anybody else in Illinois. He not only pursued Douglas on the stump in 1854 and allowed his name to help organize the opposition coalition around Springfield, but also directed several other races for antislavery candidates across the state.

After Lincoln won his own state house contest, he resigned without serving to pursue a seat in the U.S. Senate once it became clear that the new legislature might offer a majority for an anti-Douglas candidate. For months, he and his allies bombarded legislators with appeals for support. With meticulous care, he prepared notebooks for his principal lieutenants that categorized all one hundred members of the incoming General Assembly by their anticipated political affiliation. The effort paid off, not in personal victory, but as a framework for organizing the emerging Republican coalition. In an eleventh-hour decision that enraged some of his supporters (including his wife), Lincoln dropped out of the stalemated balloting for senator and threw his support to an antislavery Democrat named Lyman Trumbull who was subsequently elected by a slim majority. It was a bold sacrifice for a former Whig leader and earned Lincoln deep gratitude from the small but powerful cadre of ex-Democrats who had bolted their party over Douglas's controversial repeal of the Missouri Compromise.

Over the next year, Lincoln, practically alone among mainstream political leaders in Illinois, worked to unite the disparate elements of the Republican forces into a formal state party organization. For example, when a snowstorm disrupted a meeting of pro-Republican newspaper editors in 1856, Lincoln was the only major political figure who bothered to attend. Again and again he stepped forward to deliver speeches, recruit candidates, plot strategy, raise funds, or perform any of the demanding chores inherent to basic political organizing. The members of the Illinois Republican delegation attempted to reward his efforts when they promoted him for a spot on the party's first national ticket as the 1856 vice-presidential nominee under candidate John Fremont. He finished second in the balloting but garnered an impressive tally of more than one hundred votes.

These details are important, because most accounts of Lincoln's path to the presidency do not usually begin in earnest until 1858 when he participated in a now-famous series of debates with Stephen Douglas. By that point, however, Lincoln had already ironed out most of his stylistic wrinkles, had essentially set his strategic political course, and had clearly established his place as a party leader. In fact, it was his assertive leadership of the Illinois Republicans that netted him a virtually unprecedented early endorsement for the U.S. Senate seat then held by Douglas. This was the head-to-head matchup that had been brewing for years, and the public excitement was palpable. The two men met for seven debates, literally dozens of hours of speeches that sometimes drew outdoor audiences of more than ten thousand. In addition, newspapers across the North carried breathless reports of the impressive exchanges. Consequently, Lincoln's national reputation grew, despite the fact that the fall election returns failed to change the complexion of the legislature quite enough to unseat Douglas.

In the years since the Lincoln-Douglas debates, a great deal of mythology has developed around them. For one thing, it has become easy to forget that they had only an indirect impact on the result of the senatorial decision. For another, despite many moments of high drama and powerful eloquence, there were also tedious stretches of repetition. In addition, the text commonly accepted for the debates might not accurately reflect the words that listeners heard. A few years ago, historian Harold Holzer produced a new version that used Republican newspaper accounts for Douglas's speeches and Democratic transcripts for Lincoln's. The result was that both men appeared more human, prone to the verbal slips, awkward phrases, and garbled digressions that their own partisan reporters apparently edited away without hesitation. Finally, according to the so-called Freeport Doctrine, Lincoln sacrificed the Senate seat but secured his election to the presidency by placing a shrewd question to Douglas during their second debate in Freeport on August 27, 1858. On that day, Lincoln queried his opponent about the meaning of the Supreme Court's controversial decision in the Dred Scott case (*Scott v. Sanford*) delivered the year before. By ruling that slavery in the territories was a property right beyond the interference of Congress, the majority on the high court had seemed to imply that Douglas's policy of territorial referendum (as well as the Republican position of containment) was unconstitutional. Lincoln simply asked Douglas if there was "any

lawful way" that territorial residents could exclude slavery in the aftermath of the Court's ruling (Basler 1953, 3:43; see Document 2.11). The incumbent senator replied that prohibition could always be maintained through local regulations that discouraged slaveholding.

Douglas's answer worked well in Illinois, where ambivalence on slavery was often appreciated, but it reportedly destroyed him as a national candidate because his words upset Southerners. This exchange explains the origins of the theory that Lincoln traded the contest in Illinois for a bigger prize down the line. In fact, Republicans had every reason to believe that by forcing Douglas to speak out on the Dred Scott decision they would hurt him in the immediate campaign. After all, his position acknowledging the role of unfavorable local regulations put him at odds with the official policy of President James Buchanan, who supported the Court's decision wholeheartedly. Buchanan, the nation's leading Democrat, subsequently set out to destroy Douglas whom he considered a selfish and arrogant rival.

Lincoln proved quite adept at exploiting divisions among his opponents and throughout the campaign exhibited a cool, calculated approach to practically all of the potential problems that developed. The Douglas-Buchanan feud, for example, initially struck some eastern Republicans as a golden opportunity to approach the Senate's leading figure about switching parties. This would have been a disaster for Lincoln, but rather than curse the indifference of national party leaders he dispatched his law partner to New York City on a discreet lobbying mission and mobilized the rest of his local supporters to set up the unprecedented early endorsement convention.

During the campaign, Lincoln not only attempted to put his rival on the rhetorical defensive, but also authorized agents to work covertly with Buchanan's men in an unholy alliance to dump Douglas. As election day approached and fears multiplied that the Democrats might attempt to flood the polls with unregistered voters, Lincoln calmly offered what he called a "bare suggestion." In a secret memo, Honest Abe wrote that the party should hire someone of the " 'detective' class" to trick the mostly foreign-born transients used by the Democratic operatives into supporting Republican legislative candidates (Basler 1953, 3:329–330; see Document 2.12).

Once the contest was concluded and Douglas had retained his seat, the state Republican Party fell into debt. In response, Lincoln dutifully kicked extra funds into the coffers and reluctantly asked others for more money. But most important, after the party's defeat became apparent, he rallied his downcast supporters by reminding them that the "fight must go on" and confidently predicting that "we shall have fun again" (Basler 1953, 3:336, 342).

SEEKING THE PRESIDENCY, 1859–1860

As Lincoln matured, he developed such humble personal mannerisms that it became easy to underestimate his ambition. "I do not think myself fit for the presidency," he concluded to more than a few supporters in the aftermath of the 1858 Senate campaign (Basler, 1953, 3:377, 395). Yet in the year after the contest, he gave political speeches in five states outside of Illinois. He bought a German-language newspaper which he turned over to a local editor with strict instructions not to print anything "designed to injure the Republican party" until after the 1860 presidential election (Basler 1953, 3:383). He quietly made plans to have his debates with Douglas published in book form and distributed nationally. He initiated correspondence with some national political leaders and, despite a stated desire to focus on his law practice, maintained an active role in state party affairs. Repeatedly, he warned Republicans to avoid divisions while predicting that the Democrats were bound to break apart sooner or later over the slavery question. He continued to monitor Stephen Douglas closely, certain that the Illinois senator would become the Democratic presidential nominee in 1860.

Although the presidential election was clearly on his mind, Lincoln stubbornly refused to acknowledge any personal interest in the contest (see Document 2.13). His humble denials, however, began to sound increasingly empty. When asked to provide a biographical sketch for Northern newspapers he demurred, saying there was "not much of me" but then penned a shrewd note that highlighted every aspect of his background that might appeal to different states or groups across the North (Basler 1953, 3:511). Meanwhile, he encouraged Norman Judd, the Illinois state Republican chairman and one of the former Democrats he had been cultivating for years, to win approval from national party leaders for holding the 1860 Republican national convention in Chicago.

Even more telling, Lincoln gave a series of political speeches in the Northeast, beginning with what would become the famous Cooper

Union address at an institute for higher learning in New York City. In that speech, he attempted to explain why the Republican policy against the extension of slavery represented the moral center of the national debate. Using a litany of historical examples, compelling logic, and sober rhetoric, he condemned radicals of all stripes—including abolitionists like the recently martyred John Brown—and managed to make the Republican argument sound conservative. It was an especially deft accomplishment for an undeclared presidential candidate visiting the home state of his party's frontrunner, New York senator and former governor William H. Seward, a man whose primary weakness was that some leading Republicans considered him too controversial. Lincoln then gained additional momentum by venturing through New England, ostensibly to visit his eldest son, who was attending boarding school in New Hampshire.

For someone who supposedly considered himself unfit for the presidency, Lincoln was proving to be quite effective as a potential nominee. Republican leaders began to give the Springfield attorney serious consideration. In many ways, he was an obvious choice. The party had to win in 1860 at least two of the three key states—Illinois, Indiana, and Pennsylvania—that had gone against it in the previous election. Lincoln grew up in Indiana and lived in Illinois. If the Democrats nominated Douglas, as most expected, then only a strong local candidate like Lincoln would offer them any shot of saving Illinois's eleven electoral votes. Meanwhile, Republicans in Pennsylvania and Indiana were divided over various "favorite son" possibilities, none of whom had much appeal outside of their home states. The two leading national figures in the Republican Party, Seward and Ohio governor Salmon P. Chase, were considered too radical for most voters in the Northern border states, which had a reputation for rewarding moderates on the slavery questions. If the Republicans wanted to nominate someone who would appeal to the lower North, then Lincoln was probably their safest choice.

Complicating the situation even further was a dying third party organization built around the nativist movement called the Americans or "Know-Nothings" because of their habitual secrecy. In 1856 many Republicans blamed Millard Fillmore, the American Party presidential candidate, for splitting the anti-Democratic vote in the lower North and costing them the election. The Americans had lost significant political ground in the four years since, but Republicans still wanted to find a nominee who would appeal to, or at least refrain from alienating, former

Know-Nothings. Seward had publicly opposed bigotry against Catholics and foreigners, earning the enmity of many so-called Americans. Lincoln had been more practical, insisting that despite his sincere opposition to the principles of nativism, he would do nothing publicly to jeopardize the fragile opposition coalition. In fact, during the 1850s Lincoln worked with Know-Nothing politicians in Illinois and was regarded by most nativists as an ally. Some historians now believe that his support among this group might have been the deciding factor in both his nomination and his election.

Still, most experts of the day rated Lincoln as a long shot heading into the Chicago convention. There were no primary contests to raise name recognition, and he was out of office and less well known than his leading rivals. In addition, one of the biggest factors working against him was money. Seward and his principal aide, Albany newspaper editor Thurlow Weed, controlled a sizable campaign war chest. Some Republicans attributed their defeat in the 1856 presidential contest to what had been an overwhelming Democratic financial advantage. They did not want to wage another national campaign without better access to campaign funding sources, mostly concentrated among eastern businessmen. On this front, prairie attorney Lincoln was at a competitive disadvantage. "I can not enter the ring on the money basis," he admitted in a letter to one potential convention delegate (Basler 1953, 4:31–32; see Document 2.14). To another correspondent, he wrote, "I could not raise ten thousand dollars if it would save me from the fate of John Brown" (Basler 1953, 4:33). A second potential blow to Lincoln's chances came in April 1860 with unexpected news from the Democratic national convention in Charleston, South Carolina. Neither Douglas nor any candidate had been able to win the necessary two-thirds supermajority for nomination, and Southern delegates, upset over a platform they considered too ambivalent on slavery, had walked out. It now seemed less certain that Illinois would be ground zero of the electoral contest, and Democrats appeared on the brink of chaos. Under these circumstances, the chances for Republican frontrunner Seward grew more likely.

Thus when the Republicans met in Chicago on May 16, 1860, for only their second national nominating convention, they had the luxury of considering themselves ahead in the presidential contest. They adopted a moderate platform designed to hold their commanding position in the North and set forward a winning legislative agenda. Filled with expectation, Seward's forces initially gained the upper hand, but Lincoln's team of advisers proved more resourceful. They commandeered a suite at the city's best hotel and entertained delegates in high style—as the invoices for cigars and whiskey still attest. Using their prerogatives as hosts of the convention, they also delayed the presidential balloting for a day to provide some extra time in their last-ditch efforts to unite the anti-Seward forces. Meanwhile, the local Chicago newspapers trumpeted Lincoln's winning qualities, paying special attention to his reputation for honesty and hard work. Just a week before, he had been dubbed the "rail splitter" at a state party convention in honor of his youthful experiences as a frontier laborer. It was the kind of popular image that helped to win nineteenth-century political campaigns, and it did not go unnoticed by the pragmatic delegates from the lower North. And finally, leaving almost nothing to chance, Lincoln's managers toyed with the seating chart and even printed a phony set of admission tickets to the convention hall to guarantee that their nominee had more observers, and supportive cheering, once the balloting began.

Lincoln himself was not present for any of these behind-the-scenes maneuvers. It was still considered inappropriate for a presidential candidate to solicit votes in his own behalf. Instead, he waited impatiently in Springfield, but the underlying strategy was one that he had defined from the outset. He had written: "Our policy, then, is to give no offence to others—leave them in a mood to come to us, if they shall be compelled to give up their first love" (Basler 1953, 4:33–34; see Document 2.15). Simply put, Lincoln and his advisers positioned him as the second choice for anyone opposed to Seward. It was the classic strategy for toppling a front-runner and worked in this case with textbook precision. The New York senator led on the first ballot, about sixty votes short of the simple majority of delegates required by Republican Party rules. But Lincoln gained on Seward in the second round and by the third was winning decisively. Ever since, speculation has run high that Lincoln's men accomplished this trick with more than just whiskey and cigars, but it is difficult to imagine that they could have offered any deals or bargains that would not have been made with equal effect by any other serious contender. Lincoln biographer David Herbert Donald believes a credible case can be made for only one secret arrangement—a deal with the Pennsylvania delegation (the convention's second largest) to provide crucial support for Lincoln on the second ballot in exchange for giving Sen. Simon Cameron a seat in the cabinet. There is no clear-cut proof of this alleged trade, but the controversial Pennsylvania politician did ultimately receive a cabinet post despite fierce objections from other leading Republicans.

By modern standards, the campaign itself was anticlimactic—or at least, predictable. The Democratic Party reconvened in June but broke apart again almost immediately. This time, however, Douglas finally secured his long-awaited nomination from the remaining Northern delegates and a few Southern participants who had been produced by his managers. Most leading Democrats from the Deep South bolted the party and nominated the incumbent vice president, John Breckinridge of Kentucky, as their candidate. The collapse of the national Democratic organization essentially guaranteed a Republican victory in November. Without Southern electoral votes, Douglas had no chance of success. Breckinridge actually had a larger base of support, but faced stiff competition in upper Southern states from another splinter group, the Constitutional Union Party, formed during the election by ultraconservative Whigs and Know-Nothings. Led by nominee John Bell, a former U.S. senator from Tennessee, the Constitutional Union movement earned substantial backing from voters frightened by the overt sectionalism of the major parties. There was some hope of forming what was called a Fusion ticket, combining the various opposition forces aligned against the Republicans, but coordination proved too elusive and by October, Douglas, for one, acknowledged his impending defeat.

From his law office in Springfield, Lincoln also appeared to recognize that he was about to become president. With exceptional self-discipline, he kept quiet and provided Douglas with no ammunition to use against him. He gave no speeches, attended only a handful of local campaign events, and provided correspondents and reporters with nothing but vague, innocuous statements (see Document 2.16). For a man who had spent so many years in the middle of intense political combat, it was an extremely difficult assignment. According to his closest friends, boredom became one of his principal enemies. Perhaps that explains why, just over two weeks before election day, the presidential candidate found time in his schedule to answer a letter from an eleven-year-old girl who had written asking if he had any daughters and suggesting that he follow the fashion of the day by growing a beard. "As to the whiskers," Lincoln replied, after listing the ages of his three sons, "do you not think people would call it a piece of silly affection?" (Basler 1953, 4:129).

The beardless, prepresidential Lincoln no longer occupies much space in the public consciousness. However, the youthful rail-splitting image was central to his appeal as a presidential candidate. After all, the electorate in 1860 was not only all male and lily white, but also substantially younger than it is today. Only 8 percent of the population was over fifty years old according to the 1860 census. Taking heed, Republicans targeted their efforts toward younger male voters, using paramilitary-style clubs called Wide-Awakes to organize parades and bonfires in the popular tradition of the earlier Whig and Democratic campaigns. The ideological contest was about slavery, and to a lesser degree about secondary issues such as the tariff, westward expansion, and government corruption, but the spirit of the battle was over competing notions of virility. Each party created its own fraternity. In an era before professional sports, tight-knit alumni networks, and compulsory military service, nineteenth-century American white men tended to express their primary male bonds through politics.

The result was that election day in mid–nineteenth-century America offered an exciting spectacle (see Document 2.17). Over 80 percent of eligible voters cast ballots on November 6, 1860—that is, more than 4.7 million Americans participated in what was arguably the nation's most important election to date. For months, Southern newspapers and politicians had warned that a Republican victory would destroy the Union. Without a doubt, the results confirmed their complaint that the United States had become hopelessly divided along sectional lines. The Republicans did not even field presidential electors on the ballots in ten out of fifteen slave states, and therefore won absolutely no electoral votes and only a smattering of popular votes across the South. But there was no need for a Southern strategy. Lincoln carried all eighteen free states except New Jersey, which he split with Douglas. Although he won only about 39 percent of the popular vote nationwide, he carried 54 percent of the popular ballots in the North. In the electoral college, Lincoln secured 180 out of 303 votes and would have won an electoral majority even if the vote totals of all three of his major opponents had been combined.

The 1860 election was unlike any other in American history because of what happened in its aftermath. For the first and only time in the nation's history, the losers of a contest refused to accept the results as legitimate. Some Northern politicians panicked and attempted to broker a deal, but President-elect Lincoln would have none of it. He had been engaged in the struggle for too long. "Let there be no compromise on the question of *extending* slavery," he insisted. "The tug has to come, & better now than any time hereafter" (Basler 1953, 4:150). Later, within a month and a half of the election, states from the Deep South, led by South Carolina, began to secede from the Union. Lincoln refused to acknowledge their right to leave, arguing that it was "the essence of anarchy" (Basler 1953, 4:268). Uneasily, the nation prepared for a war to settle a dispute that, for once, politics could not seem to resolve.

RUNNING FOR REELECTION, 1863–1864

The first two years of the Lincoln administration were disastrous politically. A little more than a month after the inauguration (then held in March) war broke out between the states. Despite the fact that the Confederacy was only a few months old, rebel generals and troops seemed better prepared for the conflict than their federal counterparts. Although Republicans controlled Congress once Southerners walked out, the new president still had a stormy relationship with Capitol Hill. Many of the top Republican legislators considered him too slow and indecisive, especially on controversial matters such as emancipation of the slaves and military strategy, and treated his public actions with "undisguised contempt," according to one leading journalist (Burlingame 1998, 22–23). Personal problems added to the president's woes. His wife was unpopular and drew criticism for overspending the White House budget. Even more devastating, at the end of the war's first year the Lincoln family endured the death of a child, twelve-year-old Willie, from what may have been typhoid fever.

The midterm elections of 1862 generally confirmed the political trend against the president. Northern Democrats gained thirty-two seats in the House, a fairly typical upswing for the out-of-power party, but nevertheless an impressive public relations victory. Republicans also lost key gubernatorial races and control of the state assemblies in Illinois and Indiana. The Northern antiwar movement became emboldened and Lincoln faced difficult choices about maintaining civil liberties in the face of plunging Union morale. The winter of 1862–1863 was miserable. In Europe, leading statesmen debated whether to intervene in the stalemated conflict. Back home, Republican governors, senators, and congressmen met separately in private caucuses to criticize the course of the administration and plot ways to dump some of the president's advisers or, ultimately perhaps, the commander in chief himself.

At least initially, there was little discussion about whether Lincoln would seek reelection. No president had served a second term since Andrew Jackson, over thirty years earlier. The perception of failure seemed too ingrained in the overmatched administration to consider another political campaign. As the war dragged on, however, the inherent strengths of the president and the federal side became increasingly apparent. Northern advantages in manpower, industrial capacity, and financial resources started to wear down the rebels. When Gen. Robert E. Lee's Confederate forces suffered defeat at Gettysburg, Pennysylvania, in July 1863, almost at the same time that Gen. Ulysses S. Grant's Union forces effectively seized control of the Mississippi River, the tide of the conflict finally seemed to have shifted in the Union's favor. Moreover, the president's halting embrace of an emancipation policy for Southern slaves actually seemed to have allowed passions to cool. Lincoln was also popular with the troops and the public, considered down-to-earth, kind, and wise and known widely as "Father Abraham." By late summer 1863, John Hay, one of Lincoln's top aides, reported in his diary a rising chorus of political talk in favor of a second term for his boss.

One way to approach Lincoln's campaign for reelection is to consider practically everything through the lens of the battlefield. Union victories translated into higher morale, which meant bolstered public confidence in the president. Defeat simply reversed the process. When most of the military news was bad, as it was during the first two years of the war, Lincoln was unpopular. But as federal troops captured more territory, especially under Grant's command in the Mississippi Valley, Lincoln's prospects improved. When Grant was transferred east in the spring of 1864 and given control over all Union armies, the president's standing probably reached its apex. Republicans, acting now as the Union Party, renominated him with an overwhelming consensus. Then a long summer of bloody stalemate between Grant's and Lee's armies plunged Northern public opinion once again into despair. By August 1864, Lincoln faced the real prospect that he might be removed as the Union coalition's nominee. Only the fall of Atlanta in early September appeared to rally the public and save his campaign. As federal troops prepared for a final assault on the heart of the Confederacy, Lincoln cruised to a land-slide victory in November.

Such a mechanistic interpretation, however, ignores a fundamental truth about the election: it never had to happen. At any point before the start of the fall campaign in 1864, Lincoln might have stepped or stumbled aside and allowed a handful of equally ambitious Republican politicians to lead the Union effort. Yet despite repeated military and political disasters, he never yielded his post nor appeared to lose his self-confidence. But even more impressive than his own decision to run was his conviction that an election itself was possible, even necessary, in the middle of a Civil War. The Lincoln administration suspended civil liberties on several occasions during the conflict and ultimately authorized the military arrest of more than fourteen thousand people. Union leaders were not shy about taking measures to stomp out whatever they considered a potential breeding ground for treason. It is quite possible that if the president had attempted to suspend the 1864 elections, he would have received support from both the Congress and the Northern public. Instead, he plunged ahead on sheer faith.

Even a brief review of the campaign suggests that what grounded Lincoln more than anything else was his experience. He knew how to win. For example, there was the problem of his Treasury secretary and former 1860 presidential rival, Salmon Chase. From early on, the president—and everybody else in Washington—realized that a member of his own cabinet aspired to replace him. But instead of reacting with fury or self-pity, Lincoln calmly set about taking care of his own political business while allowing Chase to destroy himself. In November 1863, the secretary hosted a wedding for his daughter, who was marrying a wealthy senator from Rhode Island. The event brought together most of official Washington and might have served as a launch pad for his prospective campaign had not the president himself arrived, with gift in hand, to enjoy the festivities and conduct a little of his own networking. A week later, Lincoln again demonstrated his single-minded determination by traveling to Pennsylvania, despite a sick child and over his wife's objections, to help dedicate the new military cemetery at Gettysburg. What made this trip so important, besides the memorable speech, was the fact that several Northern governors attended the ceremony. Between the Chase wedding and the Gettysburg dedication, Lincoln was able to meet in person with most of the major political figures in the North. It was the

regional and personal disputes that complicated party management. Finding a single candidate who could unite the various factions was extraordinarily difficult, and there was virtually no chance that disgruntled Republicans would identify an alternative to Lincoln who was acceptable to everyone. The only serious contender for the role besides the president was General Grant, but Lincoln monitored him closely and knew that his potential rival could not win political support unless he achieved more progress on the battlefield—a development that would simultaneously help alleviate criticism of the White House.

Instead, with grim determination the president prayed for Democratic divisions to reveal themselves. He did not have to wait long. The Democratic national convention, held in Chicago at the end of August, proved to be a fiasco. The so-called Peace Democrats wrote a party platform that bitterly attacked the war as "four years of failure" (Zornow 1954, 132). Yet pro-Union Democrats succeeded in winning the presidential nomination for Gen. George B. McClellan, who was closely identified with the war effort because he had commanded the Army of the Potomac for more than a year before clashing with Lincoln over strategy. The general favored continuing the conflict, although not on the president's terms. A novice politician, McClellan simply tried to ignore the dissonance within his own party and proved indifferent to most of the campaign's requisite politicking.

The irony is that if the dates of the national nominating conventions had been reversed—that is, if the Democrats had met in June and the Unionists in August—then an entirely different result might have occurred. Instead, the Democrats emerged from their convention at the worst possible moment, denouncing the administration just as Union forces finally achieved their long-awaited breakthrough. Gen. William T. Sherman's army captured Atlanta in early September, a result that reinvigorated Northern morale and convinced most observers that Lincoln's reelection was finally secure.

Nonetheless, the campaign was fiercely contested. Partisan newspapers on each side unleashed a full-throttle political contest. In those days, newspapers provided the principal communications tools for the parties. The Union campaign chairman, for example, was Henry Raymond, who also served simultaneously as editor of the *New York Times*.

At times, the tone of the contest became shrill. Northern Democrats accused Lincoln of having assumed dictatorial powers during the war.

The administration responded by issuing a special report from Judge Advocate General Joseph Holt documenting widespread allegations of domestic treason. A couple of Democratic operatives attempted a race-baiting hoax that they thought would embarrass the president. They secretly produced a pamphlet, entitled "Miscegenation," which they attributed to abolitionists who supposedly endorsed the sexual and social intermingling of the races as a likely future for postemancipation America. Then they mailed the document to leading antislavery figures, including the president, requesting supportive statements of the fanciful proposal. The president's aides shelved his copy and the hoax was eventually exposed, but Democrats repeatedly tried to stir the racist fears of Northern whites during the contest. Pro-Union newspapers also engaged in some bigoted attacks. The *New York Times* claimed, for example, that the Democratic Party had fallen into the hands of "foreign Jew bankers" because the organization's campaign committee was headed by August Belmont, an adviser to the famous Rothschild family (Ferguson 1999, 115).

Although Lincoln once again stayed out of the public fray, he worked behind the scenes on several key campaign projects. One of the attacks against him was quite personal, rehashing an old allegation that he had shown disrespect for dead Union soldiers by swapping jokes and singing songs with his entourage while visiting the bloody battlefield at Antietam, Maryland, in 1862. Lincoln called his friend and frequent companion Ward Hill Lamon into the White House to discuss the events, and the president carefully prepared an affidavit for Lamon denying the charges. On another occasion, the president told one of his top aides that he had dispatched power broker Thurlow Weed on a special trip related to opposition research. The goal, according to the president, was to find evidence that would prove a rumor that General McClellan had once signed a letter pledging to slow the progress of his armies in exchange for Democratic backing in the 1864 contest. Weed, who had been Seward's right-hand man in 1860, was now proving useful to Lincoln. The New York–based power broker also collected tens of thousands of dollars in campaign funds from Union army contractors. By this point in his career, the president well understood the power of money and even allowed party fund-raisers to demand hundreds of dollars each from the members of his cabinet.

The results of election day on Tuesday, November 8, 1864, confirmed the wisdom of Lincoln's tactics and his faith in the process (see Documents 2.20 and 2.21). He won 55 percent of the popular vote and more than 90 percent of the electoral vote. McClellan carried only three states—Delaware, Kentucky, and New Jersey. Meanwhile, Republican candidates in other races also had done extremely well. The party won 145 out of 185 seats in the House and regained almost all of the losses suffered in the previous midterm and off-year contests. By most accounts, the key to the landslide was the overwhelming pro-Union vote from soldiers. Nineteen states allowed troops to vote in the field or by absentee ballot. Not all of the states tabulated the soldier vote separately, but among those that did, Lincoln scored nearly 80 percent of the ballots— a remarkable testament to the commander in chief's popularity among his own subordinates.

For Lincoln, winning reelection under these circumstances was especially gratifying. He had risked a great deal for himself and the nation. "We can not have free government without elections," he said afterwards, "and if the rebellion could force us to forego, or postpone a national election, it might fairly claim to have already conquered and ruined us." Some Americans of that era denigrated what Lincoln called a "political war" as divisive and unnecessary. Yet from his perspective it was the only possible foundation for the nation's freedom (Basler 1953, 8:100–101; see Document 2.22).

Unfortunately, Lincoln paid a personal price for achieving the power that popularity and esteem brought him. His victory demonstrated his indispensability to the Union cause and made him a target for anyone determined to destroy the federal government. As the Confederacy collapsed, embittered rebels increasingly focused their rage against the man who, more than any other single person, was responsible for their impending defeat. Some of those around the president realized the danger and tried to protect him. One of the most poignant scenes of the election appears in the diary of John Hay, Lincoln's personal secretary. He noted that on election night Lincoln's unofficial bodyguard, Ward Lamon, instinctively came to the White House after the results were announced and sat outside the president's bedroom door with "a small arsenal of pistols & bowie knives around him." He stayed all night before finally slipping away early in the morning (Burlingame and Ettlinger

1997, 246; see Document 2.23). It was a touching gesture during an era when ballots were sadly often followed by bullets.

SELECTED PRIMARY SOURCES

Basler, Roy P., ed. *The Collected Works of Abraham Lincoln*. 9 vols. New Brunswick: Rutgers University Press, 1953.

Burlingame, Michael, ed. *Lincoln Observed: Civil War Dispatches of Noah Brooks*. Baltimore: Johns Hopkins University Press, 1998.

Burlingame, Michael, and John R. Turner Ettlinger, eds. *Inside Lincoln's White House: The Complete Civil War Diary of John Hay*. Carbondale: Southern Illinois University Press, 1997.

Herndon, William H., and Jesse W. Weik, *Herndon's Life of Lincoln*. 1888. Reprint, New York: Da Capo, 1983.

Holzer, Harold, ed. *The Lincoln-Douglas Debates: The First Complete Unexpurgated Text*. New York: HarperCollins, 1993.

Mitgang, Herbert, ed. *Abraham Lincoln: A Press Portrait*. 1956. Reprint, New York: Fordham University Press, 2000.

Pratt, Harry E., ed. "Illinois as Lincoln Knew It: A Boston Reporter's Record of a Trip in 1847." *Transactions of the Illinois State Historical Society* (1937): 109–141.

SECONDARY SOURCES

Boritt, Gabor S. *Lincoln and the Economics of the American Dream*. Memphis: Memphis State University Press, 1978.

Ferguson, Niall. *The House of Rothschild: The World's Banker 1849–1999*. New York: Viking, 1999.

Gienapp, William E. *The Origins of the Republican Party, 1852–1856*. New York: Oxford University Press, 1988.

Howe, Daniel Walker. *The Political Culture of the American Whigs*. Chicago: University of Chicago Press, 1979.

Johannsen, Robert W. *Lincoln. The South, and Slavery: The Political Dimension*. Baton Rouge: Louisiana State University Press, 1991.

Long, David E. *The Jewel of Liberty: Abraham Lincoln's Re-Election and the End of Slavery*. Mechanicsburg, Pa.: Stackpole Books, 1994.

Paludan, Phillip Shaw. *The Presidency of Abraham Lincoln*. Lawrence: University of Kansas Press, 1994.

Riddle, Donald W. *Congressman Abraham Lincoln*. Urbana: University of Illinois Press, 1957.

Schwartz, Thomas F. " 'An Egregious Political Blunder': Justin Butterfield, Lincoln and Illinois 'Whiggery.' " *Papers of the Abraham Lincoln Association* 8 (1986): 9–19.

Silbey, Joel H. " 'Always a Whig in Politics': The Partisan Life of Abraham Lincoln." *Papers of the Abraham Lincoln Association* 8 (1986): 21–42.

Waugh, John C. *Reelecting Lincoln: The Battle for the 1864 Presidency*. New York: Crown, 1997.

Wiebe, Robert H. "Lincoln's Fraternal Democracy." In *Abraham Lincoln and the American Political Tradition*, edited by John L. Thomas. Amherst: University of Massachusetts Press, 1986.

RECOMMENDED READING

Donald, David Herbert. *Lincoln*. New York: Simon and Schuster, 1995.

Out of literally thousands of biographies on Abraham Lincoln, this single volume probably offers the most reliable and comprehensive analysis of the great president's political career, especially for the campaigns of 1860 and 1864.

Beveridge, Albert J. *Abraham Lincoln, 1809–1858*. 2 vols. Boston: Houghton Mifflin, 1928.

Written by a sitting U.S. senator, this impressive two-volume work still contains valuable insight into Lincoln's prepresidential career.

Gienapp, William E. "Who Voted for Lincoln?" In *Abraham Lincoln and the American Political Tradition*, edited by John L. Thomas. Amherst: University of Massachusetts Press, 1986.

For number crunchers and political junkies, this essay is heaven-sent, providing a detailed breakdown of the demographic factors at stake in the 1860 election.

Zornow, William Frank. *Lincoln and the Party Divided*. Norman: University of Oklahoma Press, 1954.

Although there are more recent and equally readable books on the 1864 election, Zornow's work still stands as the most meticulous accounting of that exciting race.

Document 2.1   Lincoln's Career Electoral Record

Year	Office	Party	Result
1832	State representative	Whig	Loss
1834	State representative	Whig	Win
1836	State representative	Whig	Win
1838	State representative	Whig	Win
1840	State representative	Whig	Win
1846	U.S. representative	Whig	Win
1854	State representative	Anti-Nebraska/Fusion	Win[a]
1860	President	Republican	Win
1864	President	Union	Win
Total			8 wins, 1 loss

[a] Lincoln resigned before serving as a state representative to enter the contest for the U.S. Senate.

Source: Compiled by the author.

Document 2.2   Lincoln's Record in Contests Determined by Legislative Ballot

Year	Office	Party	Result
1838	Speaker of state house	Whig	Loss
1840	Speaker of state house	Whig	Loss
1855	U.S. senator	Anti-Nebraska/Fusion	Loss[a]
1859	U.S. senator	Republican	Loss

[a] Lincoln lost but preserved victory for another Fusion candidate.

Source: Compiled by the author.

Document 2.3   Lincoln's Record as Candidate for Government Positions

Year	Office	Result
1832	Captain, Illinois militia	Elected
1833	Postmaster, New Salem, Ill.	Appointed
1833	Deputy county surveyor, Sangamon	Appointed
1849	Commissioner, U.S. General Land Office	Rejected
1849	Secretary, Oregon Territory	Offered[a]
1849	Governor, Oregon Territory	Offered[a]
1852	Claims commissioner, Illinois and Michigan Canal	Appointed

[a] Lincoln declined each offer to serve in the Oregon Territory.

Source: Compiled by the author.

Document 2.4   Selections from First Campaign Document (1832)

This announcement appeared in the Sangamo Journal *on March 15, 1832, less than eight months after Lincoln arrived in New Salem, Illinois. In those days elections for the Illinois state legislature took place in early August and whatever campaigning occurred was usually conducted over the summer. Political parties were not yet firmly established. Lincoln thus promoted himself to his neighbors in Sangamo (later Sangamon) County, Illinois, as an eager problem solver who understood the importance of local issues such as improving transportation. His concluding paragraphs suggest that behind his characteristic veil of humility Lincoln was both exceptionally ambitious and earnest.*

To the People of Sangamo County March 9, 1832

FELLOW-CITIZENS: Having become a candidate for the honorable office of one of your representatives in the next General Assembly of this state, in accordance with an established custom, and the principles of true republicanism, it becomes my duty to make known to you—the people whom I propose to represent—my sentiments with regard to local affairs. Time and experience have verified to a demonstration, the public utility of internal improvements. That the poorest and most thinly populated countries would be greatly benefitted by the opening of good roads, and in the clearing of navigable streams within their limits, is what no person will deny. But yet it is folly to undertake works of this or any other kind, without first knowing that we are able to finish them—as half finished work generally proves to be labor lost. There cannot justly be any objection to having rail roads and canals, any more than to other good things, provided they cost nothing. The only objection is to paying for them; and the objection to paying arises from the want of ability to pay. . . .

. . . But, Fellow-Citizens, I shall conclude. Considering the great degree of modesty which should always attend youth, it is probable I have already been more presuming than becomes me. However, upon the subjects of which I have treated, I have spoken as I thought. I may be wrong in regard to any or all of them; but holding it a sound maxim, that it is better to be only sometimes right, than at all times wrong, so soon as I discover my opinions to be erroneous, I shall be ready to renounce them.

Every man is said to have his peculiar ambition. Whether it be true or not, I can say for one that I have no other so great as that of being truly esteemed of my fellow men, by rendering myself worthy of their esteem. How far I shall succeed in gratifying this ambition, is yet to be developed. I am young and unknown to many of you. I was born and have ever remained in the most humble walks of life. I have no wealthy or popular relations to recommend me. My case is thrown exclusively upon the independent voters of this county, and if elected they will have conferred a favor upon me, for which I shall be unremitting in my labors to compensate. But if the good people in their wisdom shall see fit to keep me in the background, I have been too familiar with disappointments to be very much chagrined.

Your friend and fellow-citizen, New Salem, March 9, 1832. A. LINCOLN.

Source: Abraham Lincoln, "Communication to the People of Sangamo County," March 9, 1832, in *The Collected Works of Abraham Lincoln,* 9 vols., ed. Roy P. Basler (New Brunswick: Rutgers University Press, 1953), 1:5–9.

Document 2.5   Rough-and-Tumble Early Campaigns (1836)
This copy of an undated handbill was found in the papers of one of Lincoln's contemporaries, but the text indicates that it was probably issued by the future

president sometime near the end of the 1836 state legislative campaign. At the time, Lincoln was seeking his second term in the Illinois General Assembly as a representative of Sangamon County, which was in the central part of the state. The tone is defiant and contains more than a little malice, illustrating the contentiousness of many of Lincoln's early political contests.

TO THE PEOPLE OF SANGAMON COUNTY

Fellow Citizens:

I have this moment been shown a handbill signed "Truth Teller," in which my name is done up in large capitals. No one can doubt the object of this attack at this late hour. An effort is now made to show that John T. Stuart and myself opposed the passage of the bill by which the Wiggins loan was paid. The handbill says—"The only vote taken on the bill when the yeas and nays were taken, was upon engrossing the bill for a third reading." That's a lie. Let the reader refer to pages, 124, 125 & 126 of the Journal, and he will see that the yeas and nays were taken *twice* upon the bill *after* the vote referred to by this lying Truth Teller. And he will also see that my course toward the bill was anything but unfriendly. It is impossible to make a lengthy answer at this late hour. All I have to say is that the author is a *liar* and a *scoundrel,* and that if he will avow the authorship to me, I promise to give his proboscis a good wringing.

A.LINCOLN.

Source: Abraham Lincoln, "To the People of Sangamon County," c. 1836, in *The Collected Works of Abraham Lincoln,* 9 vols., ed. Roy P. Basler (New Brunswick: Rutgers University Press, 1953), 8:429.

Document 2.6   Political Opponents
Criticize Lincoln's "Clownishness" (1839)

The Illinois State Register *was the principal Democratic newspaper in Springfield, Illinois. As one of the town's leading Whig politicians, Lincoln endured frequent criticism from the journal. In 1839, after a series of debates with Stephen A. Douglas, who at that time was a promising young Democratic politician, Lincoln received stinging criticism from the* Register *for relying too heavily, in its opinion, on sarcasm and mimicry to score points in his political speeches. Lincoln shrugged off the complaints, but as the years wore on he projected more gravity in his public addresses.*

From the *Illinois State Register* (Springfield), November 23, 1839:

. . . Mr. Lincoln's argument was truly ingenious. He has, however, a sort of *assumed clownishness* in his manner which does not become him, and which does not truly belong to him. It *is assumed*—assumed for effect. Mr. Lincoln will sometimes make his language correspond with this clownish manner, and he can thus frequently raise a loud laugh among his Whig hearers; but this entire game of buffoonery convinces the *mind* of no man, and is utterly lost on the majority of his audience. We seriously advise Mr. Lincoln to correct this clownish fault before it grows upon him. . . .

Source: Illinois State Register (Springfield), November 23, 1839; reprinted in *Abraham Lincoln: A Press Portrait*, ed. Herbert Mitgang (1956; reprint, New York: Fordham University Press, 2000), 17–18.

Document 2.7   Positioning to Run for Congress (1846)

In the spring of 1843 Lincoln began an aggressive behind-the-scenes campaign to win the Whig nomination for Congress. Because the Whigs dominated the central region of Illinois but usually lacked the votes to win statewide offices, the congressional nomination in his district was highly coveted. The incumbent was a relatively young local Whig leader named John Hardin, who exhibited no interest in leaving office. Moreover, Lincoln was not the only aspiring congressman in the Whig ranks. His close friend Edward Baker, respected in the area as an eloquent orator, also wanted a chance to serve in Washington.

At a party convention in Pekin, Illinois, Lincoln and Baker succeeded in earning Hardin's agreement to step aside and allow Baker to run as the Whig candidate. After Baker's term in Congress, Lincoln expected the principle of "turn about" to work in his favor, but discovered that Hardin now denied there had been any permanent agreement over rotation in office. Almost frantically, Lincoln began writing a series of letters to supporters such as Dr. Robert Boal, urging them to prevent Hardin from recapturing the Whig nomination. Ultimately, Hardin withdrew from the contest to serve in the

Mexican War where he was killed in battle and Baker, seeking greater oppor-
tunities, moved away from Springfield, leaving Lincoln as the local party's
undisputed leader.

To Robert Boal
Dear Doctor Springfield Jany. 7 1846.

Since I saw you last fall, I have often thought of writing you as it was then
understood I would, but on reflection I have always found that I had nothing new to tell you. All has happened as I then told you I expected it
would—[Edward] Baker's declining, [John] Hardin's taking the tract, and
so on.

If Hardin and I stood precisely equal—that is, if *neither* of us had been
to congress, or if we *both* had—it would only accord with what I have
always done, for the sake of peace, to give way to him; and I expect I
should do it. That I *can* voluntarily postpone my pretentions, when they
are no more than equal to those to which they are postponed, you have
yourself seen. But to yield to Hardin under present circumstances, seems
to me as nothing else than yielding to one who would gladly sacrifice me
altogether. This, I would rather not submit to. That Hardin is talented,
energetic, usually generous and magnanimous, I have, before this, affirmed
to you, and do not now deny. You know that my only argument is that
"turn about is fair play". This he, practically at least, denies.

If it would not be taxing you too much, I wish you would write me,
telling the aspect of things in your county, or rather your district; and also
send the names of some of your whig neighbours, to whom I might, with
propriety write. Unless I can get some one to do this, Hardin with his old
franking list, will have the advantage of me. My reliance for a fair shake
(and I want nothing more) in your county is chiefly on you, because of
your position and standing, and because I am acquainted with so few others. Let this be strictly confidential, & any letter you may write me shall be
the same if you desire. Let me hear from you soon.

Yours truly
A. LINCOLN

Source: Abraham Lincoln to Robert Boal, January 7, 1846, in *The Collected Works
of Abraham Lincoln,* 9 vols., ed. Roy P. Basler (New Brunswick: Rutgers University Press, 1953), 1:352–353.

Document 2.8   Handbill Replying
to Charges of Lack of Piety (1846)

Lincoln ran for Congress in 1846 against Democrat Peter Cartwright, a well-known Methodist preacher and former state legislator. The race received relatively little coverage in the local press, but the last-minute accusations it generated about Lincoln's religious beliefs infuriated him so much that he not only issued a handbill denying the charges, but also authorized local newspapers to reprint the text of his statement after he won the election.

To the Voters of the Seventh Congressional District.

FELLOW CITIZENS:

A charge having got into circulation in some of the neighborhoods of this District, in substance that I am an open scoffer at Christianity, I have by the advice of some friends concluded to notice the subject in this form. That I am not a member of any Christian Church, is true; but I have never denied the truth of the Scriptures; and I have never spoken with intentional disrespect of religion in general, or of any denomination of Christians in particular. It is true that in early life I was inclined to believe in what I understand is called the "Doctrine of Necessity"—that is, that the human mind is impelled to action, or held in rest by some power, over which the mind itself has no control; and I have sometimes (with one, two or three, but never publicly) tried to maintain this opinion in argument. The habit of arguing thus however, I have, entirely left off for more than five years. And I add here, I have always understood this same opinion to be held by several of the Christian denominations. The foregoing, is the whole truth, briefly stated, in relation to myself, upon this subject.

I do not think I could myself, be brought to support a man for office, whom I knew to be an open enemy of, and scoffer at, religion. Leaving the higher matter of eternal consequences, between him and his Maker, I still do not think any man has the right thus to insult the feelings, and injure the morals, of the community in which he may live. If, then, I was guilty of such conduct, I should blame no man who should condemn me for it; but I do blame those, whoever they may be, who falsely put such a charge in circulation against me.

July 31, 1846.
A. LINCOLN.

Source: Abraham Lincoln, "Handbill Replying to Charges of Infidelity," July 31, 1846, in *The Collected Works of Abraham Lincoln,* 9 vols., ed. Roy P. Basler (New Brunswick: Rutgers University Press, 1953), 1:382.

Document 2.9
Lobbying to Become Commissioner
of the General Land Office (1849)

After his term in Congress Lincoln attempted to win an appointment in the administration of President Zachary Taylor, a Whig general whom he had helped to nominate and elect in 1848. Lincoln wanted to become commissioner of the General Land Office, a position that promised what was at the time a significant annual salary of $3,000, plus lucrative commissions on government land sales. It also was a post that offered abundant power by allowing the commissioner to reward loyal party workers with patronage appointments in the agency's various field offices. Lincoln's principal competitor for the position was an attorney from Chicago named Justin Butterfield, who was well connected nationally but whose local track record was questioned bitterly by Springfield Whigs. In 1849 Lincoln addressed his concerns in the following letter to an old friend from Congress and the new secretary of navy, William B. Preston. After an intense lobbying campaign and after being summoned to Washington to meet with the president directly, Lincoln lost the appointment to Butterfield and returned to Springfield to resume his law practice.

To William B. Preston
Hon: W. B. Preston: Springfield, Ills.
Dear Sir: May 16, 1849

It is a delicate matter to oppose the wishes of a friend; and consequently I address you on the subject I now do, with no little hesitation. Last night I received letters from different persons at Washington assuring me it was not improbable that Justin Butterfield, of Chicago, Ills, would be appointed Commissioner of the Genl. Land-Office. It was to avert this very thing, that I called on you at your rooms one sunday evening shortly after you were installed, and besought you that, so far as in your power, no man from Illinois should be appointed to any high office, without my being at least heard on the question. You were kind enough to say you thought my request a reasonable one. Mr. Butterfield is my friend, is well qualified, and, I suppose, would be faithful in the office. So far, good. But now for the objections. In 1840 we fought a fierce and laborious battle in Illinois, many of us spending almost the entire year in the contest. The general victory came, and with it, the appointment of a set of drones, including this same Butterfield, who had never spent a dollar or lifted a finger in the fight. The place he got was that of District Attorney. The defection of Tyler came, and then B. played off and on, and kept the office till after Polk's election. Again, winter and spring before the last, when you and I were almost sweating blood to have Genl. Taylor nominated, this same man was ridiculing the idea, and going for Mr. Clay; and when Gen: T. was nominated, if he went out of the city of Chicago to aid in his election, it is more than I ever heard, or believe. Yet, when the election is secured, by other men's labor, and even against his effort, why, he is the first man on hand for the best office that our state lays any claim to. Shall this thing be? Our whigs will throw down their arms, and fight no more, if the fruit of their labor is thus disposed of. If there is one man in this state who desires B's appointment to any thing, I declare I have not heard of him. What influence opperates for him, I can not conceive. Your position makes it a matter of peculiar interest to you, that the administration shall be successful; and be assured, nothing can more endanger it, than making appointments through old-hawker foreign influences, which offend, rather than gratify, the people immediately interested in the offices.

Can you not find time to write me, even half as long a letter as this? I shall be much gratified if you will.

Your Obt. Servt.
A. LINCOLN

Source: Abraham Lincoln to William B. Preston, May 16, 1849, in *The Collected Works of Abraham Lincoln,* 9 vols., ed. Roy P. Basler (New Brunswick: Rutgers University Press, 1953), 2:48–49.

Document 2.10   Selections from Lincoln's Stump Speech (1854)

After passage of the Kansas-Nebraska Act in 1854, a bill authored by Sen. Stephen A. Douglas of Illinois, Lincoln returned to the public limelight as an opponent of this controversial plan to open the Great Plains territories by repealing the Missouri Compromise of 1820. Douglas had agreed to abandon the old Missouri Compromise restrictions on the extension of slavery, replacing them with a new doctrine he labeled "popular sovereignty." This doctrine took the question of territorial slavery out of the hands of Congress and put it into the domain of local referendum.

For Lincoln, this policy was merely a covert way of spreading slavery across the continent, a development he considered evil and worth fighting at all costs. During the autumn of 1854, he gave several speeches urging all factions that opposed the spread of slavery to unite against Douglas and his "Nebraska bill." The principal text for these speeches comes from an address he gave at Peoria—one that followed a speech made earlier the same day by Senator Douglas. Ultimately, it was this desire to unite the opponents of slavery that led to the formation of the Republican Party in Illinois and elsewhere across the North.

October 16, 1854 (at Peoria, Illinois):

. . . The repeal of the Missouri Compromise, and the propriety of its restoration, constitute the subject of what I am about to say.

As I desire to present my own connected view of this subject, my remarks will not be, specifically, an answer to Judge Douglas; yet, as I proceed, the main points he has presented will arise, and will receive such respectful attention as I may be able to give them.

I wish further to say, that I do not propose to question the patriotism, or to assail the motives of any man, or class of men; but rather to strictly confine myself to the naked merits of the question.

I also wish to be no less than National in all the positions I may take; and whenever I take ground which others have thought, or may think, narrow, sectional and dangerous to the Union, I hope to give a reason, which will appear sufficient, at least to some, why I think differently.

And, as this subject is no other, than part and parcel of the larger general question of domestic-slavery, I wish to MAKE and to KEEP the distinction between the EXISTING institution, and the EXTENSION of it, so broad, and so clear, that no honest man can misunderstand me, and no dishonest one, successfully misrepresent me. . . .

. . . Preceding the Presidential election of 1852, each of the great political parties, democrats and whigs, met in convention, and adopted resolutions endorsing the compromise of '50; as a "finality," a final settlement, so far as these parties could make it so, of all slavery agitation. Previous to this, in 1851, the Illinois Legislature had indorsed it.

During this long period of time Nebraska had remained, substantially an uninhabited country, but now emigration to, and settlement within it began to take place. It is about one third as large as the present United States, and its importance so long overlooked, begins to come into view. The restriction of slavery by the Missouri Compromise directly applies to it; in fact, was first made, and has since been maintained, expressly for it. In 1853, a bill to give it a territorial government passed the House of Representatives, and, in the hands of Judge Douglas, failed of passing the Senate only for want of time. This bill contained no repeal of the Missouri Compromise. Indeed, when it was assailed because it did not contain such repeal, Judge Douglas defended it in its existing form. On January 4th, 1854, Judge Douglas introduces a new bill to give Nebraska territorial government. He accompanies this bill with a report, in which last, he expressly recommends that the Missouri Compromise shall neither be affirmed nor repealed.

Before long the bill is so modified as to make two territories instead of one; calling the Southern one Kansas.

Also, about a month after the introduction of the bill, on the judge's own motion, it is so amended as to declare the Missouri Compromise inoperative and void; and, substantially, that the People who go and settle there may establish slavery, or exclude it, as they may see fit. In this shape the bill passed both branches of congress, and became a law.

This is the *repeal* of the Missouri Compromise. The foregoing history may not be precisely accurate in every particular; but I am sure it is sufficiently so, for all the uses I shall attempt to make of it, and in it, we have before us, the chief material enabling us to correctly judge whether the repeal of the Missouri Compromise is right or wrong.

I think, and shall try to show, that it is wrong; wrong in its direct effect, letting slavery into Kansas and Nebraska—and wrong in its prospective principle, allowing it to spread to every other part of the wide world, where men can be found inclined to take it.

This *declared indifference*, but as I must think, covert *real* zeal for the spread of slavery, I can not but hate. I hate it because of the monstrous injustice of slavery itself. I hate it because it deprives our republican example of its just influence in the world—enables the enemies of free institutions, with plausibility, to taunt us as hypocrites—causes the real friends of freedom to doubt our sincerity, and especially because it forces so many really good men amongst ourselves into an open war with the very fundamental principles of civil liberty—criticising the Declaration of Independence, and insisting that there is no right principle of action but *self-interest.*

Before proceeding, let me say I think I have no prejudice against the Southern people. They are just what we would be in their situation. If slavery did not now exist amongst them, they would not introduce it. If it did now exist amongst us, we should not instantly give it up. This I believe of the masses north and south. Doubtless there are individuals, on both sides, who would not hold slaves under any circumstances; and others who would gladly introduce slavery anew, if it were out of existence. We know that some southern men do free their slaves, go north, and become tip-top abolitionists; while some northern ones go south, and become most cruel slave-masters.

When southern people tell us they are no more responsible for the origin of slavery, than we; I acknowledge the fact. When it is said that the institution exists; and that it is very difficult to get rid of it, in any satisfactory way, I can understand and appreciate the saying. I surely will not blame them for not doing what I should not know how to do myself. If all earthly power were given me, I should not know what to do, as to the existing institution. My first impulse would be to free all the slaves, and send them to Liberia,—to their own native land. But a moment's reflection would convince me, that whatever of high hope, (as I think there is) there may be in this, in the long run, its sudden execution is impossible. If they were all landed there in a day, they would all perish in the next ten days; and there are not surplus shipping and surplus money enough in the world to carry them there in many times ten days. What then? Free them all, and keep them among us as underlings? Is it quite certain that this betters their condition? I think I would not hold one in slavery, at any rate; yet the point is not clear enough for me to denounce people upon. What next? Free them, and make them politically and socially, our equals? My own feelings will not admit of this; and if mine would, we well know that those of the great mass of white people will not. Whether this feeling accords with justice and sound judgment, is not the sole question, if indeed, it is any part of it. A universal feeling, whether well or ill-founded, can not be safely disregarded. We can not, then, make them equals. It does seem to me that systems of gradual emancipation might be adopted; but for their tardiness in this, I will not undertake to judge our brethren of the south. . . .

. . . But Nebraska is urged as a great Union-saving measure. Well I too, go for saving the Union. Much as I hate slavery, I would consent to the extension of it rather than see the Union dissolved, just as I would consent to any GREAT evil, to avoid a GREATER one. But when I go to Union saving, I must believe, at least, that the means I employ has some adaptation to the end. To my mind, Nebraska has no such adaptation. . . .

. . . Some men, mostly whigs, who condemn the repeal of the Missouri Compromise, nevertheless hesitate to go for its restoration, lest they be thrown in company with the abolitionist. Will they allow me as an old whig to tell them good humoredly, that I think this is very silly? Stand with anybody that stands RIGHT. Stand with him while he is right and PART with him when he goes wrong. Stand WITH the abolitionist in restoring the Missouri Compromise; and stand AGAINST him when he attempts to repeal the fugitive slave law. In the latter case you stand with the southern disunionist. What of that? You are still right. In both cases you are right. In both cases you oppose [expose?] the dangerous extremes. In both you stand on middle ground and hold the ship level and steady. In both you are national and nothing less than national. This is good old whig ground. To desert such ground, because of any company, is to be less than a whig—less than a man—less than an American. . . .

Source: Speech at Peoria, Illinois, October 16, 1854, in *The Collected Works of Abraham Lincoln,* 9 vols., ed. Roy P. Basler (New Brunswick: Rutgers University Press, 1953), 2:247–283.

Document 2.11   Lincoln-Douglas Debates and the Freeport Questions (1858)

Lincoln and Douglas debated several times during their respective careers, but none of their exchanges produced more fire than their famous debates during the 1858 campaign when Illinois voters were preparing to elect the legislature that would in turn select one of them as the state's next U.S. senator. The two politicians met seven times across the state, but their second debate at Freeport was arguably the most famous, because Lincoln offered a series of questions to Douglas that appeared to pin the Democratic senator down about inconsistencies and contradictions in his controversial policy of popular sovereignty for the territories.

Second Debate with Stephen A. Douglas at Freeport, Illinois

August 27, 1858

. . . I now proceed to propound to the Judge the interrogatories, so far as I have framed them. I will bring forward a new installment when I get them ready. [Laughter.] I will bring them forward now, only reaching to number four.

The first one is—

Question 1. If the people of Kansas shall, by means entirely unobjectionable in all other respects, adopt a State Constitution, and ask admission into the Union under it, *before* they have the requisite number of inhabitants according to the English Bill—some ninety-three thousand—will you vote to admit them? [Applause.]

Q. 2. Can the people of a United States Territory, in any lawful way, against the wish of any citizen of the United States, exclude slavery from its limits prior to the formation of a State Constitution? [Renewed applause.]

Q. 3. If the Supreme Court of the United States shall decide that States can not exclude slavery from their limits, are you in favor of acquiescing in, adopting and following such decision as a rule of political action? [Loud applause.]

Q. 4. Are you in favor of acquiring additional territory, in disregard of how such acquisition may affect the nation on the slavery question? [Cries of "good," "good."]

Source: Second Debate with Stephen A. Douglas at Freeport, Illinois, August 27, 1858, in *The Collected Works of Abraham Lincoln*, 9 vols., ed. Roy P. Basler (New Brunswick: Rutgers University Press, 1953), 3:38–76.

Document 2.12   Lincoln Offers a "Bare Suggestion" (1858)
During the 1858 campaign, leaders of the new Republican Party worried incessantly about the prospect of fraud at the polls. In particular, Republicans feared that Democrats would attempt to use their influence with Irish-born railroad laborers to produce illegal votes in sections where the contests

might be especially close. Near the end of the tense campaign Lincoln wrote to Norman B. Judd, the Republican state chairman, offering what he called a "bare suggestion." He argued that if the Democrats tried to use "Celtic gentlemen" against them, the party should hire someone of the "'detective' class" to out-bribe them to win their votes. For someone who prided himself on his own integrity, it was an uncharacteristic flash of political cynicism.

Hon. N. B. Judd Rushville, Oct. 20, 1858

My dear Sir: I now have a high degree of confidence that we shall succeed, if we are not over-run with fraudulent votes to a greater extent than usual. On alighting from the cars and walking three squares at Naples on Monday, I met about fifteen Celtic gentlemen, with black carpet-sacks in their hands.

I learned that they had crossed over from the Rail-road in Brown county, but where they were going no one could tell. They dropped in about the doggeries, and were still hanging about when I left. At Brown County yesterday I was told that about four hundred of the same sort were to be brought into Schuyler, before the election, to work on some new Railroad; but on reaching here I find Bagby thinks that is not so.

What I most dread is that they will introduce into the doubtful districts numbers of men who are legal voters in all respects except *residence* and who will swear to residence and thus put it beyond our power to exclude them. They can & I fear will swear falsely on that point, because they know it is next to impossible to convict them of Perjury upon it.

Now the great remaining part of the campaign, is finding a way to head this thing off. Can it be done at all?

I have a bare suggestion. When there is a known body of these voters, could not a true man, of the "*detective*" class, be introduced among them in disguise, who could, at the nick of time, control their votes? Think this over. It would be a great thing, when this trick is attempted upon us, to have the saddle come up on the other horse.

I have talked, more fully than I can write, to Mr. Scripps, and he will talk to you.

If we can head off the fraudulent votes we shall carry the day.

Yours as ever A. LINCOLN

Source: Abraham Lincoln to Norman B. Judd, October 20, 1858, in *The Collected Works of Abraham Lincoln*, 9 vols., ed. Roy P. Basler (New Brunswick: Rutgers University Press, 1953), 3:329–330.

Document 2.13   Lincoln Attempts to Quell Presidential Talk (1859)

Not long after the 1858 campaign Lincoln and his friends began contemplating a presidential bid for him despite their defeat by Stephen A. Douglas and the Democrats in the critical legislative elections. Illinois was a key state, and Lincoln was the undisputed leader of the state's Republican movement. Any shrewd observer could see that he had a chance to win a long shot nomination despite his relatively paltry national resume. However, in an era in which ambitions for office were not often openly espoused, Lincoln was careful to warn supporters against promoting his cause too aggressively. In April 1859, he wrote to Thomas J. Pickett, a Republican newspaper editor from northern Illinois, pointedly declining to endorse what he called any "concerted effort" aimed at securing him the presidency.

T. J. Pickett, Esq Springfield,

My dear Sir. April 16. 1859.

Yours of the 13th. is just received. My engagements are such that I can not, at any very early day, visit Rock-Island, to deliver a lecture, or for any other object.

As to the other matter you kindly mention, I must, in candor, say I do not think myself fit for the Presidency. I certainly am flattered, and gratified, that some partial friends think of me in that connection; but I really think it best for our cause that no concerted effort, such as you suggest, should be made.

Let this be considered confidential. Yours very truly

A. LINCOLN—

Source: Abraham Lincoln to Thomas J. Pickett, April 16, 1859, in *The Collected Works of Abraham Lincoln*, 9 vols., ed. Roy P. Basler (New Brunswick: Rutgers University Press, 1953), 3:377

Document 2.14   Discussing Money in Politics (1860)

Even in the mid–nineteenth century campaigns cost money. Weeks before the Republican national convention in Chicago, Lincoln received a letter from an old acquaintance in Kansas, Mark W. Delahay, who offered to attend the convention as a delegate if Lincoln would pay his way. Responding to the audacious request, Lincoln expressed his ambivalent views on money in politics but offered to give his friend $100. When the fast-talking Delahay arrived in Chicago without an appointment as a delegate, Lincoln paid for his trip anyway.

Dear [Mark] Delahay—Springfield, Ills—Mar—16, 1860

. . . As to your kind wishes for myself, allow me to say I can not enter the ring on the money basis—first, because, in the main, it is wrong; and secondly, I have not, and can not get, the money. I say, in the main, the use of money is wrong; but for certain objects, in a political contest, the use of some, is both right, and indispensable. With me, as with yourself, this long struggle has been one of great pecuniary loss. I now distinctly say this. If you shall be appointed a delegate to Chicago, I will furnish one hundred dollars to bear the expences of the trip.

Present my respects to Genl. [James] Lane; and say to him, I shall be pleased to hear from him at any time. Your friend, as ever

A. LINCOLN—

Source: Abraham Lincoln to Mark W. Delahay, March 16, 1860, in *The Collected Works of Abraham Lincoln,* 9 vols., ed. Roy P. Basler (New Brunswick: Rutgers University Press, 1953), 4:31–32.

Document 2.15   Lincoln Outlines
a Nomination Strategy (1860)

Even though he had spent most of his adult life practicing law in central Illinois, Lincoln had a surprising number of friends and contacts across the North. Samuel Galloway, a former congressman and attorney from Ohio, was part of his national network of correspondents and supporters. For almost a year before the 1860 Republican convention Galloway had been pressing Lincoln on a presidential bid. In the following letter the supposedly reluctant candi-

date finally details for his friend and former business associate his strategy on how to emerge as the second choice of the majority of the convention's delegates. This was an especially sensitive document because Galloway was a leader among Ohio Republicans, who were expected to support the favorite-son candidacy of Lincoln's more prominent rival, Gov. Salmon P. Chase.

Hon. Samuel Galloway Chicago, March 24 1860
My dear Sir:

I am here attending a trial in court. Before leaving home I received your kind letter of the 15th. Of course I am gratified to know I have friends in Ohio who are disposed to give me the highest evidence of their friendship and confidence. Mr Parrott of the Legislature, had written me to the same effect. If I have any chance, it consists mainly in the fact that the *whole* opposition would vote for me if nominated. (I dont mean to include the pro-slavery opposition of the South, of course.) My name is new in the field; and I suppose I am not the *first* choice of a very great many. Our policy, then, is to give no offence to others—leave them in a mood to come to us, if they shall be compelled to give up their first love. This, too, is dealing justly with all, and leaving us in a mood to support heartily whoever shall be nominated. I believe I have once before told you that I especially wish to do no ungenerous thing towards Governor [Salmon] Chase, because he gave us his sympathy in 1858, when scarcely any other distinguished man did. Whatever you may do for me, consistently with these suggestions, will be appreciated, and gratefully remembered.

Please write me again. Yours very truly

A. LINCOLN

Source: Abraham Lincoln to Samuel Galloway, March 24, 1860, in *The Collected Works of Abraham Lincoln,* 9 vols., ed. Roy P. Basler (New Brunswick: Rutgers University Press, 1953), 4:33–34.

Document 2.16   Brief Remarks during the Presidential Campaign (1860)

In the nineteenth century, presidential candidates did not customarily give speeches or make public appearances during campaigns. Responding to the disruption of the national Democratic Party, Stephen A. Douglas violated this tradition by campaigning actively in both the North and South. Lincoln, however, largely remained quiet in Springfield. These following remarks constitute one of his few public statements during the contest.

Remarks at a Republican Rally, Springfield, Illinois
August 8, 1860

My Fellow Citizens:—I appear among you upon this occasion with no intention of making a speech.

It has been my purpose, since I have been placed in my present position, to make no speeches. This assemblage having been drawn together at the place of my residence, it appeared to be the wish of those constituting this vast assembly to see me; and it is certainly my wish to see all of you. I appear upon the ground here at this time only for the purpose of affording myself the best opportunity of seeing you, and enabling you to see me.

I confess with gratitude, be it understood, that I did not suppose my appearance among you would create the tumult which I now witness. I am profoundly gratified for this manifestation of your feelings. I am gratified, because it is a tribute such as can be paid to no man as a man. It is the evidence that four years from this time you will give a like manifestation to the next man who is the representative of the truth on the questions that now agitate the public. And it is because you will then fight for this cause as you do now, or with even greater ardor than now, though I be dead and gone. I most profoundly and sincerely thank you.

Having said this much, allow me now to say that it is my wish that you will hear this public discussion by others of our friends who are present for the purpose of addressing you, and that you will kindly let me be silent.

Source: Remarks at Republican Rally, Springfield, Illinois, August 6, 1860, in *The Collected Works of Abraham Lincoln*, 9 vols., ed. Roy P. Basler (New Brunswick: Rutgers University Press, 1953), 4:91–92.

Document 2.17   Election Results (1860)

Candidate (party)	All states		Free states (18)			Slave states (15)	
	Popular vote	Electoral vote	Popular vote	Electoral vote		Popular vote	Electoral vote
Abraham Lincoln (Republican)	1,864,735	180	1,838,347	180		26,388	0
Opposition	*2,821,157*	*123*	*1,572,637*	*3*		*1,248,520*	*120*
John Breckinridge (Southern Democratic)	669,472	72	99,381	0		570,091	72
John Bell (Constitutional Union)	576,414	39	76,973	0		499,441	39
Stephen A. Douglas (Northern Democratic)	979,425	12	815,857	3		163,568	9
Fusion[a]	595,846	—	80,426	—		15,420	—

[a] In some states, voters had the option of supporting a Fusion ticket.

Source: Compiled by the author.

Document 2.18   Union Politicians Fear Defeat (1864)

The Republican Party (renamed the Union or National Union Party for the 1864 contest) renominated President Lincoln for a second term at a national convention in Baltimore in June 1864. At the time, Unionists had high hopes that the Civil War would soon be finished, but the conflict dragged on throughout the summer and public morale plummeted. Republican leaders panicked and began considering whether to replace Lincoln as their candidate. Thurlow Weed, one of the party's principal fund-raisers and organizers, told the president directly that his reelection was "an impossibility." Henry Raymond, editor of the New York Times *and national party chairman, claimed "all is lost." Weed reported on this angst in a dismal note to his old friend and ally Secretary of State William H. Seward near the end of August.*

Thurlow Weed to William Seward, New York, August 22, 1864:

When, ten or eleven days since, I told Mr Lincoln that his re-election was an impossibility, I also told him that the information would soon come to him through other channels. It has doubtless, ere this, reached him. At any rate, nobody here doubts it; nor do I see any body from other States who authorises the slightest hope of success. Mr. [Henry] Raymond, who has, just left me, says that unless some prompt and bold step be now taken, all is lost. The People are wild for Peace. They are told that the President will only listen to terms of Peace on condition Slavery be "abandoned." Mr. [Leonard] Swett is well informed in relation to the public sentiment. He has seen and heard much. Mr Raymond thinks commissioners should be immediately sent, to Richmond, offering to treat for Peace on the basis of Union. That *something* should be done and promptly done, to give the Administration a chance for its life, is certain.

Source: Thurlow Weed to William H. Seward, August 22, 1864, in *Abraham Lincoln Papers at the Library of Congress*, Manuscript Division (Washington, D.C.: American Memory Project, Library of Congress, 2000–2002); memory.loc.gov/ammem/alhtml/alhome.html

Document 2.19   Lincoln's "Blind Memorandum" (1864)

Practically the only Union politician who seemed unwilling to consider "swapping horses" over the gloomy summer of 1864 was Lincoln himself. The president was shrewd enough to perceive that without more victories on the battlefield, his defeat was "exceedingly probable," but he did not allow this anxiety to change his immediate course of action. Instead, he reacted by planning for the future with grim determination.

The day after Thurlow Weed wrote Secretary of State William H. Seward about the campaign's extensive problems (see Document 2.18), Lincoln summoned members of his cabinet to sign a note detailing the administration's plans in case a Democrat was elected in November. The Democratic Party had not yet nominated Gen. George B. McClellan, but the president was aware that his opponents were aligned against the war effort and that their victory would only encourage the Confederates to keep fighting. So Lincoln asked his cabinet officers to sign the following memorandum "blind," or without seeing its contents, and filed the document away in his desk. After the election, presidential aide John Hay recorded in his diary the scene when Lincoln finally revealed the contents of the "blind memorandum" to his incredulous advisers.

Executive Mansion
Washington, Aug. 23, 1864.

This morning, as for some days past, it seems exceedingly probable that this Administration will not be re-elected. Then it will be my duty to so co-operate with the President elect, as to save the Union between the election and the inauguration; as he will have secured his election on such ground that he can not possibly save it afterwards.

A. LINCOLN
[The original autograph is endorsed on the verso with autograph signatures of cabinet members and Lincoln's autograph date.]

[John Hay's *Diary* records under date of November 11, 1864, the cabinet meeting of that date at which the memorandum was opened. . . .

"At the meeting of the Cabinet today, the President took out a paper from his desk and said, 'Gentlemen, do you remember last summer when I asked you all to sign your names to the back of a paper of which I did not show you the inside? This is it. Now, Mr Hay, see if you can get this open without tearing it?' He had pasted it up in so singular style that it required some cutting to get it open. He then read as follows: [memorandum]

"The President said, 'You will remember that this was written at a time (6 days before the Chicago nominating Convention) when as yet we had no adversary, and seemed to have no friends. I then solemnly resolved on the course of action indicated above. I resolved, in case of the election of General McClellan, being certain that he would be the candidate, that I would see him and talk matters over with him. I would say, "General, the election has demonstrated that you are stronger, have more influence with the American people than I. Now let us together, you with your influence and I with all the executive power of the Government, try to save the country. You raise as many troops as you possibly can for this final trial, and I will devote all my energies to assisting and finishing the war.'"

"Seward said, 'And the General would answer you "Yes, Yes;" and the next day when you saw him again and pressed these views upon him, he would say, "Yes, Yes;" & so on forever, and would have done nothing at all.'

"'At least,' added Lincoln, 'I should have done my duty and have stood clear before my own conscience.' . . ."]

Source: Abraham Lincoln, "Memorandum Concerning His Probable Failure of Re-Election," August 23, 1864, in *The Collected Works of Abraham Lincoln*, 9 vols., ed. Roy P. Basler (New Brunswick: Rutgers University Press, 1953), 7:514.

Document 2.20   National Election Results (1864)

Candidate (Party)	Popular vote	Percent	Electoral vote
Abraham Lincoln (Republican)	2,219,924	55	212
George B. McClellan (Democratic)	1,814,228	45	21

Source: Compiled by the author.

Document 2.21   State-by-State Election Results (1864)

State	Electoral votes	Winner	Margin of victory
California	4	Lincoln	18,293
Connecticut	5	Lincoln	2,405
Delaware	3	McClellan	612
Illinois	16	Lincoln	31,138
Indiana	13	Lincoln	20,189
Iowa	8	Lincoln	40,533
Kansas[a]	3	Lincoln	3,939
Kentucky	11	McClellan	36,515
Maine	7	Lincoln	24,491
Maryland	7	Lincoln	7,423
Massachusetts	12	Lincoln	77,997
Michigan	8	Lincoln	16,917
Minnesota	4	Lincoln	7,685
Missouri	11	Lincoln	41,965
Nevada[a]	2	Lincoln	3,232
New Hampshire	5	Lincoln	3,561
New Jersey	7	McClellan	7,291
New York	33	Lincoln	6,740
Ohio	21	Lincoln	59,586
Oregon	3	Lincoln	1,341
Pennsylvania	28	Lincoln	90,568
Rhode Island	4	Lincoln	4,625
Vermont	5	Lincoln	29,440
West Virginia[a]	5	Lincoln	12,766
Wisconsin	8	Lincoln	10,689

[a] States added to the Union during the Civil War.

Source: Compiled by the author.

**Document 2.22   Lincoln's Reflections on
Wartime Elections (1864)**

*Shortly after the 1864 election Lincoln gave a sober speech on the importance
of the contest. He had won a decisive victory over Gen. George B. McClellan,
but there is little in his public statement that strikes an exultant note. The war
was practically over and the devastation of the conflict was still being calculated, but it was obviously immense and tragic. Lincoln could only repeat his
support for the principle that elections mattered and that democracy could
function in times of grave national crisis.*

Response to Serenade, November 10, 1864:

It has long been a grave question whether any government, not *too* strong
for the liberties of its people, can be strong *enough* to maintain its own existence, in great emergencies.

On this point the present rebellion brought our republic to a severe test;
and a presidential election occurring in regular course during the rebellion
added not a little to the strain. If the loyal people, *united,* were put to the
utmost of their strength by the rebellion, must they not fail when *divided,*
and partially paralized, by a political war among themselves?

But the election was a necessity.

We can not have free government without elections; and if the rebellion could force us to forego, or postpone a national election, it might
fairly claim to have already conquered and ruined us. The strife of the election is but human-nature practically applied to the facts of the case. What
has occurred in this case, must ever recur in similar cases. Human-nature
will not change. In any future great national trial, compared with the men
of this, we shall have as weak, and as strong; as silly and as wise; as bad
and good. Let us, therefore, study the incidents of this, as philosophy to
learn wisdom from, and none of them as wrongs to be revenged.

But the election, along with its incidental, and undesirable strife, has
done good too. It has demonstrated that a people's government can sustain a national election, in the midst of a great civil war. Until now it has
not been known to the world that this was a possibility. It shows also how
sound, and how *strong* we still are. It shows that, even among candidates
of the same party, he who is most devoted to the Union, and most opposed

to treason, can receive most of the people's votes. It shows also, to the extent yet known, that we have more men now, than we had when the war began. Gold is good in its place; but living, brave, patriotic men, are better than gold.

But the rebellion continues; and now that the election is over, may not all, having a common interest, re-unite in a common effort, to save our common country? For my own part I have striven, and shall strive to avoid placing any obstacle in the way. So long as I have been here I have not willingly planted a thorn in any man's bosom.

While I am deeply sensible to the high compliment of a re-election; and duly grateful, as I trust, to Almighty God for having directed my countrymen to a right conclusion, as I think, for their own good, it adds nothing to my satisfaction that any other man may be disappointed or pained by the result.

May I ask those who have not differed with me, to join with me, in this same spirit towards those who have?

And now, let me close by asking three hearty cheers for our brave soldiers and seamen and their gallant and skilful commanders.

Source: "Response to Serenade," November 10, 1864, in *The Collected Works of Abraham Lincoln,* 9 vols., ed. Roy P. Basler (New Brunswick: Rutgers University Press, 1953), 8:100–101.

Document 2.23   Election Night with Lincoln (1864)

Because most state elections preceded the November presidential contest by a month or more, Lincoln was already expecting victory on election day, although his advisers feared the results might be too close for comfort. Presidential aide John Hay accompanied the generally calm president as they awaited returns in the War Department's Telegraph Office, located across a courtyard from the White House. After news of Lincoln's victory, and after some nerve-wracking mistakes in the reporting of results, the assembled men ate oysters and the president retired late to the White House for some rest. Fearing the worst, Ward Hill Lamon, his friend and unofficial bodyguard, poignantly stood guard outside the door of the president's bedroom that night. The entire scene is recorded memorably in John Hay's diary.

Tuesday, November 8, 1864:

The House has been still and almost deserted today. Every body in Washington, not at home voting seems ashamed of it and stays away from the President.

I was talking to him today. He said "It is a little singular that I who am not a vindictive man, should have always been before the people for election in canvasses marked for their bitterness; always but once: When I came to Congress it was a quiet time: But always besides that the contests in which I have been prominent have been marked with great rancor." . . .

. . . At night, at seven oclock we started over to the War Department to spend the evening. Just as we started we received the first gun from Indianapolis, showing a majority of 8000 there, a gain of 1500 over Morton's vote. The vote itself seemed an enormous one for a town of that size and can only be accounted for by considering the great influx since the war of voting men from the country into the state centres where a great deal of Army business is done. There was less significance in this vote on account of the October victory which had disheartened the enemy and destroyed their incentive to work.

The night was rainy steamy and dark. We splashed through the grounds to the side door of the War Department where a soaked and smoking sentinel was standing in his own vapor with his huddled up frame covered with a rubber cloak. Inside a half-dozen idle orderlies: up stairs the clerks of the telegraph. As the President entered they handed him a despatch from Forney claiming ten thousand Union Majority in Philadelphia. "Forney is a little excitable." Another comes from Felton, Baltimore, giving us "15,000 in the city, 5000 in the State. All hail, Free Maryland." That is superb. A message from Rice to Fox followed instantly by one from Sumner to Lincoln claiming Boston by 5000 and Rice's & Hooper's elections by majorities of 4000 apiece. A magnificent advance on the chilly dozens of 1862. . . .

. . . Despatches kept coming in all the evening showing a splendid triumph in Indiana showing steady small gains all over Pennsylvania, enough to give a fair majority this time on the home vote. Guesses from New York and Albany which boiled down to about the estimated majority against us in the city 35,000 and left the result in the state still doubtful.

A despatch from Butler was picked up & sent by Sanford saying that the City had gone 35000 McC & the State 40,000. This looked impossible.

The state had been carefully canvassed & such a result was impossible except in view of some monstrous and undreamed of frauds. After a while another came from Sanford correcting former one & giving us the 40000 in the State. . . .

. . . Towards midnight we had supper, providing by Eckert. The President went awkwardly and hospitably to work shovelling out the fried oysters. He was most agreeable and genial all the evening in fact. Fox was abusing the coffee for being so hot—saying quaintly, it kept hot all the way down to the bottom of the cup as a piece of ice staid cold till you finished eating it. . . .

. . . Capt. Thomas came up with a band about half past two, and made some music. The President answered from the window with rather unusual dignity and effect & we came home. I wrote out the speech & sent it to Hanscom.

W[ard] H. L[amon] came to my room to talk over the Chief Justiceship; he goes for Stanton & thinks, as I am inclined to think, that the President cannot afford to place an enemy in a position so momentous for good or evil.

He took a glass of whiskey and then refusing my offer of a bed went out & rolling himself up in his cloak lay down at the President's door; passing the night in that attitude of touching and dumb fidelity with a small arsenal of pistols & bowie knives around him. In the morning he went away leaving my blankets at my door, before I or the President were awake.

Source: John Hay, diary entry, November 8, 1864, in *Inside Lincoln's White House: The Complete Civil War Diary of John Hay,* ed. Michael Burlingame and John R. Turner Ettlinger (Carbondale: Southern Illinois University Press, 1997), 243–246.

The first reading of the Emancipation Proclamation before the cabinet.

CHAPTER THREE

Administration Policies

A though the Lincoln administration was consumed by the crisis of a domestic rebellion, it would be a mistake to overlook the importance of non-military policy in the Civil War era.

FOREIGN POLICY

Union and Confederate officials carefully scrutinized developments in the European capitals, convinced that "favor or disfavor" from abroad, in President Lincoln's words, might have "material influence" on the outcome (Basler 1953, 6:64). In particular, the rebel government hoped for recognition, and even support, from the British.

Great Britain was the most dominant power in the world at the time and a voracious importer of Southern cotton. Over 75 percent of the cotton used in British textile mills came from plantations in the American South. The British cabinet seriously considered proposals to mediate between the sides and even, on at least one occasion, to protect its interests by force. Most observers expected Britain to set the tone for any European response, but the French government also contemplated, on its own, the costs and opportunities of political and military intervention. This was no idle threat. In 1861 three European powers (Britain, France, and Spain) had sent a military expedition to collect unpaid debts from the neighboring Republic of Mexico. The French essentially remained, installing Ferdinand Maximilian, an Austrian prince related to their emperor, as a puppet ruler, while drawing up plans for a new "Grand Design for the Americas."

There were, of course, other nations besides the European powers, but it is probably fair to conclude that President Lincoln had little interest in the wider panorama of international affairs. "I don't know anything about diplomacy," Lincoln assured one foreign visitor. "I will be very apt to make blunders." (Fehrenbacher and Fehrenbacher 1996, 390). Indeed, he frequently sounded rather breezy in conducting the nation's international business. "I still have no name for Solicitor to go to Peru," he wrote to Charles Sumner, R-Mass., the Senate Foreign Relations Committee chairman, "Have you?" (Basler 1953, 6:134) When the king of Siam graciously offered to supply the U.S. government with breeding elephants, the president's response was a tongue-in-cheek demurral, noting that the geography of the country did not "favor the multiplication of the elephant" (Basler 1953, 5:126).

Most historians therefore have tended to emphasize Lincoln's disengagement from foreign affairs. A recent spate of diplomatic studies, however, has offered a newfound appreciation for the president's hidden-hand style of foreign policy leadership. Historians such as Howard Jones and Dean B. Mahin have written important books that explain how Lincoln's domestic antislavery ideology also shaped his foreign policy and how his overriding prudence—embodied by the maxim "one war at a time"—contributed to a generally coherent and effective global approach (Jones 1999; Mahin 1999). It was an especially impressive performance from a national executive who spoke no foreign languages and had never traveled beyond U.S. borders.

Relations with Great Britain

During the first year of the American Civil War, tensions between the U.S. government and Great Britain reached their highest point since the War of 1812. After the outbreak of the rebellion, the problems between the two countries began almost immediately; on May 13, 1861, Queen Victoria announced her nation's intention to remain neutral in the American conflict. The royal proclamation, ostensibly drafted in response to the Union blockade of Southern ports, had the effect of granting what was known as belligerent status to the Confederacy. To Union officials, this diplomatic formality suggested recognition of the rebels as a sovereign power—a fact they deplored with gusto. Senate Foreign Relations

Committee chairman Sumner quickly labeled the proclamation "the most hateful act of English history since the time of Charles II" (Jones 1999, 46). Secretary of State William H. Seward was even hotter. "God damn them," he reportedly exclaimed, when he learned that the British were meeting with Confederate envoys (McPherson 1988, 388).

Most diplomatic historians now believe that Northerners badly overreacted. In their haste to denounce the action, they failed to understand that the policy was, in the words of British foreign minister Lord John Russell, "one, not of principle, but of fact" (McPherson 1988, 388). In many ways, neutrality actually favored the Union, locking some of their initial advantages into the status quo and, most important, forestalling any further moves in London toward full recognition of the new government in Richmond. Across the Atlantic, there was an official wait-and-see approach to the rebellion. Still, for nervous politicians in besieged Washington this studied indifference did not sit well.

Seward drafted formal instructions for the new U.S. ambassador to Great Britain that blasted the queen's proclamation as "wrongful," claiming that the president was "surprised and grieved" by the decision (Basler 1953, 4:377). According to historian Phillip Shaw Paludan, the novice chief executive then revised the document with deft skill that demonstrated his superb negotiator's instincts. Lincoln changed "wrongful" to "hurtful" and "surprised and grieved" to "regrets" (Paludan 1994, 91). But most important, he instructed the American ambassador, Charles Francis Adams, to deliver the information orally rather than in writing, thereby further diminishing its hostile tone and allowing one of his few capable diplomats to use vital discretion. The result was a strong message from Washington, but not an offensive one.

The sensitive nature of U.S.–British relations was on display again toward the end of 1861, when a headstrong American naval officer nearly set off a war between the two countries. In November, Capt. Charles Wilkes arrested two Confederate diplomats, James Mason and John Slidell, while they were aboard a British ship in the Caribbean; the diplomats were attempting to evade the Union blockade so they could travel to Europe. The search of the *Trent,* a neutral ship, was a clear violation of international law and an insult to British sovereignty. It also was immensely popular across the North, especially when the Confederate diplomats were hauled off and incarcerated in a Boston jail. When the British demanded an apology and the release of Mason and Slidell, a confrontation loomed.

Outwardly, the standoff appeared to be a major crisis. Great Britain mobilized troops to sail for Canada, and Northern newspapers beat the drums for war. Privately, however, the two sides worked to ease tensions. Lord Russell sternly warned the British ambassador in Washington to "abstain from anything like menace" (Paludan 1994, 92). At about the same time President Lincoln tried to convince his advisers that he could handle the problem himself by showing the British envoy "in five minutes that I am heartily for peace"(Donald 1995, 322). Reluctantly, the president agreed to act more deliberately, and after a series of tense meetings, he made known his intention to release the rebel emissaries and acknowledge that Captain Wilkes acted without authority.

One reason for the apparent gravity of this pseudo-crisis was the reputation of the respective national leaders. Lincoln was regarded as too parochial and inexperienced for such high-stakes international gamesmanship. Just a few months before, U.S. ambassador Charles Francis Adams had confided in his diary that he saw within the administration "nothing but incompetency" and that the president was simply "not equal to the hour" (Paludan 1994, 61). By contrast, the British prime minister, Lord Palmerston (Henry Temple), was nearly eighty years old, highly experienced, and notorious for exercising British power with impunity. It was not inconceivable that the American president might accidentally provoke the irascible British leader into launching a full-scale war.

But Lincoln wanted "one war at a time" and Palmerston just as cautiously insisted that the British "continue merely to be lookers-on" until the situation became more settled (Jones 1999, 130). For the prime minister, a hardened realist, the fate of intervention hinged largely on the results of the battles. Palmerston believed that Britain must not become entangled in the American conflict unless both sides were prepared to acknowledge the need for mediation. Only in the face of a crushing defeat, he knew, would the North under President Lincoln consent to such interference from abroad. Thus, when Union forces repelled the rebel invasion of Maryland at the Battle of Antietam on September 17, 1862, Palmerston understood that the best case for a British role had, for the time being, evaporated.

Not everyone in the British government immediately grasped this insight. Chancellor of the Exchequer William Gladstone detailed the case for European intervention in a speech delivered on October 7, 1862, but before the results at Antietam were fully known across the Atlantic. "We may have our own opinions about slavery," he conceded, "we may be for or against the South." Yet, he added, "there is no doubt that Jefferson Davis and other leaders of the South have made an army; they are making, it appears, a navy; and they have made what is more than either—they have made a nation" (Jones 1999, 122). Gladstone was attempting to win an internal cabinet debate over the merits of intervention by going public with his position—a risky strategy. Palmerston felt betrayed. "Gladstone ought not to have launched into Confederate acknowledgement," the prime minister wrote tersely to Lord Russell, as he settled more stubbornly into his wait-and-see approach (Jones 1999, 125).

Emancipation, coming as it did on the heels of the Antietam battle, only added weight to the case against foreign involvement. The British Empire had abolished slavery in the 1830s, and most European nations, with the exception of Russia, regarded slavery as an odious relic of the past. Although a significant element of upper-class English society identified with Southern plantation owners, and secretly enjoyed the spectacle of American disunion, many workers and liberals in Britain recognized that if the rebellion perpetuated slavery then it was wrong and should not be encouraged. The Lincoln administration's embrace of emancipation in late 1862 thus helped to neutralize the remaining humanitarian arguments for intervention that had been gaining some currency across the Atlantic as the stalemate had continued and the rebellion had grown bloodier.

As soon as he issued his famous Emancipation Proclamation, President Lincoln used the new doctrine as a tool in cultivating opinion in Europe; he wrote public letters to "workingmen" in Manchester and London who had publicly expressed their antipathy to slavery (after some covert encouragement from American agents). Recognizing the sacrifices made by these workers, many of whom had endured unemployment caused by the Union blockade, the president praised their "sublime Christian heroism" and identified human freedom as a global ideal (Basler 1953, 6:64–65; see Document 3.1).

Ultimately, Palmerston, the aging interventionist, convinced others in the cabinet that without a clear-cut moral imperative or request from the warring parties, the British government must forgo mediation and continue its policy of watchful waiting. Nonetheless, Southerners always seemed to believe that they were only one major victory away from international recognition—and it was this misconception that helped drive Lee's army first into Maryland in 1862 and then into Pennsylvania in 1863. Instead, the British government increasingly accepted the inevitability of a Union victory and worked to avoid offending Washington during the second half of the war.

A new crisis arose between the two nations in 1863—over Confederate warships called the "Laird rams" which were outfitted illegally in the British port of Liverpool by the Laird shipbuilding company. This time, however, it was London that backed down. The British government halted the operation and ultimately paid millions of dollars to the Americans for damages inflicted by British-made rebel ships. The dispute over the illegal warships revealed the extent to which the balance of power had shifted since the *Trent* affair in late 1861. Great Britain remained the world's superpower, but the United States was now clearly the world's rising power.

Relations with France

During the American Civil War, France was a nation beginning to come apart as a result of the grandiose ambitions of its emperor. In 1848 the country had survived a turbulent revolution against its monarchy and had managed to inaugurate the Second Republic, but as in the First Republic, a Bonaparte soon seized control of this brief experiment in democracy. Napoleon III (nephew of the original Napoleon) crowned himself emperor in 1852 and ruled until 1871. From the beginning of his reign, the French ruler exhibited expansionist impulses, involving his country in foreign wars and imperialistic adventures.

France had not maintained a significant presence in the New World since the days of the Louisiana Purchase in 1803. By the 1860s, Napoleon III believed that circumstances had changed enough to rekindle hopes for a French empire in the Americas. There was widespread political unrest in both Mexico and the United States.

The bitter Mexican conflict, known as the War of the Reform (1858–1861), had preceded the Confederate rebellion and wreaked so much havoc that it had contributed in a small degree to Lincoln's fears about secession. As president-elect, he had warned a reporter from the *New York Herald* that any compromise with the Southern rebels would bring the U.S. system "down to a level with the existing disorganized state of affairs in Mexico" (Basler 1953, 4:176). The chaos south of the border was so severe that it had disrupted Mexico's ability to repay its debts. As a result, its principal European creditors sponsored a joint military expedition in 1861 to take control of the port of Veracruz and regain some of their money. Whereas Great Britain and Spain approached the operation as a temporary necessity, France's Napoleon III viewed the situation as a golden opportunity for conquest. He sent more than 35,000 troops, who helped to overthrow the liberal government led by Mexican revolutionary Benito Juarez. By 1864 pro-French forces had succeeded in engineering the selection of thirty-two-year-old Austrian prince Ferdinand Maximilian as emperor of Mexico.

The conquest was a gross violation of the Monroe Doctrine, but the Lincoln administration was in no position to defend the rest of the Western Hemisphere from imperialism. Instead, Secretary of State Seward protested the French actions, but also "dropped vague hints," in the words of historian James McPherson, that if Napoleon III withheld recognition from the Confederacy, the United States might eventually come around to accepting Maximilian's rule (McPherson 1992, 342). For his part, the French emperor, who had been unsuccessfully urging European intervention to end the American Civil War, finally realized that he was alone in defying the wishes of the Union government. He admitted privately that war with the United States "would spell disaster" for French interests and decided, like Palmerston, that his government should remain "lookers-on" for the time being (Jones 1999, 183). The Confederates, who had explored the possibility of an alliance with French dominated Mexico, were bitterly disappointed. Ultimately, the French emperor lost interest in the "grand design" altogether, abandoning his support for his nephew Maximilian and cruelly leaving him to his own devices. By 1867 the young Austrian had lost both his borrowed empire and his own life, and Mexico returned to a limited form of republican government.

ECONOMIC POLICY

The Civil War was an expensive proposition. From 1861 to 1865, the federal government allocated over $3 billion to the war. Government outlays rose by 700 percent in the first year of the conflict alone, conferring on Lincoln the distinction of being the first president to spend more than $1 million a day. Paying for this explosion in expenditures was one of the great tasks of the war and required immense skill and superb coordination. The obstacles were staggering. In that era of tight-fisted monetary policies, payments by the government were limited to gold or silver coin called specie. In the meantime, a recession, unrelated to the political crisis, had preceded the rebellion; the federal Treasury was already running a deficit at the outbreak of hostilities.

There were few signs early on that the new administration had onboard the necessary financial or administrative talent to overcome these problems. The president's managerial experience consisted largely of running a two-man law firm. He was a successful attorney who had represented some major corporations, but Lincoln the Rail-splitter was not the embodiment of a Wall Street president. Once when Salmon P. Chase, the secretary of Treasury, harassed him with economic minutiae, the president shrugged lamely, saying, "You understand these things. I do not" (Boritt 1994, 199). Chase certainly cut a more imposing figure at the time, but he was best known for his antislavery views, not his commercial genius. Moreover, he spent a good portion of the war angling to replace his boss, using the patronage of the Treasury Department to build a personal political machine. In those days, there was no White House staff to speak of, so Lincoln and Chase, plus a handful of deputies and departmental clerks, constituted the administration's entire economic team.

From this unlikely set of circumstances, however, emerged not only a successful wartime fund-raising effort, but also a striking revolution in the nation's financial system. Relying heavily on key Capitol Hill figures such as Rep. Justin Morrill, R-Vt., and Sen. William Pitt Fessenden, R-Maine, the Lincoln administration developed a combination of creative reforms that generated revenue, stabilized the banking system, and even helped to cultivate patriotism on the home front.

Taxation

There was no national income tax before the Civil War; the federal government raised its revenues primarily from tariffs and land sales. For most of the nineteenth century, these fund-raising methods were more than satisfactory for the relatively small national budget. But even before Lincoln's arrival at the White House, the Northern-dominated Congress had moved to secure additional revenues to meet the recession shortfall by raising tariff rates. A trend toward higher tariffs continued during and after the war for both economic and political reasons. Increased taxes on imported goods not only generated revenue, but also helped to protect developing industries that were concentrated in Northern states such as Massachusetts and Pennsylvania. As the nation became increasingly industrialized, a powerful lobby for a high protective tariff developed within the Republican Party, setting the stage for several postwar economic battles with the more agrarian Democrats.

Early in the Civil War, however, it became apparent that taxing foreign trade would not be enough. In August 1861, Congress adopted the nation's first income tax, a flat rate of 3 percent for all annual earnings over $800. The income figure was arbitrary, but it represented a substantial amount in that era. The new tax was implemented slowly and collection efforts did not begin until the next year. By then, the need for revenues appeared even greater, and the rates were modified as part of the landmark Internal Revenue Act of 1862. The new law established a graduated income tax of 3 percent for incomes between $600 and $10,000 and 5 percent for annual earnings above $10,000. As the war continued, the pressure to raise taxes only mounted. The rates were increased again in 1864, creating three brackets with a top rate of 10 percent. After the war, the tax was repealed.

Scholars report that during the existence of the new income tax compliance was high, owing mainly to the high degree of patriotism. Nonetheless, the revenue generated from income only accounted for about 8 percent of the funds needed to finance the war. Additional taxes were required. Thus as part of the Internal Revenue Act, Congress also adopted a wide-ranging excise tax on hundreds of goods, an inheritance tax, and various new fees and licensing costs. Altogether, according to historian Russell F. Weigley, the various taxes helped the Union pay for over 21 percent of its war effort (Weigley 2000, 208). The taxes also created a lasting institutional legacy, because the new law established the Bureau of Internal Revenue, forerunner of the Internal Revenue Service (IRS).

Banking and Currency

Although taxes were the first revenue stream to receive serious legislative attention, they were not immediately effective in raising funds. By December 1861, the Union was mired in a financial crisis. Soldiers and contractors often worked without payment. "The treasury is nearly empty," Secretary Chase glumly informed Congress in February 1862 (Paludan 1994, 109). The hard-money policies inherited from an earlier era were simply inadequate to the demands of wartime mobilization. The answer, reluctantly embraced by former Democrats such as Chase and Senate Finance Committee chairman Fessenden, was to create a paper currency and move toward nationalization of the banking system.

The Legal Tender Act won congressional approval on February 25, 1862. It was a hard-fought battle that required a major departure from previous thinking. The United States had never before issued paper banknotes that served as legal tender—that is, counted as real money. Most Americans in the mid–nineteenth century paid their bills with state or private banknotes. The result was a confusing patchwork of several thousand types of paper notes issued by more than sixteen hundred different banks. The government had been operating under even tougher restraints, limiting itself to payments by specie only. To print what was called "fiat money" seemed to be a disconcerting gamble to many national politicians. "The thing is wrong in itself," concluded Senator Fessenden, "but to leave the government without resources at such a crisis is not to be thought of" (McPherson 1992, 205). President Lincoln sounded equally circumspect. He supported the legislation but promised a "return to specie payments . . . at the earliest period compatible with due regard to all interests concerned" (Basler 1953, 5:522; see Document 3.2).

The first print run of government money was $150 million in notes. Valid for all transactions except import duties and interest payments on government bonds, the bills, printed in green ink on one side only, became known affectionately as "greenbacks." Most wartime greenbacks carried Secretary Chase's picture on them and were intended as a temporary measure. By the end of the conflict, however, the Treasury had printed nearly $450 million in legal tender notes, turning them into an icon of the popular culture. Despite some pressure after the war to end the experiment in paper currency, greenbacks, in one form or another, remained in permanent circulation in the United States.

Once the federal government began printing its own money, the arguments for a national banking system grew more intense. Banks had always been a controversial topic in American politics, especially in the aftermath of the "Bank War" of the 1830s when President Andrew Jackson almost single-handedly destroyed the Bank of the United States by vetoing its recharter. The Bank had originally been established through the efforts of Alexander Hamilton and was a privately run depository for public funds which was supposed to function as a stabilizing force in the nation's loose monetary network. Jacksonian Democrats viewed the national Bank as corrupt and exploitative of the country's farmers and workers. By contrast, the Whigs were generally supporters of the Bank, and banks in general, arguing that they provided the vital capital resources, such as sound or elastic currencies, necessary for commercial development.

Abraham Lincoln had entered politics as a Whig who supported banks and elastic currency. He believed in the availability of credit, especially for public works projects such as canals or railroads that would encourage business growth. Despite his habitual claims of ignorance about financial matters, Lincoln actually became quite familiar with commercial banking issues while serving in the Illinois legislature, according to historian Gabor S. Boritt (Boritt 1994). As president, Lincoln continued to maintain his interest in the topic and saw immediately that greenbacks would suffer terrible inflationary pressure unless an organized central bank, or association of banks, was able to monitor the flow of currency across the nation. In 1863, when Secretary of Treasury Chase urged Congress to adopt a national banking law, President Lincoln said he "had taken an especial interest" in the project. According to Lincoln, Chase "frequently consulted him in regard to it," and although he "generally delegated to Mr. C. exclusive control" of his own department, he believed that he "shared in, to some extent," the credit for reinaugurating a national banking system (Burlingame and Ettlinger 1997, 133–134).

The National Bank Act of 1863, and its revisions in June 1864 and March 1865, set up a national monetary structure that essentially remained in place until the creation of the Federal Reserve system in 1913. The law set procedures for granting federal charters to participating banks. To encourage greater participation in the system, the 1865 amendment to the original act placed a 10 percent tax on state banknotes. Within a few years the proliferation of paper currencies had vanished and the national greenback reigned supreme.

The legislation implementing the new legal tender and the national banking system was passed along strict party lines. Republicans were overwhelmingly in favor of the measures; Northern Democrats were strongly opposed. If Southern congressmen had been present in Washington during the wartime period, it is unlikely that any of the major financial reforms would have been achieved.

War Bonds

Governments can raise funds through various types of taxation, by printing their own money, through sales and fees, and by soliciting loans. During the Civil War, the federal government borrowed money from major banks, but also from the general public through massive war bond drives in which the Treasury Department sold various bonds to the Northern public and foreign creditors. The most popular bond was known as the "five-twenty" or the "5-20-sixes," which meant the bond matured anywhere between five and twenty years from the date of purchase at 6 percent interest. Bond drives were such an enormous undertaking that Treasury Secretary Chase turned to investment bankers, such as Jay Cooke of Philadelphia, to help organize the campaign. Cooke, who had experience marketing state bonds, established a network of 2,500 agents and bombarded Northern newspapers with advertisements. Historian James M. McPherson claims that Cooke "democratized the purchase of government securities," pointing out that by the end of the war nearly 25 percent of Northern families owned some type of war bond (McPherson 1992, 206).

The principal result of these various economic policies was that the Union effort to finance the war was more balanced than its Confederate counterpart. Faced with the same types of obstacles, the rebels elected to pay for most of their mobilization with fiat money. Consequently, the South was ravaged by inflation during the war, more than 9,000 percent compared with about 80 percent over four years in the North. A second major effect of Union economic policies, however, was less quantifiable. Before 1861 the average American had little day-to-day contact with the federal government. Other than the postal system, most citizens hardly needed, or wanted, any service provided by Washington. War changed that relationship. The new taxes, the greenbacks, and the war bonds all combined to insert federal sovereignty into daily life. Higher taxes aggravated some Northerners, but for most the opportunity to sacrifice for their endangered nation was considered a welcome opportunity.

SOCIAL POLICY

"From the first taking of our national census to the last are seventy years," Abraham Lincoln stated in his first annual message to Congress, "and we find our population at the end of the period eight times as great as it was at the beginning." He added, proudly, that there were "already among us those, who, if the Union be preserved, will live to see it contain two hundred and fifty millions" (Basler 1953, 5:53). Not until after 1990 did the Census Bureau announce that the U.S. population exceeded 250 million, but President Lincoln's optimism in 1861, after nine months of rebellion, was characteristic of mid–nineteenth-century American political culture. Adult white males had an almost boundless faith in the social and economic opportunity of their society.

Lincoln considered himself living proof of America's promise. He had been an uneducated farm boy who rose to become a self-taught legislator, lawyer, and ultimately president. He provided his family with a standard of living in the top 2 percent of the nation. He was a respectable embodiment of the Protestant work ethic and the American zeal for self-improvement. Despite his rough frontier origins, the president did not drink, smoke, or chew tobacco. He was not a church member, but he was an occasional churchgoer and took matters of faith seriously.

If anything distinguished Lincoln's social outlook from that of the typical middle-class adult male it was his natural generosity of spirit. Although he never acknowledged as much in public, the president seemed to understand intuitively that there was a dark side to the American promise in the nineteenth century. He endorsed policies that drove Indians from their lands, and authorized harsh punishment when they resisted, but he also seemed capable of recognizing the humanity of Native Americans when they visited the White House, or when he contemplated pardoning their captured warriors. Even as he supported the colonization of freed slaves—a policy he abandoned midway through the war—Lincoln still believed in the fundamental human rights of blacks. The president, who had worked with anti-immigrant politicians earlier in his career, now welcomed recent European arrivals and encouraged their participation in the armed conflict. Although he often called for days of prayer and thanksgiving, President Lincoln refrained from invoking his version of God against either his opponents or religious minorities within the Union coalition. When anti-Semitism arose, the president firmly dispatched it.

As a young boy he had been sensitive, unwilling even to shoot turkeys, and as commander in chief during the nation's bloodiest conflict, he continued to demonstrate the capacity to both exemplify the culture that had spawned him and to rise above most of its limitations.

Westward Expansion

As the "free soil" party, Republicans had always promoted westward expansion. Before the war, congressional Republicans, led by future Speaker Galusha Grow, R-Pa., had repeatedly introduced homestead legislation designed to encourage white settlement in the Great Plains territories, only to find their efforts thwarted by southern Democrats. After secession, they seized their political opportunity and managed to secure a pioneering Homestead Act on May 20, 1862. The legislation in its final form provided a quarter section of free public land (160 acres) to loyal settlers who would maintain a residence for five years. Eventually, according to historian James McPherson, the law helped Americans occupy more than 80 million acres of frontier land (McPherson 1988, 451). The president had little role to play in passage of the actual legislation, but he cheered its arrival. "Our abundant room—our broad national homestead—is our ample resource," he proclaimed in his 1862 annual message (Basler 1953, 5:532).

The Republican-dominated Congress pressed for several other laws to fulfill the national expansion that earlier generations had labeled their "manifest destiny." On July 1, 1862, the Pacific Railroad Act provided major railroad companies with nearly $500 million in free public lands to encourage them to complete a rail line from Sacramento, California, to Omaha, Nebraska, that would finally connect West and East via modern transportation. It was a bigger giveaway than the Homestead Act and probably more important in shaping the future of the American West. The next day, Congress adopted the Land-Grant College Act, a measure that provided portions of unused federal land to the states for resale, authorizing them to utilize the profits to build institutions of higher education. A major federal initiative to support public education, the act ultimately helped midwestern and western states to develop several world-class universities.

The push to conquer the American frontier came at a great cost for Native Americans. White settlers encroached on Indian lands with little regard for previous treaties. Promises of annual payments or supplies were routinely discarded. Several tribes, most notably the Sioux in Minnesota, increasingly exhibited what Lincoln referred to in his annual message as a "spirit of insubordination." An uprising among the Sioux in 1862 resulted in the death of more than 350 whites, an assault the president labeled "wholly unexpected" and conducted "with extreme ferocity" (Basler 1953, 5:525–526; see Document 3.3). Lincoln dispatched Gen. John Pope, who vowed "to exterminate" the rebellious Indians and treat them "as maniacs or wild beasts" (Donald 1995, 392–393). By November, the bloodthirsty general had rounded up over three hundred Sioux warriors for public execution. Under intense pressure from Minnesota political leaders, the president carefully worked through the list of condemned men, wielding his pardon power generously. Ultimately, only thirty-eight men were executed, although, according to historian David Herbert Donald, it was still the largest single instance of public execution in American history (Donald 1995, 394).

Lincoln appeared to have a romantic but patronizing view of Native Americans. When a delegation of Pottowatomies visited the White House in 1861, aide John Hay recorded the comical scene in his diary. He noted that the president "amused" the visitors "by airing the two or three Indian words he knew." Hay found himself chuckling over Lincoln's "awkward efforts to make himself understood by speaking bad English," reporting that the commander in chief uttered phrases such as "Where live now?" or "When go back Iowa?" (Burlingame and Ettlinger 1997, 14). In his public addresses, Lincoln occasionally referred to Native Americans as "savage" or "inferior," but generally he refrained from the kind of vicious metaphors that poured out of contemporaries such as General Pope. During one prepresidential lecture on great discoveries, however, his sense of superiority assumed a harder tone. "[W]hy did yankees, almost instantly, discover gold in California," he asked rhetorically, "which had been trodden upon, and over-looked by Indians and Mexican greasers, for centuries?" (Basler 1953, 3:358). Still, for a man whose grandfather had been killed by Native Americans and who had participated as a young man in a brief frontier conflict, Lincoln's outlook appeared surprisingly absent of malice.

Immigration and Ethnicity

The United States in Lincoln's time was a nation of immigrants. According to estimates from the U.S. Census Bureau, during the Civil War almost 15 percent of U.S. residents were foreign-born. In addition, this population was highly concentrated in the Northern states, where nearly one-third of adult males were immigrants. The foreign-born residents—mainly Irish, German, and English—constituted a special interest in the divided nation and played a critical role in putting down the rebellion.

More than 25 percent of the Union army was foreign-born. Other immigrants provided critical labor on the western railroads and in thousands of factories in the North. President Lincoln acknowledged their contribution in his 1864 annual message. "I regard our emigrants as one of the principal replenishing streams which are appointed by Providence," he wrote, "to repair the ravages of internal war, and its wastes of national strength and health" (Basler 1953, 8:141; see Document 3.4).

Earlier in his political career, Lincoln had been less certain about his support for immigration. As a young Whig, he had been more concerned about Democratic efforts to stuff the ballot boxes with immigrant votes than about celebrating aliens' role as "replenishing streams." Those fears lasted through his 1858 campaign against Stephen A. Douglas when he warned the state Republican chairman about the "Celtic gentlemen" who appeared to be preparing to vote illegally (Basler 1953, 3:330). For Lincoln, immigration was as much a political matter as a social one. Democrats had always cornered the market on foreign-born voters, especially among the German and Irish. For that reason, he was frequently put in the position of resisting rules that made it easier for immigrants to participate in antebellum elections.

The problem for Lincoln came when a wave of immigration in the 1840s and 1850s created a backlash among some Northern voters at the same time that a political realignment was being spearheaded by the new, antislavery Republican Party. The American, or Know-Nothing, Party had a brief but vibrant life in national politics during the mid-1850s. Called "Know-Nothings" because they claimed to "know nothing" about their controversial organization, the movement supported nativist laws designed to prescribe the rights of immigrants, especially Catholic immigrants. They backed measures to lengthen the period of naturalization, impose restrictions on office holding by foreign-born citizens, prohibit the spread of parochial schools, and restrict the sale of alcohol. The Know-Nothings secured major electoral victories in states such as Massachusetts and Pennsylvania; they won the city of Chicago in 1855;

and they established a minor foothold in Illinois for about three years, from 1854 to 1856.

Lincoln regarded the Know-Nothings in Illinois as a nuisance, an obstacle in his plans to create a Republican free soil coalition that focused more on limiting slaveholders than European laborers. The nativists split the anti-Democratic vote and scared away German immigrants, who were otherwise opposed to the increasingly proslavery policies of the Democratic Party. Nonetheless, they represented a significant element of public opinion, and Lincoln carefully avoided antagonizing them. According to news coverage of his speechmaking in the 1850s, Lincoln ducked the topic by joking about their secrecy. "If there was an order styled the Know-Nothings, and there was any thing bad in it, he was unqualifiedly against it;" he reportedly offered, "and if there was anything good in it, why, he said God speed it!" (Basler 1953, 2:234). He was so solicitous of the anti-immigrant forces, that several Illinois political observers mistakenly believed he was a member of the Know-Nothings.

The Rail-splitter's reluctance to confront an organization composed mostly of "old political and personal friends" (Basler 1953, 2:316) proved to be one of the reasons for his 1860 nomination by the Republican Party (see Document 3.5). The delegates to the Chicago convention also feared alienating nativist voters and consequently turned away from frontrunner William H. Seward, who had bravely defended Catholic schools in New York. Instead, they chose the lesser-known attorney from Illinois who appeared to have made no implacable enemies. Political historian William E. Gienapp credits the former nativist vote with providing Lincoln's margin of victory in the 1860 general election (Gienapp 2002).

Thus President Lincoln's acceptance of immigrants was a surprise to many of his contemporaries. He proved to be far more open-minded and tolerant than his reputation had predicted. When a Jewish leader questioned the president about the rules limiting chaplain positions in the Union army to Christian ministers, he was thoroughly accommodating, even if somewhat awkward in his usage. "I shall try to have a new law broad enough to cover what is desired by you in behalf of the Israelites," he wrote to Arnold Fischel (Basler 1953, 5:69). The president's only handicap with religious minorities appeared to be his unfamiliarity with their customs. He began a letter to Catholic Archbishop John Hughes with "Rt. Rev. Sir," and then apologized for his "ignorance" in not knowing the "technical correctness" of his title (Basler 1953, 4:559; see Document 3.6).

The war changed many minds about the value of immigration and helped ease the process of assimilation. Congress established the first immigration agency within the Department of State in 1864 and legalized the importation of contract laborers. But, of course, not all of the prejudice disappeared. Upset over illegal trading conducted within Union-occupied territory, Gen. Ulysses S. Grant issued his infamous Order No. 11 in December 1862 expelling "Jews, as a class" from his military department (McPherson 1992, 382). When informed of the command, President Lincoln insisted that it be rescinded. General in Chief Henry W. Halleck explained the reversal in a letter to Grant. "The President has no objection to your expelling traitors and Jew peddlers," he wrote, "which, I suppose, was the object of your order; but, as it is in terms proscribed an entire religious class, some of whom are fighting in our ranks, the President deemed it necessary to revoke it" (Basler 1953, 6:71).

"The Almighty has His own purposes," Lincoln concluded gracefully in his second inaugural address (Basler 1953, 8:333). In an era in which religious bigotry was accepted without comment, the president was not defensive at all about his own faith. He was guilty of the occasional awkward or even prejudicial reference, but the spirit of his approach to social and religious diversity was well intentioned and usually well received.

EMANCIPATION

The most vexing social question in nineteenth-century America concerned the fate of slavery. Like most mainstream politicians, Abraham Lincoln spent the bulk of his electoral career before the Civil War evading the subject. When he did confront the issue, he usually described himself as an opponent of slavery who was also uncomfortable with abolitionism. He knew slavery was wrong, but he believed those who advocated its immediate abolition only made the situation worse. Lincoln was skeptical that freed blacks could live on equal terms with whites. Even though more than 500,000 free blacks were residing in the nation on the eve of the Civil War—holding jobs, owning property, and even, in a handful of states, wielding the right to vote—racist stereotypes and fears dominated popular culture.

Lincoln was not himself guilty of race baiting, but neither did he risk political capital to defend what he thought white Northern audiences were not yet prepared to hear. Instead, he denied that opposition to slavery required any type of fundamental social revolution. He protested against what he termed "that counterfeit logic" which claimed that "because I do not want a black woman for a *slave* I must necessarily want her for a *wife*" (Basler 1953, 2: 405; see Document 3.7). He supported what was known as "colonization" for freed slaves, sending them to Liberia or practically anywhere outside the country where they could live on their own. As for slave owners, he acknowledged their constitutional property rights, but predicted that eventually they would come to understand their moral error and abandon their reliance on human chattel.

The election of Lincoln in 1860 was therefore a victory for the free soil movement, but not necessarily for abolitionists. Wary of Northern public opinion, Republicans had carefully crafted their message to focus on the promotion of white labor—not equal rights for blacks. Republicans argued that by preventing the extension of slavery into western territories, they would make the West safe and prosperous for hardworking white people. Their ranks included a number of abolitionists, but their appeal was not grounded in a commitment to interracial equality, or even in an assault on the institution of slavery where it already existed.

This background is vital for understanding why President Lincoln approached the question of wartime emancipation with so much hesitation. He was not only facing some of his own racist demons, but also was overcoming three decades of public rhetoric denying the necessity for what he was about to do. He had never supported the abolition of slavery through violence or political compulsion. From the beginning of his career, he had asserted that one could—and must—oppose slavery without abandoning the Constitution. But once war arrived, the pressures to lash out against the "slave power" became far more intense. The need for free black laborers, and their service in the military, grew much greater as well. Some Republicans on Capitol Hill, generals in the Union army, and abolitionists across the North combined to help force the president's hand. By the end of the conflict, he had become the central figure in the movement not only to abolish slavery, but also to guarantee equality for blacks. His final public speech contained a promise to enfranchise educated black men and those who had served in the Union army.

It was both a beginning for black civil rights and an end for Lincoln. Actor John Wilkes Booth was present at the April 11, 1865, address, and reportedly left muttering that it would be "the last speech he will ever make" (Donald 1995, 588).

The Politics of Freedom, 1861–1862

The road Lincoln traveled to become the Great Emancipator was first traveled by runaway slaves. After the outbreak of hostilities, fugitives seeking shelter behind Union army lines created a political problem for a federal coalition that included four of the fifteen slave states. Moderate Republicans such as President Lincoln believed the Union had to uphold fugitive slave laws to maintain the loyalty of border slave states and therefore had to return runaways to their masters. Yet nobody wanted to aid the rebellion. In May 1861, Union general Benjamin F. Butler took matters into his own hands by declaring that he considered runaways "contraband of war," not subject to federal fugitive statutes (McPherson 1988, 355). Northern newspapers delighted in the phrase, and runaway slaves soon became known as "contrabands." In August, Congress passed a Confiscation Act that attempted to ratify this process, nullifying any claims on slaves who had been employed as part of the rebellion.

The president was able to accept this type of limited emancipation on the front lines of the war, but he refused to allow his military subordinates to take the next step and declare wholesale freedom for blacks. When Generals John C. Frémont and David Hunter and Secretary of War Simon Cameron all tried at various points early in the conflict to issue formal emancipation edicts for rebel-owned slaves, the president balked. Enduring the scorn of many abolitionists, he revoked these orders and continued to argue that the war's main purpose was to preserve the Union and not to abolish slavery.

He was not, however, adverse to plans that encouraged voluntary emancipation. In the spring of 1862, the president backed a series of measures on Capitol Hill designed to promote the demise of slavery. A joint resolution authorized funds for state-sponsored experiments with gradual abolition. Lincoln signed into law measures ending slavery in the District of Columbia and banning it in the western territories. The administration also negotiated a treaty with Great Britain to stop the ongoing African slave trade.

From Lincoln's perspective, three primary criteria had to be met to ensure that the abolition of slavery proceeded legally and in a fashion acceptable to the public. First, he believed that slave owners had to be compensated for their lost property. Second, always conservative by nature, Lincoln supported making the process of abolition gradual. And, third, he continued to maintain that freed slaves should be relocated abroad. At different times during the conflict, he backed funding for colonization experiments off the coast of Haiti and in present-day Panama.

Historians disagree sharply over how and why Lincoln changed his mind about these factors, but almost all agree that he had abandoned them by the end of the war. The president's thinking evolved most dramatically during a critical six-month period, from July 1862 until January 1863. In those tense months, he essentially gave up on colonization and reluctantly accepted the principle of immediate, uncompensated emancipation as a necessity of war. A handful of critics have since suggested that Lincoln quietly regretted these developments, that he was "forced into glory" by circumstances beyond his control (Bennett 1999). Yet most scholars believe the change of heart was sincere, rooted in the unexpected tragedy of the war and the intractable positions of the participants in the debate.

Despite his best efforts, for example, Lincoln could not convince politicians from loyal slave states to back his initial proposals for gradual, compensated emancipation. He practically begged them for support. He warned that radicals would not allow him to hold back abolition much longer. "The pressure, in this direction, is still upon me, and is increasing," he told a delegation of border state congressmen in July 1862 (Basler 1953, 5:319; see Document 3.8). They ignored his pleas. Lincoln found free blacks equally reluctant to join him in his plans. In particular, they objected to his emphasis on colonization. One month after his meeting with border state representatives, Lincoln invited a group of blacks to the White House to discuss a colonization experiment that the government was financing in Central America. Again, he was blunt. "[N]ot a single man of your race is made the equal of a single man of ours," he told them, claiming it was "a fact" that he could not alter. Even though he had admitted that blacks were "suffering . . . the greatest wrong inflicted on any people," he grimly concluded that it was "better for us both . . . to be separated" (Basler 1953, 5:370–375; see Document 3.9). The delegation was understandably unmoved.

Some historians believe Lincoln knew his proposals would fail. According to this interpretation, the president was engaged in a sophisticated game of public opinion management, using rebuffs from white

conservatives and black radicals as a prelude for making his final emancipation policy appear more moderate. This explanation gives Lincoln a
great deal of credit, but there is evidence to support it. The day after
the president met with border state congressmen in July, he told two
members of his cabinet that he had already decided to emancipate rebel-
owned slaves by proclamation, because it had become "absolutely essential for the salvation of the Union." "[W]e must free the slaves," he
stated, "or be ourselves subdued." (Beale 1960, 1:70–71). In August,
again before any public announcement of his shift in policy, the president
responded to criticism of his perceived delays with a statement that might
be interpreted as shrewdly paving the way for his eventual decree. "My
paramount object in this struggle is to save the Union," he wrote in a
letter to the *New York Tribune*, "and is not either to save or to destroy
slavery" (Basler 1953, 5:388).

By framing the issue as one of military necessity, Lincoln was attempting to accomplish two objectives. His rhetoric was aimed at softening the
political controversy that would inevitably follow an emancipation order.
Moderate Northerners who otherwise might resist the notion of unlimited freedom for blacks were more likely to back a measure that could be
explained as helping to save white lives and end the war sooner. Equally
important for the former attorney, military necessity justified the action
on a legal basis. The president was concerned that legislative action in
this area was unconstitutional. Radicals on Capitol Hill had passed a Second Confiscation Act in July that went much further than their previous effort, this time vowing to strip rebels of their property and making
all their slaves "forever free" (McPherson 1988, 500). The president
signed the bill reluctantly, asserting that the emancipation power was one
best left to the commander in chief.

Toward Emancipation, 1862–1863

For Lincoln, the lingering question was one of timing. When he
informed the cabinet on July 22, 1862, of his intention to issue an emancipation proclamation, they were supportive about practically everything
in the first draft except the scheduling of the announcement. Secretary
of State Seward strongly urged the president to delay until Union forces
had won a significant battle, warning that a decree over the summer
"would be considered our last *shriek*, on the retreat" (Carpenter 1995,
20–24; see Document 3.10). Federal troops had suffered significant set-

backs in their recent campaigns along the Virginia peninsula. And, even though troops had seen more success in the Mississippi Valley, Gen. George B. McClellan's failures in the East had overshadowed all else up to that point. Seward was hopeful that Gen. John Pope's impending march toward Richmond would rejuvenate Northern morale and provide a turning point in the war.

Instead, on August 29, 1862, Pope's forces were crushed at the Second Battle of Bull Run and the emboldened Confederates promptly invaded Maryland. With emancipation now on hold, the Union army around Washington in disarray, and European nations poised to intervene, the president struggled to maintain his equilibrium. When a delegation of ministers appeared at the White House in September to urge presidential support for the national abolition of slavery, he vented some of his frustrations. "What *good* would a proclamation of emancipation from me do," he complained, "especially as we are now situated?" (Basler 1953, 5:420). Less than one week later, on September 17, Union forces led by McClellan finally defeated Robert E. Lee's Army of Northern Virginia at the Battle of Antietam and sent them retreating back across the Potomac.

The discouraged president had told the abolitionist ministers on September 13 that these were not "days of miracles" (Basler 1953, 5:420). But after the unexpected Union victory, he seemed less certain. On September 22, Lincoln called the cabinet together, informing them that he was releasing a Preliminary Emancipation Proclamation the next day, a document that spelled out his plans and how the policy would take effect on January 1, 1863. He told them that he had "made a vow, a covenant" with God before the great battle in Maryland that if the Union forces were victorious, he would issue his much-delayed edict (Morse 1911, 1:142–145; see Document 3.11). It was an uncharacteristic explanation from a president who had never belonged to a church.

The White House announcement in late September 1862 permanently altered the nation's political calculus. The conflict was now a war for freedom. It was surprising to some Republicans how quickly they shed their old fears about antislavery extremism. White House aide John Hay noted in his diary that several members of the cabinet, meeting at Salmon Chase's home the night after publication of the document, "gleefully and merrily called each other and themselves abolitionists" (Burlingame and Ettlinger 1997, 41). Conservatives still remained wary, and Democrats pounced on this opportunity to castigate "Black Republicans," but the presidential shift on emancipation helped redefine the moderate center of American politics.

Over the next several months Lincoln's position continued to evolve. He was now essentially pursuing a two-track policy on emancipation. Beginning in 1863, he was pledged to offer immediate, uncompensated emancipation to rebel slaves. This was a wartime measure, designed to incite slave rebellion and demoralize Confederate supporters. For loyal slave owners, or for masters in territory under Union occupation, he continued to believe that he could forge a consensus behind a separate plan for gradual, compensated freedom. In his December 1, 1862, annual message, President Lincoln offered a constitutional amendment that set an absolute deadline for the national abolition of slavery within the next thirty-seven years, or by 1900. He also proposed a complicated scheme for reimbursing slave owners with government bonds. Finally, although he continued to express support for colonization, he appeared more ambivalent about the need for a physical separation of the races and rejected some of the long-held beliefs of the Republican platform. "Emancipation, even without deportation," he claimed, "would probably enhance the wages of white labor, and, very surely, would not reduce them" (Basler 1953, 5:535). Still groping for answers, he had somehow come to the conclusion that freed blacks, without the coercion of slavery, would work less diligently and produce less, thereby opening up more opportunities for whites.

The winter of 1862 was a difficult one for the president. Republicans had fared poorly in the midterm elections, creating doubt within the party about the administration's new direction. McClellan failed to follow through on his victory at Antietam. Lincoln removed him after the electoral season, but his replacement subsequently led the Army of the Potomac into one of its worst defeats, at the Battle of Fredericksburg on December 13, 1862. There was widespread concern about the continued military stalemate. Leading figures on Capitol Hill blamed Secretary of State Seward and tried to have him removed.

Despite these hard times, the pressure only seemed to intensify Lincoln's commitment to emancipation. Conservatives such as Sen. Orville Browning, R-Ill., were aghast. One of Browning's colleagues reported to him that he had finally become convinced, after making a last-minute plea at the White House to delay the proclamation, that the president was instead "fatally bent upon his course" (Pease and Randall 1925, 1:606–607). Lincoln signed the Emancipation Proclamation on New Year's Day 1863, after a long morning spent greeting visitors at the White House. According to Frederick Seward, an assistant secretary of state who witnessed the event, the president carefully steadied his tired hand before providing his signature, so that nobody would think he had any "compunctions" (Donald 1995, 407).

In many ways, the final document was more important for what it omitted than for what it ordered. There was no mention of colonization and no further proposals for gradual or compensated emancipation. Instead, the presidential decree essentially promised freedom everywhere in the nation beyond its power to control. It carefully listed the states, or parts of states, currently in rebellion, noting the various exceptions to emancipation "with all the moral grandeur of a bill of lading" in the famous phrase of historian Richard Hofstadter (Paludan 1994, 187; see Document 3.12).

There was one important new addition to the president's previous statements on emancipation. For the first time, he welcomed black men "of suitable condition" into the Union military. The previous July Congress had adopted a law that had authorized the president to employ blacks in the armed forces, but the January 1 proclamation was Lincoln's first public acknowledgement of his intention to actually recruit black soldiers. His decision served to underscore how seriously he viewed his emancipation policy as one of military necessity. Three weeks later, when Supreme Court justice David Davis, one of his closest friends, warned that the promise of freedom might have to be revoked, or modified, Lincoln sternly informed him that the proclamation was "a fixed thing" (Pease and Randall 1925, 1:616).

Keeping the Promise, 1863–1865

The president's determination to abide by his pledge did not seriously waver during the remaining years of the war. The courage of black soldiers moved Lincoln, who originally feared they would last only "a few weeks," and ultimately helped to convince him that the emancipation policy was his greatest accomplishment (Basler 1953, 5:423). By the end of the conflict, more than 180,000 blacks had served in the Union army and nearly 20,000 had fought for the Union navy. Tens of thousands more provided critical manual labor to support federal troops. During a period in the conflict when some Northern whites were rioting to avoid compulsory military service, the eagerness of free blacks to participate helped to provide a vital boost to the Union effort.

Whenever critics broached the subject of repealing emancipation, Lincoln invoked black soldiers' sacrifices on the battlefield. In 1863 he responded to complaints about the proclamation by stating the case explicitly. "I thought that whatever negroes can be got to do as soldiers," he wrote, "leaves just so much less for white soldiers to do, in saving the Union." He pointed out that "negroes, like other people, act upon motives." He then asked, "Why should they do any thing for us, if we will do nothing for them?" Arguing that the "promise of freedom" would be their "strongest motive," he concluded that "the promise being made, must be kept." (Basler 1953, 7:500). By 1864, after a series of combat incidents demonstrated the extent of black heroism, he had become even more emphatic. "There have been men who have proposed to me to return to slavery [our] black warriors . . . ," he stated, "[but] I should be damned in time & in eternity for so doing" (Basler 1953, 7:507).

Lincoln ran for reelection in 1864 on a platform that called for a constitutional amendment to abolish slavery. The proposed Thirteenth Amendment, which mandated the immediate, uncompensated, and total abolition of slavery, had the president's full support. The measure failed to pass the House of Representatives by the required two-thirds majority in June 1864, but was back on the agenda in December. The president raised the issue in his annual message, urging adoption of the proposal and allowing members of his cabinet to lobby extensively for passage of what he termed the "king's cure" for the evils of slavery (Vorenberg 2001, 176). Congress finally approved the amendment for ratification by the states in late January 1865. Although not required to do so, President Lincoln signed the document anyway, indicating his enthusiastic endorsement for a commitment to equality that had been a long time in coming.

SELECTED PRIMARY SOURCES

Basler, Roy P., ed. *The Collected Works of Abraham Lincoln*. 9 vols. New Brunswick: Rutgers University Press, 1953.

Beale, Howard K., ed. *Diary of Gideon Welles: Secretary of Navy Under Lincoln and Johnson*. 3 vols. New York: Norton, 1960.

Burlingame, Michael, and John R. Turner Ettlinger, eds. *Inside Lincoln's White House: The Complete Civil War Diary of John Hay.* Carbondale: Southern Illinois University Press, 1997.

Carpenter, F. B. *The Inner Life of Abraham Lincoln: Six Months at the White House.* 1866. Reprint, Lincoln: University of Nebraska Press, 1995.

Fehrenbacher, Don E., and Virginia Fehrenbacher, eds. *Recollected Words of Abraham Lincoln.* Stanford: Stanford University Press, 1996.

Morse, John T., ed. *Diary of Gideon Welles, Secretary of Navy under Lincoln and Johnson.* Boston: Houghton Mifflin, 1911.

Pease, Theodore C., and James G. Randall, eds. *The Diary of Orville Hickman Browning.* 2 vols. Springfield: Illinois State Historical Society, 1925–1933.

RECOMMENDED READING

Basler, Roy P., ed. *The Collected Works of Abraham Lincoln.* 9 vols. New Brunswick: Rutgers University Press, 1953.

This invaluable reference source is also available online with full text search capabilities through the efforts of the Abraham Lincoln Association (www.hti.umich.edu/l/lincoln/). Lincoln, in his own words, remains the best single starting point for any true student of his life.

McPherson, James M. *Battle Cry of Freedom: The Civil War Era.* New York: Oxford University Press, 1988.

——. *Ordeal by Fire: The Civil War and Reconstruction.* 2d ed. New York: McGraw-Hill, 1992.

Battle Cry of Freedom, part of the prestigious *Oxford History of the United States,* is arguably the best narrative survey of the Civil War era. *Ordeal By Fire* offers an updated textbook version of the story, especially suitable for college classrooms.

Weigley, Russell F. *A Great Civil War: A Military and Political History, 1861–1865.* Bloomington: University of Indiana Press, 2000.

Weigley's reliable overview offers updated information on several major Civil War topics.

GENERAL ADMINISTRATION POLICIES

Donald, David Herbert. *Lincoln.* New York: Simon and Schuster, 1995.

Paludan, Phillip Shaw. *The Presidency of Abraham Lincoln.* Lawrence: University of Kansas Press, 1994.

FOREIGN POLICY

Jones, Howard. *Abraham Lincoln and a New Birth of Freedom: The Union and Slavery in the Diplomacy of the Civil War.* Lincoln: University of Nebraska Press, 1999.

———. *Union in Peril: The Crisis over British Intervention in the Civil War.* Chapel Hill: University of North Carolina Press, 1992.

Mahin, Dean B. *One War at a Time: The International Dimensions of the American Civil War.* Washington, D.C: Brassey's, 1999.

ECONOMIC AND SOCIAL POLICY

Boritt, Gabor S. *Lincoln and the Economics of the American Dream.* 1978. Reprint, Urbana: University of Illinois Press, 1994.

Curry, Leonard P. *Blueprint for Modern America: Non-military Legislation of the First Civil War Congress.* Nashville: Vanderbilt University Press, 1968.

Gienapp, William E. *Abraham Lincoln and Civil War America: A Biography.* New York: Oxford University Press, 2002.

Nichols, David A. *Lincoln and the Indians: Civil War Policy and Politics.* Columbia: University of Missouri Press, 1978.

EMANCIPATION

Bennett, Lerone Jr. *Forced into Glory: Abraham Lincoln's White Dream.* Chicago: Johnson Publishing, 1999.

Franklin, John Hope. *The Emancipation Proclamation.* Garden City, N.Y.: Doubleday, 1963.

Vorenberg, Michael. *Final Freedom: The Civil War, the Abolition of Slavery, and the Thirteenth Amendment.* Cambridge: Cambridge University Press, 2001.

Document 3.1   Address to Workingmen of Manchester (1863)

After the announcement of the Emancipation Proclamation on January 1, 1863, a public meeting of factory workers in Manchester, England, adopted a resolution expressing "high admiration" for Abraham Lincoln's embrace of freedom as a Union war aim. The president wasted no time in reaching out to cultivate public opinion in Great Britain, a powerful foreign nation that he was determined to keep out of the American conflict.

Executive Mansion, Washington,

To the workingmen of Manchester: January 19, 1863.

I have the honor to acknowledge the receipt of the address and resolutions which you sent to me on the eve of the new year.

When I came, on the fourth day of March, 1861, through a free and constitutional election, to preside in the government of the United States, the country was found at the verge of civil war. Whatever might have been the cause, or whosoever the fault, one duty paramount to all others was before me, namely, to maintain and preserve at once the Constitution and the integrity of the federal republic. A conscientious purpose to perform this duty is a key to all the measures of administration which have been, and to all which will hereafter be pursued. Under our form of government, and my official oath, I could not depart from this purpose if I would. It is not always in the power of governments to enlarge or restrict the scope of moral results which follow the policies that they may deem it necessary for the public safety, from time to time, to adopt.

I have understood well that the duty of self-preservation rests solely with the American people. But I have at the same time been aware that favor or disfavor of foreign nations might have a material influence in enlarging and prolonging the struggle with disloyal men in which the country is engaged. A fair examination of history has seemed to authorize a belief that the past action and influences of the United States were generally regarded as having been beneficent towards mankind. I have therefore reckoned upon the forbearance of nations. Circumstances, to some of which you kindly allude, induced me especially to expect that if justice and good faith should be practiced by the United States, they would encounter no hostile influence on the part of Great Britain. It is now a pleasant duty to acknowledge the demonstration you have given of your desire that a spirit of peace and amity towards this country may prevail in the councils of your Queen, who is respected and esteemed in your own country only more than she is by the kindred nation which has its home on this side of the Atlantic.

I know and deeply deplore the sufferings which the workingmen at Manchester and in all Europe are called to endure in this crisis. It has been often and studiously represented that the attempt to overthrow this government, which was built upon the foundation of human rights, and to substitute for it one which should rest exclusively on the basis of human slavery, was likely to obtain the favor of Europe. Through the actions of our disloyal citizens the workingmen of Europe have been subjected to a severe trial, for the purpose of forcing their sanction to that attempt. Under these circumstances, I cannot but regard your decisive utterance upon the question as an instance of sublime Christian heroism which has not been surpassed in any age or in any country. It is, indeed, an energetic and reinspiring assurance of the inherent power of truth and of the ultimate and universal triumph of justice, humanity, and freedom. I do not doubt that the sentiments you have expressed will be sustained by your great nation, and, on the other hand, I have no hesitation in assuring you that they will excite admiration, esteem, and the most reciprocal feelings of friendship among the American people. I hail this interchange of sentiment, therefore, as an augury that, whatever else may happen, whatever misfortune may befall your country or my own, the peace and friendship which now exist between the two nations will be, as it shall be my desire to make them, perpetual.

ABRAHAM LINCOLN.

Source: Abraham Lincoln, "To the Workingmen of Manchester, England," January 19, 1863, in *The Collected Works of Abraham Lincoln,* 9 vols., ed. Roy P. Basler (New Brunswick: Rutgers University Press, 1953), 6:64–65.

Document 3.2   Statement on Finances (1862)

During his second annual message to Congress, presented on December 1, 1862, President Lincoln praised the nation's legislators for creating a national currency during their previous session and urged them to fight inflation by adopting a national banking law.

. . . The condition of the finances will claim your most diligent consideration. The vast expenditures incident to the military and naval operations required for the suppression of the rebellion, have hitherto been met with a promptitude, and certainty, unusual in similar circumstances, and the public credit has been fully maintained. The continuance of the war, however, and the increased disbursements made necessary by the augmented forces now in the field, demand your best reflections as to the best modes of providing the necessary revenue, without injury to business and with the least possible burdens upon labor.

The suspension of specie payments by the banks, soon after the commencement of your last session, made large issues of United States notes unavoidable. In no other way could the payment of the troops, and the satisfaction of other just demands, be so economically, or so well provided for. The judicious legislation of Congress, securing the receivability of these notes for loans and internal duties, and making them a legal tender for other debts, has made them an universal currency; and has satisfied, partially, at least, and for the time, the long felt want of an uniform circulating medium, saving thereby to the people, immense sums in discounts and exchanges.

A return to specie payments, however, at the earliest period compatible with due regard to all interests concerned, should ever be kept in view. Fluctuations in the value of currency are always injurious, and to reduce these fluctuations to the lowest possible point will always be a leading purpose in wise legislation. Convertibility, prompt and certain convertibility into coin, is generally acknowledged to be the best and surest safeguard against them; and it is extremely doubtful whether a circulation of United States notes, payable in coin, and sufficiently large for the wants of the people, can be permanently, usefully and safely maintained.

Is there, then, any other mode in which the necessary provision for the public wants can be made, and the great advantages of a safe and uniform currency secured?

I know of none which promises so certain results, and is, at the same time, so unobjectionable, as the organization of banking associations, under a general act of Congress, well guarded in its provisions.

To such associations the government might furnish circulating notes, on the security of United States bonds deposited in the treasury. These notes, prepared under the supervision of proper officers, being uniform in appearance and security, and convertible always into coin, would at once protect labor against the evils of a vicious currency, and facilitate commerce by cheap and safe exchanges.

A moderate reservation from the interest on the bonds would compensate the United States for the preparation and distribution of the notes and a general supervision of the system, and would lighten the burden of that part of the public debt employed as securities. The public credit, moreover, would be greatly improved, and the negotiation of new loans greatly facilitated by the steady market demand for government bonds which the adoption of the proposed system would create.

It is an additional recommendation of the measure, of considerable weight, in my judgment, that it would reconcile, as far as possible, all existing interests, by the opportunity offered to existing institutions to reorganize under the act, substituting only the secured uniform national circulation for the local and various circulation, secured and unsecured, now issued by them. . . .

Source: Annual Message to Congress, December 1, 1862, in *The Collected Works of Abraham Lincoln,* 9 vols., ed. Roy P. Basler (New Brunswick: Rutgers University Press, 1953), 5:518–537.

Document 3.3   Statement on Sioux Uprising (1862)

In the midst of the American Civil War, an uprising of Sioux in Minnesota left hundreds of white settlers dead; originally authorities feared more than 800 fatalities but ultimately it appeared that about 350 white settlers died. Union army officers subsequently rounded up more than 300 Sioux men for capital punishment. President Lincoln intervened, however, and whittled the list down to less than forty. It was still the largest public execution in American history. During his second annual message on December 1, 1862, Lincoln called the uprising "a massacre" that was "wholly unexpected."

. . . The Indian tribes upon our frontiers have, during the past year, manifested a spirit of insubordination, and, at several points, have engaged in open hostilities against the white settlements in their vicinity. The tribes occupying the Indian country south of Kansas, renounced their allegiance to the United States, and entered into treaties with the insurgents. Those who remained loyal to the United States were driven from the country.

The chief of the Cherokees has visited this city for the purpose of restoring the former relations of the tribe with the United States. He alleges that they were constrained, by superior force, to enter into treaties with the insurgents, and that the United States neglected to furnish the protection which their treaty stipulations required.

In the month of August last the Sioux Indians, in Minnesota, attacked the settlements in their vicinity with extreme ferocity, killing, indiscriminately, men, women, and children. This attack was wholly unexpected, and, therefore, no means of defence had been provided. It is estimated that not less than eight hundred persons were killed by the Indians, and a large amount of property was destroyed. How this outbreak was induced is not definitely known, and suspicions, which may be unjust, need not to be stated. Information was received by the Indian bureau, from different sources, about the time hostilities were commenced, that a simultaneous attack was to be made upon the white settlements by all the tribes between the Mississippi river and the Rocky mountains. The State of Minnesota has suffered great injury from this Indian war. A large portion of her territory has been depopulated, and a severe loss has been sustained by the destruction of property. The people of that State manifest much anxiety for the removal of the tribes beyond the limits of the State as a guarantee against future hostilities. The Commissioner of Indian Affairs will furnish full details. I submit for your especial consideration whether our Indian system shall not be remodelled. Many wise and good men have impressed me with the belief that this can be profitably done. . . .

Source: Annual Message to Congress, December 1, 1862, in *The Collected Works of Abraham Lincoln,* 9 vols., ed. Roy P. Basler (New Brunswick: Rutgers University Press, 1953), 5:518–537.

Document 3.4   Statement on Immigration (1864)

During the final annual message of his first term, delivered on December 6, 1864, President Lincoln abandoned some of his earlier ambivalence about foreign-born citizens and endorsed the idea of increasing immigration.

. . . The act passed at the last session for the encouragement of emigration has, so far as was possible, been put into operation. It seems to need amendment which will enable the officers of the government to prevent the practice of frauds against the immigrants while on their way and on their arrival in the ports, so as to secure them here a free choice of avocations and places of settlement. A liberal disposition towards this great national policy is manifested by most of the European States, and ought to be reciprocated on our part by giving the immigrants effective national protection. I regard our emigrants as one of the principal replenishing streams which are appointed by Providence to repair the ravages of internal war, and its wastes of national strength and health. All that is necessary is to secure the flow of that stream in its present fullness, and to that end the government must, in every way, make it manifest that it neither needs nor designs to impose involuntary military service upon those who come from other lands to cast their lot in our country. . . .

Source: Annual Message to Congress, December 6, 1864, in *The Collected Works of Abraham Lincoln,* 9 vols., ed. Roy P. Basler (New Brunswick: Rutgers University Press, 1953), 8:136–153.

Document 3.5   Lincoln's Hesitation over Confronting Know-Nothings (1855)

Abraham Lincoln had never expressed anti-immigrant or anti-Catholic sentiments before the Civil War, but he was identified by many of his contemporaries as a supporter of the Know-Nothing movement. The American Party or Know-Nothings, so nicknamed because they alleged to "know nothing" about their organization, opposed immigration. They were particularly worried about Catholic immigrants from Ireland who arrived in the United States in large numbers during the 1840s and 1850s. Lincoln was not a Know-Nothing, but he worked with leaders of their movement for political reasons—he was anxious to incorporate their following into the new Republican Party. This letter, sent to fellow Republican Owen Lovejoy on August 11, 1855, illustrates how carefully Lincoln tried to avoid antagonizing anti-immigrant politicians, even though he abhorred their views.

Hon: Owen Lovejoy: Springfield,
My dear Sir: August 11- 1855

Yours of the 7th. was received the day before yesterday. Not even you are more anxious to prevent the extension of slavery than I; and yet the political atmosphere is such, just now, that I fear to do any thing, lest I do wrong. Know-nothingism has not yet entirely tumbled to pieces — nay, it is even a little encouraged by the late elections in Tennessee, Kentucky & Alabama. Until we can get the elements of this organization, there is not sufficient materials to successfully combat the Nebraska democracy with. We can not get them so long as they cling to a hope of success under their own organization; and I fear an open push by us now, may offend them, and tend to prevent our ever getting them. About us here, they are mostly my old political and personal friends; and I have hoped their organization would die out without the painful necessity of my taking an open stand against them. Of their principles I think little better than I do of those of the slavery extensionists. Indeed I do not perceive how any one professing to be sensitive to the wrongs of the negroes, can join in a league to degrade a class of white men.

I have no objection to "fuse" with any body provided I can fuse on ground which I think is right; and I believe the opponents of slavery extension could now do this, if it were not for this K. N. ism. In many speeches last summer I advised those who did me the honor of a hearing to "stand with any body who stands right"—and I am still quite willing to follow my own advice. I lately saw, in the Quincy Whig, the report of a preamble and resolutions, made by Mr. [Archibald] Williams, as chairman of a committee, to a public meeting and adopted by the meeting. I saw them but once, and have them not now at command; but so far as I can remember them, they occupy about the ground I should be willing to "fuse" upon. . . .

Source: Abraham Lincoln to Owen Lovejoy, August 11, 1855, in *The Collected Works of Abraham Lincoln,* 9 vols., ed. Roy P. Basler (New Brunswick: Rutgers University Press, 1953), 2:316 317.

Document 3.6   Lincoln's Outreach to Catholics (1861)

Aware that a diverse body of citizens was available to serve in the Union army, President Lincoln worked diligently to make individuals from different ethnic and religious groups feel comfortable. In 1861 he approached the legendary archbishop of New York, John Hughes, for advice about appointing Catholic priests as army hospital chaplains. The president approved similar positions for Jewish rabbis.

Archbishop Hughes Washington, D.C. Oct. 21. 1861.

Rt. Rev. Sir: I am sure you will pardon me if, in my ignorance, I do not address [you] with technical correctness. I find no law authorizing the appointment of Chaplains for our *hospitals;* and yet the services of chaplains are more needed, perhaps, in the hospitals, than with the healthy soldiers in the field. With this view, I have given a sort of quasi appointment, (a copy of which I inclose) to each of three protestant ministers, who have accepted, and entered upon the duties.

If you perceive no objection, I will thank you to give me the name or names of one or more suitable persons of the Catholic Church, to whom I may with propriety, tender the same service.

Many thanks for your kind, and judicious letters to Gov. Seward, and which he regularly allows me both the pleasure and the profit of perusing.

With the highest respect

Your Obt. Servt. A. LINCOLN

Source: Abraham Lincoln to John J. Hughes, October 21, 1861 in *The Collected Works of Abraham Lincoln,* 9 vols., ed. Roy P. Basler (New Brunswick: Rutgers University Press, 1953), 4:559.

Document 3.7   Lincoln on the Politics of Racial Equality (1857)

Throughout the 1850s Abraham Lincoln attempted to define his position against slavery without committing himself or the Republican Party to the even more controversial proposition of racial equality. Stephen A. Douglas, his principal political opponent, fought back by labeling Lincoln a "Black Republican" and blasting him with vicious race-baiting taunts. This extract is from one of Lincoln's lesser-known speeches, delivered in Springfield, Illinois, on June 26, 1857, as he prepared to challenge Douglas for a seat in the U.S. Senate. The passage captures his dilemma just as well as almost any other evidence from this turbulent period.

. . . Three years and a half ago, Judge Douglas brought forward his famous Nebraska bill. The country was at once in a blaze. He scorned all opposition, and carried it through Congress. Since then he has seen himself superseded in a Presidential nomination, by one indorsing the general doctrine of his measure, but at the same time standing clear of the odium of its untimely agitation, and its gross breach of national faith; and he has seen that successful rival Constitutionally elected, not by the strength of friends, but by the division of adversaries, being in a popular minority of nearly four hundred thousand votes. He has seen his chief aids in his own State, [James] Shields [D., Ill.] and [William] Richardson [D., Ill.], politically speaking, successively tried, convicted, and executed, for an offense not their own, but his. And now he sees his own case, standing next on the docket for trial.

There is a natural disgust in the minds of nearly all white people, to the idea of an indiscriminate amalgamation of the white and black races; and Judge Douglas evidently is basing his chief hope, upon the chances of being able to appropriate the benefit of this disgust to himself. If he can, by much drumming and repeating, fasten the odium of that idea upon his adversaries, he thinks he can struggle through the storm. He therefore clings to this hope, as a drowning man to the last plank. He makes an occasion for lugging it in from the opposition to the Dred Scott decision. He finds the Republicans insisting that the Declaration of Independence includes ALL men, black as well as white; and forth-with he boldly denies that it includes negroes at all, and proceeds to argue gravely that all who contend it does, do so only because they want to vote, and eat, and sleep, and marry with negroes! He will have it that they cannot be consistent else. Now I protest against that counterfeit logic which concludes that, because I do not want a black woman for a *slave* I must necessarily want her for a *wife*. I need not have her for either, I can just leave her alone. In some respects she certainly is not my equal; but in her natural right to eat the bread she earns with her own hands without asking leave of any one else, she is my equal, and the equal of all others.

Chief Justice [Roger B.] Taney, in his opinion in the Dred Scott case, admits that the language of the Declaration is broad enough to include the whole human family, but he and Judge Douglas argue that the authors of that instrument did not intend to include negroes, by the fact that they did not at once, actually place them on an equality with the whites. Now this grave argument comes to just nothing at all, by the other fact, that they did not at once, *or ever afterwards,* actually place all white people on an equality with one or another. And this is the staple argument of both the Chief Justice and the Senator, for doing this obvious violence to the plain unmistakable language of the Declaration. I think the authors of that notable instrument intended to include *all* men, but they did not intend to declare all men equal *in all respects*. They did not mean to say all were equal in color, size, intellect, moral developments, or social capacity. They defined with tolerable distinctness, in what respects they did consider all men created equal—equal in "certain inalienable rights, among which are life, liberty, and the pursuit of happiness." This they said, and this meant. They did not mean to assert the obvious untruth, that all were then actually enjoying that equality, nor yet, that they were about to confer it immediately upon them. In fact they had no power to confer such a boon. They meant simply to declare the *right*, so that the *enforcement* of it might follow as fast as circumstances should permit. They meant to set up a standard maxim for free society, which should be familiar to all, and revered by all; constantly looked to, constantly labored for, and even though never perfectly attained, constantly approximated, and thereby constantly spreading and deepening its influence, and augmenting the happiness and value of life to all people of all colors everywhere. The assertion that "all men are created equal" was of no practical use in effecting our separation from Great Britain; and it was placed in the Declaration, nor for that, but for future use. Its authors meant it to be, thank God, it is now proving itself, a stumbling block to those who in after times might seek to turn a free people back into the hateful paths of despotism. They knew the proneness of prosperity to breed tyrants, and they meant when such should re-appear in this fair land and commence their vocation they should find left for them at least one hard nut to crack.

Source: Speech at Springfield, Illinois, June 26, 1857, in *The Collected Works of Abraham Lincoln*, 9 vols., ed. Roy P. Basler (New Brunswick: Rutgers University Press, 1953), 2:398–410.

Document 3.8   Appeal to Border State Representatives (1862)

The Northern side during the Civil War included four border slave states (Delaware, Kentucky, Maryland, and Missouri). As President Lincoln contemplated emancipating rebel slaves in mid-1862, he worried about the impact of his decision on those critical members of the Union coalition. On July 12, he met with a group of congressman from the border states, urging them to adopt his plan for gradual, compensated emancipation. They refused, and within a few years slavery was abolished in their states without compensation or delay by the Thirteenth Amendment, ratified in December 1865.

July 12, 1862

Gentlemen. After the adjournment of Congress, now very near, I shall have no opportunity of seeing you for several months. Believing that you of the border-states hold more power for good than any other equal number of members, I feel it a duty which I can not justifiably waive, to make this appeal to you. I intend no reproach or complaint when I assure you that in my opinion, if you all had voted for the resolution in the gradual emancipation message of last March, the war would now be substantially ended. And the plan therein proposed is yet one of the most potent, and swift means of ending it. Let the states which are in rebellion see, definitely and certainly, that, in no event, will the states you represent ever join their proposed Confederacy, and they can not, much longer maintain the contest. But you can not divest them of their hope to ultimately have you with them so long as you show a determination to perpetuate the institution within your own states. Beat them at elections, as you have overwhelmingly done, and, nothing daunted, they still claim you as their own. You and I know what the lever of their power is. Break that lever before their faces, and they can shake you no more forever.

Most of you have treated me with kindness and consideration; and I trust you will not now think I improperly touch what is exclusively your own, when, for the sake of the whole country I ask "Can you, for your states, do better than to take the course I urge? ["] Discarding *punctillio* and maxims adapted to more manageable times, and looking only to the unprecedentedly stern facts of our case, can you do better in any possible even? You prefer that the constitutional relation of the states to the nation shall be practically restored, without disturbance of the institution; and if this were done, my whole duty, in this respect, under the constitution, and my oath of office, would be performed. But it is not done, and we are trying to accomplish it by war. The incidents of the war can not be avoided. If the war continue long, as it must, if the object be not sooner attained, the institution in your states will be extinguished by mere friction and abrasion—by the mere incidents of the war. It will be gone, and you will have nothing valuable in lieu of it. Much of it's value is gone already. How much better for you, and for your people, to take the step which, at once, shortens the war, and secures substantial compensation for that which is sure to be wholly lost in any other event. How much better to thus save the money which else we sink forever in the war. How much better to do it while we can, lest the war ere long render us pecuniarily unable to do it. How much better for you, as seller, and the nation as buyer, to sell out, and buy out, that without which the war could never have been, than to sink both the thing to be sold, and the price of it, in cutting one another's throats.

I do not speak of emancipation *at once,* but of a *decision* at once to emancipate *gradually.* Room in South America for colonization, can be obtained cheaply, and in abundance; and when numbers shall be large enough to be company and encouragement for one another, the freed people will not be so reluctant to go.

I am pressed with a difficulty not yet mentioned—one which threatens division among those who, united are none too strong. An instance of it is known to you. Gen. [David] Hunter is an honest man. He was, and I hope, still is, my friend. I valued him none the less for his agreeing with me in the general wish that all men everywhere, could be free. He proclaimed all men free within certain states, and I repudiated the proclamation. He expected more good, and less harm from the measure, than I could believe would follow. Yet in repudiating it, I gave dissatisfaction, if not offence, to many whose support the country can not afford to lose. And this is not the end of it. The pressure, in this direction, is still upon me, and is increasing. By conceding what I now ask, you can relieve me, and much more, can relieve the country, in this important point. Upon these considerations I have again begged your attention to the message of March last. Before leaving the Capital, consider and discuss it among yourselves. You are patriots and statesmen; and, as such, I pray you, consider this proposition; and, at the least, commend it to the consideration of your states and people. As you would perpetuate popular government for the best people in the world, I beseech you that you do in no wise omit this. Our common country is in great peril, demanding the loftiest views, and boldest action to bring it speedy relief. Once relieved, it's form of government is saved to the world; it's beloved history, and cherished memories, are vindicated; and it's happy future fully assured, and rendered inconceivably grand. To you, more than to any others, the previlege is given, to assure that happiness, and swell that grandeur, and to link your own names therewith forever.

Source: Abraham Lincoln, "Appeal to Border State Representatives to Favor Compensated Emancipation," July 12, 1862, in *The Collected Works of Abraham Lincoln,* 9 vols., ed. Roy P. Basler (New Brunswick: Rutgers University Press, 1953), 5:317–319.

Document 3.9 Lincoln Urges Colonization for Blacks (1862)

As part of his preliminary actions paving the way for the public announce-ment of his new emancipation policy, President Lincoln met with free black leaders at the White House in August 1862. He urged them to support his plans to colonize freed slaves in Central America. At that time, Lincoln was still skeptical that whites and blacks could live together as equals, and he was convinced that whether they could or not, Northern public opinion was not yet ready to support emancipation without the promise of racial separation. Resistance to colonization was evident among the free black population, and the subsequent heroism of black troops in the Union armed forces helped to con-vince the president to change his mind and abandon colonization after 1863. The following report appeared in the New York Tribune *on August 15, 1862.*

August 14, 1862

This afternoon the President of the United States gave audience to a Com-mittee of colored men at the White House. They were introduced by the Rev. J. Mitchell, Commissioner of Emigration. E. M. Thomas, the Chair-man, remarked that they were there by invitation to hear what the Exec-utive had to say to them. Having all been seated, the President, after a few preliminary observations, informed them that a sum of money had been appropriated by Congress, and placed at his disposition for the purpose of aiding the colonization in some country of the people, or a portion of them, of African descent, thereby making it his duty, as it had for a long time been his inclination, to favor that cause; and why, he asked, should the people of your race be colonized, and where? Why should they leave this country? This is, perhaps, the first question for proper consideration. You and we are different races. We have between us a broader difference than exists between almost any other two races. Whether it is right or wrong I need not discuss, but this physical difference is a great disadvan-tage to us both, as I think your race suffer very greatly, many of them by living among us, while ours suffer from your presence. In a word we suf-fer on each side. If this is admitted, it affords a reason at least why we should be separated. You here are freemen I suppose.

A VOICE: Yes, sir.

The President—Perhaps you have long been free, or all your lives. Your race are suffering, in my judgment, the greatest wrong inflicted on any people. But even when you cease to be slaves, you are yet far removed from being placed on an equality with the white race. You are cut off from many of the advantages which the other race enjoy. The aspiration of men is to enjoy equality with the best when free, but on this broad continent, not a single man of your race is made the equal of a single man of ours. Go where you are treated the best, and the ban is still upon you.

I do not propose to discuss this, but to present it as a fact with which we have to deal. I cannot alter it if I would. It is a fact, about which we all think and feel alike, I and you. We look to our condition, owing to the existence of the two races on this continent. I need not recount to you the effects upon white men, growing out of the institution of Slavery. I believe in its general evil effects on the white race. See our present condition—the country engaged in war!—our white men cutting one another's throats, none knowing how far it will extend; and then consider what we know to be the truth. But for your race among us there could not be war, although many men engaged on either side do not care for you one way or the other. Nevertheless, I repeat, without the institution of Slavery and the colored race as a basis, the war could not have an existence.

It is better for us both, therefore, to be separated. I know that there are free men among you, who even if they could better their condition are not as much inclined to go out of the country as those, who being slaves could obtain their freedom on this condition. I suppose one of the principal difficulties in the way of colonization is that the free colored man cannot see that his comfort would be advanced by it. You may believe you can live in Washington or elsewhere in the United States the remainder of your life [as easily], perhaps more so than you can in any foreign country, and hence you may come to the conclusion that you have nothing to do with the idea of going to a foreign country. This is (I speak in no unkind sense) an extremely selfish view of the case.

But you ought to do something to help those who are not so fortunate as yourselves. There is an unwillingness on the part of our people, harsh as it may be, for you free colored people to remain with us. Now, if you could give a start to white people, you would open a wide door for many to be made free. If we deal with those who are not free at the beginning, and whose intellects are clouded by Slavery, we have very poor materials to start with. If intelligent colored men, such as are before me, would move in this matter, much might be accomplished. It is exceedingly important that we have men at the beginning capable of thinking as white men, and not those who have been systematically oppressed. . . .

. . . I shall, if I get a sufficient number of you engaged, have provisions made that you shall not be wronged. If you will engage in the enterprise I will spend some of the money intrusted to me. I am not sure you will succeed. The Government may lose the money, but we cannot succeed unless we try; but we think, with care, we can succeed. . . .

. . . The practical thing I want to ascertain is whether I can get a number of able-bodied men, with their wives and children, who are willing to go, when I present evidence of encouragement and protection. Could I get a hundred tolerably intelligent men, with their wives and children, to "cut their own fodder," so to speak? Can I have fifty? If I could find twenty-five able-bodied men, with a mixture of women and children, good things in the family relation, I think I could make a successful commencement.

I want you to let me know whether this can be done or not. This is the practical part of my wish to see you. These are subjects of very great importance, worthy of a month's study, [instead] of a speech delivered in an hour. I ask you then to consider seriously not pertaining to yourselves merely, nor for your race, and ours, for the present time, but as one of the things, if successfully managed, for the good of mankind—not confined to the present generation, but as

"From age to age descends the lay,
To millions yet to be,
Till far its echoes roll away,
Into eternity."

The above is merely given as the substance of the President's remarks.

The Chairman of the delegation briefly replied that "they would hold a consultation and in a short time give an answer." The President said: "Take your full time—no hurry at all."

The delegation then withdrew.

Source: Abraham Lincoln, "Address on Colonization to a Deputation of Negroes," August 14, 1862, in *The Collected Works of Abraham Lincoln,* 9 vols., ed. Roy P. Basler (New Brunswick: Rutgers University Press, 1953), 5:370–375.

Document 3.10   Lincoln Recalls
the Emancipation Decision (1862)

In 1864 a painter named Francis Bicknell Carpenter came to the White House to create a portrait of the president reading the first draft of his Emancipation Proclamation to his cabinet in July 1862. During the course of his work on the painting, Carpenter observed the president and his cabinet and listened to their recollections of the momentous shift in policy. After the war, in 1866, Carpenter published a memoir of his experiences, originally titled, Six Months at the White House with Abraham Lincoln. According to Carpenter, this excerpt represents what Lincoln told him about the evolution of his emancipation policy.

[Lincoln recalled:] "It had got to be midsummer, 1862. Things had gone on from bad to worse, until I felt that we had reached the end of our rope on the plan of operations we had been pursuing; that we had about played our last card, and must change our tactics, or lose the game! I now determined upon the adoption of the emancipation policy; and, without consultation with, or the knowledge of the Cabinet, I prepared the original draft of the proclamation, and, after much anxious thought, called a Cabinet meeting upon the subject.

"This was the last of July, or the first part of the month of August, 1862. This Cabinet meeting took place, I think, upon a Saturday. All were present, excepting Mr. [Montgomery] Blair, the Postmaster-General, who was absent at the opening of the discussion, but came in subsequently. I said to the Cabinet that I had resolved upon this step, and had not called them together to ask their advice, but to lay the subject-matter of a proclamation before them; suggestions as to which would be in order, after they had heard it read. Mr. [Owen] Lovejoy was in error when he informed you that it excited no comment, excepting on the part of Secretary [William H.] Seward. Various suggestions were offered. Secretary [Salmon P.] Chase wished the language stronger in reference to the arming of the blacks. Mr. Blair, after he came in, deprecated the policy, on the ground that it would cost the Administration the fall elections. Nothing, however, was offered that I had not already fully anticipated and settled in my own mind, until Secretary Seward spoke. He said in substance: 'Mr. President, I approve of the proclamation, but I question the expediency of its issue at this juncture. The depression of the public mind, consequent upon our repeated reverses, is so great that I fear the effect of so important a step. It may be viewed as the last measure of an exhausted government, a cry for help; the government stretching forth its hands to Ethiopia, instead of Ethiopia stretching forth her hands to the government.' His idea was that it would be considered our last *shriek*, on the retreat.

" 'Now,' continued Mr. Seward, 'while I approve the measure, I suggest, sir, that you postpone its issue, until you can give it to the country supported by military success, instead of issuing it, as would be the case now, upon the greatest disasters of the war!' The wisdom of the view of the Secretary of State struck me with very great force. It was an aspect of the case that, in all my thought upon the subject, I had entirely overlooked. The result was that I put the draft of the proclamation aside, as you do your sketch for a picture, waiting for a victory.

"From time to time I added or changed a line, touching it up here and there, anxiously watching the progress of events. Well, the next news we had was of [Gen. John] Pope's disaster, at Bull Run. Things looked darker than ever. Finally, came the week of the battle of Antietam. I determined to wait no longer. The news came, I think, on Wednesday, that the advantage was on our side. I was then staying at the Soldiers' Home. Here I finished writing the second draft of the preliminary proclamation; came up on Saturday; called the Cabinet together to hear it, and it was published the following Monday. . . ."

". . . When I finished reading this paragraph," resumed Mr. Lincoln, "Mr. Seward stopped me, and said, 'I think, Mr. President, that you should insert after the word "recognize," in that sentence, the words "and maintain."['] I replied that I had already fully considered the import of that expression in this connection, but I had not introduced it, because it was not my way to promise what I was not entirely *sure* that I could perform, and I was not prepared to say that I thought we were exactly able to 'maintain' this. But Seward insisted that we ought to take this ground; and the words finally went in! It is a somewhat remarkable fact, he subsequently remarked, that there were just one hundred days between the dates of the two proclamations issued upon the 22d of September and the 1st of January. I had not made the calculation at the time."

Source: Quoted in F. B. Carpenter, *The Inner Life of Abraham Lincoln: Six Months at the White House* (1866; reprint, Lincoln: University of Nebraska Press, 1995), 20–24.

Document 3.11   Gideon Welles Recalls the Release of the Preliminary Proclamation (1862)

Lincoln read his initial draft of the Emancipation Proclamation to his cabinet in July 1862. They convinced him to delay a public announcement until after a Union victory. After the Confederate retreat from Maryland in September, the president readied his decree. On September 22, 1862, he read what was termed the Preliminary Emancipation Proclamation to the cabinet. Secretary of Navy Gideon Welles, who was skeptical of the decision, recorded the scene in his diary.

September 22. A special Cabinet-meeting. The subject was the Proclamation for emancipating the slaves after a certain date, in States that shall then be in rebellion. For several weeks the subject has been suspended, but the President says never lost sight of. When it was submitted, and now in taking up the Proclamation, the President stated that the question was finally decided, the act and the consequences were his, but that he felt it due to us to make us acquainted with the fact and to invite criticism on the paper which he had prepared. There were, he had found, not unexpectedly, some differences in the Cabinet, but he had, after ascertaining in his own way the views of each, and all, individually and collectively, formed his own conclusions, and made his own decisions. In the course of the discussion on the paper, which was long, earnest, and, on the general principle involved, harmonious, he remarked that he had made a vow, a covenant, that if God gave us the victory in the approaching battle, he would consider it an indication of Divine will, and that it was his duty to move forward in the cause of emancipation. It might be thought strange, he said, that he had in this way submitted the disposal of matters when the way was not clear to his mind what he should do. God had decided this question in favor of the slaves. He was satisfied it was right, was confirmed and strengthened in his action by the vow and the results. His mind was fixed, his decision made, but he wished his paper announcing his course as correct in terms as it could be made without any change in his determination. He read the document. One or two unimportant amendments suggested by [Secretary of State William H.] Seward were approved. It was then handed to the Secretary of State to publish to-morrow. After this, [Postmaster General Montgomery] Blair remarked that he considered it proper to say he did not concur in the expediency of the measure at the time, though he approved of the principle, and should therefore wish to file his objections. He stated at some length his views, which were substantially that we ought not to put in greater jeopardy the patriotic element in the Border States, that the results of this Proclamation would be to carry over those States *en masse* to the Secessionists as soon as it was read, and that there was also a class of partisans in the Free States endeavoring to revive old parties, who would have a club put into their hands of which they would avail themselves to beat the Administration. . . . For myself the subject has, from its magnitude and its consequences, oppressed me, aside from the ethical features of the question. It is a step in the progress of this war which will extend into the distant future. A favorable termination of this terrible conflict seems more remote with every movement, and unless the Rebels hasten to avail themselves of the alternative presented, of which I see little probability, the war can scarcely be other than one of emancipation to the slave, or subjugation, or submission to their Rebel owners. . . . While, however, these dark clouds are above and around us, I cannot see how the subject can be avoided. Perhaps it is not [as] desirable [as] it should be. It is, however, an arbitrary and despotic measure in the cause of freedom.

Source: Diary entry of Gideon Welles, September 22, 1862, in *Diary of Gideon Welles, Secretary of Navy under Lincoln and Johnson,* ed. John T. Morse (Boston: Houghton Mifflin, 1911), 1:142–145.

Document 3.12   Final Emancipation Proclamation (1863)

President Lincoln's Emancipation Proclamation was criticized by some for being long overdue and by others for being too rash. In the years since, numerous critics have pointed out that the decree itself freed no slaves. The document, however, promised that the Union army would free slaves as it conquered rebel territory. More important, the proclamation left out all mention of compensated or gradual emancipation. It also ignored the president's previous interest in colonization and offered freed blacks an opportunity to serve in the Union military. It was not the final word, but it was certainly a landmark event in the story of American freedom.

January 1, 1863
By the President of the United States of America:
A Proclamation.

Whereas, on the twentysecond day of September, in the year of our Lord one thousand eight hundred and sixty two, a proclamation was issued by the President of the United States, containing, among other things, the following, towit:

"That on the first day of January, in the year of our Lord one thousand eight hundred and sixty-three, all persons held as slaves within any State or designated part of a State, the people whereof shall then be in rebellion against the United States, shall be then, thenceforward, and forever free; and the Executive Government of the United States, including the military and naval authority thereof, will recognize and maintain the freedom of such persons, and will do no act or acts to repress such persons, or any of them, in any efforts they may make for their actual freedom.

"That the Executive will, on the first day of January aforesaid, by proclamation, designate the States and parts of States, if any, in which the people thereof, respectively, shall then be in rebellion against the United States; and the fact that any State, or the people thereof, shall on that day be, in good faith, represented in the Congress of the United States by members chosen thereto at elections wherein a majority of the qualified voters of such State shall have participated, shall, in the absence of strong countervailing testimony, be deemed conclusive evidence that such State, and the people thereof, are not then in rebellion against the United States."

Now, therefore I, Abraham Lincoln, President of the United States, by virtue of the power in me vested as Commander-in-Chief, of the Army and Navy of the United States in time of actual armed rebellion against authority and government of the United States, and as a fit and necessary war measure for suppressing said rebellion, do, on this first day of January, in the year of our Lord one thousand eight hundred and sixty three, and in accordance with my purpose so to do publicly proclaimed for the full period of one hundred days, from the day first above mentioned, order and designate as the States and parts of States wherein the people thereof respectively, are this day in rebellion against the United States, the following, towit:

Arkansas, Texas, Louisiana, (except the Parishes of St. Bernard, Plaquemines, Jefferson, St. Johns, St. Charles, St. James[,] Ascension, Assumption, Terrebonne, Lafourche, St. Mary, St. Martin, and Orleans, including the City of New-Orleans) Mississippi, Alabama, Florida, Georgia, South-Carolina, North-Carolina, and Virginia, (except the fortyeight counties designated as West Virginia, and also the counties of Berkley, Accomac, Northampton, Elizabeth-City, York, Princess Ann, and Norfolk, including the cities of Norfolk & Portsmouth [)]; and which excepted parts are, for the present, left precisely as if this proclamation were not issued.

And by virtue of the power, and for the purpose aforesaid, I do order and declare that all persons held as slaves within said designated States, and parts of States, are, and henceforward shall be free; and that the Executive government of the United States, including the military and naval authorities thereof, will recognize and maintain the freedom of said persons.

And I hereby enjoin upon the people so declared to be free to abstain from all violence, unless in necessary self-defence; and I recommend to them that, in all cases when allowed, they labor faithfully for reasonable wages.

And I further declare and make known, that such persons of suitable condition, will be received into the armed service of the United States to garrison forts, positions, stations, and other places, and to man vessels of all sorts in said service.

And upon this act, sincerely believed to be an act of justice, warranted by the Constitution, upon military necessity, I invoke the considerate judgment of mankind, and the gracious favor of Almighty God.

In witness whereof, I have hereunto set my hand and caused the seal of the United States to be affixed.

Done at the City of Washington, this first day of January, in the year of our Lord one thousand eight hundred and sixty three, and of the Independence of the United States of America the eighty-seventh.

By the President: ABRAHAM LINCOLN
WILLIAM H. SEWARD, Secretary of State.

Source: Emancipation Proclamation, January 1, 1863, in *The Collected Works of Abraham Lincoln,* 9 vols., ed. Roy P. Basler (New Brunswick: Rutgers University Press, 1953), 6:28–31.

*U.S. intelligence chief Allan Pinkerton, Lincoln, and Maj. Gen. John A.
McClernand stand outside a tent at Antietam, October 4, 1862.*

CHAPTER FOUR

Crises and Flash Points

O n the first day of President Lincoln's first term in office, he faced a national crisis greater than any other since the British invasion of 1814, when the federal government had been forced to evacuate Washington. A political rebellion had erupted in the Deep South, spreading fears that several states had seceded from the Union. The new executive pledged in his inaugural address that he would "hold, occupy, and possess" any property or place belonging to the federal government in the self-proclaimed Confederate states (Basler 1953, 4:266). By the next morning, however, he faced an immediate challenge to this stern commitment. He received a bleak report, dated February 28, from Maj. Robert Anderson, the commander of the Union forces at Fort Sumter, a federal outpost in the harbor of Charleston, South Carolina. Anderson said his supplies were dwindling. He feared that without significant reinforcements he would have to evacuate the fort within six weeks. The news was dramatic, because resupplying a federal fort within rebel-controlled territory might easily escalate the rising political hostility to violent conflict.

Turning to more experienced military advisers for guidance, the new president received a stunning verdict. General in Chief Winfield Scott, an army veteran of more than fifty years, said that by this late stage federal troops should probably withdraw. In military terms, fighting to save Fort Sumter might have been unwise, but Lincoln understood better than his generals that the decision was as much about political symbolism as it was about combat strategy. Several Southern states, led by South Carolina, had announced their intention to leave the Union in the aftermath of the November elections. From the president's perspective, he simply could not allow the rebels to continue to undermine the legitimacy of the federal government.

So Lincoln did what any determined executive does: he kept seeking advice until he got the recommendations he wanted. Ultimately, he turned to the brother-in-law of one of his new cabinet members, a former navy lieutenant named Gustavus Fox, who had devised an unconventional plan to resupply Fort Sumter at night using small boats. Because General Scott had originally assured the president that the effort would require a major expedition and a minimum of twenty thousand troops, Fox's plan appeared to be a much more reasonable alternative. Lincoln attempted to wring an endorsement of the daring resupply scheme from his cabinet, but wary of the consequences, they remained divided throughout the month of March. Meanwhile, Northern newspapers picked up the story, and public pressure on the young administration grew intense.

The tension crested near the end of the month when General Scott reported during a state dinner that one of the only other remaining federal strongholds in rebel territory, Fort Pickens in Florida, also would have to be abandoned sometime in the near future. On top of the other high-profile evacuations that had been occurring in Texas and elsewhere, this news shocked Lincoln. An angry president called an emergency cabinet meeting for the next morning, March 29, and later rallied a defiant majority of his department heads around a decision to authorize the resupply of Sumter and Pickens, beginning in early April.

One key figure in the cabinet, however, regretted the decision and attempted to overturn it. Secretary of State William H. Seward had been the leading contender for the Republican presidential nomination before Lincoln upset him at the Chicago convention. Now Seward was convinced that military conflict was avoidable but that his former rival was ill-equipped to head off the danger. On April 1, he dictated a memo to the president that harshly criticized the administration for being "without a policy either domestic or foreign" and suggested that the only answer was to "change the question before the Public" (see Document 4.1). In Seward's opinion, secession and the Sumter crisis were fundamentally about slavery and partisanship. He urged the president to avoid a domestic political crisis and instead rekindle national patriotism by adopting a more aggressive stance toward "European intervention" (Seward 1861, n.p.). He ended the note by implying that he, serving as a kind of substitute president, should spearhead the new internationalist policy. Indignant, the real president hastily drafted a response. "I remark that if this must be done," Lincoln wrote, "*I* must do it" (Basler 1953, 4:317; see Document 4.2). Interestingly, he never sent this message. Instead, he proceeded with his business, waiting for events to justify his course of action.

Lincoln's patience with often-contentious subordinates would become a theme of his tenure in office and was on full display as the crisis worsened. For example, in a series of embarrassing mix-ups about the directives for resupplying Sumter and Pickens, an important ship meant for one expedition was switched suspiciously to the other. Even after Lincoln attempted to correct the situation, his order was ignored on flimsy technical grounds. The president remained at least outwardly calm and proceeded to give notice to the governor of South Carolina that the resupply effort was in motion.

"This notice was accordingly given," Lincoln later related to members of Congress, "whereupon the Fort was attacked, and bombarded to its fall, without even awaiting the arrival of the provisioning expedition" (Basler 1953, 4:425). Major Anderson surrendered the federal forces at Sumter on Saturday, April 13, 1861, and then made the transfer of authority official the next day. On Monday morning, the president declared that because of "combinations too powerful to be suppressed by the ordinary course of judicial proceedings," he was asking states to send 75,000 militia troops to support the federal armies and was requesting a special session of Congress to meet on July 4 (Basler 1953, 4:332). The Civil War had begun.

APRIL–JULY 1861: WASHINGTON UNDER SIEGE

"The White House is turned into a barracks," noted presidential aide John Hay in his diary on April 18, 1861 (Burlingame and Ettlinger 1997, 1). Sen. Jim Lane, a Republican from Kansas, had lent a company of experienced militiamen from his state, known as "Jayhawkers," to provide security around the president. Soldiers from Massachusetts also arrived soon after the war proclamation and were boarded inside the empty congressional meeting rooms. Because the nation's capital was situated in a slaveholding district surrounded by two slaveholding states (Maryland and Virginia), any outbreak of violence related to the fate of slavery placed the federal government in immediate jeopardy. Mary Lincoln feared for her husband's safety and questioned his assistants about the lack of precautions taken on his behalf. "I had to do some very dexterous lying," reported Hay one week after the attack on Sumter, "to calm the awakened fears of Mrs. Lincoln in regard to the assassination suspicion" (Burlingame and Ettlinger 1997, 2–3).

Anxieties reached a fever pitch in Washington during the second week of the conflict when it became apparent that secessionist sympathizers near Baltimore had shut down the only railroad line into the capital. Even the president grew openly concerned. "I don't believe there is any North," he reportedly told some soldiers in the city. "The Seventh Regiment is a myth. R. Island is not known in our geography any longer. *You* are the only Northern realities" (Burlingame and Ettlinger 1997, 11).

In this crisis atmosphere Lincoln made some hasty decisions that bore signs of panic. On April 19, he declared a blockade of Southern ports, even though the decision, invoking principles of international law, undermined his own position that the rebellion was an insurrection of individuals and not the act of sovereign states. Then on April 27, 1861, he authorized General Scott to suspend the writ of habeas corpus along the route from Philadelphia to Washington. On July 2, he extended the decision to cover the route to New York City. By allowing the army to arrest people suspected of aiding the rebellion without providing formal charges and by authorizing military officials to detain prisoners indefinitely, the president risked defying one of the nation's most cherished civil liberties, a freedom enshrined in the Constitution itself.

Yet the Constitution also contained a provision that allowed suspension of habeas corpus "in Cases of Rebellion or Invasion." From Lincoln's perspective, there was no clearer case of rebellion than the situation confronting his administration. Nonetheless, when the army began to arrest Maryland secessionists, the chief justice of the United States, eighty-three-year-old Roger B. Taney, a native of the state and sympathetic to slaveholders, objected fiercely. In the course of reviewing the arrest of a man named John Merryman, Taney offered a blistering attack on Lincoln's actions. "The people of the United States," the chief justice concluded ominously, "are no longer under a government of laws" (Donald 1995, 299). According to his strict reasoning, the power to suspend the writ rested with the legislative branch—not the executive.

When Lincoln addressed the special session of Congress on July 4, 1861, he responded directly to Taney's criticism (see Document 4.3). He vigorously disputed the controversial chief justice's interpretation of the Constitution, but suggested that even if he had exceeded his executive authority, this was no time for "extreme tenderness" about such matters. He noted that the suspension had been employed "sparingly" (Basler 1953, 4:429–430). Regardless of the means, the ends were secured: the rail lines had reopened and Maryland had so far remained in the Union. With striking candor, the president asked the nation's lawmakers, "Must a government, of necessity, be too *strong* for the liberties of its own people, or too *weak* to maintain its own existence?" (Basler 1953, 4:426).

The question drew nothing but silence on Capitol Hill. Members of Congress, dominated by Republicans from Lincoln's own party, voted overwhelmingly to endorse his various executive decisions about the calling of troops and other military actions in behalf of the national defense. They refrained, however, from formally endorsing his decision to suspend civil liberties. But neither did they act to repudiate the decision or restrain the president from further decisive measures (see Chapter 5).

JULY 1861: BULL RUN

The decisive action that everyone waited for was a major military engagement. Key members of Congress and Northern newspaper editors had been repeatedly urging the administration to act. After the Confederates announced in May that they were moving their capital to Richmond, Virginia—just ninety miles from Washington—the pressure to launch a major offensive grew politically unbearable. Yet once again military advice to the president was restrained. General Scott advocated a patient policy of enforcing the blockade—in effect, starving the Confederates out of their rebellion. The commander of the principal federal force in the East, Gen. Irvin McDowell, complained that he needed more time to prepare for battle. Growing dismissive of his military professionals, Lincoln ordered an assault. "You are green, it is true," he reportedly told McDowell, "but they are green also; you are all green alike" (McPherson 1988, 336).

The Battle of Bull Run in mid-July at Bull Run Creek, near Manassas in northern Virginia, was the first major conflict of the war. Under orders, McDowell began moving his troops away from Washington on Tuesday, July 16. The Confederate Congress was scheduled to meet at the end of the week. Northern political observers immediately suspected that the campaign was designed to prevent the legislative session from taking place—a fact that most cheered lustily. Expectations of a quick Union victory were almost universal.

The Confederates had several advantages, however. They benefited from an impressive spy network, spearheaded by agents such as Rose O'Neal Greenhow, operating aggressively within Washington. In general, the rebels had an easier task, because they were on the defensive. But perhaps most important, especially for new armies, their field commanders were simply better and more experienced. Confederate general Pierre Beauregard had graduated from the U.S. Military Academy at West Point with McDowell in 1838, but he had finished second in the class while his counterpart had lagged behind at twenty-third. Beauregard had a degree of combat toughness, having been wounded twice during the Mexican War and having already led rebel forces during the tense crisis at Sumter. Other rebel commanders at Bull Run—figures such as Joseph E. Johnston, Thomas "Stonewall" Jackson, and J. E. B. "Jeb" Stuart—would later win significant renown over the course of the conflict. Of those who would emerge during the war as the great Union generals—men such as Ulysses S. Grant, William T. Sherman, and Philip Sheridan—only Sherman was present at Bull Run.

The outcome of the July 21 battle stunned the North. The federal troops were soundly defeated and sent back to Washington. On the Union side, about five hundred were dead, more than a thousand were wounded, and over twelve hundred were missing and presumed captured. Confederate losses were almost as severe, but the expectations game worked decidedly against the Union. If President Lincoln was shaken, however, he did not show it. Two days after the battle, he crafted a terse memorandum, outlining various changes in military policy and vowing that soon "Manassas junction . . . [should] be seized and permanently held" (Basler 1953, 4:457–458). But it was not to be—at least not until after months of struggle.

JULY 1861: DEFINING THE AIMS OF THE WAR

The day after the Battle of Bull Run the reaction from the respective centers of power illustrated the consequences of the Union defeat. Confederate legislators, now safe in Richmond, called for a day of thanksgiving. Southerners exulted in their victory and soon came to believe that they had soldiers who were better and braver than their Northern counterparts. On Capitol Hill, Congress worked quickly to demonstrate its support for the beleaguered administration. With only two dissenting votes, the House passed what would become known as the Crittenden-Johnson resolution, after its prime movers, Rep. John J. Crittenden, Unionist-Ky., and Sen. Andrew Johnson, D-Tenn. The Senate followed with its support, by a vote of 30–5, on July 25, 1861. The resolutions, intended to reinforce the president's stated policies, denounced the "present deplorable civil war" and pointedly vowed in the face of secession that the legislature would "recollect only its duty to the whole country." To quiet Southern complaints about Republican partisanship, the resolutions stated explicitly that "this war is not waged on our part in any spirit of oppression . . . nor purpose of authorizing or interfering with the rights of established institutions of the States" (Crittenden-Johnson Resolutions 1861).

Such phrases about the "rights" and "established institutions" of states were transparent code words for an acknowledgment that the Civil War was definitely not yet a war to end slavery. Both the administration and the vast majority of the legislators on Capitol Hill believed that their primary responsibility, especially after a demoralizing battlefield debacle, was to hold as many slave states in the Union coalition as possible. They also wanted to encourage whatever Unionist sentiment that might exist in the South to survive in the radicalized atmosphere of the deepening crisis.

Despite his hardening determination to prosecute a war against the rebels, Lincoln wholeheartedly supported this delicate balancing act. For this calculation, he paid a severe political price. It would take another year before Lincoln changed his mind about the need to include emancipation in the war's aims (see Chapter 3). He did so after the escalation in bloodshed convinced him that the federal government needed the labor and fighting power that emancipated slaves represented and that a war of such magnitude must have a greater purpose than simply restoring the bonds of a divided union. Until Lincoln redefined the war's aims, the so-called Radical Republicans repeatedly berated him for his reluctance to act against slavery. The leader of the radical abolitionists, William Lloyd Garrison, complained publicly that the president had "not a drop of anti-slavery blood in his veins" (McPherson 1992, 270). Yet once Lincoln reversed course, he found himself attacked with equal vehemence from the opposite side of the political spectrum. He was condemned as a wartime dictator who risked white lives for black people's rights—a trade-off many racist white Northerners considered ludicrous.

Ever since July 1861, Southern apologists have invoked the Crittenden-Johnson resolution as "proof" that the Civil War was not a war about slavery. Most historians reject this ahistorical reasoning, focusing instead on how the evolution of Union's war aims reflects the context of a struggle that grew more terrifying and ghastly than its participants had ever imagined possible.

JULY–DECEMBER 1861: ARMY OF THE POTOMAC

On July 21, two days after the Battle of Bull Run, President Lincoln underlined in his terse strategic memorandum the importance of reorganizing dispirited federal troops. "Let the forces late before Manassas, except the three months men," he wrote, "be reorganized as rapidly as possible, in their camps here and about Arlington" (Basler 1953, 4:457). Some historians have described the battle as a wake-up call for Lincoln, pointing out that he had originally called for a mere 75,000 militia troops or "three months men." But as Lincoln biographer David Herbert Donald has noted, the president had been required by law to limit the term of service for militia troops, and as early as May 3 he had authorized the recruitment of 42,000 additional volunteers at full three-year terms (Donald 1995, 296). During the July special session of Congress, after he requested approval for 400,000 more three-year volunteers, lawmakers granted him authority to enlist one million. Altogether, these steps marked a dramatic transformation. At the outset of the fighting in April 1861, there had been fewer than 20,000 federal troops. Moreover, nearly one-third of the officer corps had immediately defected to the Confederacy. The Union had therefore begun the Civil War with hardly enough organized troops to wage a single large military action. By the end of the conflict, the federal army was the largest fighting force in the Western world (see Chapter 5).

The man most responsible for shaping the new recruits into soldiers was thirty-four-year-old Union general George B. McClellan. He was a

Philadelphia native who had been trained as an engineer at West Point and had served in the Mexican War (1846–1848). During the 1850s, McClellan had been a railroad executive whose company had occasionally retained Springfield attorney Abraham Lincoln. After Bull Run, McClellan was assigned to create a new federal fighting force called the Army of the Potomac, which would become the principal Union military contingent in the Washington–Richmond corridor. Over the summer, his efficient administration and sharp sense of discipline impressed Northern reporters and turned McClellan into a national celebrity. "I seem to have become *the* power of the land," he wrote to his wife (Sears 1988, 95).

At first, President Lincoln appeared relieved to shift the burden of military leadership to such an appealing popular commander. He had been disappointed with General Scott's passivity and frustrated by the failures at Bull Run. When the aging general in chief finally retired in November, the president happily transferred the senior advisory title to the youthful McClellan. When he asked McClellan if the burdens of commanding armies in the field while serving simultaneously as the president's chief military adviser would prove too much, McClellan, nicknamed "Young Napoleon," arrogantly replied, "I can do it all" (Burlingame and Ettlinger 1997, 30; see Document 4.4).

Almost immediately, the president discovered that McClellan's overconfidence was utterly misplaced. When Congress returned to session in December 1861, the president and the new commander faced an angry political reckoning. According to most of the Republicans on Capitol Hill, the war had dragged on too long without major success. For his part, McClellan seemed unmoved and determined to drill his troops at his own pace. Distracted by other problems, Lincoln allowed the criticism to escalate. The Republican leadership established a Joint Committee on the Conduct of the War to investigate the nation's military policies and perceived battlefield miscues. Ultimately, the political and public relations pressures unnerved McClellan and contributed to his eventual dismissal in late 1862 (see Chapter 5).

NOVEMBER–DECEMBER 1861: THE *TRENT* AFFAIR

The principal distraction for the president near the end of 1861 was a brewing foreign policy crisis with Great Britain. A week after McClellan's elevation to general in chief in November, an American naval vessel stopped a British ship travelling through the Caribbean, discovering two Confederate diplomats, James Mason and John Slidell, and their families onboard. In violation of international law, the Union captain, Charles Wilkes, placed the diplomats under arrest, escorting them first to Union-controlled Fort Monroe in Virginia and then to prison in Boston. The British government learned of the incident at the end of November and began demanding the unconditional release of Mason and Slidell by mid-December. Despite Secretary of State Seward's original desire to inflame tensions with Europe as a distraction for divided Americans, he now feared the prospect of war with Great Britain. So did the majority of the cabinet and key congressional leaders. Still, most Northern newspapers hailed the arrest as a victory, scorning the British and the arcane rules of international law. After heated behind-the-scenes discussions, President Lincoln finally determined to weather the domestic political fallout and release the Confederate emissaries. He announced the decision to Lord Lyons, the British ambassador, on the day after Christmas, thus ending a potentially devastating foreign policy crisis (see Chapter 3).

JANUARY–JULY 1862: PENINSULA CAMPAIGN

Responding to increasing pressure from Capitol Hill and his own disgust with the lack of battlefield progress, President Lincoln issued General War Order No. 1 on January 27, 1862, calling for a wide-ranging military offensive by Washington's Birthday, February 22. For Lincoln, the need for such an aggressive campaign seemed self-evident. Writing to Don C. Buell, a leading Union general, he expressed what he called his "general idea of this war." The Union side had "*greater* numbers," he noted, whereas "the enemy" had "the *greater* facility of concentrating forces upon points of collision." The president warned that all Union efforts would fail "unless we can find some way of making *our* advantage an over-match for *his*," adding emphatically that this goal could be achieved only "by menacing him with superior forces at *different* points, at the *same* time" (Basler 1953, 5:98–99; see Document 4.5).

This was a good strategy, and one essentially adopted by Ulysses S. Grant during the final year of the conflict, but it was not an outlook endorsed by General McClellan. He considered the President's Washington's Birthday scheme amateurish and resented interference from the White House. In particular, he objected to Lincoln's enthusiasm for another overland assault along the Washington–Richmond corridor. If any major action was imminent, McClellan preferred the campaign to begin along the Virginia peninsula. He proposed to shuttle the Army of the Potomac down the Chesapeake Bay, actually landing the federal force south of Richmond. The bold proposal was designed to surprise the rebels and provide the Union army with the shortest possible land route to the Confederate capital.

Lincoln worried about the danger of a counterattack against Washington, but McClellan lobbied strenuously for his plan. The stakes were high. Meanwhile, McClellan, a Democrat, grew more and more paranoid, convinced that Lincoln and other leading Republicans were conspiring to destroy him. In fact, during this period congressional Republicans actually considered a resolution calling for the dismissal of the once-popular general. The president was less impatient than many others, but he was still becoming irritated with his vain, overly cautious commander. By the time McClellan finally executed his long-awaited movement toward the peninsula in mid-March, the rebels were no longer surprised and his relationship with the White House was poisoned. The president suddenly announced that his leading field commander could no longer serve simultaneously as general in chief. McClellan found out about his demotion through the newspapers.

The peninsula campaign was conceived in dissension, executed with relentless bickering, and abandoned amid great recriminations. Among many other problems, there was near constant haggling over numbers. McClellan and his intelligence chief, Allan Pinkerton, badly overestimated the size of the Confederate forces arrayed against them, leading to repeated and much criticized requests for reinforcements. Eventually, their miscalculations became public, causing the general great embarrassment. Meanwhile, the president and McClellan also got involved in a bitter argument over how many troops the general had promised to leave behind to defend Washington. Ultimately, suspecting betrayal, Lincoln overrode some of McClellan's orders, redirecting thousands of troops to ensure that Washington would remain well protected. The general insisted that these decisions guaranteed his failure. "You have done your best to sacrifice this army," he wrote bitterly in a statement intended to reach the secretary of war (Sears 1988, 214).

The truth, however, is that failure came on the battlefield, not from Washington. The Army of the Potomac engaged in a series of decisive actions around Richmond in late June and early July (known as the Seven Days Battles, June 25–July 1, 1862) that ended the Union's hopes of quick victory and literally changed the nature of the war. During McClellan's final attempt to capture the rebel capital, the Army of the Potomac suffered more than sixteen thousand casualties. This was actually less than the Confederate total (estimated at about twenty thousand), but the limits of McClellan's strategy were now painfully clear. He could not dislodge the rebel forces, nor could he out-general the new Confederate field commander, Robert E. Lee.

Most military historians mark this period of intense carnage as the beginning of the move toward total war. The underlying problem for the Union was that McClellan was too much of an engineer and not enough of a warrior to lead troops in such a grisly forum. In mid-July, President Lincoln visited his demoralized general at his Virginia peninsula headquarters. They had a tense exchange as McClellan handed his commander in chief a letter warning that the rest of the war should be fought only "upon the highest principles known to Christian Civilization" (Sears 1988, 227). Lincoln was not in such a civilized mood. Just a week before he had asked state governors to provide the Union with an additional 300,000 soldiers. Now he was being lectured on morality by an unsuccessful general. Lincoln returned to Washington convinced that he needed a new military leader and an even tougher strategy toward the stubborn rebels (see Chapter 5).

JULY–SEPTEMBER 1862: CONFEDERATE INVASION

The day after his return from the disappointing visit to McClellan's headquarters, Lincoln named Henry W. Halleck as his new general in chief. Halleck, nicknamed "Old Brains," was no great warrior himself, but he had been the senior Union military figure in the western theater of the war, where federal troops had secured most of their only significant victories to date. Lincoln seemed to be searching for any combination of generals that might change the direction of the conflict. The month before he had ordered Gen. John Pope to leave his post in the Mississippi Valley to form an Army of Virginia that would finally undertake the long awaited Washington-to-Richmond campaign. The president also authorized Halleck to remove McClellan from his command altogether, but the latter declined to do so. Instead, the general once known as

"Young Napoleon" was simply ordered to leave the Virginia peninsula and provide support for Pope's impending attack.

The Second Battle of Bull Run occurred at the end of August 1862. On the way to Richmond, General Pope's forces encountered fierce resistance from Confederate soldiers, led brilliantly by General Lee and his principal corps commanders, Thomas "Stonewall" Jackson and James Longstreet. Once again, Union generals found themselves outmaneuvered and embarrassed at the unlucky creek near Manassas, Virginia. Afterward, there was widespread panic in Washington, because residents feared that this time the Confederates would certainly follow their battlefield victory with an invasion of the city. Placed in charge of the formidable network of defenses around the capital, General McClellan seriously considered demolishing the city's main bridge and preparing for a siege. Lincoln privately complained to his aides that the general had exhibited "dreadful cowardice" and seemed "a little crazy" (Burlingame and Ettlinger 1997, 37). Pope was even more adamant, publicly accusing subordinates loyal to McClellan of intentionally contributing to the defeat.

The result of the second Union failure at Bull Run was the first significant Confederate invasion of Northern territory. General Lee seized this moment to attempt a daring gamble that promised to end the conflict and secure Southern independence. The Army of Northern Virginia crossed the Potomac, heading north into western Maryland. From that position Lee could easily attack Baltimore or Washington, or his troops could continue marching toward Harrisburg, the capital of Pennsylvania. The audacious Confederate general calculated that a major victory on Northern soil would demoralize pro-Union supporters and impress European powers. Convinced that Virginia had already endured too much bloodshed, he also hoped to shift the devastation away from his native state while further isolating the federal capital.

Meanwhile, President Lincoln faced a grave dilemma. Pope had lost the trust of the soldiers. McClellan no longer had the faith of the cabinet or most of Congress. Halleck was not equipped to take control of the armies in the field. Yet the president needed someone to lead federal troops into battle against Lee's celebrated Army of Northern Virginia. With no real alternative, he settled on McClellan. "We must use what tools we have," Lincoln explained defensively to his outraged advisers (Burlingame and Ettlinger 1997, 38). Always in character, the prodigal general returned to command without any renewed sense of humility, assuring his wife that he was once again being "called upon to save the country" (Sears 1988, 263).

This time, however, McClellan enjoyed a rare intelligence advantage. A Union officer had discovered a copy of Lee's orders to his various corps commanders wrapped around three cigars, apparently misplaced in the excitement of the march. McClellan reportedly vowed that if he could not "whip Bobbie Lee" with this information, then he would "go home" (McPherson 1992, 280).

On Wednesday, September 17, 1862, the two armies met on the battlefield at Antietam (or Sharpsburg), not far from Harper's Ferry, the Union arsenal in western Virginia. It was the bloodiest day in American history. Over 4,100 soldiers were dead by nightfall, and some 2,500 wounded died within a matter of days. Another 15,500 men suffered wounds but survived. Military historians have rated the battle a draw that favored the North because Lee's army had no place to go afterward but back across the Potomac into Virginia. Consequently, the invasion ended less than three weeks after it had begun. McClellan issued exultant dispatches proclaiming Maryland and Pennsylvania "safe" from the rebels, but Lincoln found no solace in this news. He expected Lee to pay a heavier price for his gamble, believing that federal troops should have pursued the Confederates after the battle and wiped out the Army of Northern Virginia before they had withdrawn. For weeks, the president brooded over what he considered an egregiously botched opportunity. The more he reflected on the course of the war, the more Lincoln became convinced that he needed to make dramatic changes in his wartime policies.

JULY 1862–JANUARY 1863: EMANCIPATION

By far the most dramatic shift in policy during this period came over the question of emancipation. Lincoln had joined the Republican Party before the war because he believed that slavery was an evil institution that should never have been extended beyond the South. But like most Republicans, he was an agnostic on the question of what to do with slavery in the states where it had already existed for generations. He was too conservative to advocate the kind of violent social revolution that antebellum abolitionism demanded. Fortunately for him, the issue had always been abstract enough that he could avoid defining his position exactly.

Even the advent of war did not compel the president to reconsider his ambivalence about ending slavery altogether. He supported the Crittenden-Johnson resolutions of July 1861, which limited the war's aim to the reconstruction of the Union. Later, he revoked several emancipation edicts offered by various military subordinates. And he resisted attempts by congressional radicals to free slaves as part of a wide-ranging effort to confiscate rebel property.

Then came McClellan's failure on the Virginia peninsula in the spring of 1862 and the rising body count. The war now seemed too gruesome for half-measures. As the president found himself authorizing calls for hundreds of thousands of more white volunteers, he grew more open to the option of arming black men to aid in the struggle. Moreover, congressional pressure for radical action against slavery had never slackened. Throughout the summer of 1862, then, the president moved ever closer toward a decision in favor of executive emancipation of slaves.

Still, he had to consider several complications while plotting the policy shift. Emancipation could be immediate or it could be gradual. Slaveholders could or could not be offered compensation. The edict might apply to the entire nation, or just to those areas currently in revolt.

In each case, Lincoln believed that the guiding principle must be military necessity. He did not see any other alternative since the Constitution protected property rights and, by a long series of legal precedents, the rights of slave masters. Thus Lincoln decided, at least initially, to pursue a two-track policy. He planned to offer immediate, uncompensated abolition of slavery in the rebel territories and gradual, compensated emancipation for slaves in Union-controlled areas. At first, he hoped that all freed slaves would accept colonization in some foreign land, preferably at an experimental colony he had helped to establish near Panama (then part of Colombia). But that notion was later discarded.

The president spelled out this new doctrine in a series of private meetings and public documents from July 1862 until January 1, 1863. The process coincided with the new hard-line military strategy he had adopted after the Virginia peninsula debacle. It was a policy shift accelerated by congressional action, foreign pressure, and battlefield events. Passage of the Second Confiscation Act on July 17, 1862, initially forced Lincoln's hand by setting a sixty-day window before federal courts might begin hearing cases from individual slaves requesting their permanent freedom. The ticking legislative clock coincided with the outcome of the Confederate invasion of Maryland. The president thus seized on the well-timed "victory" at Antietam to issue a Preliminary Emancipation Proclamation dated September 22, 1862, thereby rendering the controversial confiscation legislation essentially irrelevant. His embrace of emancipation, coupled with the failed rebel assault, also headed off growing European criticism that the war, which was seriously disrupting Atlantic commerce, had no endgame in sight and was based on arcane constitutional matters not worthy of the escalating violence.

The September 22 edict formally announced the Lincoln administration's new two-track policy, setting January 1, 1863, as the effective date for the change (see Document 4.6). This hundred-day window gave the president time to pursue other legislative options for his much-debated intention to offer gradual, compensated emancipation in loyal slave states and territories. In theory, the delay also provided some time for states in rebellion to reconsider their position.

In fact, though, the extra time allowed only further changes in Lincoln's outlook. After facing continued resistance to his plans for ending slavery everywhere in the nation, the president simply abandoned the second track of his dual policy. The final Emancipation Proclamation contained no reference to gradual or compensated abolition, or to colonization. Instead, the document boldly announced that slaves in rebel-controlled territories were immediately free and that they were expected to "labor faithfully for reasonable wages" or, in some cases, to be "received into the armed service of the United States"(Basler 1953, 6:30). Admittedly, by focusing only on the first track of his policy Lincoln guaranteed that critics would ever after claim that his proclamation did nothing more than promise freedom only in those areas in which the federal government could not guarantee that freedom. Nonetheless, it was a monumental public document, celebrated by generations of Americans (see Chapter 3).

SEPTEMBER–NOVEMBER 1862: MIDTERM ELECTIONS

In the midst of the Confederate offensive and the controversial decision on emancipation, the Lincoln administration also attempted to influence various election contests in the fall of 1862. Incumbent American presidents face a challenge in helping fellow party members hold seats during midterm elections. The party in power often experiences a natural letdown and sometimes a serious backlash in voter sentiment. This was the dynamic that essentially played out in 1862 as the Lincoln administration struggled to help Republicans in key gubernatorial, state legislative and congressional contests.

Typically, the ebb and flow of the economic cycle determine the outcome of electoral contests, but in the midst of the Civil War the continued military stalemate appeared to drag down many Republican candidates. In addition, two political controversies—over the new emancipation policy and the suspension of civil liberties—shaped an extraordinary campaign.

A rapid-fire sequence of events in the fall of 1862 spelled trouble for the Republican Party. The Battle of Antietam on September 17 may have represented a strategic victory for the Union, but the Confederate invasion of Maryland only served to remind many Northern voters about the sorry state of the war's progress. The release of the Preliminary Emancipation Proclamation on September 22 also alienated some white Northerners who feared blacks and disliked the idea of general emancipation. But for most Northern Democrats, the key rallying point was President Lincoln's decision on September 24, 1862, to extend the suspension of habeas corpus across the entire country for any "aiders and abettors" of draft resistance or, more generally, the rebel cause. To issue such a proclamation in the middle of an election season struck many contemporary observers, and some historians since, as tyrannical (see Chapter 5).

In those years, state and federal elections did not occur on uniform dates. Some critical states held their elections in October, and the early results only added to Lincoln's burdens. Democrats gained in the critical lower Northern states such as Indiana, Ohio, and Pennsylvania. Republicans scored some important victories in Iowa, but morale among party activists plunged. The Speaker of the House of Representatives, Galusha Grow of Pennsylvania, lost his bid for reelection. Even though Southern congressmen (who were heavily Democratic) were not a factor, there appeared to be a real chance that Republicans would lose control of Congress to Northern Democrats. Waging war was difficult enough. Doing so with a divided government would have been practically impossible.

Such fears never materialized, however. Democrats gained more than thirty seats in the House, but Republicans remained in the majority. Lincoln's party actually added seats in the Senate, relying on the power of incumbent Republican state legislators (who selected U.S. senators in the years prior to passage of the Seventeenth Amendment). To be sure, there were still plenty of worrisome signs. New York, the nation's largest state, elected a Democrat, Horatio Seymour, as governor. He soon proved to be one of the administration's toughest critics. Many Republicans blamed Lincoln for the party's defeats and began casting about for other potential standard-bearers within the pro-Union coalition. Lincoln remained president and commander in chief, but his political stature by November 1862 had been severely diminished (see Chapter 2).

NOVEMBER 1862: SWAPPING GENERALS

The political season had been a tense time for the president for many reasons, not least of all because he had grown increasingly enraged over missed opportunities on the battlefield. In the autumn of 1862, the Confederates had actually invaded Kentucky, as well as Maryland, with a major supporting action along the Mississippi Valley. Just as they had done at Antietam, federal armies successfully repulsed the rebel advances in the West (Corinth, October 3–4, and Perryville, October 8), but they once again proved unable to seize the offensive themselves. Lincoln simply could not understand why his leading generals, principally McClellan in the East and Don Buell in the West, appeared so utterly incapable of destroying the enemy's overextended forces. On October 24, 1862, Lincoln dismissed Buell from command. The next day, in a famously sarcastic telegram, the president ridiculed McClellan's claims that Union army horses were too fatigued to continue. "Will you pardon me for asking," he sneered, "what the horses of your army have done since the battle of Antietam that fatigue anything?" (Basler 1953, 5:474).

Only one year after McClellan had assured a rattled president that he could "do it all," he now faced open mockery and contempt. The general did not accept the change in attitude well, complaining repeatedly to his wife about the "gorilla" in charge of the nation who failed to appreciate his worth. For his part, Lincoln vented his frustrations to close friends such as Sen. Orville Browning, R-Ill., complaining sharply about the general's excessive caution and battlefield failures. On November 7,

1862, the president relieved McClellan from active command. The general would sit out the rest of the war on the sidelines, returning to combat only in the political arena, as Lincoln's Democratic opponent in the 1864 presidential contest.

For Lincoln, the process of removing Buell and McClellan was only the end of the beginning of a series of military reorganizations and changes in the lineup of leading Union generals. Buell's Army of the Ohio was handed over to Gen. William Rosecrans and turned into the Army of the Cumberland. Within a year, Rosecrans himself was gone, replaced by Gen. George H. Thomas. McClellan's Army of the Potomac went through three more field commanders after his departure, until it was finally placed under the overall direction of Gen. Ulysses Grant in the final year of the war. With hardly any military experience himself, President Lincoln became the most active commander in chief, in both setting overall policy and making day-to-day strategic decisions, of any occupant of the Oval Office except perhaps for Lyndon B. Johnson during the Vietnam War (see Chapter 5).

DECEMBER 1862: CABINET CRISIS

"We have lost the elections," Lincoln wrote in the immediate aftermath of the 1862 midterm contests, "and it is natural that each of us will believe, and say, it has been because his peculiar views was not made sufficiently prominent" (Basler 1953, 5:493; see Document 4.7). Just as the president expected, the sense of failure around his administration in late 1862 generated an intense round of finger-pointing and second-guessing. Several overlapping problems only seemed to exacerbate each other. Some observers blamed the military for a lagging war effort. Others countered by demanding an end to the vilification of the Union's hapless generals. Emancipation thrilled Radical Republicans and horrified moderate Unionists. The controversy over civil liberties gave some of the more lukewarm members of the federal coalition an excuse to attack Lincoln. There were meetings of concerned state governors, torrents of disgruntled editorials, and many feverish behind-the-scenes discussions among leading Republican politicians.

The Northern mood darkened even further as more disappointing news arrived from the battlefield. McClellan's first successor, Gen. Ambrose Burnside, led federal troops to yet another devastating defeat in Virginia at the Battle of Fredericksburg on December 13, 1862. "If there is a worse place than Hell," Lincoln reportedly exclaimed, "I am in it" (McPherson 1988, 574).   Within a few days of the battle Republican members of Congress initiated a series of secret meetings designed to air their grievances over the administration's perceived mishandling of the war effort. Radical Republicans, frustrated over the absence of military success and emboldened by their political victory on emancipation, spearheaded the heated discussions. Because there was no practical way to remove the president or significantly curtail his behavior, they seized on a motion to censure Secretary of State William Seward.

Expressing bitterness toward Seward had become a kind of parlor game among the more Radical Republicans in Washington and even among some members of the cabinet. The controversial secretary had been considered a "radical" on the slavery question before the Civil War, but since taking office he had been increasingly identified with conservative elements of the party. The Radicals felt betrayed by the man who once spoke of "an irrepressible conflict" between freedom and slavery. In addition, Seward, an inveterate politician, was a natural charmer who seemed to be on intimate terms with the elusive Lincoln, a fact that aggravated some of his jealous fellow cabinet members. Secretary of Treasury Salmon Chase, in particular, viewed Seward as a dangerous rival, and he later leaked negative information about Seward's influence over the president to members of the Republican senatorial caucus.

On December 16, 1862, an angry group of Republican senators considered a motion to censure Seward's conduct, blaming him for exceeding his statutory authority by unduly influencing presidential decisions. After some delays and debate, they decided at a meeting the next day to send a delegation to the president to air their complaints against the secretary in person before they acted. What they did not realize was that Seward, well aware of the political sentiment building against him, had already offered his resignation. The president, however, kept Seward's decision secret. He feared that if he allowed congressional pressure to force a cabinet shuffle, he would lose effective control of the government. Always keen to the nuances of political power, Lincoln took this threat as seriously as any other during the war. "We are now on the brink of destruction," he muttered nervously to his friend Orville Browning (Donald 1995, 402).

The manner in which Lincoln escaped from this potentially crippling political trap offers an illustration of his skills as a manager. He listened to the senators' complaints in his office, but rather than responding in the heat of the moment, he asked them to return the next day after he considered their concerns more completely. When they came back to the White House, Lincoln arranged to meet them with members of the cabinet (minus Seward) present. He then denied the delegation's various charges, and pointedly asked the cabinet officers to respond to his interpretation about how administration decisions had been made and whether Seward deserved any special responsibility. Especially for Secretary Chase, it was an awkward moment. Unwilling to speak candidly as Lincoln sat there listening, the secretaries, including Chase, stumbled over each other to voice support for their president and to reassure the senators that they made important decisions together.

Even though the various testimonials had been essentially coerced, they left the Republican senators with no basis for their principal accusation that Seward had been exerting a malicious influence over the president. If the cabinet functioned as a true collective body, then how could anyone place particular blame on one member? They left the White House uncertain about how to proceed, but no longer committed to censuring the secretary. Meanwhile, Chase believed he had lost face during the episode and subsequently turned up in Lincoln's office with a resignation letter of his own. According to Gideon Welles, another cabinet officer who was present, the president grabbed the letter, almost with glee, announcing that it "cuts the Gordian knot" (Donald 1995, 405). Chase's decision allowed Lincoln to keep both men in the cabinet, because each had now volunteered to leave and those attempting to push Seward out did not want to lose their ally at Treasury in the process.

Chase and Seward represented opposite poles within the cabinet. Both had been leading contenders for the presidency before Lincoln's nomination. Actually, before 1860 they had been far more accomplished and prominent than Lincoln. In addition, over the first two years of the war they had emerged as the strongest members of the administration. Each had reason to expect an opportunity to run for president in 1864. Seward was now a favorite of the conservatives; Chase had become the leading choice among Radicals. But the cabinet crisis in late 1862 undermined both potential rivals while confirming Lincoln's executive ability to wage war in the fashion he determined. It might not have completely cut the Gordian knot, but the episode did help to salvage the president's political standing at a time when he was under near constant assault (see Chapter 5).

MAY 1863: CHANCELLORSVILLE

Challenges to Lincoln's authority in late 1862 and early 1863 did not just emanate from Capitol Hill. His relationship with the federal military entered a tense, dangerous phase. Morale in the aftermath of Fredericksburg was at an all-time low. Desertions increased and officers spoke ominously about the need for a stronger hand to run the government. An especially troubling rebellion within the Army of the Potomac was aimed at Gen. Ambrose Burnside. Several subordinate commanders, including Gen. Joseph Hooker, openly questioned his competence to lead troops. Faced with endless bickering, the president relieved Burnside less than three months after giving him his command, turning to Gen. Hooker, who had been hopefully nicknamed "Fighting Joe" (see Chapter 5).

Choosing Hooker struck many as a strange decision. He had been one of the loudest, most disruptive voices raised against both Burnside and the administration. Now he was being rewarded with the army's most important field command.

To demonstrate that he was not totally caving in to outside pressure, President Lincoln sent General Hooker a blunt letter that addressed the reported criticisms. "I have heard, in such way as to believe it," he wrote, "of your recently saying that both the Army and the Government needed a Dictator. Of course it was not *for* this, but in spite of it, that I have given you the command." Then, with a deft touch of irony, the president noted that only successful generals could "set up dictators." "What I now ask of you is military success," he wrote, "and I will risk the dictatorship" (Basler 1953, 6:78–79; see Document 4.8).

In retrospect, the letter stands as yet another example of Lincoln's shrewd patience with disgruntled subordinates. At the time, however, the president appeared to many as a weak, beleaguered figure, almost desperate to cultivate allies.

At first, the elevation of Hooker helped to stabilize a bad situation. He was a striking figure, with ramrod straight posture and piercing blue-gray eyes. Soldiers respected his cocky demeanor and appreciated his effectiveness as an administrator. Lincoln was less impressed. "This is the most depressing thing about Hooker," the president confided to a reporter. "It seems to me that he is over-confident" (Donald 1995, 434).

The great test of Hooker's self-proclaimed skills came in early May 1863 at the Battle of Chancellorsville. Here the new commander of the

Army of the Potomac squared off against Robert E. Lee and his vaunted Army of Northern Virginia. Most military historians rate Hooker's battle plan and initial moves highly, but then credit Lee with a series of bold tactical decisions that left his Union counterpart confused and indecisive. The result was another terrible defeat for the federal army, although the subsequent loss of Gen. Stonewall Jackson from battlefield wounds was a costly blow to the Confederates.

"My God! My God! What will the country say? What will the country say?" Lincoln asked in an anguished refrain that had become all too familiar after two years of repeated disappointments for the North (Donald 1995, 436).

MAY–JULY 1863: VICKSBURG AND GETTYSBURG

Victory was the only answer for a Northern public demoralized by the unexpectedly prolonged conflict. By mid-1863 the president badly needed battlefield success to sustain political support for the war effort. Fortunately, two separate but intertwined campaigns provided the necessary promise of eventual triumph.

Since Lincoln's General War Order No. 1 in early 1862, federal troops, especially under the leadership of Gen. Ulysses Grant, had been steadily gaining in their attempt to seize control of the Mississippi Valley. Their efforts won far less public attention than the frustrating and bloodier campaigns in the eastern theater of the war, but they were incredibly important for strategic reasons. Closing the Mississippi River to Southern trade would deprive the Confederacy of much-needed cash and supplies. The campaign would split apart western rebel states (Arkansas, Louisiana, Texas) from the rest of their allies and would threaten key states vital to the Southern war-making machine (Alabama, Mississippi, Tennessee). Finally, Union assaults in the western theater would draw limited Confederate resources and manpower away from other potential engagements.

Grant and his forces had made relatively quick progress through western Tennessee in 1862, but they met greater resistance as they proceeded southward down the Mississippi. Union admiral David Farragut had helped to secure the main port of New Orleans on April 29, 1862, but the two principal bodies of Union troops had been unable to completely control the great river because of the remaining Confederate forces in and around the fortified town of Vicksburg, Mississippi.

After months of brilliant maneuvers but inconclusive fighting, Grant's army settled down for a siege of Vicksburg in May 1863, about three weeks after the Union defeat at Chancellorsville. The town, which sat high on cliffs above the Mississippi River, was virtually invulnerable to assault, but residents and soldiers proved more susceptible to starvation. Weeks passed and conditions grew horrific. On June 28, Confederate soldiers sent their commanding general a petition that concluded glumly, "If you can't feed us, you had better surrender" (McPherson 1988, 636).

According to most military historians, the only serious chance the Confederates had to hold Vicksburg was to call in reinforcements from the East for a counterattack—not necessarily against Grant but somewhere in the Mississippi Valley. The rebels actually considered such a plan in May 1863 during secret high-level meetings in Richmond. Confederate president Jefferson Davis was prepared to endorse a proposal to send army divisions by train to Tennessee, but General Lee argued strenuously against diluting his fighting force.

Lee wanted all of his men available for another invasion of the North. He continued to believe that a single bold, successful stroke could sway the outcome of the war. It was a gambler's philosophy, but after the string of major victories he had achieved at the helm of the Army of Northern Virginia, the general was mesmerized by his ongoing good fortune. He was also haunted by the alternative. The South had limited resources, and Virginia, Lee's native state, had suffered terribly during the conflict. Even a cautious pragmatist could have made an argument that risking everything was smarter than enduring prolonged suffering.

In the clash of wills among the rebel high command, the legendary field commander won. The Confederates reorganized Lee's army after the death of his top subordinate, Stonewall Jackson, and prepared for another invasion. This time, however, the rebel troops crossed the Potomac heading for southern Pennsylvania. Adding to the sense of crisis, once again there was dissension within the Union military ranks. General Hooker clashed with General in Chief Halleck and Secretary of War Edwin M. Stanton and even with President Lincoln. He complained incessantly about the lack of support from Washington and the need for greater reinforcements. The Army of the Potomac, over 85,000 strong, shadowed Lee's 75,000 troops but did nothing to stop their advance into Northern territory. Unwilling to stomach any more aggravation from his field commanders, Lincoln relieved Hooker and replaced him with Gen.

George G. Meade, a native Pennsylvanian. Meade took control of the Army of the Potomac on the same day that rebel soldiers in besieged Vicksburg petitioned their commander to seek surrender, and only days before the largest engagement of the entire war.

The Battle of Gettysburg, July 1–3, 1863, marked a major turning point in the conflict. It was the first significant setback for Lee's Army of Northern Virginia since Antietam. The Confederates suffered unfathomable losses when nearly one-third of their fighting force was killed, wounded, captured, or reported missing. The fighting in Pennsylvania also reflected a strategic decision that had enormous consequences for the western theater. The day after Confederate general George Pickett's famous charge at Gettysburg, isolated rebels in Vicksburg finally surrendered. Within a week, the entire Mississippi River was under Union control.

Meanwhile, back in Washington a frustrated president remained dissatisfied. Telegraph operators recalled that he spent many long hours during this period pacing around the War Department waiting for fresh dispatches from the front. This obsession with military news overshadowed even Lincoln's concern for his wife, who suffered serious head injuries in a suspicious carriage accident on July 2, 1863.

The president was on edge, because once again he saw what he considered an opportunity to end the war slip away. On July 4, the same day Vicksburg fell, Meade issued a statement that infuriated Lincoln. "Our task is not yet accomplished," Meade wrote, "and the commanding general looks to the army for greater efforts to drive from our soil every vestige of the presence of the invader" (Basler 1953, 6:318n). To the president, this comparison sounded depressingly familiar. "Will our Generals never get that idea out of their heads?" he complained to John Hay. "The whole country is *our* soil" (Burlingame and Ettlinger 1997, 62). He wanted Meade to pursue and destroy Lee's army, but the newly elevated general proved unwilling or unable to follow up his battlefield victory. Thus, even though Vicksburg and Gettysburg together represented the greatest triumph yet for the Union cause, Lincoln struggled with continuing doubts about the competency of his military team (see Chapter 5).

JULY 1863: DRAFT RIOTS

The good news from Vicksburg and Gettysburg was not enough to satisfy the disgruntled elements of the Northern home front. Antiwar sentiment had been rising for months. Ever since their victories in the 1862 midterm elections, Northern Democrats had become more aggressive in criticizing the Lincoln administration. Their new posture encouraged the development of a serious peace movement of pro-South agitators, nicknamed "Copperheads" by the Republican press (see Chapter 5).

The suspension of civil liberties and the embrace of emancipation provided the Copperheads with plenty of ammunition to use against the administration, but it was the specter of a national draft in 1863 that briefly threatened to turn what had been a small-scale, treasonous conspiracy into a widespread popular rebellion.

Congress passed the Enrollment Act in March 1863, a law that provided for a compulsory draft of any able-bodied man between the ages of twenty and forty-five, but only if recruitment targets for local volunteers went unfulfilled. The new quota system, organized around congressional districts, authorized state and local officials to offer bounties and other types of inducements to promote enlistment.

By modern standards, this Civil War era draft does not seem terribly coercive (especially because men were allowed to pay substitutes to serve in their place), but it was unprecedented at the time and unpopular in many regions of the North. Draft resistance was strongest in urban areas, particularly among immigrant workers who were predominantly Democratic and often full of racist fears about emancipated blacks. In New York City, the prospect of the coming draft led to riots on July 13, 1863, that continued for a few days. Free blacks in the city endured the worst outrages of the mobs. As the violence escalated, the government ordered army troops participating in the Gettysburg campaign to return to New York and help put down the revolt. Hundreds probably died in the ensuing crackdown. Civil War historian James McPherson ranks the episode as "the worst riot in American history" (McPherson 1992, 358).

If the president was shaken by this public uproar against his policies, he gave no outward indication. He did send a somewhat nervous-sounding telegram checking in on Robert Lincoln, who was then staying at a hotel in Manhattan. The rationale for the note, however, was probably driven as much by concern for his wife, who was still suffering aftereffects of her recent carriage accident, as it was over any fears for the physical safety of his eldest son. A few weeks later, when New York governor Horatio Seymour requested a delay in implementing the draft within sections of the city, the president dismissed the request without any hesitation. "We are contending with an enemy, " Lincoln reminded the governor, "who, as I understand, drives every able bodied man he can reach, into his ranks, very much as a butcher drives bullocks into a slaughter-pen" (Basler 1953, 6:370).

It was true that the Confederates also had implemented a conscription law. Both sides had discovered as the war dragged on that previous customs mattered little. The only goal was victory. All means to achieve this end were open to consideration.

Still, Lincoln realized over the summer of 1863 that he needed to communicate a more persuasive vision of the war's purpose to an increasingly restless Northern public. He crafted several public documents, later distributed by the Republican Party and pro-Union officials during state elections in 1863, explaining the purpose behind his more controversial decisions—emancipation, civil liberties curtailments, and the draft. These letters, such as one to Erastus Corning on June 12, 1863, and to James Conkling on August 26, 1863, helped to quell at least some of the resistance to the draft. Ultimately, however, the Union avoided additional large-scale riots, because the overwhelming majority of men who joined the federal military service—more than 90 percent—did so voluntarily.

SEPTEMBER–DECEMBER 1863: TENNESSEE CAMPAIGN

In February 1862, Nashville, Tennessee, had been the first Confederate state capital to succumb to invading Union forces. For the next year and a half the two sides had dueled for control of this key state, which contained vital railroad lines and more white males than any other rebel state except Virginia. Dissatisfied with the progress of the campaign, President Lincoln had removed Gen. Don Buell from command in October 1862. Gen. William Rosecrans, his replacement, had attempted to dislodge Confederate forces led by Gen. Braxton Bragg, but he was unable to make any progress until the summer of 1863.

Not long after Union forces had secured critical victories in Vicksburg and Gettysburg, Rosecrans's Army of the Cumberland succeeded in maneuvering Bragg's forces nearly out of Tennessee. Federal troops enjoyed a series of relatively bloodless victories until the armies squared off for a major battle at Chickamauga Creek on September 19 and 20, 1863.

The two-day engagement, not far from the city of Chattanooga, left Rosecrans's forces badly beaten. For Lincoln, the disappointing news was not entirely unexpected. "Well, Rosecrans has been whipped," he remarked quietly to aide John Hay, "as I feared" (Burlingame and Ettlinger 1997, 85). After a summer of success, the president now prepared himself for another round of tense exchanges with a demoralized commander.

This time, however, the president and his top advisers in Washington resolved not to be overly patient and let any more opportunities slip away. When dispatches from Rosecrans continued to assume a frantic tone in the days after the battle, Secretary of War Stanton decided that the beleaguered general needed immediate reinforcements. In a dramatic scene, he sent White House aide John Hay out to the Soldiers' Home, the president's wartime retreat, late on Wednesday night, September 23, 1863. Alarmed, saying that Stanton never woke him for emergency meetings, Lincoln rushed to the War Department where he encountered the secretary, General in Chief Halleck, and several leading generals attempting to plot a scheme to send more troops to Rosecrans. Working with railroad executives, they arranged for twenty thousand men from the Army of the Potomac to be transported twelve hundred miles by rail in a matter of days—an awesome logistical accomplishment.

The new troops did help to stabilize the situation in central Tennessee, but General Rosecrans proved unable to organize a counteroffensive. Not wasting any time, the president elevated his best fighting general, Ulysses Grant, to full departmental command and authorized him to take control. Never indecisive himself, Grant immediately removed Rosecrans, replacing him with Gen. George Thomas, who had been a hero at Chickamauga Creek. They soon scored spectacular victories near Chattanooga at Lookout Mountain (November 24) and Missionary Ridge (November 25). By early December, Grant and Thomas had succeeded in forcing Bragg out of Tennessee. Dismayed by the turn of events, Confederate president Jefferson Davis relieved his principal western commander and encouraged his replacement, Gen. Joseph E. Johnston, to regain the offensive as soon as possible. But the news only grew worse. Other rebel forces, under the command of Gen. James Longstreet, also were driven out of the eastern section of the state, leaving Tennessee in Union possession by the onset of winter. Across the Confederacy, perhaps for the first time in the war, there was a rising sense of gloom.

NOVEMBER 1863: GETTYSBURG ADDRESS

By contrast, as the second year of the war drew to a close Lincoln was enjoying his first extended period of popularity since taking office. According to John Hay, the president was in "fine whack" and now seemed to most Northerners fully capable of handling his momentous responsibilities (Dennett 1988, 75–76; see Document 4.9). Talk about a second term, once almost unthinkable, suddenly became a hot topic in Washington. Results from the October elections also confirmed the new spirit of optimism among Republicans. Pro-Union candidates won in several states, including key gubernatorial races in Ohio and Pennsylvania.

Lincoln seized on this moment to reintroduce himself to leading Northern politicians and prepare the ground for his reelection campaign. In mid-November, Secretary of Treasury Salmon Chase hosted a wedding for his daughter to a millionaire senator from Rhode Island that proved to be the social event of wartime Washington. Nearly every leading figure from Capitol Hill attended. A jealous first lady stayed away, but the president showed up and even brought the young couple a gift. Because Chase was openly contemplating a campaign for the Republican presidential nomination, Lincoln's appearance was audacious and somewhat unexpected.

But the president had never allowed the niceties of protocol or social expectations to guide his behavior. While he was attending the Chase wedding, for example, he was also mentally preparing for what had been billed as merely "a few appropriate remarks" for the dedication of a new military cemetery at Gettysburg, Pennsylvania (Wills 1863). Unconcerned that he was not the keynote figure at the ceremonies, Lincoln took his obligation seriously and produced a draft of what many consider to be the finest political speech in the English language.

The ceremonies at Gettysburg drew most of the Northern state governors and dozens of top political officials and newspaper correspondents. Recognizing the importance of meeting with these figures, Lincoln was uncharacteristically nervous about his schedule, insisting that his entourage depart early enough to guarantee time for socializing. He also left Washington despite Mary Lincoln's angry objections. She was concerned that their youngest son, Tad, was ill, a fear magnified by the fact that their middle son, Willie, had died only the year before.

At Gettysburg, in ten sentences and only 272 words Lincoln offered one of the clearest and most eloquent statements of democratic conviction in American history. He emphasized the mystical bonds of national self-government forged on the battlefield and dedicated to the twin propositions of liberty and equality. With biblical cadences and grand, sweeping language, he evoked a timelessness that transcended the immediate drama of the war. After a year of experimenting with various forms of public communication, the president discovered a simple yet noble formula for defining the war's purpose as "a new birth of freedom" (Basler 1953, 7:23; see Document 4.10).

MARCH 1864: GRANT'S ASCENDANCY

Once President Lincoln found his stride as a communicator, he was able to focus on the last remaining obstacle to a successful Union war effort— finding a general fully capable of putting down the rebellion. Despite his inexperience in military matters, Lincoln had been sorely disappointed in the quality of the strategic advice he had received. He began the war relying on a general in chief in his mid-seventies—who actually napped during the Battle of Bull Run—before turning to a thirty-four-year-old megalomaniac whose perfectionist tendencies made him an inadequate combat leader. After enduring the idiosyncrasies of Winfield Scott and George McClellan for over a year, the president turned to Henry Halleck, a smart, competent administrator, but a disappointment as an overall strategist. Lincoln privately dismissed his third general in chief as a "first-rate clerk" (Burlingame and Ettlinger 1997, 192).

By the end of 1863, it was clear to nearly everyone that Grant was the star of the Union military leadership. For certain, he had suffered setbacks in his campaign to control the Mississippi Valley, but unlike so many others, he had never relented. Lincoln had been one of his most dedicated admirers, telling White House visitors simply "he fights" (McPherson 1992, 233). After Grant's spectacular victories in the Tennessee campaign, speculation about his future grew intense.

Yet some historians, such as Lincoln biographer David Donald, have concluded that the president was reluctant to elevate Grant to a position of supreme command because he feared him as a potential political rival. In early 1864, the White House made a few discreet overtures and received assurances from the professional soldier that he had no interest in politics. "You'll never now how gratifying that is to me," Lincoln reportedly announced after hearing the news. "No man knows, when that presidential grub gets to gnawing at him, just how deep it will get until he has tried it" (Donald 1995, 490–491).

In early March, Lincoln acceded to congressional pressure and commissioned Grant as the nation's highest-ranking military figure since George Washington (lieutenant general). He also named him general in chief, with Halleck to serve as his chief of staff. The decision ended Grant's dazzling tenure in the western theater. He reluctantly came east, but in characteristically low-key fashion, he refused to command the Union armies from a post in Washington. During the final year of the war, Grant directed the overall federal military effort from the field, as he worked with General Meade's Army of the Potomac in a determined effort to destroy Confederate general Robert E. Lee and the Army of Northern Virginia.

MAY–JULY 1864: LEE VS. GRANT

As general in chief, Grant devised a grand strategy in 1864 that recalled aspects of Lincoln's General War Order No. 1. On January 27, 1862, the president had directed all Union armies to advance on Washington's Birthday. At the time, most of the army's senior officers had balked at the blanket nature of the order and at, as they saw it, the irrelevant symbolism of the strategy. They objected because before the Civil War most military professionals had believed that battlefield tactics involved maneuvering massed armies in repeated attempts to turn or "flank" the enemy in order to secure strategic locations, such as ports or railroad junctions. But as technology improved, the relative isolation of armies in battle disappeared. More accurate rifles and cannons and the increased efficiency of interior lines of communication and transportation made the traditional nineteenth-century offensive style increasingly outdated. Instead, the nature of modern warfare demanded near constant pressure on the enemy's war-making capacity, targeting both armies and industrial cities for annihilation. In other words, Lincoln and Grant understood intuitively that the Western world was entering a new era of total war (see Chapter 5).

General McClellan, who had insisted that the Union war effort be conducted "upon the highest principles known to Christian Civilization," never accepted this doctrine (Sears 1988, 227). Grant did, and by implementing this all-consuming strategy in 1864, he demonstrated just how brutal such warfare could become.

The Union plan called for five separate armies to move simultaneously against Confederate forces in northern Virginia, northern Georgia, and western Louisiana. It was an ambitious strategy that involved more than 250,000 men coordinating action over a thousand miles against an enemy who was fighting desperately to protect its homeland.

At first, things went poorly. Some of the secondary campaigns were bungled. Then, as the Army of the Potomac marched southward across the Rapidan River into the heart of Virginia, Lee's forces executed a dramatic counterattack on May 5–6, 1864, that nearly devastated the federal troops. Known as the Battle of the Wilderness, the fighting actually took place at the site of the Battle of Chancellorsville almost one year earlier. Shallow graves and some skeletal remains still littered the grisly scene. In this two-day contest, both sides suffered casualties of nearly 20 percent.

"I believe that if any other General had been at the Head of that army," Lincoln confided to John Hay, "it would have now been on this side of the Rapidan" (Burlingame and Ettlinger 1997, 195). Instead, Grant pressed ahead. If anything, the carnage only escalated. The armies engaged for nearly two weeks around Spotsylvania Court House, a small town about midway between Washington and Richmond. Despite suffering one setback after another, Grant refused to concede ground, vowing publicly "to fight it out on this line if it takes all summer" (McPherson 1988, 731).

As the rebels dug in, Grant attempted a classic flanking maneuver. He moved the Army of the Potomac around Lee's forces and closer to the city of Richmond. But in a series of bloody engagements at Cold Harbor on June 3, 1864, and at various points around Petersburg, a town south of the rebel capital, the Union forces were unable to dislodge their opponents. By the end of July, they were settled into a long, frustrating siege of Petersburg, waiting for better news on other fronts.

Some Northerners began to change their opinions of the latest hero-general. "He is a butcher," Mary Lincoln reportedly said, "and is not fit to be at the head of an army" (Donald 1995, 515). The president kept his own counsel on Grant's failures, but apparently did not even consider removing him. Instead, he monitored the situation as closely as he could and tried to be supportive. In June, he visited Grant at his headquarters in the field and returned "sunburnt" but "refreshed" according to White House aide Hay. The president authorized a call in July for another 500,000 soldiers, on top of the 500,000 that had already been drafted in February and the 200,000 requested for the navy in March (see Document 4.11). It was a risky decision in an election year, but Lincoln appeared determined to see achieve victory at almost all costs.

JULY 1864: WASHINGTON UNDER ATTACK

The fact that the president visited General Grant and the Army of the Potomac in the field during the Petersburg campaign indicated both how indifferent he was to his own safety and how bored he could become within the confines of the White House. Further evidence of this somewhat reckless attitude came in July when Confederate general Jubal Early staged a surprise foray into Maryland.

Union military leaders had considered Early's raid a mere nuisance until July 8, 1864, when he suddenly turned his fifteen thousand troops south toward Washington. The city was surrounded by nearly seventy forts, but many of the regular troops assigned to the defense of the capital had been transferred to the field after Grant's forces had suffered so many heavy casualties in the Virginia campaigns. Some of the soldiers on duty at the forts were recovering from wounds themselves; they were members of what was called the Veterans Reserves (formerly known as the Invalid Corps). The rest were largely short-term local militia volunteers, ill-equipped to stand up to an army, even one as tired, hungry and poorly supplied as the rebel force.

On Sunday night, July 10, Early's troops headed toward Rockville, Maryland, not far from the Soldiers' Home, where President Lincoln and his family were in residence for the summer. Afraid for their safety, Secretary of War Stanton frantically sent messengers who roused the sleepy first family and brought them back to the White House around midnight.

Meanwhile, Chief of Staff Halleck was trying to impose some order amidst the chaos in Washington. "We have five times as many generals here as we want, but are greatly in need of privates," he announced sharply in response to telegrams from various well-meaning field commanders. "Any one volunteering in that capacity will be thankfully received" (Cramer 1948, 11).

The War Department ordered all able-bodied government clerks out to the forts. Adding to the sense of drama was an intense heat wave that left many previously deskbound young men stricken along the roads out of Washington.

By Monday afternoon, July 11, a restless Lincoln had had enough. "The President concluded to desert his tormentors today & travel around the defenses," reported John Hay in his diary (Burlingame and Ettlinger 1997, 221). During his tour, Lincoln experienced his first taste of combat at Fort Stevens, which was situated on the road between the Soldiers' Home and Rockville. Military professionals dismissed the incident outside Fort Stevens as little more than a skirmish, but for the president it was a memorable encounter. He raced back to the War Department and provided the telegraph operators with a breathless description of his exploits. Then he shared the story with his young aide. "He was in the Fort when it was first attacked, standing upon the parapet," Hay recorded, sounding almost bemused. "A soldier roughly ordered him to get down or he would have his head knocked off" (Burlingame and Ettlinger 1997, 221). The truth is that the president and the city might have been in serious danger that day had Early's forces simply pushed harder. According to the Confederate general, the main obstacle was the weather—"so exceedingly hot," he later recalled, that his men were dropping out of the march even early in the morning (Cramer 1948, 12).

The Confederates made a minor show of continuing the attack on Tuesday, July 12, but by then a regular division from the Army of the Potomac had arrived to reinforce Fort Stevens and the principal threat to the city was over. At nightfall, the Southerners began their retreat back to Virginia.

Yet before the rebels evacuated the area, they nearly succeeded in dramatically altering the course of the war. Once again, President Lincoln had gone to the parapets at Fort Stevens on Tuesday afternoon to see the fighting firsthand. Once again, he was present when the fort came under fire. This time, however, the bullets came much closer. Commenting on the scene in his diary, Secretary of Navy Gideon Welles reported that he also was present and had encountered Lincoln "sitting in the shade, with his back against the parapet towards the enemy" (Cramer 1948, 54). Asking why the president had assumed such a strange position, Welles was informed that just a few minutes before, a surgeon standing near Lincoln had been shot.

For Lincoln, the danger of Early's raid only confirmed his hardening attitude toward the prosecution of the war. He understood that for a weary Northern public, victory, at whatever price, must come soon. A week after the rebels retreated from Maryland, Lincoln issued the July call for 500,000 more troops.

JULY–AUGUST 1864: RECONSTRUCTION DEBATES

Since the beginning of the conflict, Lincoln had leaned toward a two-track approach with the slave states. He had been resolute with the extremists but encouraging toward any potential loyalists. During the Sumter crisis, for example, he refused to concede control of federal property to the secessionists, but denied any plans to overturn slavery in states where it already existed. The next year he freed slaves in rebellious territories, but offered, at least initially, to provide gradual, compensated emancipation in Union-controlled areas. He repeatedly urged his generals to destroy Southern armies, yet persistently maintained that Southerners were fellow countrymen and not foreigners. In this carrot-and-stick fashion, he presumably hoped to end the war sooner, by punishing real traitors while cultivating potential moderates.

This was the same strategy Lincoln employed when the question of reconstruction grew more pressing in 1863 and 1864. As Union forces steadily conquered Southern territory, a debate arose over how to reintegrate the former rebels. Simply holding new elections seemed inadequate to most Northerners. What was the point of fighting a war if ex-rebels could reenter Congress and continue to agitate on behalf of slavery? Yet many were repulsed by calls from Radical Republicans to punish and revolutionize the South—not only end slavery, but also impose racial equality and wholesale redistribution of wealth. For Lincoln, the answer was a middle course: insist on emancipation but make it relatively easy for white Southerners to declare their loyalty, participate in elections, and return their state to its appropriate legal status within the Union. He appointed military governors in certain areas and proceeded to assert his executive prerogative over Reconstruction policy (see Chapter 3).

In December 1863, Lincoln formally spelled out his Reconstruction plan, establishing a threshold of 10 percent for readmission to the federal government. If 10 percent of a rebellious state's 1860 voters pledged future loyalty to the Union, and the state adopted some measures that eliminated slavery (even if maintaining undefined temporary forms of servitude), then it could reenter the compact of states.

Initially, Lincoln received praise for his proposals from both conservatives and Radicals within his own party, but when Congress considered the issue more seriously in the spring of 1864, friction developed between Capitol Hill and the White House. In particular, Radical Republicans in Congress came to believe that Reconstruction was a legislative, not an executive, responsibility, and that thresholds for readmission needed to be much higher than the president had requested.

What emerged from the Congress was a measure known as the Wade-Davis bill, named after Sen. Benjamin Wade, R-Ohio, and Rep. Henry Winter Davis, R-Md. Their proposal was much tougher on Southerners than Lincoln's, imposing greater standards for loyalty, stricter rules about emancipation, and higher thresholds for readmission.

The Wade-Davis bill made it to the president's desk on the last day of the congressional session, July 4, 1864. He refused to sign it, thus employing an end-of-session device known as the pocket veto. Although not required by constitutional custom, Lincoln issued a statement indicating that his primary reason for rejecting the Wade-Davis proposal was that he believed Congress should refrain from dictating any particular Reconstruction policy, especially one that employed what he considered dubious legal provisions against slavery. He continued to believe that emancipation could only be effected either by military decree or by constitutional amendment.

Some Radicals were outraged. Lincoln had already convinced Republicans to move too far to the middle, to adopt a Union Party label, and to renominate him for president; now they felt betrayed. Coupled with the recent dismissal of Salmon Chase from the cabinet, it appeared to some that there was a new conservative (and selfish) pattern in the president's behavior. In fairness, the bitterness flowed both ways. "If they choose to make a point upon this I do not doubt that they can do harm," Lincoln admitted to John Hay. "They have never been friendly to me" (Burlingame and Ettlinger 1997, 218–219; see Chapter 5).

Wade and Davis issued a "manifesto" in early August that harshly criticized the president, suggesting his attempts to control Reconstruction were "usurpations" that held the future of the Union hostage to "the dictation of his personal ambition" (Long 1994, 185). It was clear that

the "harm" certain Radicals intended to inflict on the president was political. During an election year, they aimed to have him removed as the
Union Party nominee (see Chapter 2).

JULY–AUGUST 1864: PEACE TALKS

The irony of Lincoln's troubles with Radicals during the summer of 1864
was that he fared no better with conservatives. The latter faction considered him too obsessed with emancipation and too unwilling to nego-
tiate with Confederates over conditions for returning to the Union. Historians disagree over the president's true motivations, but in response to
the criticism from conservatives, he authorized two back-channel peace
missions and nearly sent a third high-level emissary to discuss ending the
war with Jefferson Davis.

The first attempt involved a secret trip to Richmond by James Jaquess,
a Union army officer, and John Gilmore, a Northern writer and magazine editor. The Confederate president actually gave the two men an
audience, but rejected their offer of amnesty and compensation in
exchange for reconciliation and emancipation. According to Gilmore,
Davis stated explicitly that Confederates were no longer prepared to
accept anything less than full independence.

The day after the secret Richmond meeting, President Lincoln provided a letter addressed "To Whom It May Concern" for use in a separate attempt at negotiations (see Document 4.12). There had been
reports that Confederate agents were in Niagara Falls, Canada, waiting
for an opportunity to meet with the president. Horace Greeley, the well-
known editor of the *New York Tribune,* had taken a special interest in
the Niagara channel and had written Lincoln a letter urging him to provide safe passage for the diplomats. Instead, the president turned the
tables on the gadfly editor by insisting that he venture to Canada himself on behalf of the government. Greeley objected but eventually
agreed to go.

When his reluctant envoy appeared to be delaying, Lincoln dispatched
White House aide John Hay with the open letter that finally put his position in writing. The president stated that he would entertain any "proposition which embraces the restoration of peace, the integrity of the whole
Union, and the abandonment of slavery" (Basler 1953, 7:451). Greeley
and Hay delivered the letter and returned to the States empty-handed.

By insisting on the abandonment of slavery as a precondition for negotiations, Lincoln effectively eliminated any possibility of holding serious
talks. Some historians believe that this suggests that the president never
wanted the discussions to take off in the first place. According to this
interpretation, he was playing a game with conservatives, ostensibly meeting their demand to send out peace overtures, but actually working to
lure his Confederate counterpart into making the type of statement
attributed to him by Gilmore. Once Davis was on record demanding
independence, conservatives presumably would have to acknowledge that
the rebels were truly rebellious and the war required continued vigorous
prosecution.

Yet once word of Lincoln's "To Whom It May Concern" letter
became public, many conservatives felt as betrayed as the Radicals had
been over Reconstruction policy. They dismissed the attempts at negotiation as insincere and begged the president to stop insisting on emancipation as a precondition. Whatever Lincoln might have thought he was
gaining by endorsing various efforts at peace talks was lost in the uproar
over his apparently unshakable support for black freedom.

It was at this point, however, that Lincoln's intentions became even
murkier. He drafted another letter that appeared to suggest a retreat from
his hard line on emancipation. "To me it seems plain that saying re-union
and abandonment of slavery would be considered, if offered, is not saying that nothing *else* or *less* would be considered, if offered," he wrote
in an uncharacteristic display of political doublespeak (Basler 1953,
7:499). But when he read the draft of the letter aloud to some Wisconsin politicians and then to noted black abolitionist Frederick Douglass,
he appeared to change his mind. "There have been men who have proposed to me to return to slavery the black warriors of [the Union army]
to their masters to conciliate the South," he said in his interview with the
Wisconsin politicians. His voice rising, he continued: "I should be
damned in time & in eternity for so doing" (Basler 1953, 7:507). Ultimately, the president filed the letter away, never sending it (see Document 4.13).

During this period, Lincoln also considered authorizing a third peace
mission, this one by Henry Raymond, editor of the *New York Times* and
chairman of the Union Party election campaign. The editor's charge called
for "restoration of the Union" but nothing else (Basler 1953, 7:517).
Consequently, if Raymond had gone to Richmond, this would have been

the highest level and most serious effort at negotiation to that point, but once again the president changed his mind and canceled the arrangement.

Nobody knows exactly what Lincoln was thinking during this period, but given the intense political cross-pressures on him and the continued stalemate on the battlefield, it is probably fair to conclude that he was groping for an answer, just like most of the rest of the Northern public.

AUGUST–NOVEMBER 1864: LINCOLN'S REELECTION

One answer that Lincoln never seemed to doubt was that he belonged at the head of the Union Party ticket. No president had been reelected since Andrew Jackson in 1832, but after the turning-point victories in Vicksburg, Gettysburg, and Chattanooga, the momentum behind the president appeared unstoppable.

Lincoln certainly overwhelmed Salmon Chase, his only serious competition for his party's nomination. The Baltimore convention on June 8, 1864, endorsed the president and replaced incumbent vice president Hannibal Hamlin, a Radical Republican from Maine, with Andrew Johnson, a prowar Democrat from Tennessee.

Everything was going smoothly enough for the president's reelection effort until the summer of discontent. Afflicted on both sides of the political spectrum and damaged by Grant's bloodbath in Virginia, Lincoln stumbled for the first time in the contest. Throughout August, disgruntled elements of the Union coalition engaged in secret meetings to discuss the possibility of finding a new nominee.

Ultimately, none of the factions could unite or devise a realistic way to unseat Lincoln without risking defeat to the Democrats. Even the bitterest anti-Lincoln forces within the coalition, who had bolted in May to nominate John Frémont, returned to the fold in September.

Part of what helped the Union coalition to pull together was the belated organization of the Democratic campaign. The Democrats did not meet in Chicago until the end of August, but when they did they drafted a platform that labeled the war "four years of failure." For Unionists, the harsh words out of Chicago offered a rallying cry that helped smooth over some of their internal differences. Add to that dynamic the fact that the Democrats themselves were sorely divided—nominating George McClellan, a prowar figure, for example—and suddenly the campaign looked brighter for the Lincoln forces.

But Gen. William Sherman's victory in Atlanta at the beginning of September helped to revive spirits across the board more than anything else. The Union Party proceeded to wage a vigorous campaign and secure a landslide victory for Abraham Lincoln, guaranteeing both his place in history and the ultimate triumph of the federal war effort (see Chapter 2).

DECEMBER 1864–JANUARY 1865: THIRTEENTH AMENDMENT

Despite all of the controversy surrounding the issue, the Union Party platform in 1864 endorsed the notion of a constitutional amendment to prohibit slavery across the nation. At the time, an amendment was pending before the Congress. It was a principle that had President Lincoln's full support, although not yet his full attention. Since first embracing emancipation in late 1862, he had repeatedly argued that it could only occur by presidential decree during a time of war or by the formal amendment process. He was still focused on the military necessity of emancipation, but according to Lincoln, an amendment was the "king's cure," or ultimate solution, to the problem of slavery (Vorenberg 2001, 176).

A week after the Baltimore convention, the House of Representatives failed to pass the proposed amendment to ban slavery by the necessary two-thirds majority. Yet the issue did not disappear. President Lincoln and the Republicans continued to press for abolition, supporting, for example, a referendum for a new constitution in Maryland in October 1864 that included a ban on slavery. When Congress reconvened in December 1864 after the fall elections, the administration lobbied heavily for a new effort on the proposed Thirteenth Amendment. "The next Congress will pass the measure if this does not . . . ," Lincoln noted in his annual message, "may we not agree that the sooner the better?" (Basler 1953, 149).

According to historian Michael Vorenberg, the administration went to work in behalf of the amendment, although not with excessive horse trading or backroom deals (Vorenberg 2001, 180–184). They relied on persuasion and targeted pressure. The truth was that times had changed. The North was not the only section of the country considering emancipation. Desperate Southerners were debating proposals to offer their slaves freedom in exchange for military service. Confederate desertions had reached epidemic proportions, and everyone believed that the war would finally conclude in the spring.

The final vote occurred on January 31, 1865. The House passed the constitutional amendment by a vote of 119–56, with 8 abstentions. President Lincoln was not required to sign a constitutional amendment, but he did anyway for good measure. Illinois was the first state to ratify the amendment, on February 1. Two-thirds of the states ratified by December 18, 1865, officially determining that the Thirteenth Amendment ending slavery across the nation—immediately, permanently, and without compensation—had finally become part of the U.S. Constitution.

APRIL 1865: LEE'S SURRENDER

The same day that Congress sent the Thirteenth Amendment to the states for ratification, the Confederate government named Robert E. Lee the first general in chief of the rebel armies. But it was an empty gesture. The four long years of conflict were finally drawing to a close and everyone in Richmond knew that their days in power were numbered.

"Fondly do we hope—fervently do we pray," Lincoln stated at his second inaugural on March 4, 1865, "that this mighty scourge of war may speedily pass away" (Basler 1953, 8:333; see Document 4.14). Like everyone else, the president saw the signs of a collapsing Confederacy. Gen. William Sherman's armies had taken Atlanta and marched to the sea, conquering Savannah, in his words, as a "Christmas present" for President Lincoln, and then moving forward on a path of destruction up the Atlantic coast (McPherson 1988, 811). Meanwhile, General Grant and General Meade and the Army of the Potomac continued to tighten the vise on Richmond and Lee's forces. Sporadic campaigns were occurring across Southern territory, but unless the Confederates were willing to wage a low-intensity guerrilla war from the hills and swamps of the South, the "scourge of war" was finally passing away.

By the beginning of April, it was all almost over. On April 2, 1865, a Sunday, the Confederate government evacuated Richmond. By Tuesday, President Lincoln had entered the captured city and toured the Confederate White House, sitting in Jefferson Davis's study chair. Outside on the streets of the former rebel capital, black residents strained to see "the great Messiah." "Don't kneel to me," Lincoln remonstrated gently. "That is not right" (Donald 1995, 576).

During his trip, the president conducted discussions with local leaders over the prospect of fast readmission into the Union for Virginia. He was obviously intent on heading off an underground movement of rebel insurgents, hoping that a fast Reconstruction policy would demoralize any potential guerrilla forces.

Lincoln returned to Washington on April 9, 1865, Palm Sunday, the same day that General Lee finally surrendered his forces to General Grant at Appomattox Court House. Technically, Lee's surrender did not mean the end of the war. Davis remained at large and some Confederate forces continued to fight for weeks afterward. But news of the event made Northerners ecstatic. The next day, President Lincoln asked the White House band to play the Southern tune "Dixie" while his youngest son Tad waved a rebel flag. For the first time in years it seemed appropriate to relax, and even to have some fun.

SELECTED PRIMARY SOURCES

Basler, Roy P., ed. *The Collected Works of Abraham Lincoln*. 9 vols. New Brunswick: Rutgers University Press, 1953.

Carpenter, F[rancis]. B. *The Inner Life of Abraham Lincoln: Six Months at the White House*. 1866. Reprint, Lincoln: University of Nebraska Press, 1995.

Crittenden-Johnson Resolutions 1861. "The Civil War and Reconstruction." Patrick Rael, Department of History, Bowdoin College (Bowdoin: Bowdoin College, 2002); http://www.bowdoin.edu/~prael/139/crittenden.htm.

Dennett, Tyler, ed. *Lincoln and the Civil War in the Diaries and Letters of John Hay*. 1939. Reprint, New York: Da Capo Press, 1988.

Fehrenbacher, Don E., and Virginia Fehrenbacher, eds. *Recollected Words of Abraham Lincoln*. Stanford: Stanford University Press, 1996.

Miers, Earl S., ed. *Lincoln Day by Day: A Chronology, 1809–1865*. Dayton, Ohio: Morningside, 1990.

Mitgang, Herbert, ed. *Abraham Lincoln: A Press Portrait*. 1956. Reprint, New York: Fordham University Press, 2000.

Nicolay, John G., and John Hay. *Abraham Lincoln: A History*. 10 vols. New York: Century, 1890.

Pease, Theodore C., and James G. Randall, eds. *The Diary of Orville Hickman Browning*. 2 vols. Springfield: Illinois State Historical Society, 1925–1933.

Seward, William H. "Some Thoughts for the President's Consideration," April 1, 1861. In *Abraham Lincoln Papers at the Library of Congress*, Manuscript Division (Washington, D. C.: American Memory Project, 2000–2002), memory.loc.gov/ammem/alhtml/alhome.html.

Turner, Justin G., and Linda Levitt Turner, eds. *Mary Todd Lincoln: Her Life and Letters*. New York: Knopf, 1972.

Wills, David, to Abraham Lincoln, November 2, 1863, in *Abraham Lincoln Papers at the Library of Congress*, Manuscript Division (Washington, D.C.: American Memory Project, 2000–2002), memory.loc.gov/ammem/alhtml/alhome.html.

SECONDARY SOURCES

Belz, Herman. *Reconstructing the Union: Theory and Practice during the Civil War*. Ithaca: Cornell University Press, 1969.

Cox, LaWanda. *Lincoln and Black Freedom: A Study in Presidential Leadership*. Columbia: University of South Carolina Press, 1981.

Cramer, John H. *Lincoln under Enemy Fire*. Baton Rouge: Louisiana University Press, 1948.

Guelzo, Allen C. *Abraham Lincoln: Redeemer President*. Grand Rapids: Eerdmans, 1999.

Jones, Howard. *Abraham Lincoln and a New Birth of Freedom: The Union and Slavery in the Diplomacy of the Civil War*. Lincoln: University of Nebraska Press, 1999.

Long, David E. *The Jewel of Liberty: Abraham Lincoln's Re-Election and the End of Slavery*. Mechanicsburg, Pa.: Stackpole Books, 1994.

Neely, Mark E. Jr. *The Fate of Liberty: Abraham Lincoln and Civil Liberties*. New York: Oxford University Press, 1991.

_____. *The Last Best Hope of Earth: Abraham Lincoln and the Promise of America*. Cambridge: Harvard University Press, 1993.

Randall, J. G., with Richard N. Current. *Lincoln the President*. 4 vols. New York: Dodd, Mead, 1945–1955.

Sandburg, Carl. *Abraham Lincoln: The War Years*. 4 vols. New York: Harcourt, Brace, 1939.

Sears, Stephen W. *George B. McClellan: The Young Napoleon.* New York: Ticknor and Fields, 1988.

Vorenberg, Michael. *Final Freedom: The Civil War, the Abolition of Slavery, and the Thirteenth Amendment.* Cambridge: Cambridge University Press, 2001.

Williams, T. Harry. *Lincoln and the Radicals.* Madison: University of Wisconsin Press, 1941.

Wills, Garry. *Lincoln at Gettysburg: The Words That Remade America.* New York: Simon and Schuster, 1992.

RECOMMENDED READING

Burlingame, Michael, and John R. Turner Ettlinger, eds. *Inside Lincoln's White House: The Complete Civil War Diary of John Hay.* Carbondale: Southern Illinois University Press, 1997.

   Hay was a recent college graduate lucky enough to land a job as one of the president's two personal secretaries. He kept a colorful diary that offers the most intimate portrait available of Lincoln in the White House.

Donald, David Herbert. *Lincoln.* New York: Simon and Schuster, 1995.

   This biography is especially strong on the strategy and politics of Lincoln's presidential decision making.

McPherson, James M. *Battle Cry of Freedom: The Civil War Era.* New York: Oxford University Press, 1988.

_____. *Ordeal by Fire: The Civil War and Reconstruction.* 2d ed. New York: McGraw-Hill, 1992.

   Battle Cry of Freedom, part of the prestigious *Oxford History of the United States,* is arguably the best narrative survey of the Civil War era. *Ordeal by Fire* offers an updated textbook version of the story, especially suitable for college classrooms.

Paludan, Phillip Shaw. *The Presidency of Abraham Lincoln.* Lawrence: University of Kansas Press, 1994.

   This careful study offers a clear narrative of the Lincoln presidency.

Document 4.1   Seward's April 1 Memo (1861)
The first month of the Lincoln administration was consumed by the crisis over resupplying Fort Sumter in South Carolina. Secretary of State William H.

Seward, a former political rival, sent the president a memo on April 1, 1861, that appeared to insult Lincoln and suggest that he was not capable of running the government. According to Seward's thinking at that time, the government should have used the threat of foreign war to unite divided Americans.

Some thoughts for the President's consideration
April 1. 1861.

1st. We are at the end of a month's administration and yet without a policy either domestic or foreign.

2d This, however, is not culpable, and it has been unavoidable. The presence of the Senate, with the need to meet applications for patronage have prevented attention to other and more grave matters.

3d. But further delay to adopt and prosecute our policies for both domestic and foreign affairs would not only bring scandal on the Administration, but danger upon the country.

4th. To do this we must dismiss the applicants for office. But how? I suggest that we make the local appointments forthwith, leaving foreign or general ones for ulterior and occasional action.

5th. The policy—at home. I am aware that my views are singular, and perhaps not sufficiently explained. My system is built upon this *idea* as a ruling one, namely that we must

Change the question before the Public from one upon Slavery, or about Slavery for a question upon *Union or Disunion.* In other words, from what would be regarded as a Party question to one of *Patriotism or Union.*

The occupation or evacuation of Fort Sumter, although not in fact a slavery, or a party question is so *regarded.* Witness, the temper manifested by the Republicans in the Free States, and even by Union men in the South.

I would therefore terminate it as a safe means for changing the issue. I deem it fortunate that the last Administration created the necessity.

For the rest. I would simultaneously defend and reinforce all the Forts in the Gulf, and have the Navy recalled from foreign stations to be prepared for a blockade. Put the Island of Key West under Martial Law.

This will raise distinctly the question of *Union* or *Disunion*. I would maintain every fort and possession in the South.

For *Foreign Nations.*

I would demand explanations from *Spain* and France, categorically, at once.

I would seek explanations from Great Britain and Russia, and send agents into *Canada, Mexico* and *Central America,* to rouse a vigorous continental *spirit of independence* on this continent against European intervention.

And if satisfactory explanations are not received from Spain and France,

Would convene Congress and declare war against them

But whatever policy we adopt, there must be an energetic prosecution of it.

For this purpose it must be somebody's business to pursue and direct it incessantly.

Either the President must do it himself, and be all the while active in it; or

Devolve it on some member of his Cabinet. Once adopted, debates on it must end, and all agree and abide.

It is not in my especial province.

But I neither seek to evade nor assume responsibility.

Source: William H. Seward, "Some Thoughts for the President's Consideration," April 1, 1861, in *Abraham Lincoln Papers at the Library of Congress,* Manuscript Division (Washington, D.C.: American Memory Project, 2000–2002); memory. loc.gov/ammem/alhtml/alhome.html.

Document 4.2   Lincoln's Reply to Seward (1861)

Lincoln drafted the following reply to Secretary of State William H. Seward's April 1 memorandum, but he never sent the document. Most historians believe that instead he read the paper to Seward in person. Regardless of the exact format of delivery, the style shows Lincoln asserting his authority as president with a surprisingly deft touch.

Hon: W. H. Seward: Executive Mansion April 1, 1861

My dear Sir: Since parting with you I have been considering your paper dated this day, and entitled "Some thoughts for the President's consideration." The first proposition in it is, "1st. We are at the end of a month's administration, and yet without a policy, either domestic or foreign."

At the *beginning* of that month, in the inaugeral, I said "The power confided to me will be used to hold, occupy and possess the property and places belonging to the government, and to collect the duties, and imposts." This had your distinct approval at the time; and, taken in connection with the order I immediately gave General [Winfield] Scott, directing him to employ every means in his power to strengthen and hold the forts, comprises the exact domestic policy you now urge, with the single exception, that it does not propose to abandon Fort Sumpter.

Again, I do not perceive how the re-inforcement of Fort Sumpter would be done on a slavery, or party issue, while that of Fort Pickens would be on a more national, and patriotic one.

The news received yesterday in regard to St. Domingo, certainly brings a new item within the range of our foreign policy; but up to that time we have been preparing circulars, and instructions to ministers, and the like, all in perfect harmony, without even a suggestion that we had no foreign policy.

Upon your closing propositions, that "whatever policy we adopt, there must be an energetic prossecution of it"

"For this purpose it must be somebody's business to pursue and direct it incessantly"

"Either the President must do it himself, and be all the while active in it, or"

"Devolve it on some member of his cabinet"

"Once adopted, debates on it must end, and all agree and abide" I remark that if this must be done, *I* must do it. When a general line of policy is adopted, I apprehend there is no danger of its being changed without good reason, or continuing to be a subject of unnecessary debate; still, upon points arising in its progress, I wish, and suppose I am entitled to have the advice of all the cabinet.

Your Obt. Servt. A. LINCOLN

Source: Abraham Lincoln to William H. Seward, April 1, 1861, *Abraham Lincoln Papers at the Library of Congress,* Manuscript Division (Washington, D.C.: American Memory Project, 2000–2002); memory.loc.gov/ammem/alhtml/alhome.html.

Document 4.3   Special Message to Congress (July 4, 1861)

The first violence of the Civil War broke out while Congress was out of session. President Lincoln called for a special session to meet on July 4, 1861. Between April and July he essentially acted on his own. Among other decisions, he suspended habeas corpus or civil liberties along the railroad line required to bring army troops into Washington. It was a controversial action that drew strong criticism from the chief justice of the United States, Roger B. Taney. Lincoln felt compelled to defend himself in this selection from his message to Congress.

. . . Soon after the first call for militia, it was considered a duty to authorize the Commanding General, in proper cases, according to his discretion, to suspend the privilege of the writ of habeas corpus; or, in other words, to arrest, and detain, without resort to the ordinary processes and forms of law, such individuals as he might deem dangerous to the public safety. This authority has purposely been exercised but very sparingly. Nevertheless, the legality and propriety of what has been done under it, are questioned; and the attention of the country has been called to the proposition that one who is sworn to "take care that the laws be faithfully executed," should not himself violate them. Of course some consideration was given to the questions of power, and propriety, before this matter was acted upon. The whole of the laws which were required to be faithfully executed, were being resisted, and failing of execution, in nearly one-third of the States. Must they be allowed to finally fail of execution, even had it been perfectly clear, that by the use of the means necessary to their execution, some single law, made in such extreme tenderness of the citizen's liberty, that practically, it relieves more of the guilty, than of the innocent, should, to a very limited extent, be violated? To state the question more directly, are all the laws, *but one,* to go unexecuted, and the government itself go to pieces, lest that one be violated? Even in such a case, would not the official oath be broken, if the government should be overthrown, when it was believed that disregarding the single law, would tend to preserve it? But it was not believed that this question was presented. It was not believed that any law was violated. The provision of the Constitution that "The privilege of the writ of habeas corpus, shall not be suspended unless when, in cases of rebellion or invasion, the public safety may require it," is equivalent to a provision—is a provision—that such privilege may be suspended when, in cases of rebellion, or invasion, the public safety *does* require it. It was decided that we have a case of rebellion, and that the public safety does require the qualified suspension of the privilege of the writ which was authorized to be made. Now it is insisted that Congress, and not the Executive, is vested with this power. But the Constitution itself, is silent as to which, or who, is to exercise the power; and as the provision was plainly made for a dangerous emergency, it cannot be believed the framers of the instrument intended, that in every case, the danger should run its course, until Congress could be called together; the very assembling of which might be prevented, as was intended in this case, by the rebellion. . . .

Source: Message to Congress in Special Session, July 4, 1861, in *The Collected Works of Abraham Lincoln,* 9 vols., ed. Roy P. Basler (New Brunswick: Rutgers University Press, 1953), 4:421–441.

Document 4.4   McClellan Says He Can Do It All (1861)

President Lincoln appointed thirty-four-year-old George McClellan as commander of the Army of the Potomac in July 1861 and then elevated him to general in chief of all Union armies in November 1861. In his diary, White House aide John Hay describes McClellan's smug reaction to his promotion.

[November 1861]

The night of the 1st November we went over to McClellans. The General was there and read us his general order in regard to [Gen. Winfield] Scotts resignation & his own assumption of command. The President thanked him for it and said it greatly relieved him. He added "I should be perfectly satisfied if I thought this vast increase of responsibility would not embarrass you."

"Well says the Tycoon, Call on me for all the sense I have, and all the information. In addition to your present command, the supreme command of the army will entail a vast labor upon you."

"I can do it all," McC said quietly.

Source: John Hay, diary entry [November 1861], in *Inside Lincoln's White House: The Complete Civil War Diary of John Hay,* ed. Michael Burlingame and John R. Turner Ettlinger (Carbondale: Southern Illinois University Press, 1997), 30.

<hr>

Document 4.5   Lincoln Explains His Strategic View (1862)

In attempting to get Gen. Don C. Buell, one of his commanders based in the western theater of the war, to move more rapidly on the offensive, Lincoln described his view of the war's strategy to the general in a letter dated January 13, 1862.

To Don C. Buell

My dear Sir: Washington, Jan. 13, 1862.

Your despatch of yesterday is received, in which you say "I have received your letter and Gen. [George] McClellan's; and will, at once devote all my efforts to your views, and his." In the midst of my many cares, I have not seen, or asked to see, Gen. McClellan's letter to you. For my own views, I have not offered, and do not now offer them as orders; and while I am glad to have them respectfully considered, I would blame you to follow them contrary to your own clear judgment—unless I should put them in the form of orders. As to Gen. McClellan's views, you understand your duty in regard to them better than I do. With this preliminary, I state my general idea of this war to be that we have the *greater* numbers, and the enemy has the *greater* facility of concentrating forces upon points of collision; that we must fail, unless we can find some way of making *our* advantage an over-match for *his;* and that this can only be done by menacing him with superior forces at *different* points, at the *same* time; so that we can safely attack, one, or both, if he makes no change; and if he *weakens* one to *strengthen* the other, forbear to attack the strengthened one, but seize, and hold the weakened one, gaining so much. To illustrate, suppose last summer, when Winchester ran away to re-inforce Mannassas, we had forborne to attack Mannassas, but had seized and held Winchester. I mention this to illustrate, and not to criticise. I did not lose confidence in [Gen. Irvin] McDowell, and I think less harshly of [Gen. Robert] Patterson than some others seem to. In application of the general rule I am suggesting, every particular case will have its modifying circumstances, among which the most constantly present, and most difficult to meet, will be the want of perfect knowledge of the enemies' movements. This had it's part in the Bull-Run case; but worse, in that case, was the expiration of the terms of the three months men. Applying the principle to your case, my idea is that [Gen. Henry] Halleck shall menace Columbus, and "down river" generally; while you menace Bowling-Green, and East Tennessee. If the enemy shall concentrate at Bowling-Green, do not retire from his front; yet do not fight him there, either, but seize Columbus and East Tennessee, one or both, left exposed by the concentration at Bowling Green. It is matter of no small anxiety to me and one which I am sure you will not over-look, that the East Tennessee line, is so long, and over so bad a road.

Yours very truly
A. LINCOLN.

Source: Abraham Lincoln to Don C. Buell, January 13, 1862, in *The Collected Works of Abraham Lincoln*, 9 vols., ed. Roy P. Basler (New Brunswick: Rutgers University Press, 1953), 5:98–99.

Document 4.6   Preliminary Emancipation Proclamation (1862)
It took Lincoln about a year and a half to realize that, for military reasons, he would have to use emancipation as a tool in the conduct of the war He

began to change his mind over the summer of 1862 and issued this prelimi-
nary emancipation edict on September 22 after the Union victory at Antie-
tam on September 17. Bracketed items in italics were added to the document
by other administration figures, such as Secretary of State William H.
Seward.

I, Abraham Lincoln, President of the United States of America, and Commander-in-chief of the Army and Navy thereof, do hereby proclaim and
declare that hereafter, as heretofore, the war will be prossecuted for the
object of practically restoring the constitutional relations between the
United States, and each of the states, and the people thereof, in which
states that relation is, or may be suspended, or disturbed.

That it is my purpose, upon the next meeting of Congress to again recommend the adoption of a practical measure tendering pecuniary aid to
the free acceptance or rejection of all slave-states, so called, the people
whereof may not then be in rebellion against the United States, and which
states, may then have voluntarily adopted, or thereafter may voluntarily
adopt, immediate, or gradual abolishment of slavery within their respective limits; and that the effort to colonize persons of African descent, *[with*
their consent], upon this continent, or elsewhere, *[with the previously*
obtained consent of the Governments existing there], will be continued.

That on the first day of January in the year of our Lord, one thousand
eight hundred and sixty-three, all persons held as slaves within any state,
or designated part of a state, the people whereof shall then be in rebellion
against the United States, shall be then, thenceforward, and forever free;
and the executive government of the United States, including the military and naval authority thereof, *will recognize and maintain the freedom*
of such persons], and will do no act or acts to repress such persons, or any
of them, in any efforts they may make for their actual freedom.

That the executive will, on the first day of January aforesaid, by proclamation, designate the States, and parts of states, if any, in which the people thereof respectively, shall then be in rebellion against the United States;
and the fact that any state, or the people thereof respectively, shall, on that
day be, in good faith represented in the Congress of the United States,
by members chosen thereto, at elections wherein a majority of qualified
voters of such state shall have participated, shall, in the absence of strong
countervailing testimony, be deemed conclusive evidence that such state
and the people thereof, are not then in rebellion against the United States.

That attention is hereby called to an act of Congress entitled "An act to make additional Article of War" approved March 13, 1862, and which act is in the words and figure following:

Be it enacted by the Senate and House of Representatives of the United States of America in Congress assembled, That hereafter the following shall be promulgated as an additional article of war for the government of the army of the United States, and shall be obeyed and observed as such:

Article—All officers or persons in the military or naval service of the United States are prohibited from employing any of the forces under their respective commands for the purpose of returning fugitives from service or labor, who may have escaped from any persons to whom such service or labor is claimed to be due, and any officer who shall be found guilty by a court-martial of violating this article shall be dismissed from the service.

Sec. 2. *And be it further enacted,* That this act shall take effect from and after its passage.

Also to the night and tenth sections of an act entitled "An Act to suppress Insurrection, to punish Treason and Rebellion, to seize and confiscate property of rebels, and for other purposes," approved July 17, 1862, and which sections are in the words and figures following:

Sec. 9. And be it further enacted, That all slaves of persons who shall hereafter be engaged in rebellion against the government of the United States, or who shall in any way give aid or comfort thereto, escaping from such persons and taking refuge within the lines of the army; and all slaves captured from such persons or deserted by them and coming under the control of the government of the United States; and all slaves of such persons found on (or) being within any place occupied by rebel forces and afterwards occupied by the forces of the United States, shall be deemed captives of war, and shall be forever free of their servitude and not again held as slaves.

Sec. 10. And be it further enacted, That no slave escaping into any State, Territory, or the District of Columbia, from any other State, shall be delivered up, or in any way impeded or hindered of his liberty, except for crime, or some offence against the laws, unless the person claiming said fugitive shall first make oath that the person to whom the labor or service of such fugitive is alleged to be due is his lawful owner, and has not borne arms against the United States in the present rebellion, nor in any way given aid and comfort thereto; and no person engaged in the military or naval service of the United States shall, under any pretence whatever, assume to decide on the validity of the claim of any person to the service or labor of any other person, or surrender up any such person to the claimant, on pain of being dismissed from the service.

And I do hereby enjoin upon and order all persons engaged in the military and naval service of the United States to observe, obey, and enforce, within their respective spheres of service, the act, and sections above recited.

And the executive will *[in due time]* recommend that all citizens of the United States who shall have remained loyal thereto throughout the rebellion, shall (upon restoration of the constitutional relations between the United States, and their respective states, and people, if that relation shall have been suspended or disturbed) be compensated for all losses by acts of the United States, including the loss of slaves.

[In witness whereof, I have hereunto set my hand, and caused the seal of the United States to be affixed. Done at the City of Washington, this twenty second day of September, in the year of our Lord, one thousand eight hundred and sixty two, and of the Independence of the United States, the eighty seventh. By the President: Abraham Lincoln, William H. Seward, Secretary of State]

Source: Preliminary Emancipation Proclamation, September 22, 1862, in *The Collected Works of Abraham Lincoln,* 9 vols., ed. Roy P. Basler (New Brunswick: Rutgers University Press, 1953), 5:433–436.

Document 4.7   Lincoln Explains His Political Problems (1862)

After the setbacks for the Republican Party in the 1862 midterm elections, Lincoln wrote a young German American Republican Party leader named Carl Schurz. In his note, the president attempted to reply to criticisms by Schurz and others that the administration had been too friendly to Democrats.

To Carl Schurz
Private & confidential
Gen. Schurz. Executive Mansion,
My dear Sir Washington, Nov. 10. 1862.

Yours of the 8th. was, to-day, read to me by Mrs. S[churz]. We have lost the elections; and it is natural that each of us will believe, and say, it has been because his peculiar views was not made sufficiently prominent. I think I know what it was, but I may be mistaken. Three main causes told the whole story. 1. The democrats were left in a majority by our friends going to the war. 2. The democrats observed this & determined to re-instate themselves in power, and 3. Our newspaper's, by vilifying and disparaging the administration, furnished them all the weapons to do it with. Certainly, the ill-success of the war had much to do with this.

You give a different set of reasons. If you had not made the following statements, I should not have suspected them to be true. "The defeat of the administration is the administrations own fault." (opinion) "It admit-ted its professed opponents to its counsels" (Asserted as a fact) "It placed the Army, now a great power in this Republic, into the hands of its' ene-mys" (Asserted as a fact) "In all personal questions, to be hostile to the party of the Government, seemed, to be a title to consideration." (Asserted as a fact) "If to forget the great rule, that if you are true to your friends, your friends will be true to you, and that you make your enemies stronger by placing them upon an equality with your friends." "Is it surprising that the opponents of the administration should have got into their hands the government of the principal states, after they have had for a long time the principal management of the war, the great business of the national gov-ernment."

I can not dispute about the matter of opinion. On the the [sic] three matters (stated as facts) I shall be glad to have your evidence upon them when I shall meet you. The plain facts, as they appear to me, are these. The administration came into power, very largely in a minority of the popular vote. Notwithstanding this, it distributed to it's party friends as nearly all the civil patronage as any administration ever did. The war came. The administration could not even start in this, without assistance outside of it's party. It was mere nonsense to suppose a minority could put down a majority in rebellion. Mr. Schurz (now Gen. Schurz) was about here then & I do not recollect that he then considered all who were not republicans, were enemies of the government, and that none of them must be appointed to to [sic] military positions. He will correct me if I am mistaken. It so happened that very few of our friends had a military education or were of the profession of arms. It would have been a question whether the war should be conducted on military knowledge, or on political affinity, only that our own friends (I think Mr. Schurz included) seemed to think that such a question was inadmissable. Accordingly I have scarcely appointed a democrat to a command, who was not urged by many republicans and opposed by none. It was so as to [Gen. George] McClellan. He was first brought forward by the Republican Governor of Ohio, & claimed, and contended for at the same time by the Republican Governor of Pennsylvania. I received recommendations from the republican delegations in congress, and I believe every one of them recommended a majority of democrats. But, after all many Republicans were appointed; and I mean no disparagement to them when I say I do not see that their superiority of success has been so marked as to throw great suspicion on the good faith of those who are not Republicans. Yours truly, A. LINCOLN

Source: Abraham Lincoln to Carl Schurz, November 10, 1862, in *The Collected Works of Abraham Lincoln,* 9 vols., ed. Roy P. Basler (New Brunswick: Rutgers University Press, 1953), 5:493–495.

Document 4.8   Lincoln Risks Dictatorship (1863)

In 1863 the president replaced Gen. Ambrose Burnside as commander of the Army of the Potomac with Gen. Joseph Hooker. It was a surprising decision to some, because Hooker had been quoted in the newspapers criticizing both Burnside and the administration. After making the appointment, Lincoln sent his new commander this unusually blunt letter on January 26, 1863.

Major General Hooker: Executive Mansion,

General. Washington, January 26, 1863.

I have placed you at the head of the Army of the Potomac. Of course I have done this upon what appear to me to be sufficient reasons. And yet I think it best for you to know that there are some things in regard to which, I am not quite satisfied with you. I believe you to be a brave and a skilful soldier, which, of course, I like. I also believe you do not mix politics with your profession, in which you are right. You have confidence in yourself, which is a valuable, if not an indispensable quality. You are ambitious, which, within reasonable bounds, does good rather than harm. But I think that during Gen. Burnside's command of the Army, you have taken counsel of your ambition, and thwarted him as much as you could, in which you did a great wrong to the country, and to a most meritorious and honorable brother officer. I have heard, in such way as to believe it, of your recently saying that both the Army and the Government needed a Dictator. Of course it was not *for* this, but in spite of it, that I have given you the command. Only those generals who gain successes, can set up dictators. What I now ask of you is military success, and I will risk the dictatorship. The government will support you to the utmost of it's ability, which is neither more nor less than it has done and will do for all commanders. I much fear that the spirit which you have aided to infuse into the Army, of criticising their Commander, and withholding confidence from him, will now turn upon you. I shall assist you as far as I can, to put it down. Neither you, nor Napoleon, if he were alive again, could get any good out of an army, while such a spirit prevails in it.

And now, beware of rashness. Beware of rashness, but with energy, and sleepless vigilance, go forward, and give us victories.

Yours very truly A. LINCOLN

Source: Abraham Lincoln to Joseph Hooker, January 26, 1863, in *The Collected Works of Abraham Lincoln*, 9 vols., ed. Roy P. Basler (New Brunswick: Rutgers University Press, 1953), 6:78–79.

Document 4.9   Young Aide Describes Lincoln (1863)

By the summer of 1863 Lincoln's political fortunes had improved dramatically and he seemed to be settling into the demands of the executive office. In a letter to a fellow White House aide, John G. Nicolay, dated August 7, 1863, John Hay scribbled down a memorable portrait of the president at the height of his powers.

The Tycoon is in fine whack. I have rarely seen him more serene & busy. He is managing this war, the draft, foreign relations, and planning a reconstruction of the Union, all at once. I never knew with what tyrannous authority he rules the Cabinet, till now. The most important things he decides & there is no cavil. I am growing more and more firmly convinced that he should be kept where he is till this thing is over. There is no man in the country, so wise, so gentle and so firm. I believe the hand of God placed him where he is.

Source: John Hay to John G. Nicolay, August 7, 1863, in *Lincoln and the Civil War in the Diaries and Letters of John Hay,* ed. Tyler Dennett (1939; reprint, New York: Da Capo, 1988), 75–76.

Document 4.10   Gettysburg Address (1863)

Although it is only ten sentences and 272 words long, Lincoln's speech at Gettysburg remains one of the most memorable in the English language. The president was invited to give "brief" remarks at the dedication of the military cemetery at Gettysburg, Pennsylvania, on November 19, 1863. Many of the most important Northern political figures were in attendance. Various copies of the address exist, all slightly different. The following is known as the Everett copy because Lincoln prepared it for the day's main orator, clergyman and statesman Edward Everett of Massachusetts.

Four score and seven years ago our fathers brought forth upon this continent, a new nation, conceived in Liberty, and dedicated to the proposition that all men are created equal.

Now we are engaged in a great civil war, testing whether that nation, or any nation so conceived, and so dedicated, can long endure. We are met on a great battle-field of that war. We have come to dedicate a portion of that field, as a final resting place for those who here gave their lives, that that nation might live. It is altogether fitting and proper that we should do this.

But, in a larger sense, we can not dedicate—we can not consecrate—we can not hallow—this ground. The brave men, living and dead, who struggled here, have consecrated it, far above our poor power to add or detract. The world will little note, nor long remember, what we say here, but it can never forget what they did here. It is for us, the living, rather, to be dedicated here to the unfinished work which they who fought here, have, thus far, so nobly advanced. It is rather for us to be here dedicated to the great task remaining before us—that from these honored dead we take increased devotion to that cause for which they here gave the last full measure of devotion—that we here highly resolve that these dead shall not have died in vain—that this nation, under God, shall have a new birth of freedom— and that, government of the people, by the people, for the people, shall not perish from the earth.

Source: Gettysburg Address, November 19, 1863, in *The Collected Works of Abraham Lincoln*, 9 vols., ed. Roy P. Basler (New Brunswick: Rutgers University Press, 1953), 7:17–23.

Document 4.11   Patterns of Troop Strength (1861–1865)

	Number of Union soldiers	Number of Confederate soldiers
Wartime total	2,100,000 (est.)	850,000 (est.)
As of January 1, 1861	16,367	—
As of January 1, 1862	575,917	326,768
As of January 1, 1863	918,191	449,439
As of January 1, 1864	860,737	464,646
As of January 1, 1865	959,460	400,787

Source: Adapted from E. B. Long, *The Civil War Day by Day* (1971; reprint, New York: Da Capo, 1985), 706.

Document 4.12   Conditions for Peace Negotiations (1864)

Under pressure from newspaper editor Horace Greeley who wanted to open peace discussions with the Confederates, Lincoln drafted a letter addressed "To Whom It May Concern" that outlined his conditions for such talks. Once word of the statement leaked out to the public, Lincoln was castigated by many conservatives for making emancipation a precondition for negotiations.

Executive Mansion,

To Whom it may concern: Washington, July 18, 1864.

Any proposition which embraces the restoration of peace, the integrity of the whole Union, and the abandonment of slavery, and which comes by and with an authority that can control the armies now at war against the United States will be received and considered by the Executive government of the United States, and will be met by liberal terms on other substantial and collateral points; and the bearer, or bearers thereof shall have safe-conduct both ways.

ABRAHAM LINCOLN

Source: Abraham Lincoln to Whom It May Concern, July 18, 1864, in *The Collected Works of Abraham Lincoln,* 9 vols., ed. Roy P. Basler (New Brunswick: Rutgers University Press, 1953), 7:451.

Document 4.13   Lincoln Backpedals on Emancipation (1864)

After the outcry over his "To Whom It May Concern Letter," Lincoln drafted a letter to Wisconsin newspaper editor Charles D. Robinson on August 17, 1864, that he hoped would answer his conservative critics. After some consideration, however, he never released the letter and never altered his position that emancipation was a prerequisite for peace negotiations.

Hon. Charles D. Robinson Executive Mansion,

My dear Sir: Washington, August 17, 1864.

Your letter of the 7th. was placed in my hand yesterday by Gov. [Alexander] Randall. To me it seems plain that saying re-union and abandonment of slavery would be considered, if offered, is not saying that nothing *else* or *less* would be considered, if offered. But I will not stand upon the mere construction of language. It is true, as you remind me, that in the [Horace] Greeley letter of 1862, I said: "If I could save the Union without freeing any slaves I would do it; and if I could save it by freeing all the slaves I would do it; and if I could save it by freeing some, and leaving others alone I would also do that." I continued in the same letter as follows: "What I do about slavery and the colored race, I do because I believe it helps to save the Union; and what I forbear I forbear because I do not believe it would help to save the Union. I shall do less whenever I shall believe what I am doing hurts the cause; and I shall do more whenever I shall believe doing more will help the cause." All this I said in the utmost sincerety; and I am as true to the whole of it now, as when I first said it. When I afterwards proclaimed emancipation, and employed colored soldiers, I only followed the declaration just quoted from the Greeley letter that "I shall do *more* whenever I shall believe *doing* more will help the cause." The way these measures were to help the cause, was not to be by magic, or miracles, but by inducing the colored people to come bodily over from the rebel side to ours. On this point, nearly a year ago, in a letter to Mr. [James] Conkling, made public at once, I wrote as follows: "But negroes, like other people, act upon motives. Why should they do anything for us if we will do nothing for them? If they stake their lives for us they must be prompted by the strongest motive—even the promise of freedom. And the promise, being made, must be kept." I am sure you will not, on due reflection, say that the promise being made, must be *broken* at the first opportunity. I am sure you would not desire me to say, or to leave an inference, that I am ready, whenever convenient, to join in re-enslaving those who shall have served us in consideration of our promise. As matter of morals, could such treachery by any possibility, escape the curses of Heaven, or of any good man? As matter of policy, to *announce* such a purpose, would ruin the Union cause itself. All recruiting of colored men would instantly cease, and all colored men now in our service, would instantly desert us. And rightfully too. Why should they give their lives for us, with full notice of our purpose to betray them? Drive back to the support of the rebellion the physical force which the colored people now give, and promise us, and neither the present, nor any coming administration, *can* save the Union. Take from us, and give to the enemy, the hundred and thirty, forty, or fifty thousand colored persons now serving us as soldiers, seamen, and laborers, and we can not longer maintain the contest. The party who could elect a President on a War & Slavery Restoration platform, would, of necessity, lose the colored force; and that force being lost, would be as powerless to save the Union as to do any other impossible thing. It is not a question of sentiment or taste, but one of physical force, which may be measured, and estimated as horsepower, and steam power, are measured and estimated. And by measurement, it is more than we can lose, and live. Nor can we, by discarding it, get a white force in place of it. There is a witness in every white mans bosom that he would rather go to the war having the negro to help him, than to help the enemy against him. It is not the giving of one class for another. It is simply giving a large force to the enemy, for *nothing* in return.

In addition to what I have said, allow me to remind you that no one, having control of the rebel armies, or, in fact, having any influence whatever in the rebellion, has offered, or intimated a willingness to, a restoration of the Union, in any event, or on any condition whatever. Let it be constantly borne in mind that no such offer has been made or intimated. Shall we be weak enough to allow the enemy to distract us with an abstract question which he himself refuses to present as a practical one? In the Conkling letter before mentioned, I said: "Whenever you shall have conquered all resistance to the Union, if I shall urge you to continue fighting, it will be an apt time *then* to declare that you will not fight to free negroes." I repeat this now. If Jefferson Davis wishes, for himself, or for the benefit of his friends at the North, to know what I would do if he were to offer peace and re-union, saying nothing about slavery, let him try me.

Source: Abraham Lincoln to Charles D. Robinson, August 17, 1864, in *The Collected Works of Abraham Lincoln,* 9 vols., ed. Roy P. Basler (New Brunswick: Rutgers University Press, 1953), 7:499–502.

Document 4.14   Second Inaugural Address (1865)

On March 4, 1865, Abraham Lincoln became the first president since Andrew Jackson to serve a second term. In his inaugural address, the president struck a conciliatory tone. This speech is often identified as one of the finest in American political history.

[Fellow Countrymen:] March 4, 1865

At this second appearing to take the oath of the presidential office, there is less occasion for an extended address than there was at the first. Then a statement, somewhat in detail, of a course to be pursued, seemed fitting and proper. Now, at the expiration of four years, during which public declarations have been constantly called forth on every point and phase of the great contest which still absorbs the attention, and engrosses the enerergies [sic] of the nation, little that is new could be presented. The progress of our arms, upon which all else chiefly depends, is as well known to the public as to myself; and it is, I trust, reasonably satisfactory and encouraging to all. With high hope for the future, no prediction in regard to it is ventured.

On the occasion corresponding to this four years ago, all thoughts were anxiously directed to an impending civil-war. All dreaded it—all sought to avert it. While the inaugeral address was being delivered from this place, devoted altogether to *saving* the Union without war, insurgent agents were in the city seeking to *destroy* it without war—seeking to dissol[v]e the Union, and divide effects, by negotiation. Both parties deprecated war; but one of them would *make* war rather than let the nation survive; and the other would *accept* war rather than let it perish. And the war came.

One eighth of the whole population were colored slaves, not distributed generally over the Union, but localized in the Southern part of it. These slaves constituted a peculiar and powerful interest. All knew that this interest was, somehow, the cause of the war. To strengthen, perpetuate, and extend this interest was the object for which the insurgents would rend the Union, even by war; while the government claimed no right to do more than to restrict the territorial enlargement of it. Neither party expected for the war, the magnitude, or the duration, which it has already attained. Neither anticipated that the *cause* of the conflict might cease with, or even before, the conflict itself should cease. Each looked for an easier triumph, and a result less fundamental and astounding. Both read the same Bible, and pray to the same God; and each invokes His aid against the other. It may seem strange that any men should dare to ask a just God's assistance in wringing their bread from the sweat of other men's faces; but let us judge not that we be not judged. The prayers of both could not be answered; that of neither has been answered fully. The Almighty has His own purposes. "Woe unto the world because of offences! for it must needs be that offences come; but woe to that man by whom the offence cometh!" If we shall suppose that American Slavery is one of those offences which, in the providence of God, must needs come, but which, having continued through His appointed time, He now wills to remove, and that He gives to both North and South, this terrible war, as the woe due to those by whom the offence came, shall we discern therein any departure from those divine attributes which the believers in a Living God always ascribe to Him? Fondly do we hope—fervently do we pray—that this mighty scourge of war may speedily pass away. Yet, if God wills that it continue, until all the wealth piled by the bond-man's two hundred and fifty years of unrequited toil shall be sunk, and until every drop of blood drawn with the lash, shall be paid by another drawn with the sword, as was said three thousand years ago, so still it must be said "the judgments of the Lord, are true and righteous altogether."

With malice toward none; with charity for all; with firmness in the right, as God gives us to see the right, let us strive on to finish the work we are in; to bind up the nation's wounds; to care for him who shall have borne the battle, and for his widow, and his orphan—to do all which may achieve and cherish a just, and a lasting peace, among ourselves, and with all nations.

Source: Second Inaugural Address, March 4, 1865, in *The Collected Works of Abraham Lincoln,* 9 vols., ed. Roy P. Basler (New Brunswick: Rutgers University Press, 1953), 8:332–333.

A crowd of 30,000 gathers outside the unfinished U.S. Capitol building to watch Lincoln's inauguration on March 4, 1861.

CHAPTER FIVE

Institutional Relations

W hen Abraham Lincoln went to Gettysburg to deliver his now legendary address, Congressman Thaddeus Stevens, R-Pa., was not impressed and reportedly scoffed, "Let the dead bury the dead" (Carpenter 1995, 38). Such disdain from "Old Thad," who was chairman of the House Ways and Means Committee, offered an ominous illustration of the president's low standing on Capitol Hill. For long stretches of the wartime period Lincoln had few congressional allies and was forced to endure the scorn of vocal, powerful rivals.

CONGRESS

By ordinary partisan calculations, the Republican president's political situation should have been much stronger. Once Southerners seceded, Northern Republicans dominated both houses of Congress, controlling about 60 percent of the remaining legislative seats (see Document 5.1). Yet in several ways Lincoln was unable to capitalize on his party's strengths. Although Republicans managed to push through a series of social and financial reforms during the wartime period that had been bottled up by Democratic forces, Lincoln was not the prime mover behind these initiatives. As was customary for that era, the president did not typically propose domestic legislation. He cheered the passage of measures such as the Homestead Act and the Land-Grant College Act, but he did not deserve much credit for them.

Instead, he focused on prosecuting the war and maintaining the Union coalition. It was in those areas that Lincoln encountered resistance from Capitol Hill legislators. Part of the problem was the inevitable result of bad news. The fighting often went poorly for federal troops during the first two years of the conflict. Any commander in chief would have received harsh criticism after debacles like the ones at Bull Run or Fredericksburg. With his own paltry military experience—just a few months in the state militia as a would-be Indian fighter—Lincoln was especially vulnerable to second-guessing. In addition, his more arrogant military subordinates, such as Gen. George B. McClellan, often provoked congressional hostility. The subsequent establishment of a Joint Committee on the Conduct of the War, organized by Republicans to monitor the Republican administration, represented a major incursion into executive authority by the legislative branch. In late 1862, when Republican senators pressed the president to reorganize his cabinet, he feared for the independence of his administration. "We are now on the brink of destruction," he concluded darkly (Donald 1995, 402).

Sorting out constitutional authority for critical wartime decisions proved to be exceedingly difficult. In particular, legislators clashed with the president over emancipation policy and Reconstruction policy. These disputes had several political and personal crosscurrents, but a fundamental divide was the opposing views on the separation of powers. For a politician who had spent his entire public career in legislative bodies, Lincoln was surprisingly protective of his executive prerogatives. He insisted that the issues of emancipation and Reconstruction were best handled as questions of military necessity, to be decided under his authority as commander in chief and without congressional interference, or even, in some cases, consultation.

The result was coolness in the relationships down Pennsylvania Avenue that superceded party affiliation. Republican committee chairmen such as Thaddeus Stevens of Pennsylvania exhibited little personal loyalty to the president and often openly opposed his plans. Reconstruction offered the best example of their intransigence. Sen. Ben "Bluff" Wade, R-Ohio, who chaired the Joint Committee, considered the president's plan for rehabilitating former Confederate states as far too lenient. Along with Maryland congressman Henry Winter Davis (a

Unionist politician), he offered an alternative that was passed and sent to the White House in early July 1864. Lincoln refused to sign the Wade-Davis bill, employing an end-of-session pocket veto and issuing a rare public statement explaining his decision. Warned that congressional members of his own party would punish him for this move, the president sounded a defiant note. "They have never been friendly to me," he told White House aide John Hay, "& I don't know that this will make any special difference as to that" (Burlingame and Ettlinger 1997, 219).

There was no formal caucus of Republicans opposed to Lincoln, but most observers labeled the loose-knit group "Radicals" or "Jacobins," after the extremists of the French Revolution. The general impression was that the key Republicans aligned against the president were more radical on political questions—both more determined to end slavery and more committed to punishing Southern rebels. "I am a Radical and I glory in it," Senator Wade stated (Neely 1982, 321). Historians have since debated exactly how sharp the political differences were between Lincoln and the so-called Radical Republicans—some have questioned whether the distinction was more imagined than real—but there was without a doubt a shifting set of Republican congressman and senators who considered the president too cautious and ineffective. Stevens and Wade were two of the leading Radical figures. Senators Zachariah Chandler, R-Mich., and Charles Sumner, R-Mass., were two others.

Sumner was one of the few Radicals on Capitol Hill who maintained good personal relations with President Lincoln. Partly this development was the result of Mary Lincoln, who assiduously flattered the gifted and vain senator. He was often her escort at social functions that the president could not attend. Mary Lincoln later recalled that Sumner "was a constant visitor at the W.H.," although his presence was typically at her request rather than the president's (Donald 1995, 476). From his perspective, the worldly senator found conversation with the self-educated executive awkward, what he termed "a constant puzzle" (Donald 1995, 321). Still, he appeared to value their friendship and usually kept his public criticism of administration policies restrained.

Senator Chandler also recognized the value of cultivating Lincoln's personal friendship, and the two men had a civil relationship. The Michigan politician frequently laced his complaints about policy with humor or combined them with ostentatious praise. "You are today Master of the situation," he wrote Lincoln in 1863, adding pointedly, "if you stand firm" (Lincoln 1863). After the confrontation between the president and Senator Wade over Reconstruction policy in 1864, Chandler tried to arrange a truce. He described his efforts in a series of vivid letters to his wife that reflected both the extent of his commitment to the Union and his patronizing attitude toward Lincoln. "I am trying to do my duty & save the country," he wrote. "If it was only Abe Lincoln I would say, go to _____" (Long 1994, 240). Historians remain divided over the impact of Chandler's backroom maneuvering, but the deal that he believed he forged involved the withdrawal of a third party candidate in the presidential race who was aligned with some of the Radicals in exchange for the dismissal of a conservative member of the cabinet.

It would be a mistake, however, to reduce the president's strained relationship with Congress to ideological principles. Many of Lincoln's problems with congressmen were personal. In those days, there was hardly any buffer between a president and his Capitol Hill constituents. Lincoln had no congressional liaison. His entire White House staff consisted of a handful of personal secretaries, generally young and inexperienced. When senators or representatives wanted to influence an appointment for postmaster or customs agent, they went to see Lincoln personally. If he kept them waiting for more pressing military concerns, or ignored their request for political reasons, then he created deep, sometimes lingering, resentments. Congressman Isaac N. Arnold, R-Ill., also noted that the president's habit of extending short visits with jokes and stories left self-important Washington politicians exasperated. He recalled that when "a crowd of senators and members of Congress waiting their turn" gathered outside of the president's office, they would become unduly provoked by hearing "the loud ringing laugh of Mr. Lincoln" from inside the chamber (Clark 1925, 89).

The other principal obstacle for the president was the opposition party. For the most part, Northern Democrats did not enter into a coalition government with the Republicans. The irony is that the best chance for such a united front might have been lost with the death of Lincoln's longtime rival senator Stephen A. Douglas, D-Ill. Despite his reputation as a fierce partisan, Douglas put loyalty to nation ahead of any personal interests once he realized that the political crisis over slavery was leading to war. At the end of the 1860 campaign, he took to the stump in key Southern states urging Democratic voters to reject secession. After Lincoln's victory, Douglas worked desperately in Washington to craft some type of final compromise. And once war came, he pledged support to the administration. "Every man must be for the United States or against it," he said. "There can be no neutrals in this war, *only patriots— or traitors*" (McPherson 1992, 274). Such unwavering support from a leading Northern Democrat would have been invaluable to the Lincoln administration, but Douglas never lived long enough to provide it. He died in June 1861, just over two months after the firing on Fort Sumter.

Instead, many Northern Democrats on Capitol Hill fell in behind Rep. Clement Vallandigham, D-Ohio. He was generally acknowledged as leader of the antiwar faction known as the "Peace Democrats," or more derisively, as the "Copperheads." According to one Washington correspondent of the era, the controversial politician "underwent a physical transformation" when he delivered his fiery speeches. His "somewhat delicate features," in the words of pro-Union journalist Noah Brooks, became contorted, "his face wore an expression at times almost repulsive, and his voice rose to a wild shriek" (Brooks 1894, 143). Lincoln, who once referred to Vallandigham as a "wiley [sic] agitator," did not stand by idly and accept the abuse of Northern Democrats (Basler 1953, 6:266). He authorized the suspension of civil liberties and allowed the arrest of Democratic newspaper editors and party activists when they appeared to disrupt the war effort. Federal elections continued during the wartime period, but Democratic-controlled legislatures were suspended temporarily in the key states of Indiana and Illinois. Vallandigham himself was arrested and banished from the country in 1863 while he was running for governor of Ohio. He remained on the ballot and lost after conducting most of his campaign from Canada.

John Usher, Lincoln's second secretary of the interior, told the president's official biographers that only once did he hear the usually self-controlled executive give vent to his frustration with legislators. "Then I am to be bullied by Congress am I?" the president reportedly exclaimed during a wartime cabinet meeting. "I'll be damned if I will" (Fehrenbacher and Fehrenbacher 1996, 449). Like many other Oval Office occupants, Lincoln struggled to maintain good relations with Capitol Hill lawmakers. Ultimately, he discovered that he was beset by too many problems, and had too little to offer, to fully placate the needs and egos at the opposite end of Pennsylvania Avenue. Having few other options, he simply accepted their disdain and continued to perform his job.

THE SUPREME COURT

As an attorney in Springfield, Illinois, Lincoln had always preached respect for the law. He was a great believer in the essential justice of the American legal system. But then in the 1850s he witnessed what he considered a terrible perversion of constitutional principles over the question of slavery. Along with many other Republicans, he was scandalized by the Supreme Court ruling in *Scott v. Sanford* (1857), a contentious decision that invalidated the Missouri Compromise and declared that blacks were not capable of citizenship.

The author of that controversial verdict was Chief Justice Roger B. Taney, a Maryland slaveholder whose political views put him on a collision course in 1861 with the incoming Republican administration. On April 27, days after the fall of Sumter, President Lincoln suspended the writ of habeas corpus along the railroad line from Washington to Philadelphia. He considered this measure necessary to help military authorities secure safe passage for Union troops arriving to defend the national capital. Because Maryland was a slave state with a reasonably strong secessionist movement, federal officials feared the worst.

John Merryman was among the first rebel sympathizers arrested under Lincoln's order. In those years, Supreme Court justices also served on the federal circuit, hearing cases individually. While attending to the circuit covering Maryland, Taney received an appeal on Merryman's arrest and issued a blistering opinion against the suspension of civil liberties. "The people of the United States are no longer under a government of laws," he declared ominously (*Ex parte Merryman* 1861; see Document 5.2). On July 4, 1861, the lawyer-turned-president responded in a blunt address to Congress; he claimed it was no time for "extreme tenderness" about such matters (Basler 1953, 4:430). He then ignored the ruling and continued to invoke Article I, Section 9, Clause 2, of the Constitution, which he believed granted him general authority to suspend habeas corpus "in Cases of Rebellion or Invasion." Congress remained uncharacteristically silent on the issue of military arrests until 1863, when the legislative body finally endorsed, with some limits, the unprecedented executive action. In the aftermath of the conflict, the full Court issued the landmark ruling *Ex parte Milligan* (1866), which generally supported Lincoln's actions but curtailed presidential authority by declaring that military tribunals for civilians should not be convened when civil courts were still functioning (see Document 5.3).

Because the unanimous *Milligan* verdict represented a partial rebuke of Lincoln administration policy, it was noteworthy that the author was David Davis, one of Lincoln's five appointees to the high court (see Document 5.4). Before the outbreak of the Civil War, the nine-member Supreme Court had been dominated by Southern slaveholding Democrats. Taney, for example, had forged a 7–2 majority for his politically charged Dred Scott decision largely on a regional and partisan basis. If the Court had maintained the same composition throughout the war, then Lincoln's actions would have undoubtedly faced much more hostile scrutiny from the bench. Instead, a series of deaths, and the temporary decision in 1863 to expand the Court to ten members, enabled the president to alter the political makeup of the institution, diffusing any potential for confrontation. In the only significant wartime decision on presidential power, the Lincoln-dominated Court ruled in the *Prize Cases* (1863) that the president had acted within his constitutional authority at the outset of the rebellion when declaring a blockade of Southern ports. Lincoln's decision had been controversial because he made it in the absence of a formal declaration of war and without explicit congressional approval.

Chief Justice Taney died on October 12, 1864, just a few weeks before Lincoln's reelection. His death provided the president with an opportunity to gain some measure of political retribution in the appointment of his replacement. In seeking a new chief justice, Lincoln turned to his former secretary of Treasury, Salmon P. Chase, who was about as far removed from Taney on the political spectrum as possible. Unlike the pro-Southern jurist, Chase had earned his national reputation as an antislavery lawyer and as an ambitious Republican politician. By the time of his own death, Lincoln had reshaped the Supreme Court through the appointment power and his own stubborn indifference to what he perceived as the political hostility of his judicial critics.

THE MILITARY

At the outbreak of the Civil War, the general in chief of the Union army was in his mid-seventies and near retirement. Winfield Scott was practically a national military icon, but he had been in the service since 1808 and was exhausted by the secession crisis. The aging general had repeatedly urged the James Buchanan administration to reinforce federal forts in the South, but was ignored. By the time Abraham Lincoln entered office, Scott considered the situation too far gone to rectify easily and advised the new president to abandon Fort Sumter. Lincoln declined this advice and war soon came. Initially, the aging general warned of a prolonged conflict and recommended a policy of slow, steady pressure on the rebels coupled with an aggressive move to control the Mississippi Valley. Dismissed as the "Anaconda Plan" by the Northern press, the suggestion went unheeded. Instead, the president pushed for an early overland attack on Confederate forces stationed between Washington and Richmond. But the results were disastrous and the Union forces were routed. Even worse, while waiting for news of the doomed battle, Lincoln discovered that his principal military adviser, General Scott, had left to take a nap.

The president quickly realized that he needed to reorganize his military command. He added a respected young general, George B. McClellan, to the inner circle, placing him in command of the newly formed Army of the Potomac. In the autumn, Lincoln went further by naming the thirty-four-year-old engineer as a replacement for General Scott, who had reluctantly retired. Before long, however, McClellan was under political attack himself. Thus began Lincoln's three-year search for a team of field commanders and military advisers capable of shaping a victorious strategy. Historians tend to regard this often frustrating quest in two ways. The majority praises Lincoln's intuitive strategic sense and generally finds his military subordinates to be woefully lacking, at least until the elevation of Ulysses S. Grant to the position of general in chief in 1864. A dissenting minority, however, criticizes the president's incessant meddling and points out that alternative strategies for subduing the rebellion might have proved far less costly but equally effective over the long haul.

From Lincoln's perspective, putting down the Southern revolt always seemed maddeningly simple. At first, he believed the issue would be decided if federal troops captured the rebel capital. Based on this reasoning, he urged the ill-fated "march toward Richmond" in the summer of 1861. In response to that catastrophe, his strategic view grew more ambitious but remained just as single-minded; he began to realize that the Union really needed to attack the determined rebels "with superior forces at *different points,* at the *same* time" (Basler 1953, 5:98).

He unveiled this new outlook in early 1862 with a directive known as General War Order No. 1. It ordered all Union armies to move simultaneously on February 22, Washington's Birthday (see Document 5.5). In particular, he hoped this command would spur the slow-moving general McClellan into action.

Ultimately, this political pressure did succeed in forcing the Army of the Potomac into the field, but the disappointing results altered the president's thinking once again. After mid-1862, he increasingly disdained what he termed "strategy" and pushed almost exclusively for Union generals to focus on capturing or killing Confederate armies, particularly the dangerous forces led by Gen. Robert E. Lee. "My last [request for an] attempt upon Richmond was to get McClellan, when he was nearer there than the enemy was, to run in ahead of him," Lincoln wrote to his top military adviser in 1863. "Since then I have constantly desired the Army of the Potomac, to make Lee's army, and not Richmond, it's objective point" (Basler 1953, 6:467).

Making Lee's army the "true objective," as he later explained it to Gen. Joseph Hooker, allowed the president to view the Confederate general's occasional incursions into Northern territory as great opportunities rather than mortal threats. Lee's Army of Northern Virginia crossed the Potomac in September 1862 and June 1863. During both invasions, President Lincoln hoped that his military commanders would capture and destroy the legendary Confederate force. On each occasion, however, he was bitterly disappointed. After Lee's troops escaped from their defeat at Gettysburg, Lincoln bitterly told his eldest son, Robert, "If I had gone up there, I could have whipped them myself" (Burlingame and Ettlinger 1997, 63).

Inside the walls of the White House and the War Department, Lincoln's aggravation over his military subordinates became a near constant refrain. He complained that McClellan did nothing to make himself "either respected or feared." (Burlingame and Ettlinger 1997, 41). He dismissed Henry W. Halleck, his third general in chief, as little more than "a first-rate clerk" (Burlingame and Ettlinger 1997, 191–192). By the president's calculation, Gen. John C. Frémont, who had been the Republican Party's first presidential nominee, was "the damdest biggest scoundrel that ever lived but in the infinite mercy of Providence he was also the damdest biggest fool" (Burlingame and Ettlinger 1997, 197–198). He worried about Gen. Joseph Hooker, claiming that "Fighting Joe" had a tendency to get "excited." What amazed Lincoln more than anything else was the absence of mental fortitude in his leading generals. At moments of crisis, he found too often that they appeared frightened or panicked, looking to evade responsibility. He considered the situation ironic. "I who am not a specially brave man," he pointed out to John Hay, "have had to sustain the sinking courage of these professional fighters in critical times" (Burlingame and Ettlinger 1997, 191).

Not all of the presidential complaints were vented behind closed doors. During McClellan's increasingly contentious reign at the head of the Army of the Potomac, Lincoln dictated several blunt or coldly sarcastic telegrams. When Gen. Lorenzo Thomas attempted in the aftermath of the Battle of Gettysburg to defend his less than impressive efforts to collect Union regiments for the pursuit of fleeing rebels, the president issued a stinging response. He wrote that the whole endeavor promised "no immagineable service" until the troops moved "with a little more expedition." Lincoln concluded sarcastically, in his "unprofessional opinion," that unless the pace picked up, the men would be "as likely to capture the Man-in-the-Moon, as any part of Lee's Army" (Basler 1953, 6:321–322).

For much of the war, the suspicions worked both ways. Leading Union generals questioned Lincoln's abilities and resented his interference in their decision making. McClellan offered the most striking example of a military figure who seriously disdained the commander in chief. One evening in November 1861, for example, President Lincoln, Secretary of State William H. Seward and White House aide John Hay called on McClellan at his home. The general was out at a wedding reception, so the group waited in his parlor. When he returned, however, McClellan ignored his guests and marched upstairs. Uncertain as to what was happening, the trio waited about half an hour before asking a servant to remind the general of their presence. Word came back that McClellan "had gone to bed." Hay nervously called the general's rude behavior "a portent of evil to come." But Lincoln seemed indifferent, telling his young aide that it was no time for "points of etiquette & personal dignity" (Burlingame and Ettlinger 1997, 32). Later in the war, the president was compelled to lecture Gen. Joseph Hooker that although he needed all the "professional skill" of his various generals and advisers, the endless "suspicions" of each other and him hampered the war effort (Basler 1953, 6:281).

"We cannot help beating them if we have the man," Lincoln once told Secretary of Navy Gideon Welles. "How much depends in military matters on one mastermind!" (Fehrenbacher and Fehrenbacher 1996, 478). The president worked through three different generals in chief (Scott, McClellan, and Halleck), four different commanders of the Army of the Potomac (McClellan, Ambrose Burnside, Hooker, and George G. Meade), and several other temporary advisers or favored field generals before he finally found his mastermind. Ulysses S. Grant started the war as a colonel in the 21st Illinois Volunteers and rose to become the only indispensable Union military figure. "Unconditional Surrender" Grant, as he was dubbed by the press, marched through Kentucky and western Tennessee in early 1862, scoring some of the federal army's only victories during the frustrating first half of the war. He then spearheaded a lengthy, but brilliant, campaign against Vicksburg, one of the last remaining Confederate strongholds on the Mississippi River. In his rumpled field uniform, chewing on his perpetual cigar, Grant did not appear to many observers as a mastermind.

It was easy to underestimate the genius of Grant's bulldog-like tenacity. Some observers tended to view him as simple-minded in his strategic approach. He was not, however, someone who merely ordered bloody assaults and then relied on the brutal math of greater numbers for his victories. The Vicksburg campaign of 1862–1863 demonstrated that he was capable of deft maneuvers and creative deployments. President Lincoln acknowledged his achievement by telling a reporter in 1863 that the operation "stamps [Grant] as the greatest general of the age, if not of the world." (Fehrenbacher and Fehrenbacher 1996, 11). When the commander continued to have success in the autumn of 1863 as the overall head of the army's Western Department, the president needed no more convincing. He chose to elevate Grant to general in chief and bring him east in early 1864.

For the final year of the war, tensions between the civilian executive and military high command lessened considerably. There were still occasional flare-ups, during Jubal Early's surprise raid on Washington in 1864, for example, or during the dismal summer months prior to Gen. William T. Sherman's pivotal victory at Atlanta, but competent field leadership, coupled with generally good news, helped alleviate much of the old mutual distrust. Lincoln and Grant developed a deep respect for each other. They hardly ever worked together in person or even conversed directly, but the president's willingness to trust his top general marked a significant breakthrough.

Where the two plainspoken midwesterners saw eye to eye was on the grand strategy; they shared a straightforward insight. By 1864 both understood that the key to victory was to escalate the conflict beyond the capacity of the rebels to endure. Union armies needed to take advantage of their superior numbers and resources, bringing coordinated, relentless pressure against the Confederate war-making machinery. Grant proposed an ambitious offensive strategy that was in many ways reminiscent of Lincoln's 1862 order directing the movement of all Union armies simultaneously. Grant also authorized aggressive cavalry raids deep into rebel territory. Both president and general in chief accepted the inevitability of what was then called "hard war" or what is known now as total war. The result was brutal and effective. The war's final year was also the war's bloodiest year and yet it was undoubtedly the destructiveness of those terrible campaigns that ultimately broke the Confederacy.

Although it took Lincoln some time to find his partnership with Grant, his bond with the regular Union soldier developed almost immediately. Known as "Father Abraham," after a wise old figure from Benjamin Franklin's beloved *Poor Richard's Almanack,* the president quickly developed an enduring popular image as empathetic and down to earth. For weary soldiers who learned to see past the allure of the Union army's spit-and-polish approach, Lincoln's homespun integrity offered an appealing alternative. He was seen as one of them and came to personify the sacrifices the men had made for their leader (Gibbons 1862):

> We are coming Father Abraham, three hundred thousand more,
> From Mississippi's winding stream and from New England's shore,
> We leave our plows and workshops, our wives and children dear,
> With hearts too full for utterance, with but a silent tear;
> We dare not look behind us, but steadfastly before,
> We are coming Father Abraham, three hundred thousand more.

And whereas the intensity of support for the president certainly wavered with the ups and downs of the war, there was no better evidence of his strength among the average soldiers than the results of the 1864 election. Even though he was running against their former commander, George McClellan, President Lincoln won an estimated 70 percent of the vote from troops in the Army of the Potomac. In the overall military vote, Lincoln's share approached 80 percent. He was truly the soldiers' president.

THE PRESS

For about six months in 1864 President Lincoln allowed a painter named Francis Bicknell Carpenter to turn one of the White House dining rooms into a studio for a portrait commemorating the origins of the Emancipation Proclamation. Carpenter later wrote a memoir of his experience where he recalled that one day he was showing the president and a group of visitors his initial progress on the painting when one of the ladies present remarked that the newspapers had been mistakenly reporting that he was nearly finished. The artist recalled that he responded with something "commonplace" about how "papers were not always reliable." At this point, the president interjected by joking that "reliable" newspapers simply meant that "they *lie*, and then they *relie!*" (Carpenter 1995, 155–156).

Sooner or later, all presidents find themselves frustrated by the capital press corps. Even George Washington reportedly once picked up a copy of an opposition newspaper that claimed he had "debauched" the nation and responded by throwing the offensive issue down on the floor and yelling "Damn!" in front of his secretary of state (Weisberger 2000, 205). Lincoln was no exception to this rule. In fact, he probably endured greater scorn than most.

During the mid–nineteenth-century, newspapers were still considered partisan tools. Some independent journals did attempt to provide objective reporting, but most existed to serve their political party. The relationship between newspaper correspondents and politicians was entirely symbiotic. White House aide John Hay frequently contributed anonymous reports to Republican-leaning journals. Reporter Noah Brooks worked for a California newspaper for three years during the war and then planned to take over for Hay and former journalist John G. Nicolay as Lincoln's top assistant in 1865. Influential *Washington Chronicle* publisher John Forney also served as secretary of the Senate. The chairman of the president's reelection campaign was none other than Henry Raymond, editor of the *New York Times*.

Before he became president, Lincoln himself had been a regular contributor to Springfield newspapers. He wrote unsigned editorials, general reports, and satirical pieces for the leading Whig and Republican journals. In the late 1850s, he even briefly became a small-time media magnate, quietly purchasing a German-language newspaper that he hoped to use to attract immigrant voters to his party's side for the 1860 presidential contest.

Inside the White House, Lincoln proved generally accessible to reporters. One correspondent recalled that the president had a policy of allowing friendly journalists on deadline to interrupt his meetings by submitting questions on the back of visiting cards with the help of a butler who would then take them inside the office. Lincoln would then either craft a brief written answer or sometimes sneak out the door for a quick conversation.

Nevertheless, the media-friendly president encountered the same problems of ego and ideology that he had in his dealings with congressmen and generals. Many prominent editors had strong personalities and declined to buckle under Lincoln's charm offensive. James Gordon Bennett of the *New York Herald,* the nation's most widely read newspaper, frequently criticized the president, at one point labeling him a "mediocre talent" (Neely 1982, 23). Horace Greeley, editor of the rival *New York Tribune,* also proved irritating at times. Greeley began the war agitating for emancipation and then evolved into a determined advocate for a negotiated peace settlement—a strange evolution since a premature end to hostilities would have surely meant the continuation of slavery.

It was another New York editor, however, who proved to be the most important behind-the-scenes figure in the Lincoln administration. Thurlow Weed began his public career as head of the *Albany Evening Journal.* He then joined forces with William Seward and helped him to become governor and senator from New York. Weed was a journalist, campaign manager, fund-raiser, power broker, and lobbyist, all rolled into one. Consequently, President Lincoln worked diligently to remain in his good graces. Whenever Weed complained about administration policies, Lincoln quickly tried to smooth things over. "I have been both pained and surprised recently at learning that you are wounded because a suggestion of yours as to the mode of conducting our national difficulty, has not been followed," the president wrote in March 1864. He sent the apologetic note with John Nicolay for personal delivery. The aide reported back that Weed was upset because he believed Lincoln "only regarded him with a certain degree of leniency" and merely considered him "as being not quite so great a rascal as his enemies charged him with being" (Basler 1953, 7:268–269; see Document 5.6).

The truth is that Lincoln probably viewed many leading members of the press as colorful, but necessary, rascals. Weed was notorious as the "wizard of the lobby." Horace Greeley was eccentric and unreliable. John Hay once labeled James Gordon Bennett, whose irascibility was legendary, as "too pitchy to touch" (Burlingame and Ettlinger 1997, 230). John Forney was in the habit of getting drunk and making indiscreet comments. Noah Brooks was more dependable, but had a tart wit and frequently skewered lesser administration figures in his columns. Without doubt, they were a lively group that appeared, for the most part, to have an affectionate, if not strictly respectful, attitude toward the president. Like many Americans, their view of Lincoln evolved dramatically only after his death, when their laudatory obituaries finally helped to transform his image into that of a national icon.

SELECTED PRIMARY SOURCES

Basler, Roy P., ed. *The Collected Works of Abraham Lincoln*. 9 vols. New Brunswick: Rutgers University Press, 1953.

Brooks, Noah. "Washington in Lincoln's Time," *Century 49* (November 1894): 140–149.

Burlingame, Michael, ed. *Lincoln Observed: Civil War Dispatches of Noah Brooks*. Baltimore: Johns Hopkins University Press, 1998.

Burlingame, Michael, and John R. Turner Ettlinger, eds. *Inside Lincoln's White House: The Complete Civil War Diary of John Hay*. Carbondale: Southern Illinois University Press, 1997.

Carpenter, F. B. *The Inner Life of Abraham Lincoln: Six Months at the White House*. 1866. Reprint, Lincoln: University of Nebraska Press, 1995.

Ex parte Merryman, 17 Fed. Cas. No. 9487 (1861).

Fehrenbacher, Don E., and Virginia Fehrenbacher, eds. *Recollected Words of Abraham Lincoln*. Stanford: Stanford University Press, 1996.

Gibbons, James Sloan. "We Are Coming Father Abraham." *New York Evening Post*, August 16, 1862.

Lincoln, Abraham, Abraham Lincoln Papers at the Library of Congress. Manuscript Division. Washington, D.C.: American Memory Project, 2000–2002.

SECONDARY SOURCES

Bogue, Allan G. *The Congressman's Civil War*. Cambridge: Cambridge University Press, 1989.

———. *The Earnest Men: Republicans of the Civil War Senate*. Ithaca: Cornell University Press, 1981.

Clark, Allen. "Abraham Lincoln in the National Capital." *Records of the Columbia Historical Society* 27 (1925): 1–174.

Donald, David Herbert. *Lincoln*. New York: Simon and Schuster, 1995.

Long, David E. *The Jewel of Liberty: Abraham Lincoln's Re-Election and the End of Slavery*. Mechanicsburg, Pa.: Stackpole Books, 1994.

McPherson, James M. *Ordeal by Fire: The Civil War and Reconstruction*. 2d ed. New York: McGraw-Hill, 1992.

Neely, Mark E. Jr. *The Abraham Lincoln Encyclopedia*. New York: McGraw-Hill, 1982.

———. *The Last Best Hope of Earth: Abraham Lincoln and the Promise of America*. Cambridge: Harvard University Press, 1993.

Paludan, Phillip Shaw. *The Presidency of Abraham Lincoln*. Lawrence: University of Kansas Press, 1994.

Weisberger, Bernard. *Jefferson, Adams, and the Revolutionary Election of 1800*. New York: HarperCollins, 2000.

Williams, Kenneth P. *Lincoln Finds a General: A Military Study of the Civil War*. New York: Macmillan, 1949.

Williams, T. Harry. *Lincoln and the Radicals*. Madison: University of Wisconsin Press, 1941.

RECOMMENDED READING

Abraham Lincoln Papers at the Library of Congress. Manuscript Division. Washington, D.C.: American Memory Project, 2000–2002, memory.loc.gov/ammem/alhtml/alhome.html.

This is the best source for absorbing the comments Lincoln received in letters and reports from congressmen, generals, and journalists. The collection also includes hundreds of thousands of letters from ordinary citizens commenting on every topic under the sun.

Mitgang, Herbert, ed. *Abraham Lincoln: A Press Portrait*. 1956. Reprint, New York: Fordham University Press, 2000.

This has become a classic collection of newspaper coverage from throughout Lincoln's career. Readers will come away surprised at the abuse the president endured from friends and critics alike.

\Neely, Mark E. Jr. *The Fate of Liberty: Abraham Lincoln and Civil Liberties.* New York: Oxford University Press, 1991.

Most scholars now regard this Pulitzer Prize–winning book as the best, most comprehensive study on the controversial question of Lincoln's decisions to suspend civil liberties during the wartime period.

Sears, Stephen W. *George B. McClellan: The Young Napoleon.* New York: Ticknor and Fields, 1988.

There have been many excellent studies of Lincoln's relationship with the military, but this biography of his most contentious subordinate provides a subtle, yet compelling window into the complicated problem of finding a capable general for a most difficult war.

Tap, Bruce. *Over Lincoln's Shoulder: The Committee on the Conduct of the War.* Lawrence: University Press of Kansas, 1998.

In an important new study, Tap explores the operations of the somewhat notorious congressional oversight body that was dominated by Capitol Hill radicals.

Document 5.1   Political Composition of Civil War Era Congresses (1859–1867)

Southern secession created a tremendous military conflict, but also provided the Republican Party with a political bonanza on Capitol Hill. Republicans had actually gained control of the House of Representatives before the war, but they solidified their standing in the 1860 election and, for the first time, secured a majority in the Senate.

House of Representatives

Congress	Total members	Republicans	Democrats	Others	Vacant
36th (1859–1861)	237	113	101	23	—
37th (1861–1863)	178	106	42	28	2
38th (1863–1865)	183	103	80	—	—
39th (1865–1867)	191	145	46	—	—

Senate

Congress	Total members	Republicans	Democrats	Others	Vacant
36th (1859–1861)	66	26	38	2	2
37th (1861–1863)	50	31	15	3	1
38th (1863–1865)	52	33	10	9	—
39th (1865–1867)	54	39	11	4	—

Source: Office of the Clerk, "Political Divisions of the House of Representatives (1789 to Present)" (2001), clerkweb.house.gov/histrecs/househis/lists/divisionh.htm; Senate Historical Office, "Majority and Minority Parties (Party Division)" (2001), www.senate.gov/learning/stat_13.html.

Document 5.2   Chief Justice Roger B. Taney Condemns Lincoln's Suspension of Civil Liberties (1861)

In the 1861 case of Ex parte Merryman, *Chief Justice Roger B. Taney condemned President Lincoln's decision to suspend the writ of habeas corpus at the outset of the war. The jurist believed that Article I, Section 9, of the Constitution clearly indicated that only Congress could authorize such actions in times of war or rebellion. Lincoln, who was convinced that Taney was a Southern sympathizer attempting to undermine the Union effort, simply ignored the ruling, which was issued from the circuit and not by the full Supreme Court. Congress allowed Lincoln's actions to stand and essentially confirmed them in law with the Habeas Corpus Act of 1863. What follows is a selection from Taney's opinion.*

But the documents before me show, that the military authority in this case has gone far beyond the mere suspension of the privilege of the writ of habeas corpus. It has, by force of arms, thrust aside the judicial authorities and officers to whom the constitution has confided the power and duty of interpreting and administering the laws, and substituted a military government in its place, to be administered and executed by military officers. For, at the time these proceedings were had against John Merryman, the district judge of Maryland, the commissioner appointed under the act of congress, the district attorney and the marshal, all resided in the city of Baltimore, a few miles only from the home of the prisoner. Up to that time, there had never been the slightest resistance or obstruction to the process of any court or judicial officer of the United States, in Maryland, except by the military authority. And if a military officer, or any other person, had reason to believe that the prisoner had committed any offence against the laws of the United States, it was his duty to give information of the fact and the evidence to support it, to the district attorney; it would then have become the duty of that officer to bring the matter before the district judge or commissioner, and if there was sufficient legal evidence to justify his arrest, the judge or commissioner would have issued his warrant to the marshal to arrest him; and upon the hearing of the case, would have held him to bail, or committed him for trial, according to the character of the offence, as it appeared in the testimony, or would have discharged him immediately, if there was not sufficient evidence to support the accusation. There was no danger of any obstruction or resistance to the action of the civil authorities, and therefore no reason whatever for the interposition of the military.

Yet, under these circumstances, a military officer, stationed in Pennsylvania, without giving any information to the district attorney, and without any application to the judicial authorities, assumes to himself the judicial power in the district of Maryland; undertakes to decide what constitutes the crime of treason or rebellion; what evidence (if indeed he required any) is sufficient to support the accusation and justify the commitment; and commits the party, without a hearing, even before himself, to close custody, in a strongly garrisoned fort, to be there held, it would seem, during the pleasure of those who committed him.

The constitution provides, as I have before said, that "no person shall be deprived of life, liberty or property, without due process of law." It declares that "the right of the people to be secure in their persons, houses, papers and effects, against unreasonable searches and seizures, shall not be violated; and no warrant shall issue, but upon probable cause, supported by oath or affirmation, and particularly describing the place to be searched, and the persons or things to be seized." It provides that the party accused shall be entitled to a speedy trial in a court of justice.

These great and fundamental laws, which congress itself could not suspend, have been disregarded and suspended, like the writ of habeas corpus, by a military order, supported by force of arms. Such is the case now before me, and I can only say that if the authority which the constitution has confided to the judiciary department and judicial officers, may thus, upon any pretext or under any circumstances, be usurped by the military power, at its discretion, the people of the United States are no longer living under a government of laws, but every citizen holds life, liberty and property at the will and pleasure of the army officer in whose military district he may happen to be found.

Source: Ex parte Merryman, 17 Fed. Cas. No. 9487 (1861).

Document 5.3   *Ex parte Milligan* Decision
Restricts Military Tribunals (1866)

Lamben P. Milligan was a civilian arrested and tried by Union military authorities in Indiana during the course of the Civil War. After the conflict ended, the Supreme Court ruled in a unanimous decision that in areas where civil courts were still functioning, military tribunals could not be used to convict civilians. The verdict, written by Lincoln's former campaign manager David Davis, was a partial rebuke to the administration's expansive wartime approach to the suspension of civil liberties. The decision did not, however, condemn the president for suspending the writ of habeas corpus. What follows is a selection from the landmark opinion.

The importance of the main question presented by this record cannot be overstated; for it involves the very framework of the government and the fundamental principles of American liberty.

During the late wicked Rebellion, the temper of the times did not allow that calmness in deliberation and discussion so necessary to a correct conclusion of a purely judicial question. Then, considerations of safety were mingled with the exercise of power; and feelings and interests prevailed which are happily terminated. Now that the public safety is assured, this question, as well as all others, can be discussed and decided without passion or the admixture of any element not required to form a legal judgment. We approach the investigation of this case, fully sensible of the magnitude of the inquiry and the necessity of full and cautious deliberation. . . .

The controlling question in the case is this: Upon the facts stated in Milligan's petition, and the exhibits filed, had the military commission mentioned in it jurisdiction, legally, to try and sentence him? Milligan, not a resident of one of the rebellious states, or a prisoner of war, but a citizen of Indiana for twenty years past and never in the military or naval service, is, while at his home, arrested by the military power of the United States, imprisoned, and, on certain criminal charges preferred against him, tried, convicted, and sentenced to be hanged by a military commission, organized under the direction of the military commander of the military district of Indiana. Had this tribunal the legal power and authority to try and punish this man?

No graver question was ever considered by this court, nor one which more nearly concerns the rights of the whole people; for it is the birthright of every American citizen when charged with crime, to be tried and punished according to law. The power of punishment is, alone through the means which the laws have provided for that purpose, and if they are ineffectual, there is an immunity from punishment, no matter how great an offender the individual may be, or how much his crimes may have shocked the sense of justice of the country, or endangered its safety. By the protection of the law human rights are secured; withdraw that protection, and they are at the mercy of wicked rulers, or the clamor of an excited people. If there was law to justify this military trial, it is not our province to interfere; if there was not, it is our duty to declare the nullity of the whole proceedings. The decision of this question does not depend on argument or judicial precedents, numerous and highly illustrative as they are. These precedents inform us of the extent of the struggle to preserve liberty and to relieve those in civil life from military trials. The founders of our government were familiar with the history of that struggle; and secured in a written constitution every right which the people had wrested from power during a contest of ages. By that Constitution and the laws authorized by it this question must be determined. The provisions of that instrument on the administration of criminal justice are too plain and direct, to leave room for misconstruction or doubt of their true meaning. Those applicable to this case are found in that clause of the original Constitution which says, "That the trial of all crimes, except in case of impeachment, shall be by jury"; and in the fourth, fifth, and sixth articles of the amendments. . . .

Have any of the rights guaranteed by the Constitution been violated in the case of Milligan? And if so, what are they?

Every trial involves the exercise of judicial power; and from what source did the military commission that tried him derive their authority? Certainly no part of the judicial power of the country was conferred on them; because the Constitution expressly vests it "in one supreme court and such

inferior courts as the Congress may from time to time ordain and establish," and it is not pretended that the commission was a court ordained
and established by Congress. They cannot justify on the mandate of the
President; because he is controlled by law, and has his appropriate sphere
of duty, which is to execute, not to make, the laws; and there is "no unwrit-
ten criminal code to which resort can be had as a source of jurisdiction."

But it is said that the jurisdiction is complete under the "laws and usages
of war."

It can serve no useful purpose to inquire what those laws and usages
are, whence they originated, where found, and on whom they operate; they
can never be applied to citizens in states which have upheld the authority
of the government, and where the courts are open and their process unobstructed. This court has judicial knowledge that in Indiana the Federal
authority was always unopposed, and its courts always open to hear criminal accusations and redress grievances; and no usage of war could sanction a military trial there for any offence whatever of a citizen in civil life,
in nowise connected with the military service. Congress could grant no
such power; and to the honor of our national legislature be it said, it has
never been provoked by the state of the country even to attempt its exercise. One of the plainest constitutional provisions was, therefore, infringed
when Milligan was tried by a court not ordained and established by Congress, and not composed of judges appointed during good behavior. . . .

It is claimed that martial law covers with its broad mantle the proceedings of this military commission. The proposition is this: that in a time of
war the commander of an armed force (if in his opinion the exigencies of
the country demand it, and of which he is to judge), has the power, within
the lines of his military district, to suspend all civil rights and their reme-
dies, and subject citizens as well as soldiers to the rule of his will; and in
the exercise of his lawful authority cannot be restrained, except by his superior officer or the President of the United States.

If this position is sound to the extent claimed, then when war exists, foreign or domestic, and the country is subdivided into military departments
for mere convenience, the commander of one of them can, if he chooses,
within his limits, on the plea of necessity, with the approval of the Executive, substitute military force for and to the exclusion of the laws, and punish all persons, as he thinks right and proper, without fixed or certain rules.

The statement of this proposition shows its importance; for, if true,
republican government is a failure, and there is an end of liberty regulated
by law. Martial law, established on such a basis, destroys every guarantee

of the Constitution, and effectually renders the "military independent of and superior to the civil power"—the attempt to do which by the King of Great Britain was deemed by our fathers such an offence, that they assigned it to the world as one of the causes which impelled them to declare their independence. Civil liberty and this kind of martial law cannot endure together; the antagonism is irreconcilable; and, in the conflict, one or the other must perish.

This nation, as experience has proved, cannot always remain at peace, and has no right to expect that it will always have wise and humane rulers, sincerely attached to the principles of the Constitution. Wicked men, ambitious of power, with hatred of liberty and contempt of law, may fill the place once occupied by Washington and Lincoln; and if this right is conceded, and the calamities of war again befall us, the dangers to human liberty are frightful to contemplate. If our fathers had failed to provide for just such a contingency, they would have been false to the trust reposed in them. They knew—the history of the world told them—the nation they were founding, be its existence short or long, would be involved in war; how often or how long continued, human foresight could not tell; and that unlimited power, wherever lodged at such a time, was especially hazardous to freemen. For this, and other equally weighty reasons, they secured the inheritance they had fought to maintain, by incorporating in a written constitution the safeguards which time had proved were essential to its preservation. Not one of these safeguards can the President, or Congress, or the Judiciary disturb, except the one concerning the writ of habeas corpus.

It is essential to the safety of every government that, in a great crisis, like the one we have just passed through, there should be a power somewhere of suspending the writ of habeas corpus. In every war, there are men of previously good character, wicked enough to counsel their fellow-citizens to resist the measures deemed necessary by a good government to sustain its just authority and overthrow its enemies; and their influence may lead to dangerous combinations. In the emergency of the times, an immediate public investigation according to law may not be possible; and yet, the peril to the country may be too imminent to suffer such persons to go at large. Unquestionably, there is then an exigency which demands that the government, if it should see fit in the exercise of a proper discretion to make arrests, should not be required to produce the persons arrested in answer to a writ of habeas corpus. The Constitution goes no further. It does not say after a writ of habeas corpus is denied a citizen, that he shall be tried otherwise than by the course of the common law; if it had intended this result, it was easy by the use of direct words to have accomplished it. The illustrious men who framed that instrument were guarding the foundations of civil liberty against the abuses of unlimited power; they were full of wisdom, and the lessons of history informed them that a trial by an established court, assisted by an impartial jury, was the only sure way of protecting the citizen against oppression and wrong. Knowing this, they limited the suspension to one great right, and left the rest to remain forever inviolable. But, it is insisted that the safety of the country in time of war demands that this broad claim for martial law shall be sustained. If this were true, it could be well said that a country, preserved at the sacrifice of all the cardinal principles of liberty, is not worth the cost of preservation. Happily, it is not so.

It will be borne in mind that this is not a question of the power to proclaim martial law, when war exists in a community and the courts and civil authorities are overthrown. Nor is it a question what rule a military commander, at the head of his army, can impose on states in rebellion to cripple their resources and quell the insurrection. The jurisdiction claimed is much more extensive. The necessities of the service, during the late Rebellion, required that the loyal states should be placed within the limits of certain military districts and commanders appointed in them; and, it is urged, that this, in a military sense, constituted them the theatre of military operations; and, as in this case, Indiana had been and was again threatened with invasion by the enemy, the occasion was furnished to establish martial law. The conclusion does not follow from the premises. If armies were collected in Indiana, they were to be employed in another locality, where the laws were obstructed and the national authority disputed. On her soil there was no hostile foot; if once invaded, that invasion was at an end, and with it all pretext for martial law. Martial law cannot arise from a threatened invasion. The necessity must be actual and present; the invasion real, such as effectually closes the courts and deposes the civil administration.

It is difficult to see how the safety of the country required martial law in Indiana. If any of her citizens were plotting treason, the power of arrest could secure them, until the government was prepared for their trial, when the courts were open and ready to try them. It was as easy to protect witnesses before a civil as a military tribunal; and as there could be no wish to convict, except on sufficient legal evidence, surely an ordained and established court was better able to judge of this than a military tribunal composed of gentlemen not trained to the profession of the law.

It follows, from what has been said on this subject, that there are occasions when martial rule can be properly applied. If, in foreign invasion or civil war, the courts are actually closed, and it is impossible to administer criminal justice according to law, then, on the theatre of active military operations, where war really prevails, there is a necessity to furnish a substitute for the civil authority, thus overthrown, to preserve the safety of the army and society; and as no power is left but the military, it is allowed to govern by martial rule until the laws can have their free course. As necessity creates the rule, so it limits its duration; for, if this government is continued after the courts are reinstated, it is a gross usurpation of power. Martial rule can never exist where the courts are open, and in the proper and unobstructed exercise of their jurisdiction. It is also confined to the locality of actual war.

Source: Ex parte Milligan, 71 U.S. 2 (1866).

Document 5.4   Lincoln's Supreme Court Appointees (1862–1864)

President Lincoln named five men to the Supreme Court during his administration, including one chief justice. The appointments helped to shift the balance of power on the Court toward a position more sympathetic to Lincoln and the Republican Party. Note that during the war, Congress authorized an expansion of the bench from nine members to ten, a decision it rescinded only a few years later.

Name	State	Replaced	Date of appointment	Years on bench
Noah H. Swayne	Ohio	McLean	Jan. 21, 1862	19
Samuel F. Miller	Iowa	Daniel	July 16, 1862	28
David Davis	Illinois	Campbell	Dec. 1, 1862	14
Stephen J. Field	California	(new seat)	March 6, 1863	34
Salmon P. Chase[a]	Ohio	Taney	Dec. 6, 1864	8

[a] Appointed chief justice.

Source: Supreme Court Historical Society, "Presidential Nominees" (2001), www.supremecourthistory.org/fp/courtlist.htm.

Document 5.5   Lincoln's General War Order No. 1 (1862)

Frustrated by the absence of progress in the Union war effort, especially in the eastern theater of the conflict, President Lincoln issued in late January 1862 General War Order No. 1, which commanded the simultaneous movement of federal armies on Washington's Birthday, February 22. Many of his generals, especially George B. McClellan, objected to civilian authorities interfering in their plans and ridiculed the political symbolism of the directive. Nevertheless, the order had its intended effect and produced a series of offensives that proved far more successful in the West than the East.

Executive Mansion,
President's General War Order No. 1
Washington, January 27, 1862

Ordered that the 22nd. day of February 1862, be the day for a general movement of the Land and Naval forces of the United States against the insurgent forces.
That especially—
The Army at & about, Fortress Monroe.
The Army of the Potomac.
The Army of Western Virginia
The Army near Munfordsville [sic], Ky.
The Army and Flotilla at Cairo.
And a Naval force in the Gulf of Mexico, be ready for a movement on that day.

That all other forces, both Land and Naval, with their respective commanders, obey existing orders, for the time, and be ready to obey additional orders when duly given.

That the Heads of Departments, and especially the Secretaries of War and of the Navy, with all their subordinates; and the General-in-Chief, with all other commanders and subordinates, of Land and Naval forces, will severally be held to their strict and full responsibilities, for the prompt execution of this order.

ABRAHAM LINCOLN

Source: General War Order No. 1, January 27, 1862, in *The Collected Works of Abraham Lincoln,* 9 vols., ed. Roy P. Basler (New Brunswick: Rutgers University Press, 1953), 5:111–112.

Document 5.6   Lincoln's Attempt to Placate
Power Broker Thurlow Weed (1864)

Thurlow Weed was an influential newspaper editor and lobbyist from Albany who helped to manage William H. Seward's political career. Once Lincoln defeated Seward for the Republican presidential nomination in 1860, Weed began a complicated relationship with the Illinois politician. Lincoln carefully tried to cultivate Weed's loyalty. The following exchange demonstrates his concern and offers a fascinating window into Weed's mind. After hearing rumors that Weed was upset over administration policies, Lincoln crafted a brief apology and had his top White House aide, John G. Nicolay, deliver the message in person to the power broker at a hotel in New York City. Nicolay later prepared a memorandum summarizing his conversation with Weed, who seems to have been in a strangely reflective mood.

Hon. Thurlow Weed Executive Mansion,

My dear Sir: Washington, March 25. 1864.

I have been both pained and surprised recently at learning that you are wounded because a suggestion of yours as to the mode of conducting our national difficulty, has not been followed—pained, because I very much wish you to have no unpleasant feeling proceeding from me, and surprised, because my impression is that I have seen you, since the last Message issued, apparantly feeling very cheerful and happy. How is this? Yours truly

A LINCOLN

Report from presidential aide John G. Nicolay:

Mr. Weed was here at the Astor House on my arrival last Saturday morning and I gave him the note you sent him.

He read it over, carefully once or twice and then said he didn't quite understand it. He had written a letter to Judge [David] Davis, which the Judge had probably shown you, but in that he had said nothing except about Custom House matters.

He said that all the solicitude he had was in your behalf. You had told him in January last that you thought you would make a change in the Collectorship here, but that thus far it had not been done. He had told you he himself had no personal preference as to the particular man who is to be his successor. He did not think Mr. [Hiram] Barney a bad man but thought him a weak one. His four deputies are constantly intriguing against you. Andrews is doing the same. Changes are constantly being made among the subordinates in the Custom House, and men turned out, for no other real reason than that they take active part in primary meetings & c., in behalf of your re-nomination.

His only solicitude, he said, was for yourself. He thought that if you were not strong enough to hold the Union men together through the next Presidential election, when it must necessarily undergo a great strain, the country was in the utmost danger of going to ruin.

His desire was to strengthen you as much as possible and that you should strengthen yourself. You were being weakened by the impression in the popular mind that you hold on with such tenacity to men once in office, although they prove to be incapable and unworthy. This feeling among your friends also raises the question, as to whether, if re-elected, you would change your Cabinet. The present Cabinet is notoriously weak and inharmonious—no Cabinet at all—gives the President no support. [Secretary of the Navy Gideon] Welles is a cypher, [Attorney General Edward] Bates a fogy, and [Postmaster General Montgomery] Blair at best a dangerous friend.

Something was needed to reassure the public mind and to strengthen yourself. [Salmon P.] Chase and [Gen. John C.] Frémont, while they might not succeed in making themselves successful rivals might yet form and lead dangerous factions. Chase was not formidable as a candidate in the field, but by the shrewd dodge of a withdrawal is likely to turn up again with more strength than ever.

He had received a letter from Judge Davis, in which the Judge wrote him that he had read his (Weed's) letter to you, but that you did not seem ready to act in the appointment of a new Collector, and that he (the Judge) thought it was because of your apprehension that you would be merely getting "out of one muss into another."

A change in the Custom House was imperatively needed because one whole bureau in it had been engaged in treasonably aiding the rebellion.

The ambition of his life had been, not to get office for himself, but to assist in putting good men in the right places. If he was good for anything, it was as an outsider to give valuable suggestions to an administration that would give him its confidence. He feared he did not have your entire confidence—that you only regarded him with a certain degree of leniency; that you only regarded him as being not quite so great a rascal as his enemies charged him with being.

The above are substantially the points of quite a long conversation. This morning I had another interview with Mr. Weed.

He had just received Gov. [Edwin] Morgan's letter informing him of the nomination of Hogeboom to fill McElrath's place, and seemed quite disheartened and disappointed. He said he did not know what to say. He had assured your friends here that when in your own good time you became ready to make changes, the new appointments would be from among your friends; but that this promotion of one of your most active and malignant enemies left him quite powerless. He had not yet told any one, but knew it would be received with general indignation, & c & c.

I shall remain here a day or two longer.

Source: Abraham Lincoln to Thurlow Weed, March 25, 1864, and Report by John G. Nicolay, in *The Collected Works of Abraham Lincoln,* 9 vols., ed. Roy P. Basler (New Brunswick: Rutgers University Press, 1953), 7:268–269.

THE ASSASSINATION OF PRESIDENT LINCOLN.
AT FORD'S THEATRE WASHINGTON. D.C. APRIL 14TH 1865.

Published by Currier & Ives, 152 Nassau St. New York

John Wilkes Booth assassinates Lincoln in Ford's Theatre as Mary Todd Lincoln and two friends look on, April 14, 1865.

CHAPTER SIX

Assassination

The assassination of Abraham Lincoln remains one of the great murder mysteries of American history. Actor John Wilkes Booth shot and killed the president. But beyond that critical fact, vexing details continue to stir debate. Some of the more paranoid students of the episode believe, for example, that Booth actually escaped from federal authorities and died an old man. Then there are the loyal descendants of one or two of his convicted co-conspirators who persist in claiming innocence for their ancestors, and a few die-hard conspiracy theorists who claim that Vice President Andrew Johnson or Secretary of War Edwin M. Stanton had some role in the gruesome affair.

Generations of Americans debated these questions and others, until they became little more than stale parlor games. Over the last several years, however, the topic of Lincoln's assassination has developed a new sense of urgency. Historians have engaged in heated discussions over what role, if any, the Confederate government played in the Booth plot and whether the assassination should properly be regarded as an act of revenge for earlier Union schemes to kidnap or kill Confederacy president Jefferson Davis. These explosive claims remain unproven, but after years of relegating the Lincoln murder conspiracies to the fantasies of true crime sleuths, serious historians are finally reexamining the case.

PRESIDENTIAL SECURITY

Lincoln's life was in danger even before he became president. During his preinaugural trip to Washington in early 1861, reports surfaced about a plot in Baltimore to murder him when he transferred trains. In the heated atmosphere of the secession period, these threats seemed credible. Security chief Allan Pinkerton and incoming secretary of state William H. Seward convinced the president-elect to depart from his public schedule and slip into Washington unannounced, and partially disguised, on a train originating in Pennsylvania. The story was too rich for the nation's newspapers to ignore, and some Democratic-leaning journals ridiculed Lincoln for what they considered his pathetic and cowardly entrance to power (see Document 6.1).

The criticism stung. From that moment on, Lincoln generally made a show of ignoring security concerns about himself and even his family. During the first tense weeks of the war, a unit of Kansas militiamen known as the "Jayhawkers" were sent to the White House by Sen. James H. Lane, R-Kan., to protect the president. Otherwise, Lincoln passed the first year of the conflict with no extraordinary measures taken in his behalf. He had no Secret Service protection (not yet offered to presidents) and no military or police guard. Some of those close to the president grew concerned. White House aide John Hay reported that he had to do some "very dexterous lying" to Mary Lincoln to calm her fears about what he called "the assassination suspicion" (Burlingame and Ettlinger 1997, 2–3).

The situation changed in the autumn of 1862; yet it was not assassins but whole armies that threatened the president. After the Union defeat at the Second Battle of Bull Run on August 29, the entire city of Washington braced for a Confederate assault. Shortly after that engagement, Gen. Robert E. Lee's Army of Northern Virginia crossed the Potomac, setting the stage for the most critical confrontation of the war's first phase.

During that chaotic period, Union army officials ordered a cavalry detail to accompany the president whenever he traveled outside of the city and assigned a unit from the Army of the Potomac to serve as a permanent guard for the Lincoln family. At the time, the first family was in residence at the Soldiers' Home, a complex of government-owned cottages situated on shaded hills a few miles outside of the sweltering city.

According to the young Pennsylvania soldiers assigned to the new security detail, as they nervously protected their president they could actually hear the distant cannon fire from the peripheral skirmishes of the Confederate invasion.

For the rest of the war, Company K from the 150th Pennsylvania Volunteers was stationed with the Lincolns, either at the Soldiers' Home or at the White House. The family quickly grew fond of the young men (see Document 6.2). Tad Lincoln played at their campsites, enjoying the camaraderie with the troops and the generous handouts of his favorite treat, bread and jam. Once or twice the soldiers intervened to rescue the president from overly aggressive visitors, but they were not considered true bodyguards and usually kept their distance as he conducted his daily business. A prominent journalist recalled that in the middle of the war he once witnessed Lincoln wandering alone on Pennsylvania Avenue, apparently in search of a newsboy and the morning's headlines. Within the city itself, the president and his wife frequently traveled without any escort, especially when they attended the theater—the one social outlet they allowed themselves to enjoy during the conflict.

A series of near misses ultimately convinced the War Department to tighten protection around the president. In July 1863, Mary Lincoln suffered serious head injuries from a carriage accident that appeared to be the result of sabotage. Another incident allegedly took place near the Soldiers' Home as the president rode alone one night. According to the most reliable version of the story, sentries near the presidential cottage heard a rifle shot and then noticed Lincoln riding toward them hatless and in great haste. He assured them it was only a random noise that had scared his horse, but the next day they discovered his trademark stovepipe hat with a bullet hole through the crown. When they confronted the president with the evidence, he demanded that they keep the episode quiet (see Document 6.3). Equally disturbing, during the course of the war the White House received an ever-increasing number of letters threatening assassination, kidnapping, or general mayhem. By 1864 concerned Union army officials had stationed a special cavalry unit from Ohio, the Union Light Guard, to complement the security detail already in place at the White House. In the autumn of that year, they also assigned members of the recently established Washington police force to accompany the president whenever he walked or rode about town.

Lincoln fought almost all of these measures. When the cavalry detail was first assigned to him in 1862, he complained to the War Department that he and Mary Lincoln "couldn't hear themselves talk" over the clatter of swords and horses (Carpenter 1995, 67). He repeatedly dismissed the troops and traveled without them. To anyone who would listen, he joked that his life was in greater jeopardy from the novice guards—who might discharge their guns by accident—than from any hostile threat by the rebels. During a Confederate raid against Washington in July 1864, the president ignored all suggestions that he remain inside the White House and twice was present while the city's defenses were under hostile enemy fire.

As the war drew to a close in the spring of 1865, Lincoln continued to shrug off concerns for his safety. Just one day after Union forces had secured Richmond in April 1865, the president arrived to tour the defeated Confederate capital. To close friends and associates, he had the same answer for any objections to his riskier comings and goings. "I cannot be shut up in an iron cage and guarded," he reportedly declared. "The truth is if any man has made up his mind that he will give his life for mine, he can take mine" (Swett 1887, 187–188; see Document 6.4).

BOOTH'S CONSPIRACY

The man who ultimately gave his life to take Lincoln's was a celebrity before he became a killer. At the time of the assassination, John Wilkes Booth was a successful twenty-six-year-old actor from a family of famous actors. Born in Maryland, a slave state, he had discovered an even deeper affinity for Southern life while touring the region as part of a successful theater company in the months before the war. Coupled with his natural interest in politics, Booth quickly found himself absorbed by the crisis of the rebellion. In 1862 he was arrested in St. Louis for reportedly announcing that "he wished the whole dammed Government would go to hell" (Hanchett 1983, 41). However, he was soon released and even had the honor of appearing before the president in late 1863 in a play called "The Marble Hart," performed at Ford's Theatre in Washington.

Despite his treasonous views, Booth seemed to have little trouble earning money as an actor by night while engaging in subversive activities by day. He served as an occasional rebel spy, helped to smuggle medicine to the South, and apparently even met with Confederate agents in Canada during the autumn of 1864 to plan still more ambitious schemes to help derail the Union.

According to traditional accounts of the Booth assassination conspiracy, he organized a small group of former rebel soldiers on his own initiative and plotted in Washington over the winter of 1864–1865 to kidnap or kill the president and some members of his cabinet. Relying on his fame as an actor, Booth strolled unchallenged into the presidential box at Ford's Theatre in mid-April and committed murder. A handful of other Southern agents based in Maryland helped the assassin temporarily escape. Booth had dispatched other agents to murder the vice president and secretary of state, but both failed. One would-be assassin got drunk and never even made an attempt. This account was essentially the theory of the case developed by the prosecution during the military trials used to convict Booth's co-conspirators.

Some evidence suggested that the assassination plot had been conceived originally as a kidnapping scheme and had been backed by the Confederate government in Richmond but prosecutors failed to make that connection. It was not until 1988 that a book appeared with enough credible information to seriously challenge the official verdict of an isolated conspiracy. *Come Retribution,* by three former federal employees (including one ex-spymaster), offered a detailed argument suggesting that Booth had been an active agent of the Confederate Secret Service and would not have moved to assassination without at least tacit approval from rebel leaders. Since publication of this account, a series of new books and public exchanges over the merits of the case have emerged, implicating the Confederate high command in the plot to kill Lincoln.

The main problem with this latest theory is that the evidence linking Booth to the rebel government is circumstantial. Moreover, determining the substance of his conversations with Confederate agents, if they took place at all, requires a healthy degree of speculation. It is true that during the final months of the war the Confederate Secret Service considered several schemes to kidnap President Lincoln. It is also true that many in Richmond believed the Union government had already raised what was called the "black flag" of state-sanctioned terrorism. In early 1864, a failed federal cavalry raid on Richmond resulted in the publication of documents (possibly forged) that indicated a Union plan to burn the city and assassinate Jefferson Davis and his cabinet. That episode is still shrouded in mystery, but there is no doubt that during the last year of the war there was widespread talk of revenge and murder.

Yet many historians consider it unlikely that such a high-level assassination conspiracy could have existed without leaving someone, especially after the war, willing to testify to its existence. In fact, the best testimony for viewing the conspiracy within a more limited framework probably comes from Booth himself, who kept a diary as he was being hunted down by federal authorities in the final days before his own death (see Document 6.5). "Our country owed all her troubles to him," he wrote bitterly, referring to Lincoln, "and God simply made me the instrument of his punishment." He claimed that he "struck" for his country and "that alone," but nowhere in the cramped, rushed confession did he allude to a larger conspiracy. Quite the contrary, he seemed full of delusions of grandeur, almost shocked that he was being "hunted like a dog" and treated no better than a "common cutthroat" (Rhodehamel and Taper 1997, 154–155; see Document 6.5).

There is conceivably a middle ground between theories. In his diary—which prosecutors decided not to produce at the trial—Booth explained that his decision to assassinate the president came only after other kidnapping schemes had collapsed. "For six months we had worked to capture [Lincoln]," he wrote, "but our cause being almost lost, something decisive and great must be done." What is revealing about this explanation is that Booth then blamed unnamed "others" whom he claimed "did not strike for their country with a heart" (Rhodehamel and Taper 1997, 154–155; see Document 6.5). It is possible that Booth was aware of Confederate discussions about kidnapping the president, and perhaps even received covert assistance in his own initial schemes, but that ultimately—with naturally dramatic flair—he decided to act on his own murderous initiative when the professionals failed to deliver on their promises.

LINCOLN'S DEATH AND AFTERMATH

The fact that a famous actor entered the presidential box at Ford's Theatre during the evening performance on Friday, April 14, 1865, should have surprised no one familiar with Lincoln's security arrangements. The Washington police assigned to him almost never followed their subject inside city buildings. That night, the president and the first lady sat unprotected, accompanied only by a young couple whom Mary Lincoln had invited and a valet.

Not long after 10 p.m. Booth showed his card to the valet who allowed him to enter the box. He approached the president, holding a small derringer pistol. "I shouted Sic Semper [tyrannis] before I fired," Booth noted in his diary, referring to the Latin phrase (and Virginia state motto) meaning "Thus always to tyrants" (Rhodehamel and Taper 1997, 154–155; see Document 6.5). He shot Lincoln once in the head, struggled with the young man seated near him, and then leaped to the stage, breaking his leg in the process and, according to various accounts, shouting something else at the confused audience (see Document 6.6). An army surgeon quickly rushed to aid the president but initially felt no pulse. "He was being held upright in his chair by Mrs. Lincoln who was weeping bitterly," the doctor recalled. Still, despite catastrophic injuries to his brain, Lincoln clung to life.

A group of men carried the president's body across the street to the home of William Peterson, a German immigrant who owned a three-story boarding house on Tenth Street. During the course of the evening, dozens of high-level Union figures filled the large row house while hundreds, perhaps thousands, of people waited anxiously outside. From the beginning, the doctors who treated Lincoln expected him to die (see Document 6.7). It was an eerie scene with Mary Lincoln sobbing in uncontrollable agony, while Secretary of War Edwin Stanton grimly organized the initial investigation. Lincoln finally stopped breathing at 7:22 on the morning of April 15.

Secretary of Navy Gideon Welles, who had spent the night with the others at the Peterson house, noted in his diary that after the president's death he returned home for breakfast and then went to the White House where his wife was attempting to comfort Mary Lincoln. "There was a cheerless cold rain and everything seemed gloomy," he recorded. "On the Avenue in front of the White House were several hundred colored people, mostly women and children, weeping and wailing their loss." Welles made his way through the crowd into the Executive Mansion where he encountered the president's twelve-year-old son, Tad. "Oh, Mr. Welles," the boy cried out, "who killed my father?" The gruff cabinet officer admitted in his diary that on hearing this sad question, he could no longer restrain his tears, "nor give the poor boy any satisfactory answer" (Beale 1960; see Document 6.8).

As usual, it was the efficient and ruthless Stanton who had most of the necessary answers. The Union officer who transcribed eyewitness accounts for the secretary of war's initial investigation reported that they knew their culprit from the very beginning. "In fifteen minutes, " he recalled, "I had testimony enough down to hang John Wilkes Booth" (Steers 2001, 129). Yet the assassin slipped out of Washington and managed to elude federal authorities for nearly two weeks before a group of men organized by Union detective Lafayette Baker was finally able to corner the fugitive at Richard Garrett's farm in northern Virginia (see Document 6.9). Although under strict orders to bring Booth back alive, a sergeant in the expedition shot and killed the assassin as he resisted arrest.

By the time of Booth's death, government officials had arrested seven men and one woman for participating in the Lincoln murder conspiracies. Despite some opposition from within the cabinet, Secretary of War Stanton convinced the newly elevated president, Andrew Johnson, to authorize a special military tribunal to try the civilian defendants (see Document 6.10). The military officers heard testimony from nearly four hundred witnesses and conducted most of their proceedings in open session. In fact, the tribunal typically followed civil court procedure and the defendants were represented by some of the most prominent attorneys in the nation. Yet there was little doubt about the ultimate verdict. The prosecution won convictions against all eight figures. Four were hanged (including Mary Surratt, the owner of the boardinghouse where the conspiracies had been developed), and four were sentenced to long terms in federal prison. Another alleged co-conspirator was arrested in 1867, but a hung jury in civilian court allowed him to go free.

Simultaneously, the federal government also mounted a public relations campaign against Jefferson Davis and several other Confederate officials. Even before Booth was captured and killed, the War Department issued a statement claiming that it had "information that the President's murder was organized in Canada and approved at Richmond" (Hanchett 1983, 64). However, Northern newspaper reporters soon exposed the government's principal witnesses in support of this theory as liars and frauds. Davis was never convicted of anything—even treason—and was released after serving two years in prison. The single Confederate official executed after the war was Henry Wirz, commandant of the notorious Andersonville prisoner of war camp.

In some ways, it is stunning that Union officials did not exhibit a greater lust for blood. The war cost the federal government billions of dollars. An estimated 360,000 Union troops died, and another 275,000 survived their wounds. Altogether, there were more than one million American casualties. The nation endured its first presidential assassination. Secretary of State William Seward also suffered serious injuries during the simultaneous attempt on his life. And yet many former rebels, including Jefferson Davis, remained defiant, celebrating their defeat as a "Lost Cause." It is true that Reconstruction of the nation proceeded on harsher political terms than Lincoln had offered as wartime president, but the reign of Radical Republicans intent on punishing the South was short-lived. Within a few years after the war, most Southern states were operating largely as before (although at least without slavery), and by 1877 the federal government had recalled all remaining troops occupying the region.

The most poignant reminder of Lincoln's tragic death was the fate of the surviving members of his family. For years, Mary Lincoln struggled to convince the government to provide her with a sizable pension. And before Congress finally relented, she even endured the humiliation of holding a public auction of her possessions. Her life seemed doomed to tragedy. Less than six years after her husband's death, Mary Lincoln watched her youngest son, Tad, then only eighteen, succumb to a respiratory illness. She was distraught, seeking guidance from psychics and exhibiting signs of severe depression. Her only remaining son, Robert, demonstrated little sympathy for his troubled mother, and even had her briefly committed to an asylum in 1875. She was released to the care of her sister and brother-in-law, with whom she lived quietly for the last several years of her life. Robert Lincoln, the only surviving descendent of the president, enjoyed a distinguished career as secretary of war, foreign diplomat, and corporate executive, but never seemed capable of emerging from the shadow of his great father. He died without producing any children.

Ultimately, the most enduring legacy of the assassination was what historians have labeled the "apotheosis" or deification of Lincoln within American popular culture. The shooting, on Good Friday, evoked powerful emotions within an exhausted nation. Newspaper editorials and Easter sermons lauded Lincoln's good works and humble bearing. Although the president had been unpopular for long stretches of the conflict, the juxtaposition of his untimely death and final Union victory elevated him above petty partisan sniping. He became an icon of American democracy, and even his former critics acknowledged in retrospect his greatness as a national leader (see Document 6.11). If Lincoln had died an old man, his accomplishments would still surely be celebrated, but the abrupt ending of his life infused his story with an element of tragic poetry that keeps his well-told tale compelling to this day.

SELECTED PRIMARY SOURCES

Beale, Howard K., ed. *Diary of Gideon Welles: Secretary of Navy under Lincoln and Johnson.* 3 vols. New York: Norton, 1960.

Brooks, Noah. *Washington in Lincoln's Time.* New York: Century, 1895.

Burlingame, Michael, and John R. Turner Ettlinger, eds. *Inside Lincoln's White House: The Complete Civil War Diary of John Hay.* Carbondale: Southern Illinois University Press, 1997.

Carpenter, F. B. *The Inner Life of Abraham Lincoln: Six Months at the White House.* 1866. Reprint, Lincoln: University of Nebraska Press, 1995.

Doster, William E. *Lincoln and Episodes of the Civil War.* New York: Putnam's, 1915.

Gerry, Margarita Spalding, ed. *Through Five Administrations: Reminiscences of Colonel William H. Crook, Body-Guard to President Lincoln.* New York: Harper and Brothers, 1910.

Good, Timothy S., ed. *We Saw Lincoln Shot: One Hundred Eyewitness Accounts.* Jackson: University Press of Mississippi, 1995.

Lamon, Ward Hill. *Recollections of Abraham Lincoln, 1847–1865.* Edited by Dorothy Lamon Teillard. Washington, D.C., 1911.

Mitgang, Herbert, ed. *Abraham Lincoln: A Press Portrait.* 1956. Reprint, New York: Fordham University Press, 2000.

Pitman, Benn, ed. *The Assassination of President Lincoln and the Trial of the Conspirators.* 1867. Reprint, New York: Funk and Wagnalls, 1954.

Rhodehamel, John, and Louise Taper, eds. *"Right or Wrong, God Judge Me": The Writings of John Wilkes Booth.* Urbana: University of Illinois Press, 1997.

Swett, Leonard. "The Conspiracies of the Rebellion." *North American Review* 144 (February 1887): 179–190.

SECONDARY SOURCES

Bishop, Jim. *The Day Lincoln Was Shot*. New York: Harper, 1955.

Bryan, George S. *The Great American Myth*. New York: Carrick and Evans, 1940.

Chesebrough, David B. *"No Sorrow Like Our Sorrow": Northern Protestant Ministers and the Assassination of Abraham Lincoln*. Kent: Kent State University, 1994.

Cramer, John Henry. *Lincoln under Enemy Fire: The Complete Account of His Experiences during Early's Attack on Washington* (Baton Rouge: Louisiana State University Press), 1948.

Donald, David Herbert. *Lincoln*. New York: Simon and Shuster, 1995.

McPherson, James M. "A Failed Richmond Raid and Its Consequences." *Columbiad* 2 (winter 1999).

Schultz, Duane. *The Dahlgren Affair: Terror and Conspiracy in the Civil War*. New York: Norton, 1998.

Tidwell, William A. *April '65: Confederate Covert Action in the American Civil War*. Kent: Kent State University Press, 1995.

Turner, Thomas Reed. *The Assassination of Abraham Lincoln*. Malabar, Fla.: Krieger, 1999.

RECOMMENDED READING

Hanchett, William. *The Lincoln Murder Conspiracies*. Urbana: University of Illinois Press, 1983.

Hanchett provides a good, readable summary of the major conspiracy theories that have lingered over Lincoln's assassination.

Steers, Edward Jr. *Blood on the Moon: The Assassination of Abraham Lincoln*. Lexington: University Press of Kentucky, 2001.

Steers has strong opinions—on the guilt of some of Booth's co-conspirators, for example—but he supports his claims with extensive documentation and solid research.

Tidwell, William A., James O. Hall, and David Winfred Gaddy. *Come Retribution: The Confederate Secret Service and the Assassination of Lincoln*. Jackson: University Press of Mississippi, 1988.

This monograph by three retired federal employees and devoted assassination historians helped to persuade some Civil War scholars to reexamine the argument that the Confederate government might have been behind Booth's plot.

Turner, Thomas R. *Beware the People Weeping: Public Opinion and the Assassination of Abraham Lincoln*. Baton Rouge: Louisiana State University, 1982.

Turner rejects the grand conspiracy theories, offering a strong, reliable overview of the infamous murder plot and the trial of Booth's co-conspirators.

Winik, Jay. *April 1865: The Month That Saved America*. New York: Harper-Collins, 2001.

Winik offers an engaging narrative of the final days of the conflict.

Document 6.1   The Baltimore Plot (1861)

In February 1861, President-elect Lincoln traveled by train from Springfield, Illinois, to Washington, D.C. As he passed through Pennsylvania, word reached his party that officials had discovered a plot in Baltimore to assassinate him as he changed trains. A reluctant Lincoln agreed to the entreaties of his Secretary of State–designate William H. Seward and security expert Allan Pinkerton that he depart from his public schedule and that he pass unannounced through Baltimore, a city full of secessionists, on his way to the capital. Rumors spread that the president-elect also traveled in disguise. Northern Democratic and Southern newspapers ridiculed the incoming president's unheralded entry into the city. The following excerpt appeared in the Charleston, South Carolina, Mercury on February 26, 1861.

Washington. February 23.—Abraham Lincoln, President elect of the Northern States, crept into Washington most unexpectedly by the daylight train from Baltimore. It is well understood that he was in dread of an attack on the way. To guard against this, he gave out that he would arrive by to-night's train, and, in the meantime, he took measures to come incognito twelve hours earlier. Everybody here is disgusted at this cowardly and undignified entry.

Source: Mercury (Charleston, South Carolina), February 26, 1861, in Abraham Lincoln: A Press Portrait, ed. Herbert Mitgang (1956; reprint, New York: Fordham University Press, 2000), 234.

Document 6.2   Lincoln Calls Military Guard "Very Agreeable" (1862)

The president and his family received no full-time military protection until the autumn of 1862 when Confederate troops temporarily invaded Maryland. Although Lincoln objected to the decision at first, he quickly became fond of the soldiers from Company K, 150th Pennsylvania Volunteers, led by Capt. David V. Derickson. When there was discussion of replacing the troops with another unit, the president wrote a strong letter of endorsement of the Company K soldiers. As a result, the men remained stationed with the Lincoln family, at the White House and at their summer retreat, for the duration of the war.

Executive Mansion,
Whom it may concern Washington, Nov. 1, 1862

Capt. [David] Derrickson [sic], with his company, has been, for some time keeping guard at my residence, now at the Soldiers Retreat. He, and his Company are very agreeable to me; and while it is deemed proper for any guard to remain, none would be more satisfactory to me than Capt. D. and his company.

A. LINCOLN

Source: Abraham Lincoln to Whom It May Concern, November 1, 1862, in *The Collected Works of Abraham Lincoln,* 9 vols. ed. Roy P. Basler (New Brunswick: Rutgers University Press, 1953), 5:484–485.

Document 6.3   Sentry Recalls Lincoln's Narrow Escape (1864)

After the Civil War, a handful of figures claimed that Lincoln had once narrowly escaped an assassin's bullet while riding alone near the Soldiers' Home, his family's wartime retreat at the edge of the District of Columbia. Some versions of the story have contradicted one another, but the most reliable appears to come from Private John W. Nichols, a soldier in the Pennsylvania company assigned to guard the Lincoln family. His story was reprinted in the New York Times, *April 6, 1887.*

One night about the middle of August [1864] Mr. [John W.] Nichols [Pvt., Company K] was doing sentinel duty at the large gate to the grounds of the home. About 11 o'clock he heard a rifle shot, and shortly afterward Mr. Lincoln dashed up to the gate on horseback. The President was bareheaded and as he dismounted he said, referring to his horse: "He came pretty near getting away with me, didn't he? He got the bit in his teeth before I could draw the rein." Mr. Nichols asked him where his hat was, and he replied that somebody had fired a gun off at the foot of the hill, and his horse had become scared and jerked his hat off. "Thinking the affair rather strange," said Mr. Nichols, "a corporal and myself went down the hill to make an investigation. At the intersection of the driveway and main road we found the President's hat—a plain silk one—and upon examining it we discovered a bullet hole through the crown. The shot had been fired upward and it was evident that the person who fired the shot had secreted himself close by the roadside. The next day I gave Mr. Lincoln his hat and called his attention to the bullet hole. He remarked rather unconcernedly that it was put there by some foolish gunner and was not intended for him. He said, however, that he wanted the matter kept quiet, and admonished us to say nothing about it. We felt confident that it was an attempt to kill him, and a well nigh successful one, too. The affair was, of course, kept quiet in compliance with the President's request. After that the President never rode alone."

Source: New York Times, April 6, 1887.

Document 6.4   Lincoln Declines the "Iron Cage" (1862)

The president repeatedly told his friends and associates that there was nothing he could do in the face of a determined effort to assassinate him. One of his closest friends, Leonard Swett, recalled after the war that Lincoln said he refused to be "shut up in an iron cage." Other reminiscences noted the president employing similar sentiments on other occasions. Swett's recollection first appeared in the North American Review, *February 1887.*

On one occasion, in the summer of 1863, if I remember rightly [probably in 1862], the writer of this article had occasion, with William H. Hanna, of Bloomington, Ill., to ride to the Soldiers' Home, about four miles from

Washington, to call upon Mr. Lincoln in the evening. Our driver missed the way, passing by the Home into the forest below. Being once in the intricacies of this labyrinth, we did not get out until two o'clock in the morning, and the question arose, why the rebels might not send a force across the river, and coming up in the woods to the Soldiers' Home, capture Mr. Lincoln and carry him within the enemy's lines. Mr. Hanna was very much concerned in reference to the situation, and I said to him, "You go and talk with Mr. Lincoln, you are a new man." The subject of his capture or assassination had been discussed until it was a sore subject between Mr. Lincoln and his friends. So, the next day, we got Marshal [Ward Hill] Lamon, and the three obtained an audience with the President. "I cannot be shut up in an iron cage and guarded," he said. "If I have business at the War Office, I must take my hat and go there; and if to kill me is within the purposes of this rebellion, no precaution can prevent it. You may guard me at a single point, but I will necessarily be exposed at others. People come to see me every day and I receive them, and I do not know but that some of them are secessionists or engaged in plots to kill me. The truth is, if any man has made up his mind that he will give his life for mine, he can take mine." We argued that, while this was true, it was his duty to the country not unnecessarily to expose himself, that, there being no guard at the Soldiers' Home, and the condition of the country below as described, it was recklessness upon his part to go there and be there without a guard. He raised various objections, and finally we said, "Somebody must do something if anything is done. Will you leave it to us three to make such disposition as we think to be prudent, and will you simply acquiesce in what we do?" Finally, in substance, he assented, and we went to Secretary Stanton and got for him the guard of cavalry, which accompanied him every evening from the White House to the Soldiers' Home, and remained at the Home all night and came in with him in the morning.

Source: Leonard Swett, "The Conspiracies of the Rebellion," *North American Review* 144 (February 1887): 179–190.

Document 6.5 Booth's Diary (1865)
On April 26, 1865, Union army officials discovered a diary on the body of John Wilkes Booth. The small volume contained a few entries, reprinted here,

that appeared to have been written in haste as the assassin was hiding in Maryland and Virginia during the days following the murder of Lincoln.

Until to day nothing was ever *thought* of sacrificing to our country's wrongs. For six months we had worked to capture. But our cause being almost lost, something decisive & great must be done. But its failure was owing to others, who did not strike for their country with a heart. I struck boldly, and not as the papers say. I walked with a firm step through a thousand of his friends, was stopped, but pushed on. A Col. was at his side. I shouted Sic semper *before* I fired. In jumping broke my leg. I passed all his pickets, rode sixty miles that night with the bones of my leg tearing the flesh at every jump. I can never repent it, though we hated to kill: Our country owed all her troubles to him, and God simply made me the instrument of his punishment. The country is not what it *was*. This forced Union is not what I *have* loved. I care not what becomes of me. I have no desire to outlive my country. . . .

. . . After being hunted like a dog through swamps, woods, and last night being chased by gunboats till I was forced to return wet, cold, and starving, with every mans hand against me, I am here in despair. And why: For doing what Brutus was honored for. What made Tell a hero. And yet I, for striking down a greater tyrant than they ever knew, am looked upon as a common cutthroat. My action was purer than either of theirs. One hoped to be great himself. The other had not only his country's but his own, wrongs to avenge. I hoped for no gain. I knew no private wrong. I struck for my country and that alone. A country that groaned beneath this tyranny, and prayed for this end. Yet now behold the cold hands they extend to me. God *cannot* pardon me if I have done wrong. Yet I cannot see my wrong, except in serving a degenerate people. The little, the very little, I left behind to clear my name, the Govmt will not allow to be printed. So ends all. For my country I have given up all that makes life sweet and holy, brought misery upon my family, and am sure there is no pardon in the Heaven for me, since man condemns me so. I have only *heard* of what has been done (except what I did myself), and it fills me with horror. God, try and forgive me, and bless my mother. Tonight I will once more try the river with the intent to cross. Though I have a greater desire and almost a mind to return to Washington, and in a measure clear my name—which I feel I can do. I do not repent the blow I struck. I may before God, but not to man.

I think I have done well. Though I am abandoned, with the curse of Cain upon me. When, if the world knew my heart, *that one* blow would have made me great, though I did desire no greatness.

To night I try to escape these bloodhounds once more. Who, who can read his fate? God's will be done.

I have too great a soul to die like a criminal. Oh, may He, may he spare me that, and let me die bravely.

I bless the entire world. Have never hated or wronged anyone. This last was not a wrong, unless God deems it so, and its with Him to damn or bless me. . . .

Source: John Wilkes Booth diary, in *"Right or Wrong, God Judge Me": The Writings of John Wilkes Booth,* ed. John Rhodehamel and Louise Taper (Urbana: University of Illinois Press, 1997), 154–155.

Document 6.6   Testimony of Major Henry Rathbone (1865)

Maj. Henry Rathbone, age twenty-eight, and his fiancée, Clara Harris, had been invited to join the president and first lady at Ford's Theatre on Friday evening, April 14, 1865. They were enjoying the comedy "Our American Cousin" until John Wilkes Booth burst into the presidential box and mortally wounded President Lincoln. In the course of the melee that followed, Booth also seriously injured Major Rathbone. The wounded guest survived, but later had a tragic life. Fifteen years after marrying Miss Harris, Rathbone murdered her and attempted suicide. He was later committed to an insane asylum, where he remained until his death in 1911. The following excerpt is taken from a transcript prepared by noted stenographer Benn Pitman of Rathbone's testimony on May 15, 1865, at the military trial of Booth's co-conspirators.

On the evening of the 14th of April last, at about twenty minutes past 8 o'clock, I, in company with Miss Harris, left my residence at the corner of Fifteenth and H Streets, and joined the President and Mrs. Lincoln, and went with them, in their carriage, to Ford's Theater, on Tenth Street. On reaching the theater, when the presence of the President became known, the actors stopped playing, the band struck up "Hail to the Chief," and the audience rose and received him with vociferous cheering. The party proceeded along in the rear of the dress-circle and entered the box that had been set apart for their reception. On entering the box, there was a large arm-chair that was placed nearest the audience, farthest from the stage, which the President took and occupied during the whole of the evening, with one exception, when he got up to put on his coat, and returned and sat down again. When the second scene of the third act was being performed, and while I was intently observing the proceedings upon the stage, with my back toward the door, I heard the discharge of a pistol behind me, and, looking round, saw through the smoke a man between the door and the President. The distance from the door to where the President sat was about four feet. At the same time I heard the man shout some word, which I thought was "Freedom!" I instantly sprang toward him and seized him. He wrested himself from my grasp, and made a violent thrust at my breast with a large knife. I parried the blow by striking it up, and received a wound several inches deep in my left arm, between the elbow and the shoulder. The orifice of the wound was about an inch and a half in length, and extended upward toward the shoulder several inches. The man rushed to the front of the box, and I endeavored to seize him again, but only caught his clothes as he was leaping over the railing of the box. The clothes, as I believe, were torn in the attempt to hold him. As he went over upon the stage, I cried out, "Stop that man." I then turned to the President; his position was not changed; his head was slightly bent forward, and his eyes were closed. I saw that he was unconscious, and, supposing him mortally wounded, rushed to the door for the purpose of calling medical aid.

Source: Testimony of Major Henry Rathbone, May 15, 1865, in *Assassination of President Lincoln and the Trial of the Conspirators,* ed. Benn Pitman (1865; reprint, New York: Funk and Wagnalls, 1954); Surratt House Museum, ww.surratt.org/su_docs.html (2001).

Document 6.7   Testimony of Dr. Robert Stone (1865)

Several doctors and army surgeons cared for President Lincoln the night of the assassination. Dr. Robert Stone was the Lincoln family physician in Washington. Shortly after the shooting, he arrived at the house on Tenth Street where Lincoln had been taken. But he soon discovered that the situation was "a hopeless one." The following excerpt is taken from a transcript prepared by noted stenographer Benn Pitman of Dr. Stone's testimony on May 16, 1865, at the military trial of Booth's co-conspirators.

I was sent for by Mrs. Lincoln immediately after the assassination. I arrived in a very few moments, and found that the President had been removed from the theater to a house of a gentleman living directly opposite; and had been carried into the back room of the residence, and was there placed upon a bed. I found a number of gentlemen, citizens, around him, and, among others, two assistant surgeons of the army, who had brought him over from the theater, and had attended to him. They immediately gave the case over to my care, knowing my relations to the family. I proceeded to examine the President, and found that he had received a gun-shot wound in the back part of the left side of his head into which I carried my finger. I at once informed those around that the case was a hopeless one; that the President would die; that there was no positive limit to the duration of his life; that his vital tenacity was very strong, and he would resist as long as man could; but that death would certainly soon close the scene. I remained with him, doing whatever was in my power, assisted by my friends, but, of course, nothing could be done, and he died from the wound the next morning at about half-past 7 o'clock.

Source: Testimony of Dr. Robert Stone, May 16, 1865, in *Assassination of President Lincoln and the Trial of the Conspirators,* ed. Benn Pitman (1865; reprint, New York: Funk and Wagnalls, 1954); Surratt House Museum, www.surratt.org/su_docs.html (2001).

Document 6.8   Welles Describes Lincoln's Death and Early Reaction (1865)

Out of all of the first-hand accounts of Lincoln's death and the immediate reaction to the news, the most poignant description arguably comes from the diary of Gideon Welles, the secretary of the navy. What follows are excerpts from his extended entry on April 15, 1865.

A little before seven, I went into the room where the dying President was rapidly drawing near the closing moments. His wife soon after made her last visit to him. The death-struggle had begun. Robert, his son, stood with several others at the head of the bed. He bore himself well, but on two occasions gave way to overpowering grief and sobbed aloud, turning his head and leaning on the shoulder of Senator [Charles] Sumner. The respiration of the President became suspended at intervals, and at last ceased entirely at twenty-two minutes past seven.

A prayer followed from Dr. [Phineas] Gurley; and the Cabinet, with the exception of Mr. [William] Seward and Mr. [Hugh] McCulloch, immediately thereafter assembled in the back parlor, from which all other persons were excluded, and there signed a letter which was prepared by Attorney-General [James] Speed to the Vice-President, informing him of the event, and that the government devolved upon him. . . .

. . . I went after breakfast [on April 15] to the Executive Mansion. There was a cheerless cold rain and everything seemed gloomy. On the Avenue in front of the White House were several hundred colored people, mostly women and children, weeping and wailing their loss. This crowd did not appear to diminish through the whole of that cold, wet day; they seemed not to know what was to be their fate since their great benefactor was dead, and their hopeless grief affected me more than almost anything else, though strong and brave men wept when I met them. At the White House all was silent and sad. Mrs. W. was with Mrs. L. and came to meet me in the library. [James] Speed came, and we soon left together. As we were descending the stairs, "Tad," who was looking from the window at the foot, turned and, seeing us, cried aloud in his tears, "Oh, Mr. Welles, who killed my father?" Neither Speed nor myself could restrain our tears, nor give the poor boy any satisfactory answer.

Source: Diary entry of Gideon Welles, April 15, 1865, in *Diary of Gideon Welles, Secretary of Navy under Lincoln and Johnson,* ed. John T. Morse Jr. (Boston: Houghton Mifflin, 1911), 2:287–290.

―――――

Document 6.9   Booth's Escape from Washington (1865)

After receiving some help from a fellow conspirator at Ford's Theatre, John Wilkes Booth hurried away from the scene of the murder on horseback. He left the city of Washington via the Navy Yard bridge where he was briefly interrogated—but ultimately passed—by Sgt. Silas Cobb, who had not yet received notice of the assassination. The sergeant was never formally reprimanded for his actions. Booth spent the next twelve days at large, hiding in Maryland and then northern Virginia. The following excerpt is taken from a transcript pre-

pared by noted stenographer Benn Pitman of Sergeant Cobb's testimony on May 16, 1865, at the military trial of Booth's co-conspirators.

On the night of the 14th of April, I was on duty at the Navy Yard bridge. At about half past 10 or 11 o'clock, a man approached rapidly on horseback. The sentry challenged him, and I advanced to see if he was a proper person to pass.

I asked him, "Who are you, sir?" he said, "My name is Booth." I asked him where he was from. He made answer, "From the city." "Where are you going?" I said; and he replied, "I am going home." I asked him where home was. He said it was in Charles. I understood by that he meant Charles County. I asked him what town. He said he did not live in any town. I said, "You must live in some town." Said he, "I live close to Bean-town; but do not live in the town." I asked him why he was out so late; if he did not know the rule that persons were not allowed to pass after 9 o'clock. He said it was new to him; that he had had somewhere to go in the city, and it was a dark night, and he thought he would have the moon to ride home by. The moon rose that night about that time. I thought he was a proper person to pass, and I passed him.

Source: Testimony of Sergeant Silas Cobb, May 16, 1865, in *Assassination of President Lincoln and the Trial of the Conspirators,* ed. Benn Pitman (1865; reprint, New York: Funk and Wagnalls, 1954); Surratt House Museum, www.surratt.org/su_docs.html (2001).

Document 6.10
Opinion on Military Tribunals for Booth's Co-conspirators (1865)

Within two weeks of the assassination, federal officials had killed John Wilkes Booth and detained eight suspects. Secretary of War Edwin M. Stanton urged that the co-conspirators face a military tribunal rather than civilian courts. There was some opposition to this idea, but Stanton's influence won over President Andrew Johnson. In July 1865, Attorney General James Speed issued a formal opinion defending the decision to try the civilians in military court.

The President was assassinated at a theater in the city of Washington. At the time of the assassination a civil war was flagrant, the city of Washington was defended by fortifications regularly and constantly manned, the principal police force of the city was by Federal soldiers, the public offices and property in the city were all guarded by soldiers, and the President's House and person were, or should have been, under the guard of solders. Martial law had been declared in the District of Columbia, but the civil courts were open and held their regular sessions, and transacted business as in times of peace.

Such being the facts, the question is one of great importance—important, because it involves the constitutional guarantees thrown about the rights of the citizen, and because the security of the army and the government in time of war is involved; important, as it involves a seeming conflict between the laws of peace and of war.

Having given the question propounded the patient and earnest consideration its magnitude and importance require, I will proceed to give the reasons why I am of the opinion that the conspirators not only may but ought to be tried by a military tribunal.

A civil court of the United States is created by a law of Congress, under and according to the Constitution. To the Constitution and law we must look to ascertain how the court is constituted, the limits of its jurisdiction, and what its mode of procedure.

A military tribunal exists under and according to the Constitution in time of war. Congress may prescribe how all such tribunals are to be constituted, what shall be their jurisdiction and mode of procedure. Should Congress fail to create such tribunals, then, under the Constitution they must be constituted according to the laws and usages of civilized warfare. . . .

. . . Congress can declare war. When war is declared, it must be, under the Constitution, carried on according to the known laws and usages of war among civilized nations. Under the power to define those laws, Congress can not abrogate them or authorize their infraction. The Constitution does not permit this Government to prosecute a war as an uncivilized and barbarous people.

As war is required by the framework of our government to be prosecuted according to the known usages of war among the civilized nations of the earth, it is important to understand what are the obligations, duties, and responsibilities imposed by war upon the military. Congress, not having defined, as under the Constitution it might have done, the laws of war, we must look to the usage of nations to ascertain the powers conferred in war, on whom the exercise of such powers devolve, over whom, and to what extent to those powers reach, and in how far the citizen and the soldier are bound by the legitimate use thereof.

The power conferred by war is, of course, adequate to the end to be accomplished, and not greater than what is necessary to be accomplished. The law of war, like every other code of laws, declares what shall be done, and does not say what may be done. The legitimate use of the great power of war, or rather the prohibitions against the use of that power, increase or diminish as the necessity of the case demands. When a city is besieged and hard pressed, the commander may exert an authority over the non-combatants which he may not when no enemy is near. . . .

. . . In all wars, and especially in civil wars, secret but active enemies are almost as numerous as open ones. That fact has contributed to make civil wars such scourges to the countries in which they rage. In nearly all foreign wars the contending parties speak different languages and have different habits and manners; but in most civil wars that is not the case; hence there is a security in participating secretly in hostilities that induces many to thus engage. War prosecuted to the most civilized usage is horrible, but its horrors are greatly aggravated by the immemorial habits of plunder, rape and murder practiced by secret, but active participants. Certain laws and usages have been adopted by the civilized world in wars between nations that are not kin to one another, for the purpose and to the effect of arresting or softening many of the necessary cruel consequences of war. How strongly bound we are, then, in the midst of a great war, where brother and personal friend are fighting against brother and personal friends, to adopt by those laws and usages.

A public enemy must or should be dealt with in all wars by the same laws. The fact that they are public enemies, being the same, they should deal with each other according to those laws of war that are contemplated by the Constitution. Whatever rule have been adopted and practiced by the civilized nations of the world in war, to soften its harshness and severity, should be adopted and practiced by us in this war. That the laws of war authorized commanders to create and establish military commissions, courts or tribunals for the trial of offenders against the laws of war, whether they be active or secret participants in the hostilities, cannot be denied. That the judgments of such tribunals may have been sometimes harsh, and sometimes even tyrannical, does not prove that they ought not to exist, nor does it prove that they are not constituted in the interest of justice and mercy. Considering the power that the laws of war give over secret participants in hostilities, such as banditti, guerillas, spies, etc., the position of a commander would be miserable indeed if he could not call to his aid the judgments of such tribunals; he would become a mere butcher of men, without the power to ascertain justice, and there can be no mercy where there is no justice. War in its mildest form is horrible; but take away from the contending armies the ability and right to organize what is known as a Bureau of Military Justice, they would soon become monster savages, unrestrained by any and all ideas of law and justice. . . .

. . . The law of nations, which is the result of experience and wisdom of ages, has decided that jayhawkers, banditti, etc., are offenders against the laws of nature and of war, and as such amenable to the military. Our Constitution has made those laws a part of the law of the land. Obedience to the Constitution and the law, then, requires that the military should do their whole duty; they must not only meet and fight the enemies of the country in open battle, but they must kill or take the secret enemies of the country, and try and execute them according to the laws of war. The civil tribunals of the country can not rightfully interfere with the military in the performance of their high, arduous and perilous, but lawful duties. That Booth and his associates were secret active public enemies, no mind that contemplates the facts can doubt. The exclamation used by him when he escaped from the box on to the stage, after he had fired the fatal shot, *sic semper tyrannis,* and his dying message, "Say to my mother that I died for my country," show that he was not an assassin from private malice, but that he acted as a public foe.

Source: Attorney General James Speed, "Opinion on the Constitutional Power of the Military to Try and Execute the Assassins of the President," July 1865; Surratt House Museum, www.surratt.org/documents/Bplact16.pdf (2001).

Document 6.11
Editorial Eulogy of Lincoln (1865)

James Gordon Bennett was a pioneering journalist who was notoriously independent and often fiercely critical of President Lincoln's policies. His editorial in the New York Herald *on April 17, 1865, headlined, "The Great Crime—Abraham Lincoln's Place in History," captures much of the sentiment behind the transformation of the president from a controversial politician to a national icon.*

Abraham Lincoln, in the full fruition of his glorious work, has been struck from the roll of living men by the pistol shot of an assassin. That is the unwelcome news which has, for the past two days, filled every loyal heart with sadness, horror, and a burning thirst for retribution. . . . Whatever judgment may have been formed by those who were opposed to him as to the calibre of our deceased Chief Magistrate, or the place he is destined to occupy in history, all men of undisturbed observation must have recognized in Mr. Lincoln a quaintness, originality, courage, honesty, magnanimity and popular force of character such as have never heretofore, in the annals of the human family, had the advantage of so eminent a stage for their display. He was essentially a mixed product of the agricultural, forensic and frontier life of this continent—as indigenous to our soil as the cranberry crop, and as American in his fibre as the granite foundations of the Apalachian [sic] range. He may not have been, and perhaps was not, our most perfect product in any one branch of mental or moral education; but, taking him for all in all, the very noblest impulses, peculiarities and aspirations of our whole people—what may be called our continental idiosyncrasies—were more collectively and vividly reproduced in his genial and yet unswerving nature than in that of any other public man of whom our chronicles bear record. . . . And surely some hundred years hence, when the staid and scholarly disciples of the historic Muse, bring their grave eyes to scan and their brief tapelines to measure the altitude and attitude, properties and proportions of our deceased Chief Magistrate, their surprise— taking them to be historians of the present type—will be intense beyond expression.

Source: New York Herald, April 17, 1865, in *Abraham Lincoln: A Press Portrait,* ed. Herbert Mitgang (1956; reprint, New York: Fordham University Press, 2000), 465–468.

Cabinet Members, Lincoln Administration

Title	Officeholder	Term
Vice president	Hannibal Hamlin	1861–1865
	Andrew Johnson	1865
Secretary of state	William H. Seward	1861–1865
Secretary of Treasury	Salmon P. Chase	1861–1864
	William Pitt Fessenden	1864–1865
	Hugh McCulloch	1865
Secretary of war	Simon Cameron	1861–1862
	Edwin M. Stanton	1862–1865
Attorney general	Edward Bates	1861–1864
	James Speed	1864–1865
Postmaster general	Montgomery Blair	1861–1864
	William Dennison Jr.	1864–1865
Secretary of the navy	Gideon Welles	1861–1865
Secretary of the interior	Caleb B. Smith	1861–1862
	John P. Usher	1863–1865

Appendix B

Notable Figures
of the Lincoln Presidency

Baker, Lafayette C. (1825–1868, b. Stafford, N.Y.)
Union spy

Baker was a controversial Union spy and chief detective during the Civil War. His principal wartime assignment in the U.S. Secret Service was to investigate disloyalty and corruption within the federal army and government. His aggressive methods drew criticism from some quarters. Adding to his dark reputation was his brooding, mysterious appearance. But it was Baker to whom Secretary of War Edwin M. Stanton turned when John Wilkes Booth escaped from Washington after the assassination of Lincoln. Two of his agents helped to corner the fugitive, and Baker received credit for organizing the successful operation. After the war, however, he became entangled in the politics of Andrew Johnson's impeachment crisis and his career suffered. Testifying before Congress, Baker offered a series of fantastic allegations designed to embarrass President Andrew Johnson, and later, according to some accounts, he implicated Secretary of War Stanton in the plot to kill Lincoln. Most observers at the time (and most historians since) found his version of events completely unbelievable. Yet some ardent conspiracy theorists believe that Baker was murdered in Philadelphia in 1867 to prevent further revelations.

For further reading: Jacob Mogelever, *Death to Traitors: The Story of General Lafayette C. Baker, Lincoln's Forgotten Secret Service Chief* (Garden City, N.Y.: Doubleday, 1960).

Bates, Edward (1793–1869, b. Goochland County, Va.)
U.S. attorney general, 1861–1864

Bates served as attorney general in the Lincoln administration from March 5, 1861, until December 1, 1864. He was the oldest member of the cabinet—almost sixty-eight at the outset of the war—and suffered a mild stroke in his final year in office. Still, he proved to be a vigorous figure at the Justice Department, defending the president, at least initially, on the key question of his right to suspend civil liberties during wartime. Bates, a resident of Missouri, had been a leading contender for the Republican Party nomination in 1860. He represented the "old line Whig" element of the party, embodying a conservative Unionism that drew its inspiration from figures such as Henry Clay and Daniel Webster. Lincoln admiringly called Bates the "Law-Officer of the government, a believer in the virtue of adhering to the law." Once President Lincoln adopted his emancipation policy and pressed forward with measures designed to help blacks achieve greater equality, however, Bates found himself increasingly at odds with the political direction of the administration.

For further reading: Howard K. Beale, ed., *The Diary of Edward Bates, 1859–1866* (Washington, D.C.: U.S. Government Printing Office, 1933).

Bennett, James Gordon (1795–1872, b. Keith, Banffshire, Scotland)
Newspaper publisher
Arguably the most influential newspaper publisher of the Civil War era, Bennett
was a pioneer of what was known as the "penny press," the inexpensive, popularly
oriented newspapers that sensationalized current events and focused heavily on
human interest stories. Bennett's vehicle was the *New York Herald,* which had
become the nation's most widely read daily newspaper by the 1850s. Bennett was
a controversial figure, vain and cantankerous, and once labeled by Lincoln aide
John Hay as "too pitchy to touch." Yet President Lincoln needed his editorial support during the war and worked diligently to cultivate the mercurial publisher. First
Lady Mary Lincoln played a role in this outreach herself, flattering Bennett in a
series of chatty letters.

Most observers considered the publisher pro-South, but he ultimately did back
the Union war effort and seemed to gain grudging respect for Lincoln during the
course of the war. The *Herald* did not endorse the president for reelection in 1864,
but most insiders considered the newspaper's ambivalent stance a slight victory for
the incumbent—even with its sarcastic put-down of both principal candidates as
"two men of mediocre talent." Further proof that the president was generally satisfied with his treatment came in early 1865 when he offered Bennett the coveted
position of ambassador to France, an offer that was declined. After Lincoln's assassination, Bennett's editorials abandoned all of their previous ambivalence and
earnestly celebrated the dead president's "quaintness, originality, courage, honesty,
magnanimity and popular force of character." A few years later the publisher
retired, leaving his beloved newspaper in the hands of his son, also named James
Gordon Bennett.

For further reading: James L. Crouthamel, *Bennett's* New York Herald *and the
Rise of the Popular Press* (Syracuse: Syracuse University Press, 1989).

Blair, Francis P., Jr. (1821–1875, b. Lexington, Ky.)
*Member, U.S. House of Representatives (R-Mo.), various periods 1857–1864;
Union general*
Frank Blair was both an important army general and a congressman during the
Civil War. Although he was a slaveholder, Blair also was an ardent nationalist who
helped to ensure that the critical slave state of Missouri remained in the Union.
The key to understanding Blair's politics, however, is his family. His father, Francis P. Blair Sr., was a longtime power broker in Washington. His oldest brother,
Montgomery, served in Lincoln's cabinet. Together they constituted their own
peculiar interest. But, according to the president, it was Frank Blair who was "their
hope and pride." The family was powerful and controversial, known for making
enemies by their aggressive self-promotion. "The Blairs have to an unusual degree
the spirit of clan," Lincoln once told a close aide. "They have a way of going with
a rush for anything they undertake."

In some cases, the president found this impetuous behavior useful. For example, when Secretary of Treasury Salmon P. Chase threatened to challenge Lincoln
for his party's presidential nomination in early 1864, Frank Blair took to the floor
of the House of Representatives with charges of corruption in the Treasury Depart-

ment. Never tied to a particular party, Blair ran as vice president on the unsuccessful Democratic ticket in 1868. Four years later, he backed the Liberal Republican Party and appeared to be making a comeback in Missouri state politics in the mid-1870s until he suffered partial paralysis and head injuries in an accidental fall that ultimately proved fatal.

For further reading: William E. Parrish, *Frank Blair: Lincoln's Conservative* (Columbia: University of Missouri Press, 1998).

Blair, Francis P., Sr. (1791–1876, b. Abingdon, Va.)
Newspaper editor and presidential adviser
Preston Blair entered Washington politics in 1830 when he arrived in the city at the request of President Andrew Jackson to launch a new pro-administration newspaper. Called the *Globe,* Blair's paper quickly gained a following within the Jacksonian movement and established him as an important party figure. However, when the political tides changed in the 1840s, Blair found himself out of favor and eventually retired to his home in Maryland. Over the next few decades, from his outpost in Silver Spring, the elder Blair remained a powerful figure who injected himself into several controversies.

Blair took a special interest in the Lincoln administration, owing to the prominence of his sons—Montgomery Blair served in Lincoln's cabinet and Frank Blair served in the army and Congress. Lincoln frequently relied on the elder Blair, using him, for example, to conduct secret negotiations with Confederacy president Jefferson Davis in late 1864. But Lincoln also ignored Blair whenever his advice proved too meddlesome, such as in the case of Gen. George B. McClellan, whose career the aging power broker tried desperately to save.

The president was both attracted and repelled by the "spirit of clan" he saw in the Blair family. He called them "a close corporation" and seemed almost envious of their loyalty to each other. He had nothing like those kinds of relationships with his own father or sons.

For further reading: Elbert B. Smith, *Francis Preston Blair* (New York: Free Press, 1980).

Blair, Montgomery (1813–1883, b. Franklin County, Ky.)
Postmaster general, 1861–1864
Before the war, Blair was best known in his role as counsel to Dred Scott, the slave who unsuccessfully sued for his freedom in a controversial case that contributed to the polarization of North and South (*Scott v. Sanford,* 1857). During the war, Blair proved to be an efficient postmaster general, an important job in an era in which his office controlled more patronage than any other department except Treasury. But Blair distinguished himself most as a fierce political infighter. From the Fort Sumter crisis forward, he was involved in one behind-the-scenes scrape after another. While describing him as "the best scholar in the Cabinet," well-known journalist Noah Brooks also ridiculed Blair as "awkward, shy, homely and repellent."

Despite his prewar reputation as an honorable antislavery advocate, Blair emerged as one of the bitterest enemies of the Radical Republicans, especially those on Capitol Hill. He agreed with the Radicals on the need to abolish slavery, but he resisted any efforts to guarantee equality for blacks. He believed firmly in the separation of the races. This view, coupled with his desire to see more lenient terms for Southern Reconstruction, led Blair to make a series of controversial speeches in 1863 and 1864 that turned him into the number-one target of disgruntled congressional Radicals. Ultimately, they forced President Lincoln to remove Blair from the cabinet as the price for their support in the 1864 election, and the controversial postmaster resigned in September 1864.

In the months that followed, the ex-cabinet officer remained loyal to the administration, hoping that he would be named chief justice of the United States upon the death of the aging Roger B. Taney. The ailing chief justice had authored the majority verdict against his client in the famous Dred Scott case. Lincoln, however, bypassed Blair and appointed leading Radical Salmon P. Chase instead. After the Civil War, Blair abandoned the Republican Party and settled into a largely quiet, scholarly life.

For further reading: Jean H. Baker, "Montgomery Blair," American National Biography; www.anb.org.

Brooks, Noah (1830–1903, b. Castine, Maine)
Journalist
During the Civil War, Brooks served as the Washington-based correspondent for the *Sacramento Daily Union*. He was not, however, a typical member of the capital press corps. A former resident of Illinois, Brooks had known some of the major figures around Lincoln, and the president himself to a degree, before the White House years. He was a strong supporter of the administration and, by most accounts, emerged as one of Lincoln's closest confidants during the wartime period. Lincoln reportedly offered him the senior post of presidential secretary when his top aides, John G. Nicolay and John Hay, were preparing to leave at the outset of the second term in 1865. Nevertheless, Brooks had a sharp eye and was unafraid to criticize cabinet officers or presidential aides in private or in print. His dispatches from wartime Washington and his later recollections constitute one of the most vivid sources on the Lincoln administration.

For further reading: Michael Burlingame, ed., *Lincoln Observed: Civil War Dispatches of Noah Brooks* (Baltimore: Johns Hopkins University Press, 1998).

Browning, Orville (1806–1881, b. Cynthiana, Ky.)
U.S. senator (R-Ill.), 1861–1863
No prominent figure in wartime Washington, including Mary Lincoln, had known Lincoln as long as Sen. Orville Browning. The two men first met as young Whig politicians and lawyers working together in Illinois during the 1830s. Their paths then crossed many times over the next three decades. This is not to say that they were close friends in the years before the Civil War; rather, they were competitive colleagues. Browning's diary suggests that he considered the future president to be his inferior as a lawyer, political thinker, and even as an orator. For his part, Lincoln seemed on friendlier terms with Browning's wife, whom he consulted for romantic advice when he was a struggling bachelor in Springfield.

Yet once the war began and Browning was appointed to fill the U.S. Senate seat vacated in 1861 by the death of Stephen A. Douglas, the two men and their wives grew closer. Browning's wartime diary is filled with references to social outings and intimate conversations with the Lincolns. One scene in particular stands out. On Tuesday, July 15, 1862, Browning noted that he found the president in the White House library looking "weary, care-worn and troubled." Speaking as an old friend, he urged him to take better care of himself. "He held me by the hand," the senator wrote, "pressed it, and said in a very tender and touching tone, 'Browning, I must die sometime.'" Near the end of the conflict, however, the relationship between the two men grew strained. Browning's political views differed from Lincoln's, and after Browning left the Senate in 1864 to become a lobbyist, a new, awkward, commercial element crept into their association. Nonetheless, Browning served as a pallbearer at Lincoln's funeral in 1865. Later, he became secretary of the interior under President Andrew Johnson.

For further reading: Theodore C. Pease and James G. Randall, eds., *The Diary of Orville Hickman Browning, 1850–1881*, 2 vols. (Springfield: Illinois State Historical Society, 1925–1931).

Burnside, Ambrose (1824–1881, b. Liberty, Ind.)
Union general

Burnside was an important but widely criticized Union general who headed the Army of the Potomac from November 1862 until January 1863. Originally from Indiana, he graduated from the U.S. Military Academy at West Point (class of 1847). Indeed, Burnside replaced McClellan as head of the Army of the Potomac in early November 1862 when President Lincoln finally decided that he had had enough of the latter's delays and inactivity. Unfortunately, when Burnside attempted to demonstrate a more offensive-minded approach for the Army of the Potomac, the results were disastrous. At the Battle of Fredericksburg on December 13, 1862, Burnside's troops suffered more than twelve thousand casualties. Determined to prove his courage and resilience, the new general announced plans to lead a counterattack himself the next day, but other senior commanders convinced him that would be unwise.

From this point on, Burnside's subordinates demonstrated an increasing lack of confidence in the general. Eventually, Burnside demanded that several of them be reassigned. Lincoln obliged, but also decided to replace the beleaguered commander with one of his loudest critics, Gen. Joseph Hooker. Burnside, however, remained in the army and continued to serve until another battlefield catastrophe in 1864 led War Department officials to strip him of his active command. He never led troops again. After the war, he settled in Rhode Island, where he was elected governor and then U.S. senator. According to popular legend, however, Burnside's greatest legacy was his peculiar facial whiskers, which gave birth to the term *sideburns*.

For further reading: William Marvel, *Burnside* (Chapel Hill: University of North Carolina Press, 1991).

Butler, Benjamin F. (1818–1893, b. Deerfield, N.H.)
Union general

Nicknamed "The Beast" by outraged Southerners, Butler was a prominent general during the Civil War who demanded special attention from President Lincoln because he was also a leading Democratic politician from Massachusetts. Butler had actually supported Jefferson Davis for president at the 1860 Democratic national convention. Yet once war began, he rallied to the Union cause and offered to help raise troops for the fight. He was then assigned to Fortress Monroe, off the coast of Virginia, a location that attracted numerous fugitive slaves. Butler, who refused to return the slaves to their owners, labeled them "contraband of war," a phrase that the Northern press soon adopted. In 1862 President Lincoln ordered Butler to the city of New Orleans where he earned his nickname through his reputation for brutality and corruption. Before long, he was reassigned to Fortress Monroe, where he engaged in politics as much as combat.

In his postwar memoir, Butler insisted that Lincoln offered him an opportunity to serve as the vice presidential nominee on the 1864 Union ticket, but most historians do not accept this claim. Butler also alleged that Lincoln spoke with him about colonizing freed slaves as late as 1865, but again, most historians reject these anecdotes as false and transparently self-serving. After the war, Butler served in Congress, where he was one of the House managers of the impeachment proceedings against Andrew Johnson. He was also elected for one term as governor of Massachusetts.

For further reading: Hans L. Trefousse, *Ben Butler: The South Called Him Beast!* (New York: Twayne, 1957).

Cameron, Simon (1799–1889, b. Lancaster County, Pa.)
Secretary of war, 1861–1862; ambassador to Russia, 1862–1863

Within the broad canvas of nineteenth-century American politics, Cameron stands out as one of the more memorable rogues. Born into poverty, Cameron became one of the wealthiest men in Pennsylvania during the years before the war. Yet he never seemed to miss an opportunity to add to his wealth, even as a public servant, and accusations of profiteering, corruption, and opportunism haunted the Pennsylvania businessman/politician throughout his career.

Cameron's election to the U.S. Senate in 1857 was marred by what rival Thaddeus Stevens termed "wholesale private bribery." Significantly, however, none of these accusations ever led to full-scale criminal charges. Thus, when President-elect Lincoln considered naming Cameron to his cabinet in 1860 (reportedly as a reward for Cameron's support at the Republican national convention), he ignored loud complaints about his ally's shady ethics, pointing to the absence of concrete evidence. After weeks of wrangling, Cameron received the appointment as secretary of war, but his management of the overwhelmed War Department drew widespread criticism and new allegations of corruption. In January 1862, the president announced somewhat abruptly that Cameron would be named the new ambassador to czarist Russia. But if the move was designed to forestall public embarrassment for the administration, it failed. On April 30, 1862, the Republican-dominated House of Representatives ignored party loyalty and passed a formal censure resolution condemning Cameron's conduct in office.

Cameron was unhappy in St. Petersburg and returned to the United States by the end of the year. Most of his official time as ambassador actually had been spent in Harrisburg politicking. He lost a bid for the U.S. Senate in January 1863, but eventually rehabilitated his political stature by promoting himself as the administration's top ally in Pennsylvania.

For further reading: Erwin Bradley, *Simon Cameron, Lincoln's Secretary of War: A Political Biography* (Philadelphia: University of Pennsylvania Press, 1966).

Chandler, Zachariah (1813–1879, b. Bedford, N.H.)
U.S. senator (R-Mich.), 1857–1875

Like Simon Cameron, Zachariah Chandler was independently wealthy, but unlike the trouble-plagued secretary of war, Chandler seemed driven by his devotion to certain core political principles. Foremost among these principles was a belief in the evils of slavery, but not far behind was an equally tenacious conviction that the South deserved severe punishment for its role in bringing on the war. Here is where Chandler and Lincoln parted ways. The Michigan senator repeatedly criticized the president for what he considered to be the administration's half-hearted approach to the destruction of slavery and its supporting apparatus. Indeed, Chandler was part of a clique of Radical Republicans who harangued the president over topics such as military command, foreign affairs, emancipation, and Reconstruction.

Unlike other presidential critics, however, Chandler tried to maintain civil relations, and during the 1864 campaign, he even worked to reduce tensions between Radicals and the president in order to help guarantee the return of a Republican administration. Chandler, however, had an ambivalent, slightly patronizing attitude toward Lincoln that was evident in the immediate aftermath of the assassination. At one point, he claimed coldly that the "Almighty continued Mr. Lincoln in office as long as he was usefull [sic]." In fact, the Michigan senator at first actually welcomed the change of White House occupants, believing—mistakenly—that Andrew Johnson would pursue a tougher policy against the former rebels.

For further reading: Mary K. George, *Zachariah Chandler: A Political Biography* (East Lansing: Michigan State University Press, 1969).

Chase, Salmon P. (1808–1873, b. Cornish, N.H.)
Secretary of Treasury, 1861–1864; chief justice, U.S. Supreme Court, 1864–1873

Chase was a prominent antislavery attorney in the years before the Civil War, and in many ways was a far more well-known public figure than Abraham Lincoln. He served as both senator and governor in Ohio, but he made critical enemies along the way and did not receive the same level of enthusiastic local support at the 1860 Republican national convention that Lincoln enjoyed from the Illinois delegates. As secretary of Treasury in Lincoln's cabinet, Chase joined several of the president's former rivals in what turned out to be a fractious but talented collection of advisers. Chase himself demonstrated enormous ability, helping to finance the war effort through innovative reforms that included public war bonds, the federal government's first income tax, a nationwide banking system, and, perhaps the secretary's most enduring popular legacy, paper currency or the "greenback."

By the winter of 1863–1864, Chase had emerged as the Radical Republicans' leading choice for president and seemed intent on using the power of his office to further improve his prospects for the upcoming contest. Lincoln exhibited no outward signs of dismay over this stunning example of betrayal within his own cabinet. "I am entirely indifferent as to his success or failure in these schemes, " the president told John Hay, "so long as he does his duty as the head of the Treasury Department." Before long, the reasons for Lincoln's confidence became readily apparent. Chase was thoroughly outmaneuvered by the president and his allies, who had quietly organized an effective endorsement campaign at the state and local levels. When Chase's congressional supporters panicked and launched a harsh counterattack against the president, the result was a public relations fiasco, and the game was essentially over. Chase withdrew from the contest, and Lincoln secured his renomination easily.

After his selection by the Union coalition, Lincoln moved decisively to rid himself of the "mutual embarrassment" Chase had created. When the secretary threatened to resign during an argument over a minor patronage matter (one of several such threats he made over the years), the president eagerly accepted his resignation, and by the end of June 1864 his longtime rival was out of office. Lincoln, however, was not quite done with Chase. Over the next several months he dangled the prospect of an appointment to the Supreme Court before his ambitious rival as a way to ensure his loyalty during the election contest. Chase obliged, and in December 1864 Lincoln named him as chief justice to replace Roger B. Taney, the controversial pro-South jurist who had died in October. It was in this post that Chase presided over the impeachment trial of Andrew Johnson in the spring of 1868.

For further reading: John Niven, *Salmon P. Chase: A Biography* (New York: Oxford University Press, 1995).

Colfax, Schuyler (1823–1885, b. New York, N.Y.)
Member, U.S. House of Representatives (R-Ind.), 1855–1869; Speaker, House of Representatives, 1863–1869

Colfax served as Speaker of the House of Representatives during the second half of the Civil War. The election of Colfax to the Speakership in December 1863 was an "exciting canvass" in the words of White House aide John Hay. His principal opponent was Elihu B. Washburne, a Republican from Illinois who had known Lincoln for years and was closely associated with Gen. Ulysses S. Grant. The president stayed neutral in the contest, at least publicly, but according to Hay was "decidedly" for Colfax.

Journalist Noah Brooks observed that the Indiana politician was "a prime favorite with the members of the House, and with the newspapermen." Yet Colfax was not powerful. Youthful in his demeanor and eager, perhaps too eager for some, the Speaker was derisively nicknamed "Smiler" Colfax. Indeed, Colfax did not inspire fear and was dominated within the Republican caucus by Pennsylvania congressman Thaddeus Stevens.

In 1868 Colfax was elected vice president and served during the first term of the Grant administration. His years in the executive branch, however, were marred by allegations of corruption. Disenchanted, he left politics and became a successful public lecturer.

For further reading: Willard H. Smith, *Schuyler Colfax: The Changing Fortunes of a Political Idol* (Indianapolis: Indiana Historical Bureau, 1952).

Davis, David (1815–1886, b. Cecil County, Md.)
Justice, U.S. Supreme Court, 1862–1877; presidential adviser

Most historians credit wealthy attorney David Davis with being Lincoln's unofficial campaign manager during his 1860 presidential bid. In 1862 the president rewarded his old friend with an appointment to the Supreme Court, where Davis served as a relatively undistinguished associate justice until 1877, when he was elected to the U.S. Senate from Illinois. By that point in his career he had become a Democrat.

Originally from Maryland, Davis moved to Illinois in the 1830s and established a law practice. He became a prominent local politician and jurist. In 1848 he was elected judge of the Eighth Judicial Circuit in central Illinois—an important post because it was there that he developed a close association with the future president who was then a circuit-riding attorney.

Lincoln called Davis his "good friend" and suggested that he was "never associated with a better man." But in the years after Lincoln's assassination, Davis would admit that he often felt distant from his colleague. "Lincoln never confided to me anything," he recalled. Nevertheless, Davis proved invaluable to Lincoln's political career. He not only was a shrewd political manager, but also had considerable wealth, some of which he was willing to use to promote his ambitious associate. After the assassination in 1865, Davis was selected to manage the Lincoln estate. In that capacity he infuriated Mary Lincoln, whom he despised, but he grew close enough to Robert Lincoln to become almost like a surrogate father.

For further reading: Willard L. King, *Lincoln's Manager: David Davis* (Cambridge: Harvard University Press, 1960).

Dennison, William, Jr. (1815–1882, b. Cincinnati, Ohio)
Governor of Ohio, 1860–1862; postmaster general, 1864–1866

Dennison, a prominent Ohio Republican, served one term as governor of the state at the outbreak of the war and then won appointment as postmaster general near the end of the conflict. The wealthy businessman and attorney took an early stand against slavery. Then during the war, he played an important role behind the scenes and remained a loyal point of contact for President Lincoln in a state supposedly dominated by rival Salmon P. Chase. Pro-administration forces rewarded Dennison by naming him chairman of the Union convention in 1864 that nominated Lincoln for a second term. When Postmaster General Montgomery Blair was forced out of the cabinet to placate Radical Republicans in September 1864, the president tapped the former Ohio governor to head the nation's postal system.

For further reading: Mark E. Neely Jr., "Dennison, William, Jr.," *Abraham Lincoln Encyclopedia* (New York: McGraw-Hill, 1982), 81–82.

Douglas, Stephen A. (1813–1861, b. Brandon, Vt.)
U.S. senator (D-Ill.), 1847–1861; presidential candidate, 1860

During the 1850s Stephen Douglas was the dominant figure in American politics. Known as the "Little Giant," the short, stout senator from Illinois captivated public attention and antagonized political opponents as nobody else could. In many ways his fame made Lincoln's rise possible.

Born in Vermont, Douglas migrated to Illinois in the early 1830s. From an early age, he was fascinated with politics and enchanted by the example of Andrew Jackson. In the relatively new state of Illinois the ambitious, energetic young populist rose rapidly through the political ranks. Within a few years of his arrival, he was serving in the state legislature (with an equally ambitious young man named

Abraham Lincoln) and developing a reputation as a rising star in the Democratic Party. By the age of twenty-seven, Douglas was serving on the state supreme court. He entered Congress in 1843 and became a senator in 1847.

As chairman of the Senate committee on the territories, Douglas promoted policies to help white settlers develop the West, and, in doing so, proposed organizing the former territories of the Louisiana Purchase (1803) to help pave the way for the construction of a transcontinental railroad. Toward that end, he introduced the controversial Kansas-Nebraska Act (1854), which later shattered the delicate sectional balance by replacing old restrictions on the spread of slavery and helped to accelerate a political realignment that created the Republican Party and increased the likelihood of a civil war.

During the political campaigns of 1854 and 1858, Lincoln and Douglas held a series of debates that centered largely on the question of whether to extend slavery into the West. Douglas promoted what he called "popular sovereignty," or essentially allowing white settlers to decide for themselves. Lincoln argued that slavery was wrong and must be limited to only those states where it already existed. Their intense arguments defined the division within the North. Ultimately, Lincoln's view prevailed as he defeated Douglas and two other candidates in the presidential election of 1860. Douglas died shortly after Lincoln's inauguration.

For further reading: Robert W. Johannsen, *Stephen A. Douglas* (New York: Oxford University Press, 1973).

Douglass, Frederick (1818–1895, b. near Easton, Md.)
Abolitionist, reform journalist, civil rights activist
Frederick Douglass never quite made up his mind about Abraham Lincoln. Before the 1860 presidential election the former slave and abolitionist orator hardly thought twice about the Illinois politician, referring to him occasionally as "Abram." After the war began, Douglass grew increasingly impatient with the decisions of the administration, especially those about emancipation. He concluded harshly for the readers of his monthly newspaper that "the action of President Lincoln has been calculated in a marked and decided way to shield and protect slavery." Yet once the president finally endorsed black freedom as a Union war aim and allowed the army to accept black soldiers, Douglass softened his criticism. Then the president invited him to a private meeting at the White House—a personal and cultural milestone. "I felt big there," he boasted afterward. He noted that Lincoln treated him with respect and carefully solicited his support. Expecting to receive a commission as the Union army's first black officer, Douglass excitedly announced the suspension of his newspaper and prepared to head South to recruit former slaves. But the administration quietly retreated from any such offer, and Douglass remained in the North, embarrassed and alienated.

In 1864 Douglass opposed Lincoln's renomination and only reluctantly endorsed the president. Lincoln then tried again to cultivate the skeptical abolitionist. At a second meeting in August 1864 they discussed political strategy and the prospect of peace talks with the Confederacy. It was a tense discussion, but it left both men aware of how much they needed each other politically. The two met once more on March 4, 1865, after Lincoln's second inaugural. They shook hands and the president asked Douglass for his opinion on the day's speech, graciously claiming that there was "no man's opinion" he valued more. Impressed, the former critic called the address a "sacred effort."

Immediately after Lincoln's death, Douglass, overwhelmed by emotion, praised him as "emphatically the black man's president." Over time, however, he grew more ambivalent. In a famous speech delivered in 1876 Douglass described Lincoln as "preeminently the white man's President" who viewed freed slaves as "only his step-children." Lincoln himself left no written statement about Douglass, but, according to one presidential adviser, he considered the great black leader "one of the most meritorious men in America."

For further reading: William S. McFeely, *Frederick Douglass* (New York: Norton, 1991); and Michael Burlingame, "Emphatically the Black Man's President: New Light on Frederick Douglass, Abraham Lincoln and Black Freedom," White House Lecture Series, National Archives, December 10, 2001.

Eckert, Thomas T. (1825–1910, b. St. Clairsville, Belmont County, Ohio)
Chief, Telegraph Office
During the Civil War, Major Eckert headed the Telegraph Office in the War Department. It was there, according to one telegraph operator, that President Lincoln "spent more of his waking hours" than any other place except the White House, seeking the latest information on the progress of the war. Although he was supposed to begin each day reading a collection of recent telegraphic dispatches, Lincoln often found himself unable to wait for the news.

Because the War Department building was situated near the Executive Mansion, the president frequently strolled over to the Telegraph Office at odd hours to send and receive information directly. As a result, Eckert's office was the setting for many critical scenes of the war. It was there that Lincoln probably drafted some early versions of his emancipation policy. He paced anxiously around the office in July 1863 awaiting news from the battle at Gettysburg. The president worked with Eckert and other leading Union military officials to arrange the logistics for reinforcing besieged federal troops near Chattanooga, Tennessee, in September 1863. John Hay recorded in his diary the jovial atmosphere in the office as the president awaited results from the 1864 presidential balloting. After the war, Eckert helped to build the American telegraph industry, rising to the position of president of Western Union.

For further reading: David Homer Bates, *Lincoln in the Telegraph Office: Recollections of the U.S. Military Telegraph Corps during the Civil War* (1907; reprint, Lincoln: University of Nebraska Press, 1995).

Fessenden, William Pitt (1806–1869, b. Boscawen, N.H.)
U.S. senator (R-Maine), 1854–1864, 1865–1869; secretary of Treasury, 1864–1865
Pitt Fessenden was a towering figure in the U.S. Senate during the mid-nineteenth century. He chaired the Finance Committee for most of the war and served as Lincoln's secretary of Treasury once Salmon P. Chase resigned. During his nine months as head of Treasury—a position that the president practically forced him to take—Fessenden managed a new bond drive that raised over $500 million to help conclude the war effort.

Fessenden and Hannibal Hamlin, Lincoln's first vice president, were bitter rivals within the state's Republican Party. There was no doubt, however, that Fessenden wielded more power during the war era. According to Ben Perley Poore, a legendary Capitol Hill reporter, Fessenden "was really the leader of the Republican party in the Upper House" and a "statesman of great power and comprehensiveness." Lincoln observed that Fessenden knew " the ropes thoroughly," which in his opinion far overshadowed the latter's "quick & irritable temper."

For further reading: Charles Jellison, *Fessenden of Maine: Civil War Senator* (Syracuse: Syracuse University Press, 1962).

Forney, John W. (1817–1881, b. Lancaster, Pa.)
Newspaper editor; secretary of the U.S. Senate, 1861–1868
Forney, a Democratic newspaper editor from Pennsylvania, moved to the Republican fold on the eve of the Civil War and became one of President Lincoln's most trusted press contacts. During the wartime period, Forney built a virtual media empire, running daily newspapers in Washington and Pennsylvania and serving as secretary of the Senate. According to historian Mark E. Neely Jr., he "had influence as great as that of any editor." Still, his relationship with Lincoln was complicated, and Forney apparently felt unappreciated at times. John Hay recorded seeing him at home one night, drunk and belligerent, telling his guests that the president "never asked me [to support him] & don't want me." "When I go to see him," he added bitterly, "he asks me what is the last good joke I have heard." Yet he also believed that Lincoln was "the most truly progressive man of the age," and the night before Lincoln delivered the Gettysburg Address Forney berated a crowd of Pennsylvania residents for failing to understand the greatness of their national executive. "Do you know what you owe to that Great man?" he asked. "You owe your country—you owe your name as American citizens."

For further reading: John W. Forney, *Anecdotes of Public Men* (New York: Harper and Brothers, 1873); and Mark E. Neely Jr., "Forney, John W.," *Abraham Lincoln Encyclopedia* (New York: McGraw-Hill, 1982), 114–115.

Fox, Gustavus V. (1821–1883, b. Saugus, Mass.)
Assistant secretary of the navy, 1861–1866
Fox was a former naval captain who played a key role in the Fort Sumter crisis and later earned an appointment as assistant secretary of the navy. Montgomery Blair, Lincoln's first postmaster general and the brother-in-law of Fox's wife, introduced Fox to the president who found him to be "a live man." In particular, Fox offered Lincoln a solution to the vexing problem of how to resupply Fort Sumter, the federal outpost in Charleston harbor that was being cut off by the Confederates. Fox's plan, which involved sending a fleet of small boats at night to accomplish the mission—a much more palatable alternative than General in Chief Winfield Scott's plan calling for an army of twenty thousand men—actually failed. But Lincoln decided his new adviser was too ingenious to let slip away and convinced Secretary of the Navy Gideon Welles to bring him into the department for the remainder of the war.

For further reading: Ari Hoogenboom, "Gustavus Vasa Fox," American National Biography Online; www.anb.org.

Frémont, John C. (1813–1890, b. Savannah, Ga.)
Union general; presidential candidate, 1864

Best known as the first presidential candidate of the Republican Party, Frémont was a thorn in Lincoln's side during the Civil War, both as an ineffective and insubordinate general and as a potential spoiler in the 1864 election.

President Lincoln asked Frémont to head the Department of the West in 1861 and authorized him to take military action to keep Missouri, a slave state, in the Union. Frémont, who struggled to achieve his objective, decided in August that he needed to issue an emancipation decree aimed at rebel slave owners to help crush the revolt. Concerned about the delicate politics of other border states, Lincoln ordered Frémont to retract the decree. At first, the general declined to do so. Then the impetuous commander arrested Frank Blair, a loyal Missouri politician whose oldest brother Montgomery was Lincoln's postmaster general. Shortly thereafter, the president relieved Frémont of his command. "His cardinal mistake," Lincoln observed shrewdly, "is that he isolates himself."

In early 1862, the president reassigned Frémont to a post in western Virginia, but by the summer the contentious general resigned rather than take orders from Gen. John Pope, a junior commander. He made himself politically available in 1864 and was nominated by a group of radicals as a third-party presidential candidate. By this point, Lincoln had lost all respect for his would-be rival; nonetheless, he worried that Frémont could siphon away enough votes away to harm his reelection chances, so he apparently consented to a deal with the radicals that got the troublemaking general out of the race in exchange for the dismissal of Montgomery Blair from the cabinet. After the war, Frémont lost his fortune in bad business ventures and struggled to survive financially.

For further reading: John C. Frémont, *Memoirs of My Life* (1887; reprint, New York: Cooper Square Press, 2001).

Grant, Ulysses S. (1822–1885, b. Point Pleasant, Ohio)
Union general and general in chief; president, 1869–1877

Grant was the greatest Union general of the Civil War. He rose from colonel of the 21st Illinois Volunteers at the outset of the fighting to general in chief of all the Union armies. His was a remarkable story, made even more compelling by the utter irrelevance that the fantastic rise to prominence had on Grant's personal style. Not much for conversation, fancy dress, or the trappings of power, he embodied the no-nonsense spirit of the American prairie. He showed up at the 1864 reception held in honor of his elevation to lieutenant general in a dirty, rumpled uniform because he did not have time to change his clothes. President Lincoln appreciated this lack of pretension and deeply admired the general's tenacity on the battlefield. "I can't spare this man," he told visitors to the White House, "he fights."

The plainspoken, fighting general graduated from U.S. Military Academy at West Point (class of 1843) but never seemed entirely comfortable with military life. He began drinking heavily while in the service and by some accounts became an alcoholic. Grant resigned from the army in the mid-1850s and attempted to support his family by farming in his native Ohio. In 1860 he relocated to Galena, Illinois, and worked in a tannery operated by his family, until the outbreak of war compelled him to return to military service.

Assigned to the western theater of the war, Grant quickly earned a reputation as a hard fighter. He scored important victories during a period in early 1862 when good news was scarce for Union forces. His greatest tactical accomplishment as a general according to most military historians came in 1863 when he engaged in a successful campaign to wrest the town of Vicksburg from Confederate control. His efforts helped to secure the Mississippi River for the Union, thus dividing the rebel territory. Additional victories in Tennessee later that year further demonstrated Grant's brilliance as a field commander, leading to his promotion as general in chief.

During the final year of the war, Grant managed the federal war effort from the field. He traveled with the Army of the Potomac, under the command of George Meade, and engaged Gen. Robert E. Lee's Army of Northern Virginia in some of the war's bloodiest confrontations. Not everyone was pleased with his performance. Mary Lincoln called him "a butcher." Her husband, however, kept his faith in Grant and was rewarded with the final, hard-earned victory in the spring of 1865.

Grant capitalized on his military success by running for president in 1868. He served two scandal-ridden terms, thus squandering much of the goodwill he built for himself during the war. Yet at the end of his life, cut short by a bout with cancer, Grant again demonstrated his heroic potential by penning the most successful memoir of the war period, a wonderfully written, best-selling work that erased his personal debt and guaranteed his family a substantial income after his death.

For further reading: Ulysses S. Grant, *The Personal Memoirs of U.S. Grant*, 2 vols. (1886; reprint, New York: Penguin, 1999); and William S. McFeely, *Grant: A Biography* (New York: Norton, 1981).

Greeley, Horace (1811–1872, b. Amherst, N.H.)
Newspaper editor

Greeley was the eccentric editor of the *New York Tribune* during the Civil War era. He was influential but unreliable, tending to bounce around the political spectrum in disconcerting fashion. Lincoln considered Greeley "an old friend, whose heart I have always supposed to be right," but found himself frequently exasperated by the gadfly editor. During the summer of 1864, when Greeley harassed the administration about opening peace negotiations with the Confederacy, Lincoln turned the tables on his frequent critic and demanded that he meet with rebel emissaries himself. Reluctantly, the editor ventured up to Niagara Falls, where he and presidential assistant John Hay delivered a generic statement from the White House indicating that the abolition of slavery was a precondition for any discussions about reunion. For that reason, the talks went nowhere.

Like many other pundits, Greeley became more enamored with Lincoln after the latter's death in 1865. He ran for president himself in 1872 under Liberal Republican Party banner, but performed poorly at the polls against the Grant reelection juggernaut. Greeley died about a month later.

For further reading: Glyndon G. Van Deusen, *Horace Greeley, Nineteenth Century Crusader* (Philadelphia: University of Pennsylvania Press, 1953).

Halleck, Henry W. (1815–1872, b. Westernville, Oneida County, N.Y.)
Union general, general in chief
Nicknamed "Old Brains," Halleck, a respected scholar of military theory, served as general in chief and chief of staff of the Union armies during the Civil War. Halleck's first assignment in the conflict was to take over the Department of Missouri (originally known as the Department of the West), a region that had been under the command of the controversial Gen. John C. Frémont. In this position, Halleck supervised Gen. Ulysses S. Grant and helped coordinate the initial Union campaign to seize control of the Mississippi Valley. President Lincoln promoted Halleck to general in chief in July 1862, hoping that he would rejuvenate the stalled federal war effort in Virginia.

But then came the disastrous defeat of Gen. John Pope's forces at the Second Battle of Bull Run on August 29, 1862, and the subsequent rebel invasion of Maryland, which, according to the president, unnerved the scholarly commander. "[E]ver since that event," Lincoln recalled two years later, "he has shrunk from responsibility whenever it was possible." When a capable administrator was urgently needed at the Union army headquarters in Washington, Halleck's service proved valuable. Once Grant became general in chief in March 1864, his former superior reverted to the more suitable position of chief of staff and, according to most accounts, performed admirably in that lesser role. Halleck continued to hold commands in the armed forces until his death in 1872.

For further reading: Stephen E. Ambrose, *Halleck: Lincoln's Chief of Staff* (1962; reprint, Baton Rouge: Louisiana State University, 1996).

Hamlin, Hannibal (1809–1891, b. Paris, Maine)
Vice president, 1861–1865
Lincoln's first vice president, Hamlin was an antislavery politician who had little influence during his single term in office. Before the Civil War, Hamlin had served in both chambers of Congress where he gained expertise in commercial matters. He occupied his Senate seat while Lincoln was a member of the House, and recalled being once introduced to the Illinois congressman. The president, however, had no memory of this encounter.

Because the vice president was something of a nonentity and because they wished to balance the ticket, at their 1864 convention in Baltimore Unionists replaced Hamlin with Tennessee Democrat Andrew Johnson as Lincoln's vice presidential nominee. Historians continue to disagree over what role, if any, President Lincoln had in removing Hamlin. White House aide John Hay claimed in his diary that the president "positively refuses to give even a confidential suggestion in regard to Vice Prest. Platform or organization," yet others close to Lincoln later claimed that he authorized them to draft Johnson. Either way, Lincoln did not speak out to keep his vice president. After his service in the administration, Hamlin became chief customs collector at the port of Boston—a relatively lucrative patronage plum. Eventually, he returned to the Senate where he remained until 1881.

For further reading: H. Draper Hunt, *Hannibal Hamlin of Maine: Lincoln's First Vice-President* (Syracuse: Syracuse University Press, 1969).

Hay, John (1838–1905, b. Salem, Ind.)
Presidential aide

John Hay was a twenty-three-year-old bachelor and recent Ivy League graduate when he got a job as a principal aide to President Abraham Lincoln. After having grown up in Illinois, Hay knew the president's senior assistant, former journalist John G. Nicolay, and found himself assigned at the outset of the administration to help the overburdened secretary. At first, the two men were almost entirely responsible for managing the president's schedule and correspondence. It was a daunting task, made even more challenging by Lincoln's disorderly habits. Hay found the president "extremely unmethodical," noting, "it was a four-year struggle on Nicolay's part and mine to get him to adopt some systematic rules. He would break through every Regulation as fast as it was made."

Technically, Hay's salary was allocated from the Pension Office because congressional rules at that time dictated only a single presidential secretary. Ultimately, the White House staff grew with the addition of several other young male clerks borrowed mainly from the Interior Department. Still, Nicolay and Hay remained at the top of the small pyramid, and because of their relative youth and self-important demeanor, they subsequently became the objects of jealous sniping from other Washington insiders. "The President is affable and kind," reported one leading journalist, "but his immediate subordinates are snobby and unpopular."

Lincoln, however, treated Hay as a surrogate son. While his family was away for summer vacations, the president spent time with his young aide, reading Shakespeare to him until the latter fell asleep or gazing at stars with him from the Naval Observatory. Both Nicolay and Hay kept beds at the White House because they often worked so late, and the president, who had difficulty sleeping, frequently wandered into their rooms seeking the latest news or friendly conversation. The two aides even socialized with the first couple, dining and attending theater with them on several occasions. Hay was in awe of the man he labeled the "Tycoon," although he was less at ease with the first lady, whom he ridiculed as "the Hell-cat."

During the war, Hay was given a few political and military assignments of some importance in addition to his regular White House duties. He traveled to Union-occupied Florida, for example, to help register loyal voters in an unsuccessful wartime effort to reconstruct the state's government. He also ventured to Canada with newspaper editor Horace Greeley in a failed effort to conduct secret peace negotiations with the Confederates in the summer of 1864. He was scheduled to leave the White House and go to Paris in 1865 as part of the American mission when President Lincoln was shot. After the war, Hay served as a diplomat and ultimately gained his greatest fame as secretary of state under presidents William McKinley and Theodore Roosevelt. With Nicolay, Hay also coauthored the official ten-volume biography of the great president and history of the Lincoln administration. He was an accomplished writer, nineteenth-century political insider, and diplomat.

For further reading: Michael R. Burlingame and John R. Turner Ettlinger, eds., *Inside Lincoln's White House: The Complete Civil War Diary of John Hay* (Carbondale: Southern Illinois University Press, 1997).

Holt, Joseph (1807–1894, b. Hardinsburg, Ky.)

Judge advocate general, Union army

Holt played a supporting role in several critical episodes of the Civil War era. He was secretary of war under President James Buchanan and delivered the devastating letter from Robert Anderson, the Union commander at Fort Sumter, that provoked the chain of events that led to the outbreak of hostilities. Originally from Kentucky, Holt then lobbied strenuously to keep his native state from seceding.

President Lincoln ultimately rewarded his loyalty with appointment as judge advocate general of the Union army, a new position designed to help streamline the system of military prosecutions. In that position, Holt became enmeshed in political controversies regarding the military arrests of civilians and death sentences for deserters. In 1864 he produced an inflammatory report in the middle of the presidential contest that alleged a vast rebel-inspired conspiracy across parts of the North. During the Lincoln murder trials, he spearheaded the government's unsuccessful attempts to prove connections between the assassins and the Confederate high command.

The president liked and trusted Holt, calling him "a good man," but the latter's involvement in so many controversies, and his hyperaggressive Unionism, ultimately tarnished his reputation among both contemporaries and historians who believed that he bent the rules to satisfy his paranoia. Lincoln offered him a chance to become attorney general when Edward Bates resigned in 1864, but both men realized that he was too controversial for the post, and Holt gracefully declined. He maintained a high opinion of Lincoln. "The President is without exception," he stated, "the most tender-hearted man I ever knew."

For further reading: Mark E. Neely Jr., "Holt, Joseph," *Abraham Lincoln Encyclopedia* (New York: McGraw-Hill, 1982), 149–150.

Hooker, Joseph (1814–1879, b. Hadley, Mass.)

Union general

"Fighting Joe" Hooker commanded the Army of the Potomac for about six months in 1863. Hooker graduated from the U.S. Military Academy at West Point (class of 1837) and served with distinction in the Mexican War. He was retired from active duty when the Civil War broke out, but rejoined quickly and was eventually commissioned as a brigade commander in the nearly formed Army of the Potomac. During the first two years of the war, he progressed steadily in rank even as Gen. George B. McClellan, the original commander and organizer of the Potomac force, found himself cast aside by President Lincoln. After McClellan's replacement, Gen. Ambrose Burnside, also ran into trouble with the president, Hooker received command of the Army of the Potomac in January 1863. It was a strange decision, because he had been a public critic of the administration and its conduct of the war.

At first, Hooker won rave reviews for his energetic leadership. But Lincoln was less impressed and found him "over-confident." Lincoln's fears proved accurate as Hooker suffered one of the worst Union defeats of the war at the Battle of Chancellorsville, May 2–4, 1863. In the aftermath of the catastrophe, Lee and the Army of Northern Virginia began an invasion of Pennsylvania. Still sensitive over his failure in Virginia, Hooker quarreled with General in Chief Henry Halleck and even the president and was relieved of command just days before the Battle of Gettysburg. Hooker was then sent to the western theater of the war, where by some accounts he performed well, but where once again he quarreled with his superior officers. "Fighting Joe" Hooker spent the last year of the war heading the quiet Northern Department in the Great Lakes region, far removed from the combat.

For further reading: Walter H. Hebert, *Fighting Joe Hooker* (1944; reprint, Lincoln: University of Nebraska Press, 1999).

Johnson, Andrew (1808–1875, b. Raleigh, N.C.)
Vice president, 1865

Johnson had served as Lincoln's second vice president for little more than one month when an assassin's bullet elevated him to the presidency and controversy beyond his imagination.

Born in North Carolina to a poor family, Johnson moved to Tennessee as a teenager after his father died, and there he launched a successful career in business and politics. He became an ardent Jacksonian Democrat and won a series of offices, including a seat in Congress, the governorship, and a place in the U.S. Senate. He supported slavery but opposed secession, and became the only senator from a Confederate state to remain loyal to the Union during the Civil War.

In 1862 President Lincoln named Johnson as the military governor of Union-occupied Tennessee. During this period, Johnson finally abandoned his support for slavery, although he never accepted the principle of racial equality. His loyalty and evolution on emancipation were enough, however, to earn him a place on the Union presidential ticket in 1864 as Lincoln's running mate. The Lincoln-Johnson electoral slate won handily in November, but the Tennessee politician stumbled at the outset of the second term when he appeared drunk at the inauguration ceremonies because he had reportedly been taking whiskey to stave off the effects of an illness. In the immediate aftermath of Lincoln's assassination, Johnson made harsh statements about the need to punish the rebels, but his later actions suggested that he had a much more lenient view of the situation than the Radical Republicans on Capitol Hill. When he began ignoring legislation designed to curtail his authority, Republicans on Capitol Hill launched the impeachment proceedings that marred the end of his term.

For further reading: Hans L. Trefousse, *Andrew Johnson: A Biography* (New York: Norton, 1989).

Lamon, Ward Hill (1828–1893, b. Frederick County, Va.)
Marshal, District of Columbia

Hill Lamon and Lincoln were fellow lawyers on the Illinois circuit during the 1840s and 1850s, and Lamon participated in his friend's various political campaigns. During the Civil War, Lamon served as the marshal of the District of Columbia, a largely honorary position. As a practical matter, he acted as the chief presidential companion, accompanying Lincoln on trips and looking after his personal safety.

In that role, Lamon frequently warned the president to take greater security precautions. And a month after the 1864 election, he advised the president not to attend the theater without any bodyguards. On the night of April 14, 1865, Lamon was in Richmond on a special assignment for the president.

In the years after the war, Lamon sought to cash in on his acquaintance with Lincoln, buying materials from the president's former law partner and hiring a ghostwriter to help shape them into a biography. The project proved to be a financial and critical failure, however, and Lamon spent his final years bitterly recalling his absence from Washington on the one night the president needed him most.

For further reading: Ward H. Lamon (ghostwritten by Chauncy F. Black), *The Life of Abraham Lincoln from His Birth to His Inauguration as President* (1872; reprint, Lincoln: University of Nebraska Press, 1999); and Ward H. Lamon, *Recollections of Abraham Lincoln*, ed. Dorothy Lamon Teillard (1911; reprint, Lincoln: University of Nebraska Press, 1994).

Lincoln, Mary (1818–1882, b. Lexington, Ky.)
First lady

Mary Todd met Abraham Lincoln in 1839. They married in 1842 and had four boys in fairly regular order; Robert (1843), Edward (1846), William (1850), and Thomas (1853). Mary Lincoln was the first presidential wife known as the first lady. In her role as the nation's leading spouse, Mary Lincoln was a controversial figure, celebrated by some as a devoted wife and mother who visited the wounded soldiers at Union hospitals, but vilified by others as extravagant in her spending and compromised by her Southern relatives. After the war, she led a troubled life, mourning her husband and three of her sons, while struggling against what she perceived as a looming financial catastrophe. In her grief, she exhibited behavior that today would probably be recognized as signs of depression, but at the time was treated as evidence of her insanity. Her only surviving son, Robert, had her briefly committed to an asylum in 1875.

Like her husband, she was born in Kentucky, but unlike him, she was raised in a wealthy family dominated by a successful father. Her mother died when she was young, however, and Mary Todd felt estranged from her stepmother. As a young woman, she settled with her sister and brother-in-law who lived in Springfield, Illinois. The two forged their romantic bond over the exciting presidential contest of 1840. Unlike most women of the era, Mary Todd was fascinated by politics. Their courtship, however, foundered over various problems and fell apart for a time, but ultimately the two reconciled and married less than three years after their initial meeting.

In Springfield, they lived a relatively normal nineteenth-century middle-class life, raising children, buying and improving their home, hiring (and occasionally firing) domestic help, entertaining guests, and arguing over time spent apart. As Lincoln became more prominent, his wife became less vital to his life. This was especially true after he became president. There was still abundant evidence of their affection for each other, but also increasing signs of alienation. In addition, Mary Lincoln suffered chronic health problems connected in part to her four pregnancies and in part to a suspicious carriage accident in 1863. She also endured lingering emotional problems that developed in the aftermath of the death of two of her sons, Eddie (1851) and Willie (1862).

Their biggest source of friction during the war years came over money. Mary Lincoln outspent the White House budget on what the president dismissed as "flub-dubs" and apparently tried to hide that fact through creative accounting and various unethical maneuvers. She also surrounded herself with a loose assortment of characters, some of whom were prominent and respected social figures in Washington, but others who preyed on her insecurities, such as the spiritualists who promised to raise the dead and the sycophants who used her for access to the president. To make matters worse, she had relatives from Kentucky who visited the White House but refused to renounce the Confederacy, an embarrassment the president swallowed out of concern for his increasingly isolated wife.

Yet it would be a mistake to dismiss the first lady as merely a liability for President Lincoln. She frequently helped him with effective outreach toward difficult characters such as editor James Gordon Bennett or Sen. Charles Sumner. In 1864 she opened the White House to public social events just in time to coincide with the reelection campaign. Despite traveling away from Washington for long stretches of time, she remained engaged in the administration's struggles and committed to her husband.

She was left distraught and grief-stricken by the assassination. Her depression only worsened when her youngest son, Tad, died of a respiratory illness in 1871. She had a distant relationship with Robert, her eldest. He seemed incapable of understanding her fears and moods and conspired with his father's oldest friends to have her committed once they thought she had become too self-destructive and eccentric. A few months later, Mary Lincoln was released into the care of her sister and brother-in-law who once again offered her shelter in Springfield. She lived quietly with them until her death in 1882.

For further reading: Jean H. Baker, *Mary Todd Lincoln* (New York: Norton, 1987); and David Herbert Donald, *Lincoln* (New York: Simon and Schuster, 1995).

Lincoln, Robert (1843–1926, b. Springfield, Ill.)
Son

The president's eldest son, Robert, spent most of the wartime period as a student at Harvard, but finished the conflict as a junior staff officer with Gen. Ulysses S. Grant. He had a strained relationship with his father. The surprising ambivalence that Father Abraham exhibited toward his own son was on display quite early in their relationship. When Robert was about three, his father described him in a letter as "short and low" and noted coldly, "I some times fear he is one of the little rare-ripe sort, that are smarter at about five than ever after." Robert Lincoln later complained that he never had enough time with his father and felt like a stranger to him. But, as usual in such cases, the blame worked both ways. Robert spent most of the war years away from Washington, either at Harvard or traveling with his friends. On one of the rare nights in July 1863 when the presidential son was in town, he went to a party at Secretary of State William H. Seward's home. Meanwhile, his father was alone at the family retreat on the outskirts of Washington where he conducted "a talk on philology" with White House aide John Hay, who was only a few years older than Robert.

Lincoln's close relationship with Hay and other young men suggests that he enjoyed playing the paternal role and would have done more for Robert if he had let him. There is some evidence that he tried to provide for his son's needs. There is a revealing letter, for example, that the president sent to General Grant in early

1865. "My son, now in his twenty second year, having graduated at Harvard," he wrote delicately, "wishes to see something of the war before it ends." Then he requested a favor which he asked Grant to consider "as though I was not President, but only a friend." He wondered if Robert might "without embarrassment to you, or detriment to the service, go into your Military family with some nominal rank, I, and not the public, furnishing his necessary means?" It was a curious and poignant moment as the president tried to navigate between his presidential office and paternal instincts.

Robert Lincoln spent about six months on Grant's staff. He became an attorney after the war and married the daughter of a leading Republican senator from Iowa. Eventually, he gained prominence on his own as secretary of war, U.S. ambassador to Great Britain, and president of the Pullman Company. Yet despite years spent as the guardian of his father's reputation, he never seemed fully reconciled to his family legacy. Robert Lincoln remains the only member of the president's immediate family not buried at their crypt in Springfield. Instead, his body rests apart at Arlington National Cemetery.

For further reading: John S. Goff, *Robert Todd Lincoln* (Norman: University of Oklahoma Press, 1969).

Lincoln, Thomas (1853–1871, b. Springfield, Ill.)
Son

Tad Lincoln was eight years old when the Civil War began, boyish enough to enjoy the excitement of the conflict and relish the attention he received as the youngest occupant of the White House to that point. During the first year of the war, he and his older brother Willie wreaked pleasant havoc around the White House with their boisterous games and assorted pets. Then both boys became seriously ill in early 1862, but only Tad recovered. After Willie's death, Tad grew increasingly dependent on his parents. He often slept with one of them and did not dress himself. Typically he tagged along during trips or events as the only child among many adults. He refused to study with his tutor and was barely able to read and write by the end of the war. Adding to his isolation was a speech impediment that resulted from a cleft palate. Often the president and first lady were the only ones who could discern the meaning of his more excited conversations. Nonetheless, testimony from servants and troops assigned to the White House indicate that Tad was a favorite among them, despite his reputation for being somewhat spoiled and rambunctious. The little boy who paraded around in his "3rd Lieutenant's" uniform, begging his father to pardon the Thanksgiving turkey or spilling ink at the Telegraph Office, was usually too adorable to punish. The president, for one, never seemed to discipline him. "He was the most indulgent parent I ever knew," recalled one family friend.

Tad was at another theater across town on the night of his father's assassination. When informed of the news, his tutor rushed him back to the White House where a member of the staff recalled that the young boy was understandably overwhelmed. "They've killed papa dead," he cried. "They've killed papa dead." He then lived with his mother in Chicago and traveled with her around Europe until he was eighteen, when on their return to the United States he contracted a fatal respiratory ailment and died. The president had called Tad "a peculiar child," but doted on him regardless and showed him the kind of unrestrained affection he never appeared to indulge in with anyone else.

For further reading: Ruth Painter Randall, *Lincoln's Sons* (Boston: Little, Brown, 1955); and Jean H. Baker, *Mary Todd Lincoln* (New York: Norton, 1987).

Lincoln, William (1850–1862, b. Springfield, Ill.)
Son

Willie Lincoln was the president's third son and his second to die as a child. His death in February 1862, probably the result of typhoid fever contracted from the polluted White House water supply, hit both parents hard. "Well, Nicolay," the president cried out to his senior aide, John G. Nicolay, on the night of his son's death, "my boy is gone—he is actually gone!" It was an especially trying time for Lincoln, as he struggled to control his emotions while he bickered with Gen. George B. McClellan over Union military strategy. Mary Lincoln was too grief-stricken to attend the funeral, let alone conduct public business. She entered deep mourning over the son many considered her favorite. "I always found my hopes concentrating on so good a boy as he," she wrote sadly afterward. The poet N. P. Willis wrote a famous memorial to the presidential child which first appeared shortly after his funeral in the *Home Journal*. "His leading trait seemed to be a fearless and kindly frankness," Willis recounted. He then extolled the boy's precocious "self-possession" and described his amazement at watching him one afternoon interrupt his play outside the White House to bow "like a little ambassador" as the secretary of state and an entourage of foreign dignitaries rode by in an official carriage.

For further reading: Ruth Painter Randall, *Lincoln's Sons* (Boston: Little, Brown, 1955); and N. P. Willis, "The President's Son," *Home Journal;* reprint, *The Living Age,* April 19, 1862; "Making of America: Cornell University Library," cdl. library.cornell.edu/moa.

McClellan, George B. (1826–1885, b. Philadelphia, Pa.)
Union general, general in chief; presidential candidate, 1864

McClellan was arguably the most controversial Union general of the war, a figure of both incredible hubris and legitimate talent, who clashed with President Lincoln and ultimately challenged him in one of the most important electoral contests in American history. A graduate of the U.S. Military Academy at West Point (class of 1846), McClellan was trained as an engineer. He served in the Mexican War and along the western frontier, and then was sent as an observer of the Crimean War (1854), a conflict that foreshadowed some of the key tactical questions raised in an era of new weapons and improved transportation. In the mid-1850s McClellan left the military to serve as an executive of the Illinois Central Railroad, a major U.S. company that also employed Abraham Lincoln as a contract attorney.

The former army captain rejoined the military in 1861 and served initially in western Virginia, helping to secure key railroad junctions. He was then quickly elevated to the position of commander of the newly organized Army of the Potomac. Nicknamed "Young Napoleon" by the Northern press, McClellan proved to be a fantastic administrator and organizer who instilled a sense of professionalism in the novice federal troops. Even the president was impressed. In November he promoted the thirty-four-year-old to general in chief of the Union armies.

McClellan was a perfectionist who excelled more at preparing his troops than leading them. He had contempt for the president, who was inexperienced in military affairs, and resented his interference. His delays in launching an offensive eventually earned him criticism from Republicans on Capitol Hill, and by the spring of 1862 even tested Lincoln's abundant patience. Subsequently, under intense political pressure, McClellan led the Army of the Potomac on a flanking maneuver that brought federal troops to the Virginia peninsula in an attempt to reach Richmond via the shortest land route possible. But the extensive campaign proved to be a catastrophe with an enormous loss of life that unnerved the young general. On July 11, 1862, he had a tense encounter with President Lincoln in which it became clear that the two men had utterly opposite views of how best to conduct the war. The president then turned to another commander, but soon another battlefield disaster, at the Second Battle of Bull Run on August 29, 1862, required that he once again call McClellan into a leadership position. The rebels were threatening to invade Washington. The commander helped to rally forces to defend the capital and, after securing a copy of Robert E. Lee's battle plans, stopped his nemesis in the Maryland town of Sharpsburg (near Antietam Creek). However, when McClellan failed to pursue Lee's retreating forces vigorously enough for the president, he was relieved from active command for the final time in the war.

McClellan spent the next year and a half in semi-exile in New Jersey and New York, plotting a return to power. A loyal Democrat, he was selected as the nominee to face Lincoln in the 1864 presidential contest. But he lost by a landslide after a bitter campaign that saw his own party divided into two factions, and he officially resigned from the army. He was not done with politics, however. In 1877 McClellan was elected governor of New Jersey, a post he held for one term.

For further reading: Stephen W. Sears, *George B. McClellan: The Young Napoleon* (New York: Ticknor and Fields, 1988).

McCulloch, Hugh (1808–1895, b. Kennebunk, Maine)
Comptroller of the currency, 1863–1865; secretary of Treasury, 1865–1869
McCulloch served as the first comptroller of the currency in the Lincoln administration—an irony because he supported the gold standard and opposed national banks—and then was named secretary of Treasury in March 1865. Originally from Maine, McCulloch was an Indiana banker with a sharp tongue and rigid views on business affairs. Like President Lincoln, he described himself as "an original Henry Clay Whig," meaning that he generally supported any procommerce policies. He became a Republican before the Civil War and joined the administration in 1863. Although McCulloch served President Lincoln as Treasury secretary for only one month in 1865, he remained in office under President Andrew Johnson until 1869. He returned to Treasury in late 1884, serving the final few months as secretary in the Chester A. Arthur administration.

For further reading: Hugh McCulloch, "Memories of Some Contemporaries," *Scribner's Magazine*, 4 (September 1888): 279–295; "Making of America: Cornell University Library," cdl.library.cornell.edu/moa.

McDowell, Irvin (1818–1885, b. Columbus, Ohio)
Union general
McDowell was the Union commander at the disastrous First Battle of Bull Run on July 21, 1861. He graduated from U.S. Military Academy at West Point (class of 1838) and served in the Mexican War. At the outset of the Civil War, McDowell received instructions to organize Union forces in northeastern Virginia for an early offensive toward Richmond, but he complained that he needed more time to prepare for battle. By July the president had lost his patience and ordered an assault. McDowell later put together a reasonably sophisticated battle plan, but poor intelligence, hot weather, and inexperience conspired to delay his doomed assault. After the defeat, McDowell was reassigned as a subordinate to Gen. George B. McClellan within the new Army of the Potomac. The hapless general continued to lead troops in battle until late August 1862, when his forces were involved in the defeat at the Second Battle of Bull Run on August 29. Following these debacles, McDowell was reassigned to duty on the West Coast.

For further reading: John T. Hubbell, "Irvin McDowell," American National Biography Online; www.anb.org.

Meade, George G. (1815–1872, b. Cadiz, Spain)
Union general
After growing up in Pennsylvania, Meade was asked to help defend the Keystone State from a Confederate invasion in 1863. He served as the fourth commander of the Army of the Potomac from June 1863 until the end of the Civil War. His most famous accomplishment was his successful leadership of Union forces at the Battle of Gettysburg, July 1–3, 1863, a confrontation that took place only days after he assumed command of the army. His achievement at Gettysburg, however, was diminished by his failure to aggressively pursue Gen. Robert E. Lee's Army of Northern Virginia as it retreated. President Lincoln initially was enraged by this missed opportunity, but in a few days he calmed down. He told a Union general less than a week later that he "now felt profoundly grateful to Meade & his army for what they had done, without indulging in any criticisms for what they had not done." He graciously called Meade "a brave & skillful officer & a true man." During the final year of the conflict, Meade was eclipsed by General in Chief Ulysses S. Grant, who traveled with the Army of the Potomac and essentially directed its movements.

For further reading: Freeman Cleaves, *Meade of Gettysburg* (Norman: University of Oklahoma Press, 1960).

Meigs, Montgomery C. (1816–1892, b. Augusta, Ga.)
Union general
Meigs, who was quartermaster for the Union army during the Civil War, has received a great deal of credit from most historians for his administrative skills. Born in Georgia, he grew up in Philadelphia and graduated from the U.S. Military Academy at West Point (class of 1836).

Before the outbreak of the rebellion, Meigs, an engineer, was assigned to the build the Capitol dome. Later, during the Fort Sumter crisis, he was sent on a special mission to reinforce Fort Pickens, another endangered federal outpost in Florida. His diary during this period offers critical evidence about President Lincoln's decision-making process. Meigs was later promoted, but he specifically requested assignment in Washington.

As quartermaster general, Meigs spent nearly $1.5 billion during the course of the war. Yet despite his impressive reputation, evidence suggests that Lincoln developed a dim view of Meigs's personal courage. In 1864 the president told John Hay "a queer story" about the quartermaster. He said that during the summer of 1862, while the Army of the Potomac remained stationed on the Virginia peninsula, Meigs, apparently energized by some rumor, woke the president one night, urging him to evacuate the troops and kill the horses "as they c[oul]d not be saved" at their location. Lincoln was appalled by his lack of nerve. "Thus often," he told his young aide, "I who am not a specially brave man have had to sustain the sinking courage of these professional fighters in critical times."

For further reading: Russell F. Weigley, *Quartermaster General of the Union Army: A Biography of M.C. Meigs* (New York: Columbia University Press, 1959).

Nicolay, John G. (1832–1902, b. Essingen, Bavaria)
Presidential aide

Nicolay, the journalist who became Lincoln's top White House aide, primarily managed the president's schedule and delivered messages to Congress, but he also performed a wide variety of sensitive political assignments, such as negotiating treaties with western Indian tribes and sorting out patronage disputes at the New York City Customs House. Nicolay and his fellow secretary, John Hay, worked long hours and forged a close bond. Hay, younger and more easygoing, called his friend "Nico."

Journalist Noah Brooks, who was scheduled to replace the burned-out Nicolay in 1865, called the presidential assistant a "grim Cerberus of Teutonic descent." Lincoln called him "entirely trustworthy." Unlike John Hay, Nicolay did not keep a regular diary, but he did send evocative letters to his fiancée and future wife, Therena Bates, that are now an indispensable source for analyzing life in the Lincoln White House. After the war, Nicolay served as an American diplomat in Paris and as marshal of the U.S. Supreme Court. The bulk of his energy, however, was dedicated to producing, along with John Hay, a ten-volume official biography of Lincoln that was finally published in 1890.

For further reading: Michael Burlingame, ed., *With Lincoln in the White House: Letters, Memoranda, and Other Writings of John G. Nicolay, 1860–1865* (Carbondale: Southern Illinois University Press, 2000).

Pope, John (1822–1892, b. Louisville, Ky.)
Union general

Pope was a Union general in the middle of what might have been the most dangerous period of the war for the Northern side. In late August 1862, Confederate forces routed troops led by Pope at the Second Battle of Bull Run and threatened to capture Washington. Gen. Robert E. Lee then launched an invasion through Maryland, confident that success would compel European powers to intervene in the conflict. Only a massive and bloody counterattack by federal troops at the Battle of Antietam on September 17, 1862, prevented what could have been a devastating catastrophe. Furious over his defeat, Pope blamed Gen. George B. McClellan and other Union commanders whom he considered insubordinate and disloyal. After graduating from the U.S. Military Academy at West Point (class of 1842), Pope served in the Mexican War as a topographical engineer. He remained in the army until the Civil War, when he was promoted to the rank of brigadier general and assigned to the Department of the West. He led troops into battle in Missouri and Mississippi before President Lincoln requested his transfer to the eastern theater of the war in mid-1862. After the debacle at Second Bull Run, Pope was reassigned to put down a Sioux uprising in the Minnesota and Dakota territories. Despite feeling betrayed by subordinates and mistreated by his superiors, he continued to serve in the army until his retirement in 1886.

For further reading: Peter Cozzens and Robert I. Girardi, eds., *The Military Memoirs of General John Pope* (Chapel Hill: University of North Carolina Press, 1998).

Scott, Winfield (1786–1866, b. Petersburg, Va.)
Union general
Scott was the most important military figure in the United States during the first half of the nineteenth century. He joined the army in 1808 and served as general in chief for twenty years, from 1841 to 1861. An imposing figure in many ways, Scott was six feet, five inches tall and probably weighed close to three hundred pounds by the end of life. His greatest achievement came during the Mexican War when he planned and led the dramatic assault on Veracruz and the subsequent campaign to capture Mexico City. He had a less successful detour in politics. In 1852 he was the final presidential nominee of the Whig Party, losing badly to Democrat Franklin Pierce.

At the outbreak of the Civil War, Scott was in his mid-seventies. President Lincoln respected his experience but rejected much of the aging general's conservative advice and quickly began to rely on younger, more aggressive commanders.

After Lincoln named thirty-four-year-old George B. McClellan to set about organizing the massive new fighting force, the disgruntled senior figure soon retired. The president did not forget about Scott, however. In June 1862, he made the extraordinary decision to travel to West Point, New York, to consult with the retired legend during an especially difficult period of the war. Scott published his memoirs during the war and lived to see the Union triumph.

For further reading: John S. D. Eisenhower, *Agent of Destiny: The Life and Times of General Winfield Scott* (New York: Free Press, 1997).

Seward, William H. (1801–1872, Florida, Orange County, N.Y.)
Secretary of state, 1861–1869
Secretary of state throughout the entire Lincoln administration, Seward was one of the founders of the Republican Party and a dynamic figure in mid–nineteenth-century American politics. He had been the frontrunner for the 1860 Republican

presidential nomination after a long career in public life that included two terms as governor (1839–1843) and nearly a dozen years in the U.S. Senate (1849–1861). He lost to Lincoln on the convention's third ballot.

Unlike Lincoln, who had few close attachments, Seward's career is impossible to analyze without reference to Thurlow Weed, the legendary newspaper editor and power broker. The two men forged a critical partnership—as anti-Masons, Whigs, and ultimately as Republicans—that dominated New York politics from the 1830s through the Civil War era. Despite his triumph over the duo in 1860, the president seemed slightly in awe of their alliance, once joking with the secretary that he had been previously advised to "do like Seward does—get a feller to run you."

The president certainly worked hard to cultivate both figures during the course of the war. Seward, for his part, proved almost infallibly loyal once he accepted the idea that the president was truly in charge of the administration.

At first, this usually self-evident fact was not clear. In the midst of the Fort Sumter crisis, the secretary sent the president a harsh memorandum that criticized the administration for being "without a policy either domestic or foreign." Lincoln ignored the slight and soon demonstrated that he was in command of the situation. "I saw a great while ago that the President was being urged to do many things," Seward recalled afterward. But instead of "running and shouting for the coming events," he admitted that he learned "to stay behind" and "share with him the criticism and the risk and to leave the glory to him and to God."

As for Seward, he certainly shared the criticism, becoming a lightning rod for disgruntled Radical Republicans who attempted to have him removed from the cabinet in late 1862. Although foreign affairs generally came second to the domestic rebellion, several tense moments between the United States and the European powers tested Seward's abilities. In addition, as secretary of state he was initially placed in charge of monitoring treason within the North—a controversial assignment he gratefully ceded to the War Department after 1862. And finally, he was a target of the Booth conspirators and narrowly escaped his own death in 1865.

The secretary continued in office under President Andrew Johnson, most notably engineering the purchase of Alaska from the Russians. His remaining years proved personally difficult, however, as he recovered slowly from his own injuries and lost both his wife and his only daughter. "I have always felt that Providence dealt hardly with me in not letting me die with Mr. Lincoln," he reportedly said. "My work was done, and I think I deserved some of the reward of dying there."

For further reading: John M. Taylor, *William Henry Seward: Lincoln's Right Hand* (New York: HarperCollins, 1991).

Smith, Caleb B. (1808–1864, b. Boston, Mass.)
Secretary of the interior, 1861–1862
Smith was secretary of the interior in the Lincoln administration from March 5, 1861, to December 31, 1862. After serving with Abraham Lincoln in the House of Representatives for two years in the late 1840s as the congressman from Indiana, Smith worked as an attorney and became a leading Republican in Indiana, along with Rep. Schuyler Colfax and future governor Henry Lane. When it came time to choose a cabinet, the president-elect wanted someone from Indiana to help cement the regional balance of his team, and Smith was simply the most available

candidate. Lane had already been elected governor, and Colfax was young. With Smith, Lincoln reportedly said, "[I]t is now or never."

The new secretary proved to be a conservative but extremely quiet voice in the cabinet. Historian Mark E. Neely Jr. dismisses him as "colorless and not well-liked." Smith suffered from poor health and became disenchanted as the president moved toward an embrace of emancipation. He was a strong supporter of colonization for freed blacks and felt increasingly uncomfortable with the direction of the administration. "Smith has no faith & no hope," David Davis reported, noting that the secretary attacked the president for consulting his cabinet "as critics only" and not for serious strategic advice. He announced his resignation at the end of 1862 and managed to convince the president to appoint him to a federal judgeship—a post he held until his death in 1864.

For further reading: Mark E. Neely Jr., "Smith, Caleb B.," *Abraham Lincoln Encyclopedia* (New York: McGraw-Hill, 1982), 282.

Speed, James (1812–1887, b. Jefferson County, Ky.)
Attorney general, 1864–1866
A Kentucky Unionist and cautious antislavery politician, Speed served as attorney general in the Lincoln administration after the resignation of Edward Bates in late 1864. Speed's brother Joshua had been Abraham Lincoln's closest friend when the two men were young bachelors living together above a grocery store in Springfield, Illinois. Joshua Speed claimed that his brother was appointed "as a representative man of the party for freedom in the slave States." After Lincoln's assassination, the attorney general endorsed the idea of trying the primary conspirators in a military tribunal, but decided that Jefferson Davis (who was never convicted) should appear before a federal civilian court in Virginia. He claimed that Lincoln was "the best and greatest man I ever knew."

For further reading: James Speed, *James Speed: A Personality* (Louisville, Ky.: Press of J. P. Morton, 1914).

Stanton, Edwin M. (1814–1869, b. Steubenville, Ohio)
Secretary of war, 1862–1868
A prominent attorney, Stanton served three presidents during the Civil War era. Attorney general during the final months of James Buchanan's administration, he returned to government service in early 1862 as Lincoln's second secretary of war, a position he continued to hold under President Johnson until his dismissal in 1868 helped to set off the impeachment crisis. Although he was originally from Ohio, Stanton became a nationally known attorney who operated out of Pittsburgh and Washington, D.C. In 1855 Lincoln and Stanton served together on an important legal case, but the future secretary of war considered the future president to be out of his depth and treated him rudely.

Stanton was a Democrat who supported the Southern Democratic presidential candidate, John C. Breckinridge, in 1860, but remained utterly devoted to the Union. He was not, however, equally devoted to incoming president Lincoln.

Yet within a year Lincoln offered him the most important cabinet post in the government and he accepted. Stanton replaced Simon Cameron, a corrupt Pennsylvania politician who was ill-equipped to deal with the massive demands of wartime mobilization. Stanton lacked Cameron's political skills, but he had abundant administrative and bureaucratic talents. Under his direction, the War Department operated more efficiently and honestly.

First and foremost, Stanton was intimidating. Noah Brooks called him "opinionated, implacable, intent, and not easily turned from any purpose." The journalist claimed that newspapermen hated him because the secretary was "inexorable as death, and as reticent as the grave." Many people in Washington apparently detested Stanton. John Usher, the second interior secretary, called him "rude and offensive" and refused to speak to him. Part of Stanton's imposing presence was physical. He was short and heavy with a long, thick beard that gave him, according to Gen. John Pope, "a shaggy, belligerent sort of look."

What truly baffled Washington insiders was Stanton's close relationship with President Lincoln. Despite his incivility and his poor first impressions of the president, Stanton developed a closer working partnership with Lincoln than any other member of the cabinet. White House staffer John Hay wrote Stanton that Lincoln "loved you and trusted you." Mary Lincoln believed that the pair was "warmly attached to each other." Robert Lincoln, who admired Stanton greatly, reported that "for ten days after my father's death in Washington, he called every morning on me in my room, and spent the first few minutes of his visits weeping without saying a word."

For further reading: Benjamin P. Thomas and Harold M. Hyman, *Stanton: The Life and Times of Lincoln's Secretary of War* (New York: Knopf, 1962).

Stevens, Thaddeus (1792–1868, b. Danville, Vt.)
Member, U.S. House of Representatives (R-Pa.), 1849–1853, 1859–1868

Called "the despotic ruler of the House" by a leading wartime journalist, "Old Thad" Stevens, a representative from Lancaster, Pennsylvania, was the leader of the Radical Republicans in Congress. During the Civil War, he chaired the all-important House Ways and Means Committee and loomed large as a factor behind the creation of the controversial congressional Joint Committee on the Conduct of the War. He believed in the abolition of slavery, equality for blacks, and punishment for white Southerners. A frequent critic of the Lincoln administration, Stevens at one point claimed that the president's ineffective policies, especially on emancipation, deserved "the condemnation of the community." He was a famously irascible figure, "argumentative, sardonic, and grim," according to one Washington correspondent. Born with a deformed foot, Stevens walked with a noticeable limp. "He was sturdy, well built," reported the newspaperman, "with dark-blue and dull-looking eyes, overhanging brow, thin, stern lips, a smooth-shaven face, and wore a dark-brown wig."

After the war, an aging, ill Stevens led the campaign to impeach Andrew Johnson. Even after Johnson was acquitted, Stevens tried to have the charges reinstated, but he died before making any headway. In his final act of defiance against white conventions, Stevens had himself buried in the only cemetery in Lancaster without restrictions on race.

For further reading: Hans L. Trefousse, *Thaddeus Stevens: Nineteenth Century Egalitarian* (Chapel Hill: University of North Carolina Press, 1997).

Sumner, Charles (1811–1874, b. Boston, Mass.)
U.S. senator (R-Mass.), 1851–1874

Massachusetts-born and Harvard-educated with an impressive transatlantic network of friends, Sumner was a Yankee intellectual who spoke out eloquently against slavery and chaired the Senate Committee on Foreign Relations during the Civil War era. In 1856 Sumner, a Republican, lashed out against proslavery Southerners and their role in undermining the rule of law in the territory of Kansas. Outraged about Sumner's vivid rhetoric, which vilified South Carolina senator Andrew Butler and likened slavery to prostitution, Democratic congressman Preston Brooks, who was Butler's cousin, stormed into the Senate chamber and, using his walking cane, beat the Massachusetts orator senseless. Sumner did not fully recover for three years. The assault contributed to the exacerbation of sectional hostilities and the coming of the Civil War.

The Massachusetts senator was unpopular with many of his colleagues, who often found him arrogant and distant. In 1862 Sen. Orville Browning recorded in his diary a private conversation he had about Sumner while on a train ride with some other members. The small group, which included both radicals and conservatives, agreed that Sumner was "cowardly, mean, malignant, tyranical [sic], hypocritical, and cringing and toadyish to every thing, and every body that had the odor of aristocracy."

The year after the war ended, Sumner married for the first time at the age of fifty-five. He was divorced within two years. First elected to the Senate in 1851, Sumner was the longest continuously serving member of that body when he died in 1874.

For further reading: David Donald, *Charles Sumner and the Coming of the Civil War* (1960; reprint, Chicago: University of Chicago Press, 1981); and David Donald, *Charles Sumner and the Rights of Man* (New York: Knopf, 1970).

Taney, Roger B. (1777–1864, b. Clavert County, Md.)
Chief justice, U.S. Supreme Court, 1835–1864

Chief justice of the United States from 1835 to 1864, Taney was a controversial figure from the time of his appointment through the final years of his tenure in office. In his home state of Maryland, Taney gained a reputation as one of the state's top lawyers. He married Anne Key, sister of national anthem composer Francis Scott Key.

Taney started out in local politics as a Federalist. Ultimately, however, he became a Jacksonian Democrat who joined the first Jackson administration as attorney general. In 1833 President Jackson fired his secretary of Treasury and offered the position to Taney, who accepted. But, with the nation in the midst of the fierce "Bank War," he found himself the object of senatorial censure and was not confirmed. Jackson then nominated the Maryland attorney to serve on the Supreme Court, but the Whig-dominated Senate again balked. When legendary chief justice John Marshall died in 1835, President Jackson once again submitted Taney's name, and this time the Senate reluctantly approved his choice.

Taney was involved in several critical cases, but the one decision that towered above all the others in importance was *Scott v. Sanford* (1857). In this case, he drafted a lengthy majority decision that denied blacks could be citizens, rejected congressional authority to limit slavery in the territories, and labeled the Missouri Compromise of 1820 as unconstitutional. It was a breathtaking verdict that scandalized Northern Republicans, including Abraham Lincoln, and contributed to the coming of the Civil War.

Taney and Lincoln clashed almost as soon as the war broke out. Taney objected to the president's decision to suspend habeas corpus, announcing from the circuit in *Ex parte Merryman* (1861) that only Congress could take such drastic action. Lincoln ignored the ruling, which did not have the weight of the full Supreme Court behind it, and Congress declined to back the controversial jurist.Taney stopped making customary social calls at the White House and reportedly began preparing to issue decisions undoing several key policy changes affected by the Republican-controlled Congress. However, he lacked the energy and the votes to stop the administration and died before there was another major constitutional confrontation between the executive and judicial branches. Lincoln attended memorial services for Taney, but did not go to the funeral. He replaced him with Salmon P. Chase, a Radical Republican whose advocacy for emancipation could not have been more at odds with the views of the proslavery justice.

For further reading: Don E. Fehrenbacher, *The "Dred Scott" Case: Its Significance in Law and Politics* (New York: Oxford University Press, 1978); and Sandra F. Van Burkleo and Bonnie Speck, "Roger Brooke Taney," American National Biography Online; www.anb.org.

Usher, John P. (1816–1889, b. Brookfield, Madison County, N.Y.)
Secretary of the interior, 1863–1865

Usher began the Civil War as assistant secretary of the interior and succeeded Caleb Smith as secretary in 1863. Usher's previous government experience consisted of a single term in the Indiana state legislature and a few months as Indiana attorney general. Once in Washington, Usher impressed few people. Salmon P. Chase dismissed him as a "nobody." Journalist Noah Brooks wickedly described him as "fair, fat, fifty and florid," although he credited the Indiana attorney with being "a good worker" and "an able lawyer." One of his few appearances within the Hay diaries concerned an embarrassing mix-up. Usher apparently attempted at the last minute to change a few paragraphs related to the Interior Department in the president's 1863 annual message, a critical document that included his new policy on Reconstruction. The result was that the secretary "spoiled eight pages of matter & forced the Message over till the next day," a maddening miscue that delayed an important announcement. After the war, Usher moved to Kansas and was eventually elected mayor of Lawrence.

For further reading: Elmo R. Richardson and Alan W. Farley, *John Palmer Usher: Lincoln's Secretary of Interior* (Lawrence: University of Kansas Press, 1960).

Vallandigham, Clement L. (1820–1871, b. New Lisbon, Ohio)
Democratic Party leader; member, U. S. House of Representatives (D-Ohio), 1858–1863

Vallandigham was the foremost Northern critic of the Lincoln administration during the Civil War. A three-term Democratic congressman from Ohio, he was considered leader of the antiwar faction known as the "Peace Democrats" or, more derisively, as the "Copperheads." When his district around Dayton, Ohio, was reapportioned in 1862, he was unable to hold the seat.

The next year Vallandigham maneuvered to run for governor of Ohio, and, according to most historical accounts, intentionally attempted to provoke federal authorities into arresting him. Regardless of Vallandigham's true strategy, Union commander Ambrose Burnside, fresh out of his disastrous experience as head of the Army of the Potomac, determined that the Copperhead orator was a threat and had him detained. The situation created a political problem for President Lincoln, who did not want to elevate the profile of the outgoing congressman, and so he ordered that Vallandigham be exiled to the Confederacy. The irrepressible agitator won the Democratic nomination for governor of Ohio anyway and subsequently campaigned from the South and Canada. His overwhelming defeat in October 1863 suggested that the appeal of the antiwar movement was waning and helped to generate early momentum for Lincoln's reelection bid.

When Vallandigham returned to the United States in 1864 and played an active role in the presidential contest, the administration studiously ignored his violation of the exile decree. After the war Vallandigham continued unsuccessfully to pursue political office. He died from a accidental self-inflicted gunshot wound.

For further reading: Frank L. Klement, *The Limits of Dissent: Clement L. Vallandigham and the Civil War* (1970; reprint, New York: Fordham University Press, 1998).

Wade, Benjamin F. (1800–1878, b. Feeding Hills, Mass.)
U.S. senator (R-Ohio), 1851–1869

"I am a Radical and I glory in it," claimed Sen. Ben Wade, one of the most powerful figures in the wartime Congress. Wade, an antislavery attorney, first entered the Senate in 1851. During the rebellion, he chaired the Joint Committee on the Conduct of the War, a vehicle frequently used by Radical Republicans in Congress to harass the administration. Wade was a persistent critic of the president, especially over the slow pace of the emancipation policy, but he did not violently break with Lincoln until 1864 when they clashed over Reconstruction policy.

After the war, Wade became even more bitterly entangled in the politics of Reconstruction. Along with other Radicals, he opposed President Andrew Johnson's policies and supported impeachment. What distinguished Wade's actions, however, was that if Johnson had been removed in 1868, the retiring Ohio senator would have become president. There was no vice president then serving under Johnson (who had succeeded to the presidency after Lincoln's assassination) and Wade was president pro tempore of the Senate—next in the line of succession. Johnson escaped conviction by one vote, and "Bluff" Ben Wade returned to Ohio where he practiced law and continued to follow politics, although now from the sidelines.

For further reading: Hans L. Trefousse, *Benjamin Franklin Wade: Radical Republican from Ohio* (New York: Twayne Publishers, 1963).

Weed, Thurlow (1797–1882, b. Greene County, N.Y.)
Newspaper editor and lobbyist

For more than three decades, Thurlow Weed edited the *Albany Evening Journal,* but his influence extended far beyond a single newspaper in upstate New

York. He was a shrewd organizer of political parties, from the Anti-Masons to the Whigs to the Republicans. In addition, he was a noted nineteenth-century influence peddler and lobbyist who wielded power with aplomb. But most important, Weed was a political insider who understood his own limitations and found his public alter ego in William H. Seward, the influential governor, U.S. senator, and secretary of state.

During the Civil War, Weed engaged in a delicate dance with President Lincoln as the two men, virtual strangers before the conflict, immediately recognized their usefulness to each other and attempted to build a relationship. They worked together efficiently during the 1860 contest—Weed helped to raise and distribute critical funds for the campaign—and, despite some glitches, found common ground in the formation of the cabinet and initial mobilization for war in 1861. However, as the president made a series of tough choices about patronage jobs and as the administration moved further away from Weed's essentially conservative outlook, tensions between the two men increased. By 1863 Lincoln seemed nearly panicked that he had permanently alienated the New York power broker. "I have been brought to fear recently that somehow, by commission or omission, I have caused you some degree of pain," he wrote in October. Weed responded coolly, expressing annoyance with the president for apparently referring to his longstanding political battles with *New York Tribune* editor Horace Greeley as a "personal quarrel." "My quarrels' are in no sense *personal*," he wrote defensively, "I am without personal object or interests." Then with a touch of braggadocio, he added, "I have done something in my day towards Electing Presidents and Governors, none of whom found me an expensive Partizan."

Weed left the *Evening Journal* in 1863, reportedly to help build a political alliance between War Democrats and Republicans, but it seems in retrospect that he was simply becoming more involved in business ventures. He relocated to New York City and soon became a millionaire. He continued to help the Lincoln administration behind the scenes, raising funds, cutting deals, and performing a variety of political assignments, but he lost much of his past influence. In August 1864, he told Lincoln that his reelection was "an impossibility" unless he opened peace negotiations with the Confederacy. The president considered, but ultimately rejected, Weed's advice and won despite the latter's pessimism. The editor and lobbyist tried to stay active in business and politics during the Reconstruction era, but poor health eventually drove him into retirement.

For further reading: Glyndon G. Van Deusen, *Thurlow Weed: Wizard of the Lobby* (1947; reprint, New York: Da Capo Press, 1969).

Welles, Gideon (1802–1878, b. Glastonbury, Conn.)
Secretary of the navy, 1861–1869

A journalist and politician from Connecticut, Welles served as secretary of the navy in the Lincoln administration. Along with William H. Seward, he was one of only two cabinet members to remain in office from the inauguration through the assassination. With his flowing white beard, Welles cut a striking figure in wartime Washington. Some ridiculed him as "Father Neptune." Journalist Noah Brooks called him "slightly fossiliferous" but also found him to be "kind-hearted, affable and accessible." If Brooks had read the secretary's private diary, however, he might have altered his opinion. Welles kept a regular journal full of biting observations about the people and events around him. He commented on the "infidelity" of Edwin M. Stanton; called *New York Times* editor Henry Raymond "an unscrupulous soldier of fortune"; ridiculed letters from Salmon P. Chase as "miffy"; and frequently reported clashes with top aide Gustavus Fox and with cabinet rival William H. Steward. A former Democrat, Welles was particularly tough on radicals and adopted a cautious attitude toward equality for blacks. Because his wife, Mary Ann Welles, was close to Mary Lincoln, his diary also noted fairly regular social outings with the president.

After the war, Welles produced several recollections of the administration, principally aimed at debunking the stature of some of his cabinet rivals, particularly Seward, whom he found overrated. Welles himself was not a central figure in the administration, but his diary is one of the two or three best sources on the workings of the cabinet.

For further reading: Howard K. Beale, ed., *Diary of Gideon Welles*, 3 vols. (New York: Norton, 1960); and John Niven, *Gideon Welles: Lincoln's Secretary of the Navy* (New York: Oxford University Press, 1973).

Key Events in Lincoln's Life

1809

February 12 Abraham Lincoln is born in Hardin County, Kentucky, the second child of Thomas and Nancy Hanks Lincoln.

1816

December The Lincoln family moves to southern Indiana, in part because Thomas Lincoln opposes slavery and resents the legal and political power of slaveholders.

1818

October 5 Nancy Lincoln, the future president's mother, dies from illness.

1819

December 2 Thomas Lincoln remarries, to Sarah Bush Johnston, a widow.

1830

March 15 The Lincoln family arrives in Macon County, Illinois, still seeking better economic opportunities.

1831

July Twenty-two-year-old Abraham Lincoln returns from a trip to New Orleans and strikes out on his own for the first time, establishing a residence in New Salem, a small trading village in central Illinois.

1832

March 15 Lincoln, then a grocery story clerk, announces his candidacy for the Illinois state legislature.

April 21–July 17 During an extended period of frontier tension, known as the Black Hawk War, Lincoln joins the state militia, serving as a captain. He sees no combat.

August 6 About one week after his return from military service, Lincoln loses his first political campaign, coming in eighth out of thirteen legislative candidates.

1834

August 4 Lincoln is elected to his first public office, winning a seat in the state house of representatives. He is reelected in 1836, 1838, and 1840.

1836

September 9 After studying law books on his own for several months, Lincoln receives his license to practice law.

1837

March 3 State representative Lincoln and fellow legislator Dan Stone propose a resolution that condemns both slavery and abolitionism. This is Lincoln's first public statement against the evils of slavery.

April 15 Lincoln moves to Springfield, the new state capital of Illinois. He becomes a junior law partner to a prominent attorney and politician, John Todd Stuart, and lives above a grocery store with his closest friend, Joshua Speed.

1841

January 1 Lincoln breaks his engagement with Mary Todd, the daughter of a prominent Kentucky businessman. Mary was living in Springfield with her sister, and they had been courting for over a year.

April 14 Lincoln forms a new law partnership, his second, this time with attorney Stephen Logan.

1842

September 22 Ensnarled in a bitter political dispute, Lincoln nearly fights a duel with Illinois state auditor James Shields. Lincoln finds the episode sobering and becomes more restrained in his political and personal behavior.

November 4 Mary Todd and Abraham Lincoln wed in a small ceremony at her sister's home.

1843

August 1 Robert Todd Lincoln is born. He will later graduate from Harvard College, serve briefly in the Union army, and ultimately become secretary of war and president of the Pullman Company.

1845

March 18 Lincoln and Herndon, a new law partnership, tries its first case. William H. Herndon, Lincoln's third partner, works with him closely for the next sixteen years and later becomes one of his most devoted biographers.

1846

March 10 The Lincolns' second son, Edward, is born. He will die only a few years later.

August 3 Lincoln is elected to Congress, defeating Peter Cartwright, a Democrat and Methodist preacher.

1849

May 22 Logical by nature and long interested in canals, Lincoln receives a patent for a device to aid steamboats in traversing shallow waterways. He is the only president ever to receive a patent.

June After his single term in Congress, Lincoln unsuccessfully competes for a position as commissioner of the General Land Office, a mid-level government job controlled by the incoming administration of President Zachary Taylor.

1850

February 1 Edward Lincoln, age three, dies after a bout with pulmonary tuberculosis.

December 21 The Lincolns' third son, William, is born. He will die as a young boy during the Civil War, probably as a result of typhoid fever.

1853

April 4 The Lincolns' fourth son, Thomas (nicknamed "Tad") is born. He has a speech impediment and develops slowly. He will die at age eighteen from pleurisy.

1854

August Lincoln resumes his career as a political candidate, this time on a Fusion ticket for the state legislature, representing an assortment of opponents to Stephen A. Douglas's controversial Kansas-Nebraska Act. Lincoln is elected, but he resigns before serving in order to campaign for a seat in the U.S. Senate.

1855

February 8 Despite being considered the frontrunner, Lincoln loses a legislative election held to determine a replacement for incumbent U.S. senator James Shields. However, by helping to elect antislavery Democrat Lyman Trumbull, Lincoln begins to build the foundations for the Republican Party in Illinois.

1856

May 29 "Anti-Nebraska" politicians, soon known as Republicans, hold their first statewide political convention in Illinois, in the town of Bloomington. Lincoln gives a stirring address that helps to mobilize delegates.

June 19 At the first national Republican nominating convention held in Philadelphia, Lincoln comes in second in the balloting for a vice presidential nominee under John C. Frémont.

1858

June 16 Republicans in Illinois break precedent and openly endorse Abraham Lincoln as their candidate in the upcoming contest for U.S. senator. At the state convention, held in Springfield, Lincoln delivers the famous, "House Divided" speech.

August 21 The first of seven joint appearances by Lincoln and incumbent senator Stephen A. Douglas takes place in Ottawa, Illinois. The seven debates capture national attention and help to elevate Lincoln's stature in Illinois and across the North.

November 2 Legislative elections in Illinois make it clear that Douglas will be reelected as U.S. senator when the state legislature meets the following January, but the party defeat does not diminish Lincoln's growing stature.

1859

December 20 Lincoln pens a brief autobiographical sketch at the request of Jesse W. Fell, an Illinois newspaper publisher who has been approached for material on Lincoln by a Pennsylvania newspaper interested in profiling potential Republican presidential candidates.

1860

February 27 Venturing into what was considered hostile territory for the aspiring western candidate, Lincoln delivers a well-received speech at Cooper Union in New York City, firmly establishing him as a top contender for the Republican presidential nomination.

May 16–18 The second Republican national convention meets at Chicago and nominates Lincoln as its presidential candidate on the third ballot.

November 6 Abraham Lincoln is elected president in a four-way contest with nearly 40 percent of the popular vote and nearly 60 percent of the electoral vote.

December 20 In response to the Republican victories at the polls, South Carolina secedes from the Union. Over the next few months, six more states from the Deep South will follow South Carolina's lead.

1861

March 4 Lincoln is inaugurated as the sixteenth president of the United States.

March 5 Lincoln receives a letter from Maj. Robert Anderson, commander of Union forces at Fort Sumter in the harbor of Charleston, South Carolina, warning of an impending supply crisis.

March 29 After much internal debate, Lincoln announces to his cabinet that the administration will attempt to reinforce and resupply two major federal outposts in the South—Fort Sumter and Fort Pickens in Florida.

April 12 South Carolina forces fire the first shots at Fort Sumter.

April 13 Maj. Robert Anderson surrenders the federal forces at Sumter.

April 15 With Congress out of session, Lincoln announces that because of "combinations too powerful" to suppress by police action, he was calling for states to send 75,000 militia troops to Washington.

April 17 Virginia secedes from the Union, joining seven states from the Deep South already in full rebellion (Alabama, Florida, Georgia, Louisiana, Mississippi, South Carolina, and Texas).

April 19 Despite his desire to avoid conferring sovereign status on the rebels, Lincoln orders a blockade of Southern ports.

April 20 Robert E. Lee resigns from the U.S. Army and joins the Confederate forces.

April 27 Lincoln authorizes the temporary suspension of civil liberties along the line of troop movements from Philadelphia to Washington. Later, chief justice of the United States Roger B. Taney challenges his decision, but the president essentially ignores Taney's ruling.

May 6 Arkansas secedes from the Union.

May 13 England announces its neutrality in the American conflict.

May 20 North Carolina secedes from the Union.

May 21 The new Confederate government announces it will leave Montgomery, Alabama, and transfer its capital to Richmond, Virginia, only ninety miles from Washington, D.C.

May 24 Union general Benjamin Butler declares fugitive slaves arriving at Fort Monroe, Virginia, to be "contraband of war" and refuses to return them to their rebel masters. Northern newspapers soon pick up the phrase, and throughout the war runaway slaves are popularly known as "contrabands."

June 8 Tennessee secedes from the Union, the eleventh and final state to join the Confederacy.

July 2 Anxious about the fate of other border slave states, Lincoln authorizes another limited suspension of civil liberties.

July 4 With Congress back in session, Lincoln sends a stirring "War Message" to Capitol Hill that offers a vigorous defense of his administration's policies.

July 21 First Battle of Bull Run (Manassas, Virginia). Rebel forces score a surprise victory in the war's first major military action.

July 22 In a move designed to appeal to the loyalties of border slave states, Congress adopts the Crittenden-Johnson resolution, declaring that the war is being fought simply to preserve the Union—and not to abolish the institution of slavery.

July 27 Lincoln places Gen. George B. McClellan in command of federal troops in the vicinity of Washington. Over the summer McClellan will organize the Army of the Potomac.

August 5 Congress adopts the nation's first income tax, a temporary measure designed to help finance the war effort.

August 6 Congress passes what will later be known as the First Confiscation Act, nullifying claims on any fugitive slaves who had been employed in the Confederate war effort.

August 30 Union general John C. Frémont, who was the Republican nominee for president in 1856, declares martial law in Missouri, a state with divided loyalties, and orders emancipation, or immediate freedom, for the slaves of rebel sympathizers.

September 2 Lincoln, still concerned about maintaining the loyalty of border slave states, privately instructs Frémont to reverse his emancipation edict. After repeated delays and objections by Frémont and his supporters, Lincoln publicly reverses the order and transfers the controversial general out of Missouri.

October 21 Battle of Ball's Bluff (near Leesburg, Virginia). Union forces suffer a second major defeat in Virginia, losing over nineteen hundred troops.

November 1 Lincoln names Gen. George B. McClellan as general in chief of the Union armies, replacing the retiring general Winfield Scott.

December 20 Tired of depressing news from the battlefield and frustrated with what they perceive as Lincoln's conciliatory leadership, radical-leaning Republicans in Congress organize the Joint Committee on the Conduct of the War to oversee the administration's military policies.

December 26 After weeks of behind-the-scenes consultation, Lincoln determines to release two Confederate emissaries, James Mason and John Slidell, who while on board the *Trent*, a British mail ship, were captured by Union sailors. The decision placates the British government and avoids, at least temporarily, the possibility of entangling European nations in the American Civil War.

1862

January 11 Lincoln replaces Secretary of War Simon Cameron, a corrupt Pennsylvania politician, with Edwin M. Stanton, who was more efficient and honest and had served as attorney general in President James Buchanan's cabinet.

January 27 Responding to pressure from Capitol Hill, Lincoln issues General War Order No. 1, calling for a general military offensive by Washington's Birthday (February 22).

February 6 Union general Ulysses S. Grant begins a successful campaign in the Mississippi Valley with the capture of Fort Henry near the Tennessee River.

February 16 General Grant and his forces capture Fort Donelson on the outskirts of Nashville, Tennessee.

February 20 Twelve-year-old Willie Lincoln, the president's second son, dies after a long illness.

February 23 Lincoln appoints former U.S. senator Andrew Johnson as the military governor of Union-occupied Tennessee.

February 25 Unable to prevent General Grant's advances, rebel forces evacuate Nashville, Tennessee.

March 9 *Monitor* vs. *Virginia,* also known as the *Merrimac* (near Hampton Roads, Virginia). This confrontation marks the world's first hostile encounter between two ironclad warships. During the fighting, the *Virginia* is forced to withdraw and soon will be destroyed by Confederate forces anxious to avoid its capture.

March 11 Lincoln removes General McClellan as general in chief of the Union armies, but keeps him in place as commander of the Army of the Potomac. Lincoln expects McClellan to act in response to his General War Order No. 1 and begin a major offensive in Virginia.

March 13 Congress adopts amended articles of war that prohibit any federal military officer from returning fugitive slaves, or "contrabands," to rebel masters.

March 23 Confederate general Thomas "Stonewall" Jackson begins his legendary Shenandoah Valley campaign in northern Virginia, a remarkable feat of military logistics that frustrates federal military planners as they gear up for a general assault on Richmond.

April 4 The Army of the Potomac begins its long-awaited offensive against Richmond, moving from its new base on the edge of the Virginia peninsula toward Yorktown, scene of the British surrender in 1781. Over the next several weeks General McClellan will slowly position his troops forward along the peninsula toward a planned attack on the Confederate capital.

April 6–7 Battle of Shiloh (Pittsburg Landing, Tennessee). Confederate forces surprise General Grant's troops, but fail to drive them from the battlefield. Despite horrific casualties, federal soldiers hold their ground and secure a hard-fought victory.

April 25 Union navy admiral David Farragut and his forces capture the city of New Orleans.

May 20 Lincoln signs into law the Homestead Act, which helps open the western plains to white citizens by providing five-year settlers with up to 160 acres of publicly owned land at reduced prices.

May 31–June 1 Battle of Seven Pines (near Richmond, Virginia). Union forces avoid defeat, forcing a strategic stalemate in a key battle outside of the Confederate capital. Confederate general Joseph E. Johnston is severely wounded. He is replaced by General Robert E. Lee, who hurries from military headquarters in Richmond to lead the rebel troops in the field. Lee will eventually emerge as the Confederacy's most celebrated general.

June 13 By this point in June, the president and his family have moved their residence from the White House to a cottage at the Soldiers' Home, a military retirement community on the outskirts of Washington. The Lincoln family will return to the Soldiers' Home every summer during his presidency and remain in residence for a few months at a time.

June 16 Lincoln orders General Lee's former home in Arlington, Virginia, to be converted into a military hospital. The grounds will eventually be used to create a new national military cemetery.

June 23–June 25 Lincoln travels to West Point, New York, to confer with retired general Winfield Scott over the continued failure of Union military forces to secure victory over the rebels.

June 26 Union general John Pope receives an order from Lincoln authorizing him to organize the Army of Virginia, a new federal force designed to prepare the way for an overland assault on Richmond.

June 26–July 2 Seven Days' Battle (near Richmond, Virginia). Only a few weeks after taking command, General Lee succeeds in outmaneuvering General McClellan in a series of bloody engagements over the course of a fateful week. Union troops withdraw back along the waterways outside of Richmond, confirming for most observers that McClellan's much-anticipated peninsula campaign has been a failure.

June 27 Having transferred most of Gen. John Frémont's forces to the new command under General Pope, Lincoln orders that Frémont be relieved of his military command entirely. Later, a disgruntled Frémont will enter the 1864 election as a third party candidate.

July 1 Congress passes the Pacific Railway Act, which authorizes the nation's first transcontinental railroad, a project that will be completed in 1869.

July 2 Lincoln signs into law the Morrill Act, which provides federal land to states for the creation of "land-grant" agricultural colleges. The new law leads to the establishment of numerous public universities, widening access to higher education in the United States.

July 7–July 10 Lincoln visits General McClellan at his headquarters in Harrison's Landing on the Virginia peninsula. They have a tense exchange of views that convinces the president that McClellan is not fit to execute the current military policy.

July 11 Lincoln appoints Gen. Henry W. Halleck as general in chief of the Union armies, a position that had been vacant since General McClellan's demotion in March.

July 12 Congressional representatives from border states meet with Lincoln at the White House to hear his plan for voluntary, gradual, and compensated emancipation of the slaves. The president is promoting this plan as an alternative to the prospect of more radical legislation likely to emerge from Capitol Hill.

July 13 Lincoln reportedly discusses his plans to issue an immediate emancipation proclamation for rebel-controlled territories with two members of his cabinet, William H. Seward and Gideon Welles, while riding together to a funeral for the child of Secretary of War Stanton.

July 17 After much behind-the-scenes wrangling, Lincoln signs into law the Second Confiscation Act, which imposes tougher penalties on Southern rebels and includes a provision that designates any fugitive slaves of rebel owners as "forever free." The law provides for the courts to resolve confiscation or emancipation questions and is written to take effect after sixty days' notice from the president.

July 22 The entire cabinet hears of Lincoln's change of heart about emancipation policy at its regular meeting. Secretary of State Seward reportedly convinces Lincoln to delay announcing his new policy until the Union armies have achieved a decisive victory on the battlefield.

July 25 Lincoln issues the sixty days' notice required by the new Second Confiscation Act. He now has until the end of September to decide whether he will preempt congressional action on emancipation with his own proclamation or allow the legislature to seize control of the controversial policy.

August 14 Free black leaders meet with Lincoln at the White House. He urges them to support his administration's colonization efforts, particularly a program to resettle freed slaves in Central America.

August 22 Despite having already secretly discussed his intentions to issue an emancipation proclamation, Lincoln informs Northern newspaper readers in an open letter that his "paramount object" is to save the Union—and not to end slavery.

August 22 Union general Benjamin F. Butler, now stationed in New Orleans, organizes the "Native Guard," the first functioning federal black military units in occupied Louisiana.

August 30 Second Battle of Bull Run (Manassas, Virginia). Union forces are once again routed near the location of the war's first battle. Furious at his defeat, Gen. John Pope will accuse Gen. George B. McClellan and various subordinates of sabotaging his battlefield plans out of spite and disloyalty. Emboldened by their success, the Confederates prepare for a multipronged offensive against Union positions.

September 2 Amid chaos in the city of Washington after the Union defeat, Lincoln orders General McClellan to take command of the capital's defenses and reorganize the dispirited federal troops.

September 4 The Confederate Army of Northern Virginia, under the direction of General Lee, begins crossing the Potomac River, launching its first major invasion of Northern territory.

September 17 Battle of Antietam (near Sharpsburg, Maryland). In the bloodiest single day in American military history—over 25,000 combatants killed, wounded, or reported missing—General McClellan's Army of the Potomac halts the rebel advance. Shortly after, the Army of Northern Virginia recrosses the Potomac. McClellan's troops are too tired and shaken to pursue the rebels.

September 22 Lincoln formally decides to issue the Preliminary Emancipation Proclamation, announcing that all slaves in rebel territories will be considered "forever free" after January 1, 1863.

September 24 Lincoln orders a general suspension of civil liberties to help combat Northern "aiders and abettors" of the rebels. This declaration, coupled with the emancipation policy, appears to most observers to hurt the Republican Party in the upcoming fall elections and damages Lincoln's political standing.

October 3 Battle of Corinth (Mississippi). As part of the general Confederate offensive, rebel troops in northern Mississippi advance against Union positions under General Grant's overall command. Despite some initial success, rebel troops suffer defeat at the Battle of Corinth.

October 8 Battle of Perryville (Kentucky). In late summer and early autumn, rebel troops under the command of Gen. Braxton Bragg spearhead an invasion of Kentucky that culminates in a Union counterattack at Perryville in early October. Although federal troops suffer higher casualties, the Confederates cannot dislodge them and are forced to withdraw from Kentucky.

November 5 After repeatedly urging McClellan to pursue Lee's armies after the Battle of Antietam without success, Lincoln finally relieves him of his command and appoints Gen. Ambrose Burnside to head the Army of the Potomac.

December 13 Battle of Fredericksburg (Virginia). General Burnside's first major engagement as commander of the Army of the Potomac ends in disaster as Union forces suffer horrendous casualties in a poorly coordinated assault on a Confederate stronghold.

December 19 Lincoln meets with a delegation of eight U.S. senators who want him to dismiss Secretary of State William H. Seward. Radical Republicans on Capitol Hill are upset with the failures of the administration and blame the situation on the influence that conservatives such as Seward appear to have over the president—a perception fueled by gossip from Secretary of Treasury Salmon P. Chase. When Chase fails to confirm his complaints in a meeting with the caucus staged by the president, Lincoln holds his ground and heads off the congressional coup.

1863

January 1 Lincoln signs the Emancipation Proclamation, which abolishes slavery in areas under rebel control and encourages free blacks and former slaves to enlist in the Union armies. No slaves are immediately freed by this proclamation, but the decisions to embrace emancipation and black recruitment are momentous.

January 2 Battle of Stone's River (Murfreesboro, Tennessee). Union forces are stalled in their campaign through central Tennessee toward the railway junction at Chattanooga.

January 25 Gen. Joseph Hooker replaces the unpopular Ambrose Burnside as commander of the Army of the Potomac.

January 30 Union general Grant begins his campaign to capture Vicksburg, one of the last remaining Confederate strongholds on the Mississippi River.

March 3 Congress adopts the nation's first conscription act, detailing rules for the mandatory enrollment of males between the ages of twenty and forty-five if states fail to meet voluntary enlistment goals. As customary for the era, the new law allows men to purchase substitutes to serve in their place.

May 2–May 4 Battle of Chancellorsville. Lee's Army of Northern Virginia inflicts yet another devastating defeat on federal forces, this time commanded by General Hooker, who had bragged that his army was "the finest on the planet." Lincoln is distraught by the news.

June 24 The Army of Northern Virginia crosses the Potomac River as the rebels begin their second major invasion of the North in less than a year.

June 25 Anxiety and tension grip the federal command as Lincoln replaces General Hooker with Gen. George G. Meade, just days before the eventual confrontation with the invading Southern army.

July 1–July 3 Battle of Gettysburg (Pennsylvania). The bloodiest, and arguably the most important, battle of the war, Gettysburg marks a critical turning point for the Confederacy. Lee loses nearly 28,000 men—more than one-third of his army—but fails to secure victory. Once again, rebel troops return to Virginia and once again Union forces fail to pursue them aggressively. Lincoln continues to express his dismay at what he considers the failure of his military leadership to capitalize on its advantages.

July 3 Mary Lincoln suffers various head injuries during a fall in a carriage accident while riding from the Soldiers' Home to a local hospital. Later, her wounds will become infected and she nearly dies.

July 4 Nearly thirty thousand Confederate troops surrender at the city of Vicksburg, Mississippi, marking the culmination of a six-month campaign organized by Union general Grant and widely regarded as one of the most successful of the war.

July 8 Port Hudson, Mississippi, the last significant rebel stronghold on the Mississippi River, surrenders to Union soldiers.

July 13–16 Draft riots in New York City stun the Northern public and cast a shadow over the recent victories at Gettysburg and Vicksburg.

September 9 Confederate troops evacuate Chattanooga, Tennessee, essentially conceding that the eighteen-month Union campaign to secure the state of Tennessee has finally succeeded. With this rebel retreat, federal troops now appear poised to begin an assault on Georgia and the heart of the Confederacy.

September 20 Battle of Chickamauga (Georgia). Federal troops under the direction of Gen. William Rosecrans suffer a stinging defeat and are forced to return to Chattanooga. Shortly afterward, Lincoln replaces Rosecrans with Gen. George H. Thomas, the "Rock of Chickamauga," whose troops demonstrated incredible bravery during the catastrophic battle. Rebel forces begin to converge around Chattanooga.

November 19 Lincoln delivers the Gettysburg Address at ceremonies dedicating a new military cemetery on the famous battlefield.

November 23–November 25 Seizing command of the Union forces after the defeat at Chickamauga, General Grant directs a series of maneuvers that drive the Confederate forces away from Chattanooga and once again position the federal armies for an assault on Georgia.

December 3 Confederate troops evacuate Knoxville, their last remaining significant outpost in Tennessee.

December 8 Lincoln issues a Proclamation of Amnesty and Reconstruction that offers relatively lenient terms for Southerners to return to the Union.

1864

February 1 Lincoln orders the secretary of war to make arrangements for any free blacks who want to return from the failed colonization experiment in Central America. This decision effectively marks the end of Lincoln's efforts to colonize free blacks outside of the United States.

February 28 Lincoln receives a unanimous endorsement of his reelection from a joint caucus of the Republican, or Union, members of the Ohio state legislature. This is significant news, because Lincoln's principal rival for the nomination is his own Treasury secretary, Salmon P. Chase, the former Republican governor of Ohio.

February 17 The Confederate submergible ship, the *P* launches the first submarine attack of the war, successfully torpedoing a federal ship in Charleston harbor. The small ship, however, does not resurface.

March 10 Lincoln names Grant as general in chief of the Union armies.

April 12 Confederate forces under the command of Nathan Bedford Forrest, later one of the founders of the Ku Klux Klan, massacre captured black soldiers at Fort Pillow on the Mississippi River.

April 17 General Grant halts prisoner exchanges, a tough policy designed to retaliate for the Fort Pillow massacre and weaken the Confederacy, already facing manpower shortages. Ultimately, however, the decision indirectly contributes to the death of thousands of Union prisoners held in overcrowded Southern prisons.

May 4 Union general William T. Sherman begins his campaign to secure the city of Atlanta, Georgia. He will maneuver for months before finally achieving success in the early autumn.

May 5–6 Battle of the Wilderness (Virginia). In the first great confrontation of the war between Grant and Lee, the result is a stalemate. Undeterred, General Grant directs federal armies to begin a flanking maneuver toward Richmond.

May 8–12 Battle of Spotsylvania (Virginia). Once again, the armies behind Grant and Lee clash and once again the result is a strategic draw. Grant displays his dogged determination by wiring back to Washington that, if necessary, he intends to "fight it out on this line if it takes all summer." It actually takes nearly another year before he finally achieves a breakthrough.

May 31 A small group of Radical Republicans meeting in Cleveland, Ohio, nominate former general John Frémont as a third party candidate for president.

June 3 Battle of Cold Harbor (Virginia). Grant again throws Union troops at Lee's fortified positions. There is still no movement, but the carnage shocks the Northern public. Up to this point, Grant's Wilderness campaign has cost the Union more than sixty thousand casualties.

June 7 Republicans meet for a national convention in Baltimore, rename themselves temporarily the Union Party, and renominate Lincoln as their presidential candidate. The convention's only excitement occurs when the delegates choose to skip over incumbent vice president Hannibal Hamlin of Maine and nominate Andrew Johnson, a War Democrat from Tennessee, as their new vice presidential candidate.

June 15–18 Battle of Petersburg (Virginia). Grant's armies are once more prevented from entering Richmond. The federal commander orders a siege of Petersburg, a small town south of the Confederate capital.

July 2 Congress passes the Wade-Davis bill for the reconstruction of rebel states, setting forth a policy much stricter than the one outlined by the president in his proclamation of December 8, 1863. Lincoln pocket vetoes the legislation.

July 11–12 Raid on Washington, D.C. Confederate general Jubal Early raids Maryland at the beginning of the month, creating havoc in Baltimore and Washington. On July 11 and 12, Early's troops threaten to assault the federal capital, and Lincoln briefly comes under enemy fire while viewing the skirmishes from a fort outside of the city.

July 17 Confederate president Jefferson Davis replaces Gen. Joseph E. Johnston, who has been maneuvering to keep Union general William T. Sherman's forces away from Atlanta, Georgia, with the more offensive-minded general John B. Hood.

July 18 Lincoln issues two controversial public documents. The first announces a new call for 500,000 more enlistments—a stunning indication that the war will not be over anytime soon. The second states in the form of an open letter that the "abandonment of slavery" should be considered a precondition for any negotiations on ending the war.

July 22 Battle for Atlanta (Georgia). Confederate general Hood unsuccessfully attacks Sherman's forces on July 22 and again on July 28.

July 30 Battle of the Crater (Petersburg, Virginia). During the siege of Petersburg, Union engineers attempt to tunnel under rebel lines, planting explosives that they hope will decimate the Confederate position. The result is a fiasco as unthinking Union officers direct their troops into the "crater" created by the explosives, making them easy targets for Confederate defenders.

July 30 Following up his daring raid on Maryland and Washington with another on southern Pennsylvania, Confederate general Jubal Early burns the town of Chambersburg when local residents fail to meet his demands for $500,000 in tribute.

August 5 Sen. Benjamin Wade, R-Ohio, and Rep. Henry Winter Davis, Unionist-Md., issue a strongly worded "manifesto" that attacks the president for failing to support their Reconstruction plan. Their unhappiness reflects a general discontent among many Radical Republicans with Lincoln's leadership.

August 22 Thurlow Weed, a leading Union political adviser, writes to Secretary of State William H. Seward that Lincoln's reelection is "an impossibility" because the "people are wild for peace."

August 23 Lincoln drafts a terse memorandum detailing his course of action in the event of a Democratic victory in the upcoming presidential contest, and asks all the members of his cabinet to sign the document without seeing its contents.

August 29 The Democratic national convention in Chicago nominates Gen. George B. McClellan as the party's nominee and adopts a platform denouncing the conflict as "four years of failure." Because McClellan at least nominally supports the war effort, his selection, coupled with the platform's harsh language, only serves to underline the party's internal divisions.

September 2 Fall of Atlanta (Georgia). Sherman and his troops finally enter Atlanta. Most observers consider the victory to be a decisive turning point in the campaign to reelect Lincoln.

September 19 Battle of Winchester (Virginia). Union general Philip Sheridan defeats Confederate general Jubal Early and continues over the next weeks and months to drive rebel forces out of the Shenandoah Valley in a series of engagements that represents some of the war's most intense fighting.

September 23 Lincoln removes Postmaster General Montgomery Blair from his cabinet. Most observers believe the removal of a controversial conservative is part of a deal with Radicals to remove third party candidate John C. Frémont from the presidential race.

October 13 Results of various state elections (then held separately from the presidential contest) indicate that the Union coalition will carry the North and that Lincoln can expect to win reelection.

November 8 Lincoln wins reelection handily, with 55 percent of the popular vote and 212 of 233 electoral votes.

November 16 Union general Sherman begins his "March to the Sea," taking his troops from Atlanta to Savannah and frequently destroying rebel property along the way.

November 30 Battle of Nashville (Tennessee). Confederate general John B. Hood launches a desperate counterattack on federal forces stationed in Nashville, Tennessee, but after fierce fighting his assault is repulsed and most of his troops are wounded or captured.

December 6 Lincoln nominates his former rival and cabinet officer Salmon P Chase as the Supreme Court's next chief justice, to succeed Roger B. Taney who died in October.

1865

January 16 Having completed their capture of Savannah in December, Sherman's armies now begin a march up the Atlantic coast, northward through the Carolinas.

February 3 Lincoln meets with Confederate emissaries on a ship near Hampton Roads, Virginia. The talks end without achieving any progress.

February 17 Columbia, South Carolina, burns to the ground as Sherman's troops pass grimly through the state that started the secession movement.

March 3 Congress establishes the Freedmen's Bureau to aid former slaves in their adjustment to impending freedom.

March 4 Lincoln is inaugurated for a second term and delivers an address that many consider one of his finest efforts and one of the nation's most eloquent political speeches. The theme of the speech is reconciliation.

March 13 Confederate president Jefferson Davis signs into a law a plan to offer freedom to Southern slaves who enlist in the collapsing rebel armies.

March 27–28 Lincoln meets with Generals Grant and Sherman and directs them to offer generous terms of surrender to their Southern counterparts.

April 2 General Lee abandons Petersburg and the Confederate government flees Richmond.

April 5 After the federal occupation of Richmond, Lincoln visits the city.

April 9 General Lee surrenders to General Grant at Appomattox Court House, Virginia.

April 11 Lincoln gives what will turn out to be his last public speech, urging reconciliation but also suggesting that he supports various controversial steps toward integrating former slaves into the nation's civic community.

April 14 Lincoln is shot and fatally wounded while spending an evening at Ford's Theatre with his wife and another couple.

April 15 At 7:22 a.m. Abraham Lincoln dies. Andrew Johnson becomes the nation's seventeenth president.

April 18 Confederate general Joseph E. Johnston surrenders the last significant body of rebel troops, but scattered resistance in the South will continue for weeks.

April 19 Funeral services held at the White House for Abraham Lincoln.

April 21 A train carrying Lincoln's body begins a twelve-day journey from Washington to Springfield, Illinois.

April 26 Presidential assassin John Wilkes Booth, a well-known actor, is cornered and killed at Richard Garrett's farm near Bowling Green, Virginia.

May 4 Abraham Lincoln's body is buried at Oak Ridge Cemetery near Springfield, Illinois.

May 10 Confederate president Jefferson Davis is captured in Georgia. He will remain in federal custody until his pardon by President Andrew Johnson in 1868.

May 13 The final rebel resistance west of the Mississippi River ends and the war is finally over.

Index

Text Credits

Basler, Roy P., ed. *The Collected Works of Abraham Lincoln*. 9 vols. New Brunswick: Rutgers University Press, 1953. Selections reprinted by permission of the Abraham Lincoln Association, Springfield, Illinois.

Burlingame, Michael, and John R. Turner Ettlinger, eds. *Inside Lincoln's White House: The Complete Civil War Diary of John Hay*. Carbondale: Southern Illinois University Press, 1997. Selections reprinted by permission of Brown University Library.

Long, E. B. *The Civil War Day by Day*. 1971. Reprint, New York: Da Capo, 1985. Selections reprinted by permission of Doubleday, a division of Random House Inc.

Winkle, Kenneth J. *The Young Eagle: The Rise of Abraham Lincoln*. Dallas: Taylor, 2001. Selections reprinted by permission of Taylor Trade, an imprint of Rowman and Littlefield Publishing Group.